Aesthetics of Textiles and
Advancing Multi-Disciplinary

ITAA Special publication #7

1994

Edited by

Marilyn Revell DeLong
University of Minnesota

Ann Marie Fiore
Iowa State University

© *1994*
International Textile and Apparel Association, Inc.
PO Box 1360
Monument, CO 80132-1360
USA
(719)488-3716

ISBN 1-885715-03-X

Table of Contents

Acknowledgments

This volume was a collaboration that began with a call for papers that ends today with the passing on of manuscripts to ITAA for publication. We believe we have collected an impressive grouping of topics that expand the previous aesthetic paradigms and an equally impressive listing of distinguished and soon-to-be distinguished authors. The authors who answered the call were so very cooperative in responding to the reviewers and staying with the schedule that they deserve our high praise and thanks.

The review process involved a call for papers and selection of reviewers. The review process was equally as stringent as for the *Clothing and Textiles Research Journal*, and that meant every manuscript was reviewed by 2-3 reviewers in a blind review process. Reviewers responded to the process with great vigor and enthusiastic support. We wish to thank our reviewers for their patience and diligence and also for adhering to the schedule we set for ourselves. Each who participated was truly committed to this special publication and it shows.

Though the authors receive recognition in publication, the reviewers generally do not. Manuscript reviewers were critical in the review process and we would like to acknowledge and thank them. Reviewers were as follows: Nancy Bryant, Lesle Davis Burns, Elizabeth Bye, Catherine Cerny, Catherine Daly, Marilyn DeLong, Joanne Eicher, Sandra Evenson, Ann Marie Fiore, Janet Hazard-Ambrose, Jane Hegland, Patricia Hemmis, Janet Hethorn, Robert Hillestad, Susan Kaiser, Sharleen Kato, Patricia Kimle, Sharron Lennon, Susan Michelman, Bettie Minshall, Gwendolyn O'Neal, Rachel Pannabecker, Mary Ellen Roach-Higgins, Nancy Rudd, Catherine Rutherford-Black, Susan Stark, Patricia Warner, Linda Welters and Jane Workman.

Finally we would like to thank the ITAA Council and the Publications Vice President, Margaret Rucker, and her committee for responding favorably to our initial proposal and for encouraging the project in its various stages. We have worked in close contact with Sandra Hutton Executive Director of ITAA, who has continued to remain cheerful, helpful and patient throughout the project.

In summary, we have all worked together in a synergistic manner making the whole much greater than the sum of its parts.

Marilyn DeLong and Ann Marie Fiore
April, 1994

ITAA SPECIAL PUBLICATION
LIST OF CONTRIBUTORS

Nancy O. Bryant
Oregon State University

Leslie Davis Burns
Oregon State University

Elizabeth Bye
University of Minnesota

Catherine A. Cerny
Virginia Polytechnic Institute and State University

Marilyn DeLong
University of Minnesota

Joanne B. Eicher
University of Minnesota

Tonye V. Erekosima
University of Port Harcourt, Nigeria

Ann Marie Fiore
Iowa State University

Key Sook Geum
Hong-Ik University

Jane Hegland
University of Minnesota

Patricia Hemmis
University of Minnesota

Betsy Henderson
University of Minnesota

Robert Hillestad
University of Nebraska

Elizabeth Hoffman
University of Maine

Morris Holbrook
Columbia University

Sharleen Kato
Seattle Pacific University

Patricia Anne Kimle
Iowa State University

Joseph Kupfer
Iowa State University

Karen LaBat
University of Minnesota

Sharron J. Lennon
Ohio State University

Hazel Lutz
University of Minnesota

Bettie C. Minshall
Kansas State University

Gwendolyn S. O'Neal
Ohio State University

Nancy Ann Rudd
Ohio State University

Catherine Rutherford-Black
Texas Tech University

Louann Tedrick
Compuserve, Inc., Columbus, Ohio

Patricia C. Warner
University of Massachusetts

Introduction

Ann Marie Fiore
Iowa State University

Marilyn DeLong
University of Minnesota

This special focused issue was conceived because we envision aesthetics of textiles and clothing to be more comprehensive than previously considered. We believe that research in the aesthetics area is sorely needed and that the only way to foster such research is to dispel the myths that seem to accompany aesthetics. In this publication aesthetics has not been trivialized into a mere understanding of how we can produce "pleasing" products through the relationship of line, shape and color, nor a simplification of the form to its bare object function. Rather we believe aesthetics involves understanding both the product and our response to it, the form and its meaning. Further we believe that aesthetics of clothing can be viewed from a position of both cause and effect, that is, clothing can be viewed as an expression of our values as well as help to shape our values. Aesthetics of clothing can be a catalyst for enjoyment that brings with it a higher life quality or represent bottom line economic profit. Aesthetics is not just intuitive. It is true that some aspects of our response, our likes and dislikes for example, are immediate and can be immediately expressed, but to capture our reasoning requires going well beyond likes and dislikes. As professionals we need to know far more about aesthetics than just how to clothe ourselves in garments we find pleasurable. Viewing aesthetics as understanding the response of an individual within a culture to its artifacts whose form and meaning may reach iconic or symbolic status places it within a different paradigm.

Understanding aesthetics within the field of textiles and clothing requires broadening the range of topics examined within such a paradigm. Academicians of textiles and clothing who may or may not call themselves aestheticians have submitted manuscripts to this special publication. Contributions represent a range of perspectives including anthropology, consumer behavior, consumer textiles, design, history, philosophy, semiotics, and social-psychology. The contributions exemplify a variety of methods including grounded interpretation, introspective interpretation, quantitative analysis, and visual analysis. It is only through the inclusion of these many perspectives and methods that the following objectives of this special publication could be met:

1. To define and clarify issues in aesthetics
2. To broaden the range of aesthetics topics studied in textiles and clothing
3. To foster dialogue across perspectives/disciplines
4. To encourage research in areas of aesthetics heretofore unaddressed.

Background

The field of textiles and clothing is comprised of members with diverse perspectives and areas of interest. Members representing these diverse perspectives assembled at a Special Session during the 1990 *International Textile and Apparel Association* conference to discuss a kindred interest, aesthetics. The session entitled "Aesthetics of Apparel: Subject, Form and Content" was convened by DeLong and Hillestad. The purpose of the Session was to broaden the definition of aesthetics by discussing some critical issues in aesthetics. Having sampled some issues in aesthetics, the following year at the 1991 ITAA conference, a second Special Session was planned to focus on presentation of research papers followed by discussion of their relation to aesthetics. Papers were identified through the review of research abstracts for the general conference and a panel of discussants read the manuscripts in preparation for the session. In retrospect these two sessions served purposes of dissemination of new scholarship on aesthetics and of sharing concerns, thoughts and ideas among participants.

These Special Sessions were of great value in raising questions and fostering dialogue among participants, but the limited time frame deterred any extensive development of thoughts, and ideas common to aesthetics. A routine question during the sessions, "Is that aesthetics?" represents the rudimentary level of shared understanding found among participants. It became apparent that there existed a need for a more in-depth understanding of aesthetics from perspectives of various disciplines.

In the summer of 1992 Fiore coordinated a week-long seminar on aesthetics at Iowa State University. The purpose was to discuss aesthetics of clothing from perspectives of various disciplines. Marilyn DeLong escorted participants through her systematic analysis of the Apparel Body Construct, an approach rooted in art theory and perception psychology. Morris Holbrook presented his axiology of consumption behavior which helped distinguish aesthetic value of a consumption experience from other values. Joseph Kupfer posed philosophical questions about the general nature of aesthetics and its relationship to textiles and clothing. Ann Marie Fiore discussed the evolution of anthropology of aesthetics and key theories from psychological approaches to aesthetics.

Evaluating the ITAA conference sessions and the seminar, Fiore and DeLong believed the next step was an ITAA focused publication. Such a publication would help meet the need for defining and clarifying aesthetics from various perspectives. Contributions from ITAA members would be solicited and supplemented by papers from the scholars taking part in the Iowa seminar.

Process

A call in the *ITAA Newsletter* for papers on new perspectives on aesthetics, and through encouragement to members from various specializations in textiles and clothing to submit manuscripts, we received gratifying support for our project. We publicized the prospectus outlining the framework within which we wanted to work. The five categories of Creator, Creative Process, Object, Appreciator, and Appreciation Process helped to inform and organize the sections of this publication. These arose from a comprehensive review of literature found inside and outside the field of textiles and clothing by Fiore, Kimle, & Moreno . We believe the broad definition of aesthetics used in the solicitation was responsible for the success in attracting manuscripts offering a range of perspectives:

Aesthetics is the study of human response to the non-instrumental quality of the object or event; specifically, aesthetics addresses the activated internal processes, the object or event's multi-sensory characteristics, and the psychological and socio-cultural factors affecting the response of the creator or appreciator to the object or event (Fiore, Moreno, & Kimle, in press).

We received 28 manuscripts. The peer review process was both stringent and nurturing with reviewers selected because of their knowledge of the subject of a particular manuscript. Reviewers and authors perceived the review process as a pioneering and cooperative effort with both working toward the goal of an outstanding publication focused on aesthetics. After a blind review process set up to be similar to that of *Clothing and Textiles Research Journal*, 21 manuscripts were coalesced to form this special publication. The following papers represent the work of 27 authors, many recognized as already distinguished, both within and outside the field, as well as some just entering textiles and clothing. Many authors are not necessarily recognized at this time for their contribution to aesthetics, but we hope this publication will serve to encourage continued endeavor.

Organization of the Contributions

As editors of the special publication, we believe that advancing aesthetics and the field of textiles and clothing includes exploring new topics and using an array of methodologies. The contributions are organized into five sections and an overview of general issues of concern. In **General Issues** one finds the **Fiore** paper that attempts to dispel misconceptions about the study of aesthetics of textiles and clothing. This creative writing approach was an aesthetic experience in itself.

We organized the remaining papers into sections according to the five categories of aesthetics used in the call for papers. The category was selected based upon the primary focus even though many of the papers were integrative in nature. Some papers are discussed under two categories of the introduction, but are situated in the publication in only one section noted by bold facing the author's name under the selected section heading.

Creator

Incorporated in the Creator category is literature examining the influence of psychological and socio-cultural factors of the creator on *differences* in creative ability, participation in production of aesthetic objects, processes of production, and physical manifestations of the aesthetic product. In this publication, factors found to influence the creator include personal and interpersonal experience and growth, technological development and aesthethic ideology of culture.

Warner uses an art history methodology as a foundation for analyzing and interpreting the style and content of the work of the artist, Remedios Varo. Varo's childhood experiences of sewing and designing apparel, and her short stint as a costume designer had a lasting effect on the content of her paintings. Immersion in the art movement of the time period and personal relationships with fellow artists also shaped her work, allowing dreamlike images and perspectives on the social reality of women to fill the canvas. Even though only two dimensional representations of clothing are the product of this creators work, the significance of the social effects on the physical manifestations of the work and the symbolic meaning conveyed by clothing can provide insight into the study of textile and apparel artists.

Whereas Warner focuses on how personal life experiences of the Creator can have a profound effect on the aesthetic form, **LaBat** and **Bye** discuss how technological development within a culture can maintain or promote change in aesthetic forms of dress. Materials and processes of product development and production are influenced by technology. Technological development, in turn, is spurred on by desire for change in the aesthetic form and results in a change in the standards of the aesthetic form.

Henderson supports the use of DeLong's (1987) systematic analysis to understand the aesthetic of a (sub)culture of creators and discusses implications for teaching apparel design in a post modern society. She tries to define the aesthetic of some of her design students, who's rules of aesthetics are post modern. Whereas her students adopted popular fashion trends, these students customized their own look, emulated previous time periods other cultures, and wore styles of the opposite sex in order to create their own aesthetic standards.

Creative Process

The Creative Process category contains literature that addresses internal processes that take place *within* the creator during development of ideas through to the completion of the aesthetic object. These processes consist of the logical and unconscious mental components, and the sensual, emotional, and spiritual components of aesthetic experience. Contributions to the the creative process section of this publication focus on the logical mental component of experience, but unconscious and sensual components are also discussed.

Kato, Kimle, and **Hemmis** and **Hegland** focus on the internal processes involved in creativity and the design of textiles and clothing. Kato uses a theoretical framework composed of five categories to organize literature on creativity. Three of these categories (cognitive, psychoanalytic, and psychedelic) and the scholarship discussing models of the creative process pertain to the *logical mental* and *unconscious mental* components of the Creative Process. Both Kato and Kimle examine the logical mental models of the design process of apparel forwarded by other textiles and clothing scholars. Kimle submits that design foundations are important to the design process because perceptions, thoughts, and feelings of the designer can be translated into elements and principles of design, which leads to availability of content of experience in the design process.

Hegland and Hemmis provide an introspective, interpretive look at the technological and aesthetic development of one knitwear designer. Their discussion of the journey through the creative process reveals that satisfaction, provided by particular aspects of logical and sensual components of knitwear design and production, influences techniques selected by the knitwear designer and also ultimately shapes the product of the designer. For instance, the authors explain that the method of first drafting intricate patterns on graph paper removed the knitter from the sensual pleasures of the act of knitting and the duplication of the intricate pattern distracted the knitter from the sensory qualities of knitting. The product of this process was never completed and the yarns were used in other designs.

Kato and Kimle conclude with considerations in teaching textile and apparel design, including the facilitation of the creative process in student designers through expansion of the internal processes engaged, and through attention to the individualized experience of design. The contribution of Hemmis and Hegland supports the need for attention to the individualized nature of the creative process, as creators find satisfaction in particular aspects of design and production that results in successful completion of the object and growth as a designer.

Object

The Object category includes literature exploring the formal (characteristics of composition), expressive (feeling), and referential (symbolic references to the outside world) nature of the physical object or experiential event. Formal qualities affecting aesthetic experience and referential meaning dominate this section of the publication.

In his position paper, **Hillestad** stresses the importance of considering form and referential content as inseparable in the development and evaluation of the aesthetic object. His plea for an integrated approach to form and content will insure fulfillment of human needs, abundant meaning and an enriched life. **Bryant** and **Hoffman** provide us with a critical framework for understanding wearable art as object of aesthetic appreciation. This paper shows that in evaluation one must consider the context of that object and the role of the appreciator and creator. Appropriately integrative, these authors situate the object as well as wearer and viewer in the evaluation of wearable art objects. For example, the object is not viewed for itself but as a tangible means of evaluating the success of the mental processes of the designer.

A number of contributions (DeLong & Geum; Bryant & Hoffman; **Kupfer**, and **Lutz**) in this publication support the need for understanding the multisensory nature of the aesthetic experience offered by textile and apparel products. Kupfer draws upon philosophical literature to explain universal criteria (complexity, unity, and intensity) helpful in understanding the formal, expressive, and referential aspects of aesthetic evaluations of the multisensory object. For instance, as one walks, contrasting sensations of weight between heavy boots and a lightweight insulated jacket can add complexity and aesthetic enjoyment of interactions with clothing. Lutz, in her effort to capture the spirit of the women's garments of 1910-1939, considers the effect of weight of the fabric, reflective and effect of the fabric, and layout (cut) of the garment on the aesthetic experience offered through *movement* of the clothed-body form. Lutz proposes that the sensual quality of the texture of velvet was also an important component of the aesthetic experience during this time period.

Burns and **Lennon** also discuss the importance of multisensory aspects of the object. These researchers focus upon visual and tactile aspects. They look at aesthetic perceptions, involving "sensory stimulation and the resulting preferential or affective interpretations of the sensations" (p.4). They survey methods used to measure aesthetic perception of these visual and tactile aspects. They suggest that sensations registered by sensory receptors of the wearer's body as well as sensations of the hand are critical to the assessment of the product. Burns and Lennon conclude that aesthetic response can be due to the object characteristics, environment of response, and characteristics of the consumer. Thus, characteristics of the Appreciator are as important as formal aspects of the object in our understanding of the aesthetics.

The referential nature of textiles and apparel is evident in the work of Eicher and Erekosima, Cerny, and Warner. Eicher and Erekosima explore men's clothing as a symbol for socio-political status. Cerny proposes that the textile object is a means of communication of (quilter's) connectedness in social life, hence making tangible the special social role of women in the particular time period in history. In Warner's paper images of textiles and clothing are used as tangible markers of a woman's experiences and creative spirit. Thus, representations of textiles and apparel in Varo's artwork and actual quilts become metaphors for the social reality and spirit of women.

Clothing as facilitator of aesthetic appreciation of the environment (e.g., a hat that allows you to enjoy a walk in the rain) is central to Kupfer's conceptualization of aesthetics of clothing. Thus, the object's form, expression, or meaning may not be appreciated aesthetically, but rather the object may be valued for it's functional quality, which is the intermediary to the final goal, aesthetic appreciation of the environment. **Holbrook's** paper, which looks at axiology (nature of and type of consumer value) of the product, supports the focus on the culminating experience rather than the features of the object. According to Holbrook, value lies in the consumption experience and not in the purchased product itself. This suggests a shift from the examination of the purchase or selection of textile and clothing products to the experience facilitated by these products.

Appreciation Process

The Appreciation Process includes variables similar to the Creative Process. The focus is on the internal processes that take place during the aesthetic response to an preexisting object or an event. These processes consist of the sensual, physiological, cognitive, emotional, and spiritual components of aesthetic experience.

Minshall defines the underlying dimensions and measurement of preference, an important dependent variable in the study of aesthetics. This contribution helps us better understand the nature of the Appreciation Process. The perceptual, cognitive, and affective components of evaluation are delineated, and the nature of preference change is discussed. Minshall's contribution provides a perspective on the nature of preference change related to fashion apparel. Implications for the study of the preference for apparel were included. In particular, she calls for the use of both affective and cognitive components in apparel preference research, the examination of the relative importance of these components in preference for various categories of apparel, and the understanding of the difference of 'preference for' and 'response to' apparel objects.

Cerny also explores the nature of the Appreciation Process. She introduces us to the play of tropes, the mechanism of language linking internal sensual, cognitive, and emotional experiences to the symbolic meaning of production of the object and the object itself. Language reflects and gives access to the person's conceptual world, but not in a straight forward manner. In the play of tropes words are used in a non-literal way to bring meaning to life. In aesthetic experience, sensory qualities are not only a source of hedonic pleasure, but also become a metaphor. The pleasant sensory quality of warmth is also a metaphor for the warmth of the personal relationship between the creator and the user of the quilt. Cerny advocates a cultural aesthetic where cultural meaning mediates individual perception of material objects.

Rudd and **Lennon** examine internal cognitive processes (and social processes) of evaluation of the aesthetic value of the body. Social comparison, comparison to others leading to self-evaluation, establishes the internal process of continual assessment of the aesthetic value of one's own body based upon comparison to others, particularly to the cultural ideal. Pleasure is the response to positive assessment of one's body to that of others including the cultural ideal. Rudd and Lennon propose that the cultural ideal of the body becomes the internal aesthetic standard used in social comparison. This suggests the importance of socio-cultural factors, found in the Appreciator section, on aesthetic experience.

Appreciator

The Appreciator category, similar to the Creator category, focuses on the influence of psychological and socio-cultural factors affecting aesthetic ability (sensitivity to aesthetic features), selection, preference, and evaluation of aesthetic objects. Contributions to the Appreciator section of the special publication illustrate the effects of broad cultural differences, sub-cultural influence, and gender on aesthetic ability, selection, and preference of apparel.

Looking at adolescent appearances in a high school yearbook in the U.S.(**Black** and **DeLong**) and Kalabari dress (**Eicher** and **Erekosima**), one may conclude that interpretation of aesthetic qualities of the object are influenced by socio-cultural factors, leading to a relative rather than an objective nature of aesthetic evaluation. Eicher and Erekosima point out the similarity between the structure of the form and systematic rules of dress that parallel the social order in Kalabari society. Black and DeLong discuss systematic differences in appearance of U.S. male and female adolescence, but these differences are not as extensive as found among Kalabari men.

Whereas systematic aesthetic rules of dress appear to be evident in the Kalabari culture and adolescence of the U.S., **Henderson** suggests that systematic rules are not the case for a certain segment of U.S. culture. Henderson states that the social control of aesthetic aspects of appearance in the U.S. may come up against opposing forces of postmodernism. Strict codes of aesthetics of appearance are being replaced by more individualism in appearance, and formal rules and clear cut referential meanings are dwindling due to the postmodern aesthetic.

Instead of a purely individualistic aesthetic, there appears to be differentiated aesthetics for subcultural groups, such as the differentiated aesthetic for apparel and fragrance of male homosexuals, as described by **Rudd** and **Tedrick**. Rudd and Tedrick outline how the development of aesthetic codes of appearance may relate to proclamation of personal and social identity for members of the homosexual subculture. They also present some of the socio-cultural factors that may contribute to aesthetic sensitivity and to the higher value placed upon an attractive appearance within this subcultural group.

O'Neal explains how Eurocentric standards of beauty perpetuate African-Americans as the 'other', which leads to a lack of validation of aesthetic judgments and experiences, and lack of self-definition of beauty for African-Americans. O'Neal shows that an African-American aesthetic has its foundation in the cultural and philosophical premises shared with West African cultures, including unity with nature, collective kinship, and individual uniqueness. These central beliefs lead to the notion that beauty is more than a physical quality and points to the importance of not only studying the physical form to determine the aesthetic of another culture, but to first identify the culture's definition of aesthetics and/or beauty. O'Neal submits that it is important to incorporate the aesthetic of subcultural groups, e.g. African-American, in teaching and in research of textiles and clothing, just as Henderson submits the need for sensitivity to the aesthetic of the postmodern student.

The importance of studying aesthetics in a cultural context is reinforced by the contribution of **DeLong** and **Geum**. These researchers examine the empirical aesthetic response of Korean women and the cultural influences on these aesthetic responses to a range of tradi-tional styles of Korean dress. DeLong's (1987) systematic analysis of aesthetics provides a second method. The systematic analysis allowed for insight into the preferences of the culture, interpreted in the context of traditions and beliefs of the culture. For example, Koreans' love of nature is important in explaining motifs, and preference for aesthetic features of Korean dress reflect the importance of retaining national identity while also remaining open to progress.

Because of the multisensory nature of aesthetic experience, the appreciator may be the wearer or the viewer of apparel. DeLong and Geum of U.S. and Korean cultures, respectively, provide an interesting cross-cultural analysis of aesthetic experience as the *wearers* of Korean traditional dress.

In conclusion, the array of papers found in this special publication represent the beginning of what the editors hope will grow into a new and expanded generation of research on aesthetics. This introduction provides an integrative look at the papers but doesn't speak to the riches awaiting you in the following contributions. We anxiously await the next generation of aesthetics related research from either the continued efforts of the present authors or new authors encouraged by this publication.

References

Delong, M. R. (1987). *The Way We Look: A framework for visual analysis of dress.* Ames, IA: Iowa State University Press.

Fiore, A. M., Kimle, P. A., & Moreno, J. M. (in press). *Aesthetics: A comparison of the state of the art outside and inside the field of textiles and clothing. Part one: Creator and creative process.*

Fiore, A. M., Moreno, J. M., & Kimle, P. A. (in press). *Aesthetics: A comparison of the state of the art outside and inside the field of textiles and clothing. Part three: Appreciation process, appreciator, and summary comparisons.*

Aesthetics: The James Dean of Textiles and Clothing

Ann Marie Fiore
Iowa State University

This entry serves as catharsis, expression of deep-seated thoughts and feelings, while illustrating important issues regarding aesthetics of textiles and clothing that professionals of textiles and clothing must face for the betterment of the field. Dispelling misconceptions of aesthetics of textiles and clothing is necessary to open up this avenue of literature to fortify understanding of many areas of textiles and clothing subject matter.

I will examine some of the explicit and subtle (real or imagined) messages received as a scholar of aesthetics of textiles and clothing. As I pondered these messages the intriguing similarities between aesthetics of textiles and clothing and James Dean's on-screen and off-screen personae became evident. Both aesthetics and James Dean have made invaluable contributions, but remain encumbered with fallacies. Both are *mistakenly* seen as enigmas, rebels, and ensnared in their own complexity. Aesthetics, like Dean, involves more than physical beauty. To rest comfortable with exploring only the attractiveness of (Dean's) physical appearance misses the richness of the experience.

Aesthetics and James Dean as Significant Contributors

Aesthetics holds its own, as Dean did in his three films (*East of Eden*, *Rebel Without a Cause*, and *Giant*) even against co-stars Julie Harris, Natalie Wood, Rock Hudson, and Elizabeth Taylor. Aesthetics, like Dean, is more than a "bit player" in the profession regardless of relative youth, and greatly contributes to the telling of the story (of textiles and clothing). For instance, consumers report that aesthetic aspects of apparel are of primary importance in selection and purchase of apparel (Eckman, Damhorst, & Kadolph, 1990). Aesthetic value, more than utilitarian value, is associated with U.S. consum-

ers' willingness to pay more for apparel products (Morganosky, 1984). Aesthetic aspects are relevant to other variables such as perceived quality (Fiore & Damhorst, 1992) and perceived risk (Winakor, Canton, & Wolins, 1980), which are associated with satisfaction with the product. Researchers concerned with fabric hand have made direct reference to the connection between aesthetic and physical/mechanical properties of fabric (Elder, 1977; Paek, 1979; Ukponmwan, 1987; Winakor, Kim, & Wolins, 1980). Aesthetic qualities of apparel also influence impressions of the wearer (e.g., Damhorst & Reed, 1986; Fiore & DeLong, 1984)[1]. Thus, centrality of aesthetic aspects to the story of one's experience with apparel parallels the centrality of Dean to the storyline in films.

Fallacies of Aesthetics and James Dean

The Enigmas

Both aesthetics and James Dean are viewed as enigmas, things of mystery that cannot be explained. However, effort and careful analysis can pierce the shrouded mysteries of both aesthetics and Dean. The apparent belief, that aesthetics is an enigma and thus unexplainable, is displayed in the glazed over look in the collective eye of some textiles and clothing professionals when the discussion of aesthetics is underway. I have once witnessed a respected theoretician in the field concede that she had no understanding of that (aesthetics), as if unable to comprehend the enigmatic nature of aesthetics. Aesthetics is not the simplest of topics to understand, but at the same time it should not be considered an enigma. We're scholars; we can untangle a strand of polished pearls of wisdom.

James Dean may have been a man of few words, but verbal and behavioral revelations result from careful analysis. Sal Mineo (Plato), in *Rebel Without a Cause*, said of Dean's character (Jim), "He doesn't say much, but when he does you know he's sincere." This was an accurate depiction of Dean's off-screen mannerism as well (McCann, 1991, p. 135). While Dean did not talk much about his sexuality, "He was openly and unashamedly bisexual at a time

Acknowlegments: This research is a part of the Family and Consumer Sciences Research Institute, College of Family and Consumer Sciences, Iowa State University, Ames, IA 50011. The author would like to thank Mary Lynn Damhorst, Mary Littrell, and John Littrell for their encouraging support of this non-traditional form of scholarship.

when no one else was admitting it" (Beath, 1986, p. 22). He preferred to express his deepest feelings through art and acting (McCann, 1991). Both forms of expression revealed that Dean was the embodiment of "still waters running deep." Anger and insecurity from witnessing, at the age of nine, the protracted suffering and death of his mother and only confidante, and resentment of his distant father were frequently cited reasons for his enigmatic, fascination with death and his mercurial nature (Beath, 1986; McCann, 1991). His motives were not transparent, but careful listening to his on-screen or off-screen statements offers insight into his enigmatic characteristics. For instance, at the end of *Giant* one must listen very carefully to the drunken ramblings of Dean's character (Jett Rink) to understand that his hidden unrequited desire for Elizabeth Taylor's character (Mrs. Leslie Benedict) drove him to extremes. These drunken ramblings may parallel, for some textiles and clothing professionals, the "ramblings" of aestheticians bandying concepts such as aesthetic intention, indeterminacy, or physiognomic expression.

The enigmatic image of aesthetics has been dispelled through identification and definition of concepts and theories that give order to the subject matter. There are many concepts and theories that have pierced the shrouded mysteries of aesthetics; textiles and clothing professionals must actively acquire this knowledge from aesthetics literature inside and outside the field. In a review of textiles and clothing related journals from 1970-1992, Fiore, Moreno, and Kimle (in press) found that in 63 aesthetics articles 1249 references were cited and only 284 (23%) were aesthetics related. Less than half (135) of the 284 references came from sources outside the field of textiles and clothing, a figure that suggests the need for better grounding of textiles and clothing research in aesthetics concepts and theories found in outside disciplines. Scholars of textiles and clothing should supply the reader with the theoretical underpinnings of aesthetics research. Through supporting literature, aesthetics is stripped of it's enigmatic character and is explained just as well as other complex human behaviors such as impression formation.

The Rebels

Both aesthetics and Dean are considered rebels because they are *mistakenly* thought to resist or reject the established social orders of their worlds. Aesthetics is viewed as a rebel, resisting or working outside the established rule of scientific rigor. In a recent discussion of a new description for an undergraduate course addressing aesthetics of clothing, a colleague was dismayed because I made aesthetics "sound so scientific." Aesthetics, unlike an uncivilized wolf-boy huddled in the corner afraid of fire, has embraced modern science (e.g., rigorous methods, ratings of reliability, and tests of significance). In fact, empirical studies of aesthetics grew rapidly during the late 19th and early 20th centuries (Crozier & Chapman, 1984). Further, *Empirical Studies of the Arts*, a journal first published in 1982, continues to present well-respected empirical studies of aesthetics. With the propagation of aesthetics scholarship from philosophy to an array of disciplines (e.g., anthropology, consumer behavior, and psychology) steeped in their own methodological traditions, aesthetics clearly submits to the rule of scientific inquiry. Each discipline, though favoring particular methodological traditions, shares the same cause of better understanding of aesthetics.

For Dean's rebellious generation, dissatisfied with the inadequacies of materialism, and perceived lack of parental caring, understanding, and love, James Dean embodied the spirit of the generation (McCann, 1991). Many saw Dean as a rebel on-screen and off-screen, but his on-screen characters were really in search of conformity and order offered by a conventional societal order. In *East of Eden*, Dean's character (Cal) was enamored with Julie Harris' good girl character (Abra), in *Giant* his character surprised Mrs. Benedict with his newly acquired social graces, and in *Rebel Without a Cause* his character (Jim Stark) desperately wanted the security of a family headed by a strong father and wanted to enter a conventional grown-up life. Jim laments, "If I could just have one day ...that I felt I belonged somewhere." Thus, Dean's characters want to be part of the establishment and to find stability offered by an idealized and ordered world.

Off-screen, Dean's yearning for social acceptance and his intense need for the fame (Yates, 1985) and adulation of a star (Beath, 1986, p. 22) dictated his actions. Identifying what part of his off-screen rebel persona was real and what was for effect is difficult (McCann,

1991, p. 153). Those in Dean's hometown who knew and respected a mild-mannered James Dean take great pains to dispel the image of a restless delinquent (Shaw, 1980). He called himself a serious minded and intense little devil ("James Dean", 1992), and was described by others as a "disenchanted romantic" (Thomson, 1976, p. 125). Such statements suggest Dean's desire to improve the social order rather than escape from it. Just as Dean wanted to be part of the established order, aesthetics wants to be part of the scientific community, which offers the ordered (and sometimes idealized) world of research methodology.

Aesthetics shares with Dean's characters the aspiration for *improved* social order that offers a supportive environment for its members. This supportive environment offers guidance and structure, as well as flexibility to meet individual needs. Dean's character, Cal, in *East of Eden* wanted to be loved by his father for who he was, not for his conformity to parental demands. Cal urges, "I gotta know who I am." Similarly, aestheticians have to know who they are: controlled-quantitative, inductive-qualitative, or reflective-introspective scholars. All co-exist in the supportive environment of the structured but encompassing interdisciplinary model of aesthetics offered by Fiore, Kimle, and Moreno (in press a).

No discipline should be locked out of the study of aesthetics because each provides an unique contribution to understanding this multifaceted topic. Cultural anthropology, commonly employing qualitative methods, demonstrates how aesthetic activities reflect and reinforce cultural structures and processes. Anthropology also examines how the symbolic nature of objects or activities, offering new or contradictory views of reality, transforms the order of society (Fratto, 1978). Philosophy depends heavily upon dialectical argument about concepts, principles, and descriptions of aesthetic experience (Bamossy, Johnston, & Parsons, 1985). Philosophers generally seek to clarify vague and problematic notions employed in discourse (Shusterman, 1989) and define the well rooted foundations of formal (Beardsley, 1969; Fry, 1969), expressive (Langer, 1953; Hospers, 1969; Berndtson, 1969), and general natures of aesthetic experience (Dewey, 1934; Pole, 1983). Whereas philosophy deals with the nature of aesthetics in general, art history deals with individual works, artists, schools, and historic periods for various kinds of aesthetic products (e.g., painting, music, poetry). Art history teaches about "(1) the geniusness [sic] of a specimen of art, (2) the presence of art, (3) its variety, and (4) how it has reached its current state" (Armstrong, 1989, p. 240). Psychology spawns psychoanalysis and empirical aesthetics. Psychoanalysis provides insight into the origins of aesthetic satisfaction. Empirical aesthetics, characterized by controlled experimental conditions, attempts to detect the structural properties of aesthetic stimuli and consistencies of individuals' reactions to these properties (Bamossy, Johnston, & Parsons, 1985).[1] A supportive environment, embracing a variety of these methodologies, can produce unique perspectives on aesthetics of textiles and clothing. The present special publication is comprised of scholarship using these quantitative, qualitative, and introspective methods, all enriching our understanding of aesthetics of textiles and clothing.

Ensnared in Complexity

Nothing makes me bristle more than hearing the statement, "Why do you have to make aesthetics so complicated? No one can understand aesthetics because it's been made so complex." Some professionals are annoyed by the use of concepts that move beyond elements and principles of design [e.g., viewing priorities (DeLong, 1987), complexity and novelty (Berlyne, 1974)]. Granted, some aesthetics literature is very complex and has a circuitous "Celtic knot" pattern of logic that must be unraveled (e.g., Gracyk, 1986), but the phenomenon of aesthetic experience is complex. For example, aesthetic experience is available in the process of creation as well as the process of appreciation of other-created objects or events. Aesthetic experience available during the creative and appreciation processes is not unidimensional; the experience consists of sensual, physiological, cognitive (unconscious and logical mental), emotional, and spiritual components that are frequently interrelated. Aesthetic experience is as much an experience of the body, as it is of the mind and the soul or spirit (for a discussion of the components of the creative and appreciation processes, see Fiore, Kimle, & Moreno, in press a; Fiore, Moreno, & Kimle, in press). Aestheticians do not take a simple phenomenon and make it complex; nor do they take a complex phenomenon and make

9

it simplistic. Aestheticians strive to make a complex phenomenon more *understandable*. Understanding a complex phenomenon does not ensnare, but *frees* scholars and appreciators to comprehend and experience aesthetics.

Some would rather see aesthetics resemble *Jimmy* Dean (either the [pre-star] farm boy growing up in Indiana or the sausage king) than *James* Dean. The down home, simple folk, "aw shucks" attitude of either Jimmy Dean would be seen by some as a fitting role model for aesthetics. Jimmy Dean, the sausage king, may have made his mark by staying down on the farm, but James Dean the legend never could. Moving beyond the comfort of the 'homey' elements and principles of design, with which most are acquainted, is essential to arriving at a deep understanding of aesthetics. I remember innocently asking a presenter who used stimuli made of a limited range of colors, patterns, and style detail how she would generalize beyond simple descriptive preferences of the limited range of aesthetic forms. The look of disdain on her face is etched into my memory. The response was no more gracious to the next audience member who raised the issue of proportion of the surface design to the size of garment layout of the stimuli. This sort of response is tantamount to a scholar bellowing down the halls of geography, "Why can't we use the old theory that the world is flat? It's much easier to draw maps that way."

Just a "Pretty Face"

Many equate aesthetics with the study of beauty, the ideal of physical attractiveness. This physical attractiveness may be analyzed according to composition of form such as shape, color, texture, line, size, and proportion. However, there are two other aspects, expressive and referential aspects (Fiore, Kimle, & Moreno, in press b), that contribute to aesthetic experience. The expressive aspect involves the aesthetic object's conveyance of feelings (e.g., liveliness of high intensity colors) and emotions (sadness of downward curved lines) (Kose, 1984). The referential characteristic of aesthetic objects consists of the symbolic elements conveying information about or referencing external realities (e.g., crane figure in Asian textiles symbolizing the wish for longevity of the owner).

For consumers, formal qualities appear to be more important than expressive or referential aspects of textiles and apparel (Eckman, Dam-

horst, & Kadolph, 1990; Morganosky & Postlewait, 1989; Littrell, 1980). Not surprisingly, formal qualities of dress are the most frequent topics of research in textiles and clothing. Thirty-three of the 63 aesthetics articles found in textiles and apparel related journals from 1970 to 1992 included analysis of formal qualities. Only six articles discussed expressive aspects, and eight studied referential aspects (Fiore, Moreno, & Kimle, in press). Some textbooks used in undergraduate courses on aesthetics (e.g., Kefgen & Touchie-Specht, 1986; Mathis & Connor, 1993) focus on ways dress can enhance physical attractiveness. Formal aspects are undoubtedly a constituent leading to aesthetic experience but they are not the whole story. Particularly in small scale and postmodern societies, beauty may not encompass all aspects of the aesthetic experience derived from appearance. For instance, is beauty the end goal of the postmodern individual dressing in the morning? Expressiveness or uniqueness of form may be the aesthetic goal of the postmodern individual, with little regard for resulting attractiveness of the body form. Is "cool" cool because it *isn't* beautiful? "Cool" may refer to objects that intentionally break or disregard established criteria of formal beauty (e.g., cosmetics that create a cadaverous appearance).

To disregard the importance of expressive and referential aspects of dress would be as short-sighted as disregarding the importance of these aspects to the "star quality" of James Dean. Dean was no "pretty boy." He was a scrawny fellow with regular features except for bow legs and prominent ears. Dean did not have the dashing good looks and stature of his contemporaries, such as Rock Hudson and Marlon Brando. (Dean was described as "a half-pint Brando" ["James Dean", 1992, p. 53].) Yet, Dean captured attention when appearing with these stars. When Dean was described as physically attractive ("moody good looks"; "James Dean's Hometown", 1990, p. 115), expressiveness qualifies the statement. The expressiveness of his face and mannerism was what attracted interest in Dean (McCann, 1991, p. 140). He would stand in front of the mirror and take rolls of close-up photographs of his face with only the slightest variation of expression. Dean was seeking the soul beneath the skin (McCann, 1991, p. 142). The referential images he created were so powerful that one of his biographies was entitled, *James Dean:*

American Icon (Dalton, 1984). He was described as the "brief, living manifestation of a new era" ("Obsessed by James Dean", 1989, p. 69), and the "damaged, but beautiful *soul* [italics added] of our time" by Andy Warhol (McCann, 1991, p. 125). Referential aspects of clothing even played a part in the indelible image of Dean. He carefully chose clothing to express an attitude towards society. Clothing was selected "with a painful self-consciousness that symbolized his youthful insecurities" (McCann, 1991, p.141). Thus, the contributions of expressive and referential aspects must be explored to understand and appreciate the depth of experience offered by aesthetics and Dean.

Where the Similarity Ends

There is one major difference between Dean and aesthetics of textiles and clothing; aesthetics is not going to crash and burn at an early age. This special publication is a testament to the burgeoning strength of aesthetics of textiles and clothing. My feeling may be appropriately expressed in the words of Dean's character (Jett) in a scene from *Giant* after he struck oil in a small parcel of arid land begrudgingly given to him by the powerful Jordan Benedict, "My well came in. Everyone thought I had a duster. My well came in big and there's more oil down there." The scene continues with a friend's reply to an angered Benedict who lunged towards Jett, "You should have killed him a long time ago when you had a chance. Now he's too rich to kill." Aesthetics of textiles and clothing is too rich to dismiss.

Endnote

[1] Content of this paragraph regarding aesthetics is drawn almost verbatim from Fiore, Kimle, and Moreno (in press a). Total word count of the content is less than 500 which, according to APA style, means that permission to quote is not required.
[2] Content of this paragraph regarding aesthetics is also drawn almost verbatim from Fiore, Kimle, and Moreno (in press a). Total word count of the content is less than 500 which, according to APA style, means that permission to quote is not required.

References

Armstrong, A. M. (1989). The interlacing of philosophy and history of art, *British Journal of Aesthetics, 29*(3), 239-247.

Bamossy, G., Johnston, M., & Parsons, M. (1985). The assessment of aesthetics judgment ability. *Empirical Studies of the Art, 3*(1), 63-79.

Beardsley, M. C. (1969). Reasons in aesthetic judgments. In J. Hospers (Ed.), *Introductory readings in aesthetics* (pp. 245-253). New York: Free Press.

Beath, W. N. (1986). *The death of James Dean.* New York: Grove Press.

Berlyne, D. E. (1974). *Studies in the new experimental aesthetics: Steps toward an objective psychology of aesthetic appreciation.* Washington, DC: Hemisphere.

Berndtson, A. (1969). *Art, expression, and beauty.* New York: Holt, Rinehart, and Winston.

Crozier, W. R., & Chapman, A. J. (1984). The perception of art: The cognitive approach and its context. In W. R. Crozier & A. J. Chapman (Eds.), *Cognitive processes in the perception of art* (pp. 3-23). New York: Elsevier Science.

Dalton, D. (1984). *James Dean: American icon.* London: Sidgwick & Jackson.

Damhorst, M. L., & Reed, J. A. P. (1986). Clothing color value and facial expressions: Effects on evaluations of female job applicants. *Social Behavior and Personality, 14*(1), 89-98.

DeLong, M. R. (1987). *The way we look: A framework for visual analysis of dress.* Ames, IA: Iowa State University Press.

Dewey, J. (1934). *Art as experience.* New York: Minton.

Eckman, M., Damhorst, M. L., & Kadolph, S. J. (1990). Toward a model of the in store purchase decision process: Consumer use of criteria for evaluating women's apparel. *Clothing and Textiles Research Journal, 8*(2), 13-22.

Elder, H. M. (1977). Fabric appearance and handle. *Journal of Consumer Studies and Home Economics, 1*, 171-182.

Fiore, A. M., Kimle, P. A., & Moreno, J. M. (in press a). Aesthetics: A comparison of the state of the art outside and inside the field of textiles and clothing. Part one: Creator and creative process, *Clothing and Textiles Research Journal.*

Fiore, A. M., Kimle, P. A., & Moreno, J. M. (in press b). Aesthetics: A comparison of the state of the art outside and inside the field of textiles and clothing. Part two: Object, *Clothing and Textiles Research Journal.*

Fiore, A. M., Moreno, J. M., & Kimle, P. A. (in press). Aesthetics: A comparison of the state of the art outside and inside the field of textiles and clothing. Part three: Appreciation process, appreciator, and summary comparisons, *Clothing and Textiles Research Journal.*

Fiore, A. M., & Damhorst, M. L. (1992). Intrinsic cues as predictors of perceived quality of apparel. *Journal of Consumer Satisfaction Dissatisfaction and Complaining Behavior, 5*, 168-178.

Fiore, A. M., & DeLong, M. R. (1984). Use of apparel as cues to perception of personality. *Perceptual and Motor Skills, 59*, 267-274.

Fratto, T. F. (1978). Undefining art: Irrelevant categorization in the anthropology of aesthetics. *Dialectical Anthropology, 3,* 129-138.

Fry, R. (1969). Art as form. In J. Hospers (Ed.), *Introductory readings in aesthetics* (pp. 100-114). New York: Free Press.

Gracyk, T. (1986). Sublimity, ugliness, and formlessness in Kant's aesthetic theory. *Journal of Aesthetics and Art Criticism, 45,* 49-56.

Hospers, J. (1969). The concept of artistic expression. In J. Hospers (Ed.), *Introductory readings in aesthetics* (pp. 142-166). New York: Free Press.

James Dean. (1992, July). *People,* p. 53.

James Dean's hometown revels without pause in fond memory of fairmount's favorite son. (1990, October). *People,* p. 114-115.

Kazan, E. (Producer), & Kazan, E. (Director). (1955). *East of Eden* [Film]. Burbank, CA: Warner Bros. Pictures & First National.

Kefgen, M., & Touchie-Specht, P. (1986). *Individuality in clothing selection and personal appearance* (4th ed.). New York: Macmillan Publishing.

Kose, G. (1984). The psychological investigation of art: Theoretical and methodological implications. In W. R. Crozier & A. J. Chapman (Ed.), *Cognitive processes in the perception of art* (pp. 27-44). New York: Elsevier Science.

Langer, S. (1953). *Feeling and form.* New York: Charles Scribner.

Littrell, M. A. (1980). Home economist as cross-cultural researchers: A field study of Ghanaian clothing selection. *Home Economics Research Journal, 8,* 307-317.

Mathis, C. M., & Connor, H. V. (1993). *Triumph of individual style.* Cali, Columbia: Timeless Editions.

McCann, G. (1991). *Rebel males.* London: Hamish Hamilton.

Morganosky, M. (1984). Aesthetic and utilitarian qualities of clothing: Use of a multidimensional clothing value model. *Home Economics Research Journal, 13,* 12-20.

Morganosky, M. A., & Postlewait, D. S. (1989). Consumers' evaluation of apparel form, expression, and aesthetic quality. *Clothing and Textiles Research Journal, 7(2),* 11-15.

Obsessed by James Dean, Japan's Seita Onishi makes a monument to that fallen rebel his cause. (1989, August). *People,* p. 66-67.

Paek, S. L. (1979). An analysis of sensory hands as identified by selected consumer. *Textile Research Journal, 45,* 698-704.

Pole, D. (1983). *Aesthetics, form, and emotion.* London: Gerald Duckworth.

Shaw, B. (1980, October). Dead 25 years, James Dean is given a touching hometown tribute by nostalgic fans. *People,* pp. 40-41.

Shusterman, R. (Ed.). (1989). *Analytic aesthetics.* Oxford: Basil Blackwell.

Stevens, G. & Ginsberg, H. (Producers), & Stevens, G. (Director). (1956). *Giant* [Film]. Burbank, CA: Warner Bros. Pictures.

Thomson, D. (1976). *A biographical dictionary of film* (1st ed.). New York: William Morrow and Co.

Ukponmwan, J. O. (1987). Appraisal of woven fabric quality. *Textile Research Journal, 57,* 283-298.

Weisbart, D. (Producer) & Ray, N. (Director). (1955). *Rebel without a cause* [Film]. Burbank, CA: Warner Bros. Pictures.

Winakor, G., Canton, B., & Wolins, L. (1980). Perceived fashion risk and self-esteem of males and females. *Home Economics Research Journal, 9,* 45-56.

Winakor, G., Kim, C. J., & Wolins, L. (1980). Fabric hand: Tactile sensory assessment. *Textile Research Journal, 50,* 601-609.

Yates, B. (1985, October). Far from Eden. *Car and Driver,* pp. 85-90.

The Needlework Arts in the Art of Remedios Varo

Patricia Campbell Warner
University of Massachusetts-Amherst

Introduction

Remedios Varo was a Spanish painter of the Surrealist movement who achieved fame in Mexico after World War II. In spite of the work of two American scholars, Estella Lauter and Whitney Chadwick, who included her in their collections of women artists, she remained virtually unknown in the United States until a small exhibition of her work was mounted at the New York Academy of Sciences and later traveled to the National Academy of Sciences in Washington, D.C. in 1986. But it was not until Janet Kaplan published her book, *Unexpected Journeys, The Art and Life Of Remedios Varo,* in 1988 that a broader audience saw her work.

Most writers are struck by Varo's references to science and the natural world. Certainly it was that aspect of her work that drew the attention of the Academies of Science and prompted their exhibitions.[1] Lauter and Kaplan also point to Varo's imagery of journey and the female quest, and Chadwick particularly links her imagery with women who create life and art.[2] But my field is clothing and textile history, and the major impact for me on seeing her work in Kaplan's book was her inventive and pervasive use of clothing, and of the needle arts. As is so often the case, this was an aspect ignored by other writers, except only casually, biographically. I was struck by how often Varo used the needle arts as a metaphor for women's experience, symbolizing both women's work and their escape from an enclosed, confined existence. In her work, cloth or clothing become agents to break through the boundaries, giving life to the present and intimations of the future. Thus, this paper looks at her art in terms of her use of clothing and textiles as symbols of women's experience and women's lives. Its place in this collection of papers on aesthetic aspects of dress is perhaps different from others, since it does not contemplate "real" dress, but clothing and textiles used as symbols, as metaphor in art.

I have thought about Varo's work in terms of layerings. Broadly, her vision combines commentary on women's existence, its solitary nature, its isolation, even its entrapment, with women's creativity and determination. At a secondary level fall her choice of medium, which is mostly oil painting, and her participation in the Surrealist movement. She expressed her vision in Surrealist terms, that is, in terms of the fantastic, the psychological, dream or nightmare, or through extraordinary flights of imagination. At a third level, we find the images themselves, and the symbolic use of those images. It is here that clothing and textiles perform their roles in her work. She was a classically trained painter who chose to comment on women's education and experience in part through the subject matter of needlework.

In my view, the entire set of layers expresses Varo's aesthetic. These all together present to us, her viewers, her very personal but universal message about her art, her view of her own life, her view of women's lives generally. And her centering much of her expression on a unique view of the elements and messages of dress and needlework places her firmly within the framework of this publication.

In traditional art and art criticism, "women's work", that is, the domestic efforts of women's hands rather than, say, painting or sculpture, has been relegated to craft, or non-art. It simply was never considered in discussions of what commentators liked to think of as Art. Recently, however, scholars have looked at women's artistic production with eyes educated by a feminist sensibility. As Gisela Ecker points out in the introduction of her collection of essays on the subject of feminist aesthetics, "What has been imposed on women through oppressive social conditions or prejudice should not be made part of our definition of women's art and thus be further perpetuated." She quotes Shulamith Firestone to remind us that women, confined to the house, used "wool rather than marble" for their medium. Further, she points out the "derogatory tone which seems inevitably to creep in when talking about 'wool rather than marble.'" Ecker admits that she personally finds "it extremely hard to celebrate needlework having gone through convent school education during which it became painfully clear that what we were taught wasn't elaborate hemstitch embroidery but what was thought was essential femininity."[3] Varo too commented on that same convent-bred shared history, as we shall see.

Rozsika Parker gives another view of the significance of embroidery in women's history, one also prompted by a feminist aesthetic. In her book, *The Subversive Stitch*, she drew attention to the needlework arts as expression of women's lives. Art rather than craft, women's work rather than men's, and a symbol of femininity—"docility, obedience, love of home, and a life without work"[4]—embroidery and related skills became the perfect metaphor for the quietude of a patriarchal society's perfect woman. But, Parker added, though "[t]he art of embroidery has been the means of educating women into the feminine ideal, and of proving that they have attained it, ...it has also provided a weapon of resistance to the constraints of femininity."[5] Strong words and strange, juxtaposing the delicacy of needlework with the bluntness of weaponry. Yet this very contrast is used to wonderful effect in the art of Remedios Varo, who understood completely the significant linkage between the needle arts and the enclosed world women inhabited. So much of her work incorporated the symbols of women's lives, from the generation or creation that defines women's existence to the outer, more social manifestations of their lives, like clothing and textiles. Though much of her work depicted aspects of clothing and textiles, it was done in such an unsettling way that we are forced to question the meaning behind the commonplace of the "women's work" represented.

If, as the dictionary definition suggests, aesthetics is "of or pertaining to the sense of the beautiful" or "pertaining to the criticism of taste", or even "having a love of beauty", it must clearly apply to the work of women's hands.[6] Varo makes us see the connections between the two aesthetics and women's work in her many references to them, but it is her use of the symbols of women's lives represented in needlework and the textile arts that I wish to address here.

Remedios Varo was born to a middle class family in Spain in 1908. She was a product of a typical convent education, an experience that later in life, as we shall see, she reflected on in her art.[7] She learned to sew as a child, in all likelihood influenced by her grandmother who

was a sewer. Illustrations in Janet A. Kaplan's biography of Varo, *Unexpected Journeys,* show a sketch done by a 14-year-old Remedios of her grandmother, bent over embroidery, and a photograph of the old woman intent on her work behind a home sewing machine. Early in her life, Varo developed a "consuming interest in costumes and sewing", making her own clothes from childhood on, declaring that "tailors had no idea of a woman's anatomy". She "even designed her own shoes," to the delight of her cousins. So key an element in her life was sewing and costume that, in a retrospective of her work in 1983 in Mexico City, her sewing machine was exhibited in a place of honor.[8]

Not surprisingly, an even greater lifetime interest was drawing and painting. In the mid-twenties she went to art school in Madrid, at that time a lively, innovative artistic center that drew intellectuals from all over Europe, to learn technique and hone her skills. But out of the classroom, she turned to the new Surrealism, the most avante-garde movement of the time, to express herself.[9] Wanting the life of an artist, she married a "politically committed artist" in 1930 at age 21, thereby freeing herself from the bourgeois constraints of her family. Within a year, political turmoil disrupted life in Madrid, so, when Varo graduated in 1931, the couple decided to leave for a year in Paris .[10] Returning to Barcelona, whose atmosphere was less conventional than Madrid's, Varo immersed herself more and more in the ideas and expression of Surrealism, often leftist politically oriented. Her marriage faded, but another liaison with an artist in the movement, Estaban Francés, encouraged her work. By 1937, the year after the outbreak of the Spanish Civil War, she returned to Paris, both to escape the war and for a new love, of an older, established French Surrealist poet she had met in Barcelona who was a close friend of André Breton, the guru and scribe of Surrealism. While she was in France, Franco closed Spain's borders, effectively preventing her return.[11] Kaplan tells us, "She was to dwell on the impact of this abrupt and painful break throughout the rest of her life, expressing deep remorse at having thus separated herself from her family."[12] The overpowering impressions of her upbringing and early years played out in the work done in her later years, as we shall see.

The next years spent in France, immersed in the company of Surrealist artists, enriched her own aesthetic vision. Even in those early years as an artist, her interest in clothing images is evident. One painting, "Souvenir of the Valkyrie", 1938, incorporates the ring of fire of the German legend, but instead of the entrapped and protected maiden in its center, there is a long-torsoed, empty corset lying on its side, with a lively vine and leaves springing out of it, symbol of woman, symbol of life within it. Kaplan states:

> Varo's connection with the Surrealist movement was of enormous importance to her as an artist. At a crucial moment in her development, when she was seeking a focus for her painstakingly acquired technique, Surrealism encouraged her tendency toward the imaginative and oriented her toward an attitude of questioning, experimentation, and irony.[13]

This was true, but it was to distinctly female sets of symbols that she turned, pulling her away from the traditional male-oriented (and female-destructive) symbols of most of the Surrealists.

World War II intervened, and after undergoing a series of harrowing experiences she and her companion, who both had been imprisoned, managed to escape German-occupied Paris for Vichy-controlled Marseilles. A year later in 1941, destitute and near-starving, they eventually secured passage to Mexico, which had opened its doors to "all Spanish refugees of both sexes resident in France."[14]

Many of their old friends had undergone a similar journey, and had already settled there, all part now of the émigré community in Mexico City, and separate (determinedly so on both sides) from the native Mexican art community centered around Diego Rivera and Frieda Khalo. Varo became inseparable friends with the English Surrealist painter, Leona Carrington, also an expatriate, whom she had met in Paris. Both imaginative and extraordinary women, they fed each other's creative spirit, and developed new visions based on Surrealist principles.[15] Their friendship, so important to each, clearly influenced their work, yet though both used imagery relating to women and their lives, each had a singular style of her own. Kaplan and Chadwick both tell us that

> ...the common concerns of these two women (often appearing in striking similarities of tone, point of view, and narrative focus) were developed not through shared collaboration but individually, each woman working alone, often years after leaving the Surrealist circle, when each had little or no contact with the others.

Varo and Carrington shared the sense that they were both uniquely inspired by strange inner powers, that they had been chosen for a special psychic journey. Traveling together into what the poet Adrienne Rich has called "the cratered night of female memory,"[16] they undertook a shared process of creative self-discovery, working together to probe the possibilities of woman's creative power. Through their exploration of hermetic and magical paths, they developed a common pictorial language, derived from the realms of domestic life, the fairy tale, and the dream.[17]

It is interesting to note that "each woman work[ed] alone", yet depended on the friendship for support, since this pattern is so typical of women's lives generally. Varo carried the isolation of the individual into her paintings to become a significant theme in her work.

Varo's paintings are particularly recognizable since they are filled with versions of self-portraiture. (Figure 1). Throughout her mature work, she consistently used her own distinctive features of huge almond eyes, long thin nose, small elfin chin and narrow-lipped mouth to give face to her silent, mysterious and determined young women. This signature is evident throughout her mature work, as is her use of other symbols, including those of generation or creation, and a reliance on extraordinary clothing and textiles. Carrington, on the other hand, had no real interest in that aspect in her own art.

Whitney Chadwick has written about the important women of the Surrealist movement.[18] Although many of the other Surrealist women adopted subject matter related to women's experience, (unlike the men in the group, who tended to fragment and sexualize women) only Varo gives real importance to the clothing her figures wear, or to textiles that they create. Indeed, it is to textiles and clothing she turns when she wants to symbolize the domestic sphere. So pervasive is the message of these two ele-

Figure 1. Remedios Varo, from the Mexico City years.

ing the middle ground of the painting, from right border to left, all moving and visible above a high wall that hides not only the bodies of the wearers, but even their heads. There is no explanation for them in this picture, nor even a relationship to the figures in the foreground. But the hats attest to unseen people, and help to create an atmosphere of uneasiness.

Varo and Estaban Francés, who had also emigrated to Mexico, worked for Marc Chagall on his costume designs for a Léonid Massine ballet which, because of the war, premiered in Mexico City rather than in Paris. Francés went on to costume Ballanchine productions in New York, but Varo, who gave up professional designing soon after,[21] retained the essence of theatrical costuming in her paintings throughout her life. Many of her figures, often human/animal mutations, look more like fantastic creatures designed for the ballet stage than anything else, like costumed human beings with elaborate animalistic head-dresses.

A good example of this is "Creation of the Birds" (1958) (Figure 2), which depicts an owl/woman seated in a high room, calm and engrossed, painting birds that spring to life after having a beam of light from a distant star directed on them through a prism. The paint brush is connected to a miniature guitar strung like a pendant from her neck, suggesting music's life force. The paints, the three primary colors from which all colors stem, are produced from a double-egg-shaped distiller, another symbol of life-giving, in turn connected to another distant star. The whole suggests woman, wisdom, artist, alchemist, mystery, creation, life-giving; a magical and evocative representation.

The owl/woman looks like a figure costumed for dance. Her head is an owl's head, like a head-dress, round with huge facial disks that even as they look owl-like, still retain human eyes and Varo's own features. It sits on a narrow, human neck. Her body from neck to ankles is covered with feathers, like a feathery leotard revealing her legs, but her ankles and feet are human, and bare. Her arms (not wings) are clothed in sleeves gathered at the wrist, leaving the human hands free to create. The entire impression is one of a ballet dancer, in the style of the 1950s.

This painting represents much of what is constant in Varo's mature work. Mysticism and

ments in her canvases that any viewer attuned to them is forceably struck by their messages. Where others, even Carrington, used generic robes and drapery to clothe their figures, Varo injected magical activity into cloth, imagining it springing to life of its own volition, or being the ground for germinating plant life; taking the role of body binding, rather like mummy wrapping, or creating physical barriers for her figures to break through. Clothing became metaphors for vehicles, whether boats or self-contained wheeled body enclosures. She gave life to swirling hand-made creations. Clearly, her own personal aesthetic included clothing and textiles to a prominent degree.

Early in her stay in Mexico, before she became known as an artist, she worked as a costume designer for theatrical productions. Kaplan tells us, "hats and other head coverings became her specialty."[19] Indeed, a work entitled "Coincidence"[20] has a virtual river of hats cover-

Figure 2. Creation of the Birds, 1958.

superstition combined with flights of fancy found in few other artist's work pervade her paintings. Yet often a scientific basis underlies her imagery, and a natural world gone awry but under some other order's careful control influences the quiet intensity of the figures and their activities. Usually her figures are either female or androgynous; even the male figures are slim and willowy, never sturdily masculine. However, the point of view is clearly a woman's, mainly because of the subject matter and the use of the female form. Never is that form openly revealing; usually it is in the act of something, whether creating, as here, or in questing, to use the medieval sense of the word. Almost invariably there is a feeling of isolation and silence, and often, though not here, a sense of entrapment. Almost never is emotion displayed, yet the sense of activity, of intensity sometimes almost to the point of madness, always done in silence, is usually there.

Varo had learned her craft well. Her works, small in size, recalling the egg-yolk tempera on gesso works of the high Gothic and early Renaissance, were as finely detailed and meticulous as those precursors. Her careful attention to textiles and clothing also reminds her viewers of those early masters who provided exquisite records of the textiles and clothing of their day.

Almost all of Varo's works had human or human-like figures in them. To get their correct movements and foreshortening, she used an artist's small articulated wooden mannequin for which she fashioned miniature costumes. The little outfits were perfect in detail. She would dress the little form, put it into the position she was aiming for in her painting, and use it as a clothed model.[22] Obviously, her sewing and designing skills came into play behind the scenes even more directly than in the paintings themselves.

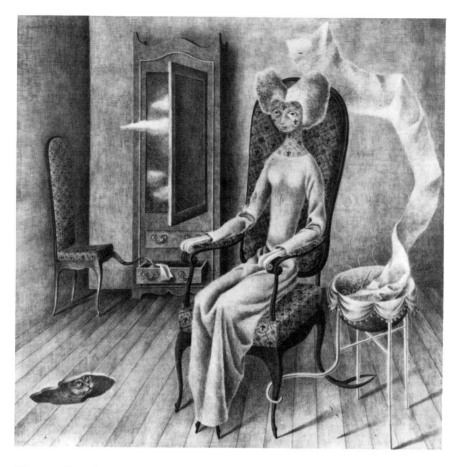

Figure 3. Mimesis, 1960.

The designer and seamstress, then, were evident in her work, and, knowing her background, might be anticipated. What could not be foreseen was her use of textiles and clothing in other ways. It is through these other uses, mystical and magical, that we see the merger of Varo's own personal understanding of womens' lives, her aesthetic and her imagination. She uses several approaches, all of them out of the ordinary. One is to use textiles as metaphor for women's environment. Often in the form of paper-as-textile, as hand-made paper is, they suggest a form of entrapment or a barrier through which a woman must pass. Another uses them as metaphor for women's creative spirit. A third takes clothing and transforms it into something else, usually a vehicle of some whimsical type. And still another fuses clothing with the natural world, creating a visible link between the two. So strong is the imagery that women recognize its power and message instantly on seeing it.

The first type, suggesting environment, is perhaps best represented by the painting, "Mimesis" (1960) (Figure 3), one of Varo's most chilling works. Here the title gives us a clue. *The American Heritage Dictionary of the English Language* quotes Susan Sontag for a definition of the word: "The earliest theory of art...proposed that art was mimesis, imitation of reality." Mimesis comes from the Greek, meaning imitation, from which the words mime, mimic, mimicry all come.[23] From the root word also comes pantomime, the ancient form of acting that depends for its effect on the total silence of the actors. The art historian and aesthetician, E.H. Gombrich, tells us, "In antiquity the conquest of illusion by art was such a recent achievement that the discussion of painting and sculpture inevitably centered on imitation, *mimesis.* "[24] In this painting, Varo seems to play on the word of the title, showing us both the imitative and the silent. But the idea of imitation turns away from the natural in order to achieve artistic reality and takes on a startling and sinister form quite opposite in effect from anything natural.

A female figure, passive almost unto terminal stillness, sits in an armchair in her bleak parlor. Here is the darker side of the calm, serious figure depicted in "Creation of Birds". Her silence is complete, her gaze deadened. Her supreme silence and immobility contrast starkly with the lively activity going on around her. In this case, it is imitation with a nightmare quality. The human element in the painting is lifeless, the inanimate objects represented by the furniture and her needlework are all crazily alive, reaching out in sinuous movement to embrace each other or fly away of their own accord. The most chilling aspect of the picture is that the woman's flesh has taken on the unhealthy, putrid green coloring and pattern of the chair she sits in. Her hands, resting on the wooden arms of the chair, have been replaced by replicas of the chair arm terminals, and her feet have become the wooden feet of the chair legs. Beside her, her work basket—comfortable symbol of women's sphere—delicately reaches out one leg to wrap around a leg of the chair, while the acid green cloth she had been working on (which is the same unappealing color as her dress) emerges of its own accord from the basket and surges above her head like a snake charmer's python, and with similar menace. Her hair is non-human in its form, resembling two large natural sponges framing her face. Even her cat, the one genuinely alive creature in the painting, has frozen into immobility under the wooden floor, afraid to enter the room.[25] This image of a woman whose essence is being drained by her rapidly animating furniture is powerful and frightening, surely a warning to those whose pride of home has taken priority in their lives. And textiles, linked here irretrievably with the woman, are utilized to bear the strong message. By titling the work "Mimesis", or imitation of reality, Varo tells us clearly of her recognition of the ambiguities of women's lives. She forces us to ask the question, Which is imitation, and which is reality?

Another example of textile as environment is actually a reversal of that concept, becoming instead environment as textile. Two paintings use this same device particularly forcefully. The first, "Solar Music" (1955) (Figure 4) shows the figure bowing a beam of light in the middle of a forest, as if the light were a giant double bass.

Her cloak, drawn up loosely around her shoulders, is an extension of the forest floor, soft, heavy, and covered with grassy plants. The other, "The Useless Science or the Alchemist" (Figure 5) from the same year, depicts a figure seated in the middle of a room with a fantastic collection of Rube Goldberglike machinery. This sexless person is huddled, clutching a cloak that covers its head and everything else, exposing only the two hands and face. As in the previous painting, the cloak is a seamless continuation of the floor, only in this case it is a black and white check tile floor that miraculously softens into textile plasticity to drape over the body. To those who consider clothing as near environment, this is clothing as environment indeed.

Textiles used in other ways are vividly portrayed in a triptych Varo conceived in 1961 and '62, "Toward the Tower" (1961), "Embroidering Earth's Mantle" (1961), and "The Escape" (1962). These three autobiographical paintings harken back to her childhood and her convent education, and show us how deeply the strong influence of those years remained with her until her death, in 1963. They are packed with symbolism and tell a story of order, duty, restriction, confinement, of longing and silent planning, and finally of escape. The first, "Toward the Tower", sets the scene with its convent background designed to look like a beehive. Buzzing out on odd little bicycles made of wheels and stiffened tails of the riders' clothing are a swarm of identical young, golden-haired women all dressed in school uniform, deep gray-blue with crisp white collars. Leading them is a nun, also riding a scooter-like machine whose handlebars are the train of her own outfit. She in turn is led by a man on a bicycle who has a huge pack on his back that is in reality not separate but all of a piece with his coat. Birds circle in and out of this pack. Of all the young women, only one challenges the event by catching the viewer's eye.

The second painting in the series is "Embroidering Earth's Mantle" (Figure 6). Here, we see the convent students trapped high in a storybook tower, guarded by a cloaked and veiled male (not the nun of the previous painting), who stirs a double-egg vessel very much like the one in "Creation of Birds" as he reads a book. From the vessel come not only floating, lively threads for the young women to use as embroidery floss, but taut, straight ones that bind them

Figure 4. "Solar Music"

almost invisibly as well. Behind the overseer, in a wall recess, is another veiled and draped figure, playing a vertical flute. The young women sit at embroidery frames, unspeaking, eyes cast down, dutifully working on endless pieces of embroidery that flow out of horizontal slits in the sides of the tower. Their completed work tumbles down the outside of the tower like a waterfall, to swirl and eddy into land- and town-scapes. The embroidered images take on 3-dimensional forms, creating the world below.

Women once again are passive here, their heads bowed over the needlework suggesting silence, work, entrapment. Once again, only one's eyes stray from the work at hand, symbolizing again both challenge and resistance. The glance draws us in, making us co-conspirators.

Figure 5. The Useless Science or the Alchemist, 1955.

woman effecting her escape as she had envisaged and embroidered it, the two of them sailing off in a little boat that looks like a cross between a furry cup and an upside-down umbrella (yet another bending of textile reality). As Roszika Parker so aptly pointed out, the iconography of women's work is rarely given the consideration it deserves.[27]

In the central painting of this triptych, we are aware of Varo's use of traditional women's work, in this case embroidery, to focus our attention on the constraint and isolation of women's lives. Rozsika Parker, writing in *The Subversive Stitch,* showed the relationship between embroidery and the feminine. She stated,

> That embroiderers do transform materials to produce sense—whole ranges of meanings—is invariably entirely overlooked. Instead embroidery and a stereotype of femininity have become collapsed into one another, characterized as mindless, decorative and delicate; like the icing on a cake, good to look at, adding taste and status, but devoid of significant content.[28]

Parker referred to embroidery as "the bearer of women's soul"[29] and linked it to sexuality (certainly, Varo would have agreed with this concept) quoting from several nineteenth century authors and painters to make her case. Speaking of John Everett Millais' painting, *Mariana,* "The whole angle of the body, the position of the arms and the gaze indicate a sexual provocativeness, an element of rebelliousness, that could only be kept in check by embroidery frames, stained glass windows, the restricted limits of the convent . . ."[30] Varo went a step further by suggesting that even the tight rein of convent restrictions was overcome by the truly defiant.

In a graphic description, Colette, as quoted by Parker, recalled another aspect of embroiderers that has seeped into the culture and was indelibly relayed in Varo's painting. Speak-

Kaplan pointed out a wonderful small detail that one can't see in the illustration. The rebellious heroine here in the centerpiece of the triptych has, in her captivity, embroidered her vision of her escape into the fabric of her work. Her secret meeting with her lover can be faintly seen upside down in the part of the cloth she has completed.[26] In the third section of the triptych, "The Escape", we see the young

Figure 6. Embroidering Earth's Mantle, 1961.

ing of her daughter, she wrote: "She is silent, and she—why not write down the word that frightens me—she is thinking." Parker continued, speaking of young embroiderers learning the art, "Maternal authority kept them there for years and years, never rising except to change the skein of silk, or to elope with a stranger. . ." She concluded, "Eyes lowered, head bent, shoulders hunched—the position signifies repression and subjugation, yet the embroiderer's silence, her concentration also suggests a self-containment, a kind of autonomy."[31] The young rebel of the paintings so aptly fits the description that we wonder if Varo was familiar with Colette's ruminations—but Varo has made her heroine a stereotype placed within a fantastic environment.

"Finally, in the nineteenth century, embroidery and femininity were entirely fused," continued Parker.

. . . Then embroidery was blamed for the conflicts provoked in women by the femininity the art fostered. By the end of the century, Freud was to decide that constant needlework was one of the factors that 'rendered women particularly prone to hysteria' because day-dreaming over embroidery induced 'dispositional hypnoid states'.[32]

Varo, a generation after Freud, would probably have agreed with him up to a point, but possibly would have come to a different conclusion. Certainly her paintings link the long hours of forced, painstaking work with the germination of ideas, perhaps even of "hypnoid states", but she funnels her thoughts toward escape, not mindless daydreaming. And the powerful message that the product of women's silent, dutiful and even forced work takes on new meaning to become the foundation of new worlds is not lost on viewers of "Embroidering Earth's Mantle".

Figure 7. Weaver of Verona, 1956.

Another work by Varo that combines women's creative aesthetic with textiles and once again pushes the metaphor beyond the normal is "Weaver of Verona" (1956) (Figure 7). Here we see several of the elements she has used in the past: a solitary woman draped in a cloak of soft material, seated, working with her hands – in this case, knitting, the title of the painting notwithstanding. The product of her handiwork flies away from her feet, taking on a life of its own. But there are differences here. The ribbed knitted strips leave her needles as flat pieces, but almost immediately begin folding in on themselves to form a 2-dimensional, cut-out paper-like figure that, as it approaches the open window, fleshes out into the head and neck of a beautiful young woman, fully 3-dimensional. The source of the yarn in this case is from a cloud hovering high in the rafters of the small, bare room, but close inspection reveals that the cloud is a drawing of the scroll-work and *f*-holes of a violin. In "Embroidering Earth's Mantle", the hint of music in the isolated tower room was certainly present in the image of the flute player; the pendant the bird/woman wore in "Creation of Birds" also reminded us of the importance of music. Here, it is suggested again in the amorphous cloud that provides the source of the magical yarn.

Varo seems to be telling us, then, that music is critical to women's lives, even necessary to aid the creative process. But two other elements are required as well: the work a woman does, as exemplified by the knitting, and escape from restriction. For it is not until the figure reaches the window, to sail through it into the quiet city and open sky, that it takes on a human shape. Up until then, it is flat, 2-dimensional. Creativity according to Varo seems to demand the combination of woman's thoughts or inspiration, her determined work, and her freedom to create as she herself sees fit.

Figure 8. Vagabond, 1958.

In "Vagabond" (Figure 8), the focus of the entire painting is on the vehicle of the central figure, this time (and rare for Varo) a man. His personal environment or vehicle is entirely his clothing, wrapped around him and extended to include wheels, propellers, a veiled hat and all the paraphernalia of his existence, even his cat curled at his feet. Wood siding supports utensils and a flower pot at chest level, and on the other side, as part of the lining of his cloak, the paneling backs a bookcase and a small portrait. Double cupboard doors open to display his face. His hat, like an inverted flower pot, has a propeller attached that connects to another one on top of the wheeled staff he carries in his right hand. His entire body is wrapped by a cloak that layers and folds around him, its buttons left open to suggest accessibility. Underneath all this, the traveler wears an outfit reminiscent of an early nineteenth century English curate, deep gray with buttons down the front and narrow, form-fitting trousers that look more like breeches and stockings. As he passes through a deep, silent forest, he appears to be utterly self-sufficient, his world contained around him in his clothing. But as Varo herself explained about this painting,

> It is a design for a vagabond's clothes, but it is for an *unliberated* vagabond. It is a very practical and comfortable set of clothes that has front-wheel drive for locomotion; if he lifts his walking stick he stops. The outfit can be hermetically sealed at night and has a little door which can be locked with a key. Some parts of the outfit are made of wood, but as I said, the man is not liberated: on one side of the outfit there is a nook which acts as a living room. Here there is a portrait hanging and three books. On his breast he wears a flower pot with a rose growing in it, a finer and more delicate plant than those he finds in these woods. But he needs the portrait, the rose (nostalgia for a little garden and a house) and his cat; he is not truly free.[33]

Once again, as in "Mimesis", Varo seems to be commenting on the relationship we have with our possessions. As long as we are tied to them, we are not free.

Another highly imaginative use of textiles, this time clothing, is in Varo's wonderful little vehicles where clothing actually becomes the mode of transportation. Students of clothing and its messages in society often refer to clothing as personal environment, or as vehicle of meaning—symbol—within a culture. Varo takes this interpretation literally in some of her more whimsical representations. We already have seen examples of this in "Toward the Tower", but two works particularly, "Vagabond" (1958) and "Exploration of the Sources of the Orinoco" (1959) show this most clearly.

The other example of clothing as vehicle is "Exploration of the Sources of the Orinoco River", (1959) (Figure 9). Here, a conventionally

24

Figure 9. Exploration of the Sources of the Orinoco river, 1959

dressed young woman wearing a khaki-colored quasi-military coat and bowler hat sits upright with earnest, even mad determination in a boat shaped like the blossom of a lady's-slipper. But instead of any organic form, this boat is fashioned like a giant overcoat. The rim of her bowler flows behind her to become the back of the armchairlike vessel, anchoring her firmly in place. The lapels of the coat are huge, spreading out like sails at the sides, the bulbous front is buttoned together around her knees. A patch pocket holds, presumably, her maps. A belt arches above her knees to hold her compass in front of her. Her navigational devices are a series of Rube Goldberglike strings and ropes that connect to various buttons on her epaulettes or through the ornamental buckles of her belt, through buttonholes in the coat/boat, and eventually to the rudder, which resembles a fish's fin. Once again, one of Varo's charac-

ters is secure in her vehicle as it takes her on a fantastic voyage. For the purposes of those who look at clothing in terms of carrier of message, it is literally vehicle here.

The contrast, particularly in "Orinoco", between the conventional and the unconventional is striking. The traveler is in part very conventional in appearance, yet she is embarked on a fantastic journey in an impossible craft made from clothing. Time and again Varo used clothing to stand for other worlds, whether on the bodies of her mystical figures, or interacting in some other ways in their lives. At the same time clothing or textiles frequently define her women in their roles, true for women everywhere. The needle arts are compelling elements of women's experience, whether in the form of clothing choice or the products of women's work. For Varo, however, they are more. They become the vehicle of the voyage, or the creation that flies away in something approaching human form seeking escape from the confines of established boundaries. Embroidery becomes not only the solid foundation of the universe but the pattern of escape as well. Perhaps Varo saw our clothing as the vehicle in which we travel our own journeys through life, defining each of us as we go.

In 1985, Gisela Eckart wrote, "It is tempting to mistake features of women's art as representations of 'women's nature'".[34] Another writer in the Eckart collection, Silvia Bovenschen, wrote, "Thus far, I have found tangible instances of what might be termed female sensitivity towards...painting...only in certain moments of female subversion, female imagination or formal constructs within various works. And I find these only when the specifics of feminine experience and perception determines the form that the work takes, not when some 'feminine concern' has merely been tacked on to the original form."[35] A generation earlier, Varo had already proved them at least in part wrong since much of the focus of Varo's work relied explicitly on "woman's nature", on her daily experience and the artifacts of it. Certainly, her perception of women's lives recurs in much of her mature work, and in Bovenschen's words, "determine the form". It would appear that neither writer was aware of Varo's work at the time of their writing. Had they been so, I believe they would have modified their statements.

It is interesting to recognize that, as with many of us, the work of Varo's maturity incorporated many aspects of her own past. The difference is, of course, that while most of us plod unimaginatively forward, in her hands, reality and metaphor were interwoven seamlessly. She who had learned to sew and design as a child never lost that fascination. Many of us recognize that attraction. But for Varo, it became a major part of her personal aesthetic, a metaphor through which she used tedious hours plying a needle to explain women's creative spirit which can survive in spite of being trapped in a social milieu. She borrowed from that early interest in making clothing to illuminate the transformations that costume can bring, adding her rich imagination's details to complete the transformation from one species to another. Fashioned through her own per-sonal filter, dress became literally the vehicle of the quest or of escape.

She refused convention's limitations, substituting instead an unresolved but supremely detailed world of her own. Much of it addressed women's experience in a dreamlike, even nightmarish formula which refused to accept the usual boundaries between woman's sphere and the larger world. Her figures are often bounded by societal limitations: architecture, clothing, domestic expectation. At the same time, her subjects defy those conventions, responding to some greater, unknown inner power. They burst through barriers into rooms, embark on fantastic journeys, produce endless creations that come alive apart from ordinary time and place. Octavio Paz understood her work well, paying tribute to her in a poem written after her death. In it, he summed up her vision in the phrase, "Remedios does not invent: she remembers."[36]

Perhaps with that insight he touched the essence of her appeal to many women who strive for self expression.

Endnotes

[1] I am indebted to biologist Margaret S. Ewing of Oklahoma State University for bringing Varo's work to my attention in 1986 at the time of the Washington, D.C. exhibition, and for many hours of subsequent conversation on the subject of Varo's work.

[2] For Varo's use of the journey, see Janet Kaplan's biography of Remedios Varo, *Unexpected Journeys, The Art and Life of Remedios Varo*, (New York: Abbeville Press, 1988); for her transformation of archetypes, see Estella Lauter, *Women as Mythmakers, Poetry and Visual Art by Twentieth-Century Women*. (Bloomington, Indiana: Indiana University Press, 1984). Whitney Chadwick, *Women Artists and the Surrealist Movement*. (Boston: Little, Brown and Company, 1985). Margaret Ewing and I are currently collaborating on a paper incorporating science and the textile arts in Varo's work.

[3] Gisela Ecker, ed. *Feminist Aesthetics*. (Boston: Beacon Press, 1986), 16. My thanks to Susan Michelman for bringing this book to my attention.

[4] Rozsika Parker. *The Subversive Stitch*. (New York: Routledge, 1984) Reprint, paper, 1989. 11

[5] Parker, Forward.

[6] *American Heritage Dictionary of the English Language*. (Boston: Houghton-Mifflin Company, 1969).

[7] All biographical information in this paper is taken from Janet A. Kaplan's *Unexpected Journeys, The Art and Life of Remedios Varo*. My descriptions and interpretations of Varo's works of art were possible because of its many excellent illustrations. Her help in securing photo permissions for this article was invaluable. I would also like to express my gratitude for Kaplan's thorough and fascinating study, which brought to light Varo's hitherto unknown body of work. Without it, this paper would have been impossible.

[8] Kaplan, 101.

[9] Kaplan, 28-30.

[10] Kaplan, 32-35.

[11] Kaplan, 35-53.

[12] Kaplan, 53.

[13] Kaplan, 67.

[14] Kaplan, 249. Kaplan's Chapter 3, "Among the Surrealists, Paris and Marseilles", 55-83, tells the movie-plot-like story of the years spent in bohemian verve and sexual freedom, poverty and political activity. (Varo had several affairs, often concurrently, while still legally married to her first husband. She had the rare gift of remaining friends with all her former partners throughout her life.) Benjamin Péret, Varo's primary companion (both were still married to others) was an avowed Communist, which caused him to be imprisoned by the Gestapo and refused admission to the United States in 1940-41 when such Surrealist figures as André Breton and others sought refuge here. The entire period of the War years in France has all the plot fascination of a thriller, including the possible intervention of Peggy Guggenheim, the American heiress and patron of the arts in New York, to provide the funds that sent Péret and Varo to Mexico via that most famous of all wartime centers of human distribution, Casablanca.

[15] Their friendship and work is described in several sources, among them: Chadwick, *Women Artists and the Surrealist Movement*, and Lauter, *Women as Mythmakers. Poetry and Visual Art by Twentieth-Century Women*.

[16] Quoting Adrienne Rich, "Re-forming the Crystal," in *Poems: Selected and New, 1950-1974* (New York: Norton, 1975), p. 228. Kaplan, 216.

[17] Kaplan, 216-217.

[18] Chadwick, op. cit.

[19] Kaplan, 98.

[20] Illustrated in Kaplan, 211; no date given.

[21] Kaplan, 98-101.

[22] Kaplan, 201, 205.

[23] *The American Heritage Dictionary of the English Language*.

[24] E.H. Gombrich, *Art and Illusion*. (Princeton: Princeton U Press, 1960), 1972 ed'n. 11.

[25] Kaplan tells us that "Varo believed throughout her life in the power of...dream images and in the blurring of boundaries between them and waking reality. She first developed these magical ideas in fanciful stories that she wrote as a child and buried for privacy beneath the stones of her bedroom floor. Thus began her preoccupation with an imagined subterranean life lived secretly under floors, behind walls, and within furniture." Kaplan, 18.

[26] Kaplan, 21.

[27] Parker, 12.

[28] Parker, 6.

[29] Parker, 15.

[30] Parker, 25.

[31] As quoted in Parker, 10.

[32] Parker, 11.

[33] Kaplan, 151, quoting Varo in Paz, *Remedios Varo*.

[34] Eckart, 17.

[35] Silvia Bovenschen, "Is There a Feminine Aesthetic?" in Eckart, 44.

[36] Kaplan, 230.

[37] I wish to thank Walter Gruen for his kind permission and help in the publication of Varo's works in this article.

References

Brockett, O. G. (1987). *History of the Theatre.* (Fifth Edn) Boston: Allyn and Bacon, Inc.

Chadwick, W. (1985). *Women Artists and the Surrealist Movement.* Boston: Little, Brown and Company.

Ecker, G. (1986). *Feminist Aesthetics.* Boston: The Beacon Press.

Gombrich, E.H. (1960). *Art and Illusion.* Princeton: Princeton University Press.

Irigaray, L. (1985). *This Sex Which Is Not One.* Ithaca, New York: Cornell University Press.

Kaplan, J. A. (1988). *Unexpected Journeys. The Art and Life of Remedios Varo.* New York: Abbeville Press

Kaplan, J. A. (1987). "Remedios Varo". Feminist Studies Vol. 13. 38-48.

Lauter, E. (1984). *Women as Mythmakers. Poetry and Visual Art by Twentieth-Century Women.* Bloomington, Indiana: Indiana University Press.

Nicoll, A. (1963). *Masks Mimes and Miracles.* New York: Cooper Square Publishers, Inc.

Parker, R. (1989). *The Subversive Stitch, Embroidery and the Making of the Feminine.* New York: Routledge.

Paz, O. & Caillois, R. (1966). *Remedios Varo.* Mexico City: Ediciones Era, S.A.

Technology: Shaping the Aesthetic Product

Elizabeth K. Bye
University of Minnesota

Karen L. LaBat
University of Minnesota

A finished product with aesthetic appeal is not completely separable from the processes of production and reproduction (Munro, 1956). In all areas of product design there is the on-going discussion of the forces of technology push versus market pull (Pannenborg, 1986) and how those two forces affect the design of a product. Much research in apparel design concentrates on how to meet the needs of the user group or target market. However, there are many examples of technological developments that have allowed the creation of new forms or that have forced new forms into the market. Technology has been an intimate partner of the apparel product since the development of the sewing machine. Mass production took apparel production out of the home and into the factory where standardization has been the emphasis. A closer examination of the effects of technology on the aesthetic form of apparel is necessary as technology advances and new tools are being introduced to the apparel designer and apparel manufacturer. Will the preferences of the consumer become secondary to the push of technological innovations that emphasize economy and productivity or will designers and manufacturers use technology to expand the possibilities for exploring new aesthetic forms?

Technology in apparel design and production has three effects on the aesthetic form of apparel. 1. Some technological developments are pursued to maintain a traditional aesthetic form, with the purpose of lowering costs or replacing scarce materials. These technologies are used to continue to provide the aesthetic forms that are desired by the market. There are several examples such as the use of fusible interfacings; a fast, inexpensive production method, that provides similar structural results and appearance of hand tailoring techniques. Silk, a scarce and costly commodity, was replaced by nylon in hosiery. Nylon maintained the sheer, conforming qualities desired in women's hosiery and added new product pos-

sibilities for thermoplastic shaping. Ultra-Suede™, a materials innovation that simulates leather, provides a traditional look with easy care properties. 2. Technology may have limiting effects on forms of apparel. For example, automated sewing machines that stitch to template forms limit the designer's choice of shapes of garment parts. 3. Technology may promote new aesthetic forms of apparel. The marriage of the increasing sophistication of technologies in synthetic fibers and knitting production resulted in the era of the polyester pant suit. The colors made possible by the dyes used for the synthetic fibers presented a new vibrancy in color whereas the resilience of the fibers combined with the knit structure presented a smooth surfaced form that seemed to reflect a modern age. These technologies "pushed" aesthetic forms of apparel in new directions.

Apparel has historically been influenced by the materials and processes of its manufacture, and the resources available to its producers. By examining the history of technology's effect on the materials and processes used in apparel design and production, it is possible to anticipate future effects of technology and to be creative in the use of technology (i.e., to use technology as a means of expanding possibilities, not limiting choices).

Technology: Materials Development

Fiber Technology

In the late 19th century chemists began working on the first manufactured fiber, rayon. The spinning box was developed in 1905 and allowed polymer filaments to be spun into yarn. The production of rayon in fabric form began in 1910. There was great interest in rayon because it gave the look of "silk" to those of modest means. Further development of synthetic fibers expanded the choices of fabrics for apparel designers. The thermoplastic property of synthetic fibers promoted new products not possible before. Hosiery was permanently shaped to mimic body form, and design features such as permanently set-in pleats were made possible with these new fibers. Polyester changed the appearance of garments with its excellent wrinkle resistance and recovery. Men's shirts could maintain a wrinkle-free appearance through-out the course of a day.

Spandex fiber, introduced by DuPont in 1958, but not vigorously promoted until the 1980's, has influenced the shape of apparel. The stretch and recovery of spandex can be used to create apparel forms, such as "stretch pants" and "bike shorts", that conform to body contours without extensive seaming and stitching.

The technology of manufactured fibers, the raw material in solution form, has also provided new opportunities in finishing and dying. Fibers can be made shiny or dull, smooth or rough-textured, thick or thin. Dyes can maintain much of their original color by being incorporated into the dope of the fiber. Dyes also provide a new range and depth in color not possible with earlier generations. Dyes have been created that change color as the body changes temperature, providing a view of the wearer's emotions or protecting the wearer from life-threatening temperature extremes.

The thermoplastic property of fibers or plastic materials has, perhaps, not been explored to the fullest extent. At this time, the heat molding possibilities of these materials have been used in small products such as bra cups and shoulder pads, but even these small products have contributed to aesthetic forms of apparel: a smooth, seamless surface. Grants from the National Science Foundation have supported research into the possibility of entire garments that are completely formed using the plastic properties of synthetics (Advanced Materials and Processes, 1989). This technology provides the possibility of a fitted apparel form without seams, darts or any fitting devices.

Synthetic fibers have reduced the cost of apparel, increased the ease of care, improved the performance and function of many garments, and influenced the shape and design of apparel. The current emphasis in fiber research seems to be in "high-tech" fiber development; fibers that provide protection from high temperature, impact, biological organisms and many other life-threatening forces. These fibers impose restrictions on the aesthetic forms of apparel as a result of their use in very specific applications; color choices as well as shaping and joining options may be limited. Eventually these new developments will find applications in broader markets, complete with possibilities and limitations.

Fabric Technology

Woven, knitted, and non-woven fabric structures have an effect on apparel forms. Each structure has possibilities and limitations. Woven fabrics impose direction in placement of the fabrics due to inherent grain characteristics. Because wovens have limited possibilities of stretch and pliability, tailored shaping has to be used to move from a boxy shape to a body conforming shape. The appearance of darts, side seams, openings using zippers, and buttons are a classic notion of the Western apparel aesthetic. Vionnet became an innovator in the 1930's when she developed a new paradigm and introduced garments constructed with the grain on the bias. This resulted in body conforming garments with more stretch, comfort, and new aesthetic options and challenges due to the difference in drape and light and shadow. Later, woven fabrics were again transformed by blending yarns with spandex to give woven apparel shape retention, comfort, and body conforming capabilities.

Knit fabrics allow and promote a closer fit to the body without the use of tailoring techniques. The stretch and pliability of knits can give a smooth conforming appearance. The improvement of knitting machines reduced the cost of knitted goods. New designers often introduce their first lines in knit fabrics because of their lower costs and ease in fit and structure. The character of the knit fabric imposes simplified silhouettes and a minimum of structured details. Knit fabrics of synthetic fibers have allowed freedom of movement and responded to increased demands for high performance sports garments. The one-legged, form-fitting, unitard worn by Olympic athlete Jackie Joyner-Kersee changed the appearance of female athletes participating in track and field events. Athletes in timed events, such as speed skating, use the conforming character of knit fabrics to increase performance, at the same time developing an aesthetic form of a sleek aerodynamic object that has become the expected standard for the sport.

Non-woven fabrics provide the advantage of low production cost, always a motivating factor for use in products. However, non-wovens have found limited applications in apparel, perhaps because they do not provide the desired aesthetic appeal of wovens and knits, in both visual and tactile terms. Non-wovens are used as interfacings and interlinings to provide internal shaping of garments. As technology progresses in non-woven structuring and perceptions change, perhaps whole-garment applications can be found.

Fiber and fabric technologies provide the most basic building blocks for the aesthetic apparel product. It is here that new visions can be developed by thinking beyond traditional fiber, yarn, and structure and expanding acceptance of materials in a variety of forms and structures to create an environment for the human body. Technology can help provide the spark needed to initiate expanded paradigms for these materials.

Fastener Technology

Buttons have provided a means of fastening garments since Roman times (Petroski, 1993, p. 96), but also serve a very important aesthetic function. Buttons are often the focal point of a garment and give visual interest and variety (DeLong, 1987). Although new fastening technologies are introduced, buttons will undoubtedly continue as the fastener of choice for apparel due to their aesthetic appeal.

Elsa Schiaparelli took an innovation previously used for shoes, boots, and industrial applications and changed the way women donned and doffed clothing. The zipper was introduced and challenged the prominent use of buttons and snaps as fasteners. Advertising campaigns to promote the zipper in the 1930's encouraged designers to avoid embarrassing "gap-osis" by using zippers, instead of buttons or snaps, as closures (Petroski, 1993, p. 12). The zipper made possible a new range of structural shapes. Garments that clung to the body, without the bulk of hooks or buttons provided a freedom of movement and a more streamlined appearance. The 1960's introduction of the "invisible" zipper gave designers a closure that complimented the smooth continuous surface of the double knit garment.

Hook-and-loop tapes are a comparatively recent technological development in fastening systems. The functional advantages of these products determine their use in apparel products, providing easy opening and closure, often invisibly. Some athletic shoe manufacturers have used hook-and-loop fasteners to replace the classic broken line of zig-zag lacings for a smooth, flat surface. The major reason for using the fastening is function, but the result is a different aesthetic for shoes. Hook-and-loop tapes have not been acceptable in an aesthetic sense in many applications due to bulk and the characteristic noise of un-doing this type of closure. Manufacturers are developing new forms of hook-and-loop to overcome some of these objections.

Exploration of innovative possibilities in fastening systems, such as magnetic attachments and biological seaming composed of living cells has been suggested by Watkins (1984, p. 209). This little researched but necessary component of clothing deserves more research. Fasteners are an aesthetic and functional feature that are often ignored, yet have historically contributed to new forms of apparel.

Technology: Apparel Product Development

As apparel designers and manufacturers accept and embrace computer technology, the possibilities for changing the aesthetic product are multiplying. Computer technology, in many forms, is being applied to every step of apparel manufacturing, from design concept to final inspection. With the advent of Expert Systems, computers are more than ever a tool that can expand creativity.

Visualizing the Product

Designers have traditionally used sketching as the means of making their design ideas visible, both to themselves and to co-workers. Numerous ideas are sketched to communicate concept, form, silhouette, color, and details. These sketches provide the basis for making decisions, selecting the best ideas to translate into three-dimensional forms. Sketching, however, is time consuming and in itself may limit the number of ideas a designer can present for evaluation. Computer technology has greatly influenced this ability to generate large quantities and a variety of initial ideas. Drawing programs provide the possibility of drawing templates that can be quickly modified providing many variations on a theme. The problem now may be wading through numerous choices and developing criteria to be selective. Older, more time consuming methods of presenting visual ideas; pen and ink, water color, etc. required that the designer sort through design ideas in their imagination before presenting their best ideas. Computer technology brings the internal ideation to the screen giving the designer the freedom to experiment. This process also makes team design more feasible as ideas can be shared in their earliest forms.

Simple sketch programs are being replaced by sophisticated graphic technologies. By 1987 computer graphics were not only faster, but had sharper images that made photo-realistic details of garments with folds, shading, texture, and highlights possible (Freedman, 1991). This meant that Computer Aided Design (CAD) systems were moving into the design department and replacing traditional visual media. Now instead of taking weeks to develop an apparel product from sketch to sample, it could be done in less than a day, including selection of coloration, fabrics, and trims. CAD greatly reduces the amount of time needed in product development, and the realistic three-dimensional quality of the graphics permits immediate evaluation of the garment without the need to produce an actual sample. A variety of colorways can be created quickly and easily so the opportunity exists to evaluate many different options that would not have been considered before due to time and cost constraints. Shapes, silhouettes, patterns, and details can be changed and evaluated quickly. Because so many ideas can be generated and reviewed quickly, designers may venture beyond traditional models to explore new color combinations or forms.

Quick-time and video incorporation are the technologies being used in many industries to explore new directions for design. Animated ideation could provide the apparel designer with the possibility of evaluating a three-dimensional form from all angles. Designers have traditionally sketched the front and back of garments and often did not consider movement of the form, except in a very rudimentary way or in the last stages of making a sample garment. Adding movement to ideation sketching could add to exploration of new forms of apparel; traditional side seams may disappear as sketches would no longer be viewed only front and back. New structures could evolve from

studying the interaction of the body with textiles. Incorporating the stretch and movement characteristics of a textile into the computer and then mapping that textile to body motion could lead to pattern shapes that are not in existence today. For example, detailed analysis of the movement of the ball and socket joint of the arm and shoulder could result in use of materials and seaming that changes the traditional set-in sleeve of tailored garments.

These tools and options should lead to quality in design because there are more choices and ideas from which to select. Input from a variety sources, including designers, marketing, and production, can be offered throughout the development process rather than just at final evaluation time (Hirsch & Thoben, 1992). This cooperative input should lead to more certain acceptance of the product by the consumer. However, it would be ill advised to assume that all designers will be more creative and productive using the available technologies. Technology is a tool which can help turn ideas into products. It can make creative professionals more productive while revealing new expressive opportunities (Hitch, 1993), but the ideas, judgment and business sense must come from the human element.

Product Shaping

The flat pattern method is often used by designers to create the pieces to form the three-dimensional garment. Two-dimensional apparel pattern design systems were introduced in the early 1980's and increased the speed with which patterns could be created. New patterns could be created or style variations generated from existing patterns. An experienced pattern maker could produce more patterns, and thus increase the turn-around time for product development. However, the new tools required an adaptation in work style that demanded patience and a willingness to succeed on the part of the pattern maker as information gained through tactile communication with paper, pencil, and ruler was replaced with a computer screen, stylus, and paper printout. This working environment has the potential to dramatically change the product development process but has been the most under-used CAD program (A. M. Cruz, personal communication, May 1993). In fact, the need for tactile information has lead CAD companies to take a step back by developing CAD systems that encourage pattern makers to work in a circular fashion from pattern input on a digitizing pattern table, to computer screen, to pattern, to test garment, and back to the computerized pattern. As a tool, the effect on the apparel product is subtle and more directly related to the ability of the operator to manipulate the program. These effects include variations in pattern shaping or experimentation with shape and structure, which may improve with increased operator experience. Stock patterns that are stored in computer memory may limit creativity, but increase speed, due to the ease with which minor design changes can be made. It is this increase in speed which will allow manufacturers to remain competitive and continue to offer the traditional aesthetic forms desired by the consumer.

Because computers can handle great amounts of data, designers may become more sophisticated in their understanding of building motion and function into garment structures. Fabric characteristics of stretch, recovery, stiffness, and pliability could be factored into the shaping of a garment, changing pattern dimensions to accommodate body movement. These types of expectations are realistic for designers to anticipate in the future, however, technology that is designed to encourage creativity and exploration of ideas could be initially limiting during a period of acceptance, learning, and skill building. Technology thus remains a tool, providing the opportunity and challenge for new ways of thinking and solving problems.

Draping is another method that designers use to create the three-dimensional form. In this method the designer manipulates the materials and relies to a large extent on tactile information to shape the product. Computer systems have been developed that simulate this process, however, the interaction of designer and material is remote and at this point, unsatisfactory. The designer has to rely on the programming of the computer to "map" the fabric onto the form. Advances in the technology of Virtual Reality could remove the boundaries of the current stiff remote computer interface. One form of Virtual Reality uses a head-mounted display (HMD) to allow an individual to move through and interact with a three-dimensional computer generated virtual world (Robinett, 1992). Current applications are in flight simulation, augmented reality and architectural design (Hodges, 1993). As

sophistication and wider application of these technologies proceed, applications in apparel design may be found. A natural consideration is the use of virtual reality as an ideation field for draping garment forms. The designer, equipped with an HMD, could enter a virtual environment where a variety of textiles could be draped on "live" mannequins.

One of the more difficult challenges in developing virtual worlds where a designer could drape simulated fabric is providing tactile feedback to the designer. Robinett (1992, p. 244) stated, "Displaying with perfect fidelity to the haptic and tactile senses presents such a daunting engineering challenge that it seems nearly impossible. Some sort of whole body exoskeleton would be needed, with integrated arrays of pressure, vibration, and temperature displays covering the entire body surface." Some of these technologies exist today in limited forms. There are tactile arrays that display texture and vibration to the finger and other skin surfaces (Linvill, 1973; Rheingold, 1991). The variety in weight and texture possible in textiles will create further challenges in developing a virtual world where draping a garment form will have applications in a real world. Creating with virtual reality fabrics may influence new technologies in real fabrics and result in exploration and acceptance of new apparel forms.

Technology: Apparel Product Production

Historically, garments were made one at a time for a specific individual with a single person responsible for the concept. design, development, and production. The aesthetic was individually determined either as the individual made their own garment or as the individual worked with a tailor or dressmaker to shape a garment that met standards of the time and also could include individual taste. With the advent of the industrial revolution, this changed, and the skills of the designer became more focused on specialized tasks, which contributed only part of the expertise needed to manufacture or create a garment (Black, 1990). For those responsible for the design of mass-produced objects, understanding what will appeal to the greatest number of people, what will receive the highest average evaluation is what matters (Berlyne, 1974). Yet, focus in the mass production mode remained on improving individual skills and increasing piecework rates rather than on the total quality and appearance of the finished apparel. Fashion became a driving force for manufacturers of mass-produced apparel because the desire for variety and change could be easily met. In the period of mass produced garments, easily recognized aesthetic forms can be identified with a point in time.

Mass production of men's garments for the military began shortly after the invention of the sewing machine in 1848 and was followed closely by the production of men's suits and shirts. Women's suits and skirts were not mass produced until the 1870's. Men had traditionally made men's clothing and women's dressmakers made garments for women. However, as garment factories began to develop, women provided the labor while men oversaw the production and design of both men's and women's garments (Banner, 1983). Men designed garments for women, borrowing menswear styling; an aesthetic change based on the social changes driven by the new technology. Suits were purchased by working women who had reduced time for their own home based production and had little choice in designs offered in the market.

This change in the production of apparel brought about the concept of standardization in both sizing and design so that garments could move rapidly through the factory system, and would appeal to the masses. It was the beginning of the end of custom designed and fitted clothing, and the acceptance of a standardized apparel aesthetic. These changes in production and the resulting product took off slowly, but it changed the way apparel was made and how it looked by limiting choice and encouraging conformity in fashion.

CAD/CAM Technology

CAD/CAM (computer aided design/computer aided manufacturing) refers to the application of computer technology to any or all aspects of production from design through manufacture. The first computer systems introduced to apparel manufacturing were designed to grade patterns. Grading a pattern provides all of the sizes necessary for production using the sample size as the starting point. This is a very time-consuming, repetitious activity which requires a high degree of accuracy. The technology offers labor, time, and cost savings as well as accuracy to a 64th of an inch, however, limitations also exist which affect the apparel product. Albrecht (1989) stated that irregular or

uneven grades are often made even to aid the computer. Similarly, there is a tendency to simplify the design to make computer processing easier (Johnson, 1982). The shape of the pattern is often distorted during the grading process, and results in a garment that is not visually proportioned for each size in the size range, particularly the further from the sample size it falls. As technology advances, computers may go beyond a mechanical, cookbook approach to sizing and grading to first analyzing the proportional relationships of garment parts and then maintaining or altering the relationships in the grade to meet the physical and visual needs of the individual consumer (Bye & DeLong, 1994). This is a step towards more customized fit in garments.

The next computerized process was developed for marker making, which is the layout of the pattern pieces for cutting. The computer has the ability to help the marker maker lay a very tight marker that results in great cost savings by saving even a few inches of fabric. The computer can be programmed to track each piece, match plaids or stripes, or maintain grainline. Because this is an interactive process, the ability exists to override set parameters, as has been the case when a marker maker tilts a pattern piece slightly off grain to make it fit more tightly into the marker. The resulting garment does not hang as intended by the designer and may even twist around the body as is often the case with pant legs. Engineering pattern pieces is a common practice to make the pieces fit more economically into the marker. Such practices as shifting the placement of seams or reducing fullness can dramatically change the appearance and quality of the apparel product intended by the designer. The original design can be altered through production and costing decisions facilitated by technology.

With the development of marker data, computerized cutting systems were introduced that increased the speed and accuracy of the cutting process. The initial intent was fast cutting of large quantities of garments in multiples. However, that same technology can be used to cut single order, custom fitted garments. This application of the technology makes possible Toffler's (1980) vision of "The Third Wave", producing a one-of-kind garment for an individual. Made-to-measure suits are currently being manufactured by Custom Cut Technologies with a laser cutter (DeWitt, 1990). This presents the opportunity for all suit buyers to be custom fitted, selecting a unique fabric and design instead of settling for a garment "off the rack" that may need to be altered and may not meet the customer's expectations for fit, function, and aesthetics.

While CAD/CAM technology in the production environment has been essential in keeping apparel manufacturers competitive and maintaining the production of traditional aesthetic forms, it has also been limiting. For the last 25 years, apparel manufacturers have been increasing the speed and reducing the cost of producing apparel, yet this technology has not encouraged new ways of thinking. Creative problem solving was overlooked as a solution and instead energies were placed into learning how to push buttons and operate the computer at its maximum potential. The same methods and thought processes that have always been used, are still being used, at an increased speed. This is not to say that the time spent learning to operate these "tools" was wasted. Acceptance of current computer technology by the human component is essential to the success of future technologies.

Technology: Expert Systems

Expert systems are developed by knowledge engineers who work with experts in a particular field extracting selected knowledge from the expert and programming that knowledge into the computer. Expert systems go beyond the current level of CAD/CAM which has automated traditional manual practices and offers the ability to transmit an expert's solutions to those users confronted by a variety of problems in the design and manufacturing environment (Fetzer, 1990). Expert systems are knowledge based systems that remove the limitations of present systems and provide opportunities for new ways of thinking and solving problems (Hayes-Roth et al., 1986). The knowledge base under development for the apparel industry will contain facts, information, and rules of judgment about designing and producing apparel. The system will be programmed to reason and offer solutions to problems, with the opportunity to expand the knowledge base and receive interactive information from the user or designer. It is this continuous improvement to the knowledge base that offers great potential for improving both the technical and design

quality of apparel. Non-experts will have an expert's advice at their fingertips, and everyone will be freed from the responsibilities of mundane, detailed, or repetitive tasks. This should create opportunities for creative thinking and problem solving and the potential for dramatic changes in the aesthetic form of apparel.

Fashion will continue to change at a rapid pace, and there will be an increased demand for fresh, new ideas, not just previous styles redone. Toffler (1981) suggested that the "Third Wave" in manufacturing will focus on the short run of partial or completely customized products. Naisbitt (1990) called it the "primacy of the consumer" with computerized manufacturing that responds with individualized products. There will be an increased demand for garments that fit individual body forms and perform according to specific requirements. Tailoring the apparel product to individual needs of the consumer will become more important and lead to production in small batches driven by customer orders. This creates a scenario that ultimately leads to one-of-a-kind production (Hirsch, 1992).

The factory of the future will be involved with one-of-a-kind production, and producing apparel products that are characterized by an increase in variety. In order for this to take place, new technologies and new paradigms for production must evolve. Concurrent production which is characterized by a focus on customer requirements is possible with the power of expert systems and advanced methods of communication. The concept of custom fitting and designing a garment for an individual will be a reality, although a huge effort will be required to develop the technology and assemble the knowledge base.

There is currently an expert system under development that will custom fit a pattern according to an individual's body form and posture (Collins et al., 1990). The knowledge base will also include information that will have an impact on the visual appearance of the pattern while adjusting for the physical dimensions of the body. Supporting technology is part of the development plan. An example of aesthetic change that has already resulted from research involved with the development of this system is a woman who now considers pants part of her personal apparel aesthetic. Until she was involved with this project, she had never worn pants of any type due to her unique body form and posture. The expert system was able to combine physical body dimensions with it's knowledge base to design a pants pattern to fit and complement her body. Computer systems of the future will combine the mind-expanding possibilities of Virtual Reality with expert systems that provide years of compiled experience. All of this power at the fingertips of the designer.

The success of future apparel companies and consumers' satisfaction with the apparel that they produce is dependent on the designer's creative ability and the company's ability to respond quickly to individual customer requests. Quality is inherent in the product and a result of continuous improvement in the process (Hirsch & Thoben, 1992). Concurrent design and production require excellent information exchange and cooperative effort, along with technological capabilities. Expert systems will be at the core of these advancements.

This concept of product synthesis will initially be approached as a method to maintain traditional aesthetic forms by allowing successful competition in the global market. Such profound changes in the apparel manufacturer's paradigm are about to take place, that the focus of this new technology will be on integrating the process and helping current and future designers and apparel workers to make the transition. They should initially be well prepared with their CAD/CAM experience.

The most immediate change in the apparel product will be the improvement of quality due to the ready access of the information needed to make technical and design decisions. For example, a customer in Seattle would be able to go to a retailer and order a pair of jeans that will be custom fitted, designed to flatter her body form, and customized with stitching and beads from a manufacturer in Greensboro. The jeans would arrive at her home within a week. This would be a vast improvement over the current practice of shopping and trying on as many as 25 pairs of jeans to find one pair that fits, flatters, and looks like everyone else's. Expert systems will guarantee that the jeans will match the physical and appearance needs of the customer. Given a personal profile of the customer, the designer can customize the jeans according to lifestyle and aesthetic requirements.

Technological limitations to design should eventually be greatly reduced or eliminated as a result of expert systems. Initially, the limitations of acceptance and transition will result in the continued maintenance of traditional forms or even perhaps a drop in aesthetic quality and variety. However, the most exciting prospect is the potential for truly new aesthetic forms. There is hope that by providing tools that will free the mind from clutter and repetition, designers will seize the opportunity to expand their visual thinking and challenge current aesthetic forms for the human body. These intelligent CAD systems would not fully automate the design process, but would provide intelligent assistance to the human designer at a much higher level than is currently provided by purely geometric modelling systems (Kerr, 1991, p. 302).

There is a real danger of losing creativity due to the need to push garments through production quickly, or working so quickly that there is little time for exploration, creative thought, and experimentation. Technology does not always work as intended, as was seen historically in those who adopted the sewing machine into their own homes. Instead of resulting in a savings of time, women used the machine to vastly expand their ability to trim and decorate their garments (Banner, 1983). The adoption of expert systems will have both positive and negative effects on the process and the resulting apparel product. The ultimate goal is to return to the creativity and quality seen in apparel that is individually crafted, but at a price and availability for all consumers. If designers and manufacturers are open to new ideas and willing to take advantage of the opportunities available, both the process and the apparel product should become more satisfying for the producer and the consumer.

Technology: The Human Component

According to Van De Bogart (1990), the future of fashion will take on a new look as designers learn of the new capabilities and innovations they can achieve with their computers. However, computer technology is still just a tool, and the real creativity remains in the minds of the people involved. Technology has the ability to extend our vision and free our mind of cluttering details by automating simple repetitive tasks so that energy can better be spent on more creative aspects of work (Hubbard, 1985).

While CAD/CAM is making the product design cycle faster, more efficient, and more accurate, management must be prepared to react more quickly to new ideas and concepts. Decisions will be made and risks taken based on the managers access to current market information. Management must provide the support needed to work hand-in-hand with designers to bring a high quality product to the consumer at the right time and price. Creativity can diminish if too much attention is given to the computer interaction. Managers must realize that the computer is a tool that requires creative human input.

Computer technology must be easy to understand and user friendly or it will become a stumbling block rather than a useful tool. Experimentation with the system can lead to creative developments, but that really remains a function of the designer/operator's own creative ability (Majcjrzak et al., 1987). Expectations for creative output should remain centered on the designers ability and even the most creative designer will burn out if expectations are too high. A good designer may come up with three to five well thought out ideas a week. By introducing a new tool, one should not expect 25 high quality ideas the following week. Current users indicate that there is more success in developing what the designer really has in mind without the time and cost of producing samples, because of the opportunities to easily and rapidly visualize the product. Consumers benefit as response time is greatly reduced, and all have the opportunity to select from the best the designer has to offer.

Technology is really a tool for our minds that encourages extensive manipulation of visual data. With the development of CAD/CAM, there is much less tactile information from a sample product at any phase of the development process. Technology has increased the need to abstract a flat image as a three-dimensional garment on a body, a skill necessary to evaluate a garment during the product development process. This abstraction has been increasing since the initial time that artisans gave up responsibility for designing and producing the entire garment and instead began to develop specialized skills.

The industrial revolution introduced a sequential mode of production in which one process was completed by one individual and then passed on to the next phase of production. The workers at the beginning of the assembly line did not often see the final product or feel pride in their contribution. This created a lack of integrative communication and thinking and resulted in difficult quality control. Before the technological revolution, an artisan had the ability to modify and improve a garment during the entire phase of production. This artisan had all the information necessary in his own mind and new information could be evaluated and taken into consideration instantly.

Most recently, CAD/CAM technology has maintained this sequential method of thinking, enabling design and production to happen at a much quicker pace. If there has been dissatisfaction with the quality, design or performance of an apparel product, it is perhaps related to a lack of readily available integrated information. Concurrent access to information would allow for simultaneous design and development, allowing all those involved in the development of an apparel product to participate at any phase of the project (Black, 1990). The simple ability to integrate and access information quickly will have an enormous effect on how apparel is conceived, designed, produced.

Conclusions

Technology has had an overall positive effect on the aesthetic apparel product, and has greatly increased the speed at which this aesthetic form changes. Technological influences do not operate in a vacuum--social, economic, and political influences will still play a part. The one-of-a-kind design and production goals can become a reality; however, the most important factor in their success is the focus on customers' requirements. Those manufacturers who focus primarily on technology will be left with many unsatisfied customers and a lot of expensive equipment. New technological developments will continue to maintain a traditional aesthetic apparel form and offer opportunities and limitations based on what is technologically possible. Beyond initial limitations, these new technologies may suggest shape, form, silhouette and color that have not been considered before. Ideally, the new technologies will enable designers and manufacturers to be creative in the use of technology as a means of expanding possibilities, not limiting choices. Although technology won't enable us to predict the future, information systems will allow us the unprecedented ability to understand our world as it is and as it might be, and build a future which each of us will find more interesting, productive (Leebaert, 1991) and aesthetically pleasing.

Required in this proposed scenario is a means of training future and current apparel producers to think and respond differently to changing sets of demands, problems, and opportunities. Multi-disciplinary training will be essential. Designers must know about manufacturing processes and available technologies. Managers and production personnel must have an element of design in their background. The critical importance of marketing should be emphasized to both (Black, 1990). All must be trained and encouraged to think beyond their individual worlds to a universe of possibilities. It is ultimately the consumer who drives and enables all this effort towards change and advancement. We may not be able to predict exactly how the apparel product will look and function, but change is inevitable given the rapid transformation of the productive and creative environment.

The aesthetic apparel product is not separable from the processes of its creation. We are moving away from the current standardized aesthetic brought on by mass production and returning to an apparel product that is more individually designed and produced for individual aesthetics and function. We are looking less for ways to maintain our traditional aesthetic and instead realizing a new one. Creative designers and manufacturers will be at the core of this consumer driven change, and technology will provide the tools to realize it.

References

Albrecht, D. (1989). Impact of technologies on the quality of apparel. *American Society for Quality Control Congress Transactions* . Toronto, Ontario, Canada, 383-390.

Banner, L. (1983). *American beauty*. Chicago: University of Chicago Press.

Berlyne, D. (1972). Ends and means of experimental aesthetics. *Canadian Journal of Psychology 26* , 303-325.

Black, I. (1990, October). Back to the future with CAD: Its impact on product design and development. *Design Studies*, 207-211.

Bye, E. and DeLong, M. (1994). A visual sensory evaluation of the results of two pattern grading methods. *Clothing and Textiles Research Journal, 12*(4), 1-7.

Collins, J., Grunes, M., Kozak, D.,Vittal, A. (1990, April 10). *System for preparing garment pattern data to enable subsequent computerized prealteration* (Patent Number 4,916,634). Washington, D.C.:United States Patent Office.

Cruz, A. (1993, May). Interview with Senior System Engineer, Gerber Garment Technology.

DeLong, M. (1987). *The way we look*. Ames: Iowa State University Press.

DeWitt, J. W. (1990, November). Custom comes of age. *Apparel Industry Magazine*, pp. 98-103.

Fetzer, J. (1990). *Artificial intelligence: Its scope and limits*. Dordrecht, The Netherlands: Kluwer Academic Publishers.

Freedman, L. (1990, April) . CAD/CAM technology paints a new picture. *Bobbin Magazine*, pp. 86-89.

Hayes-Roth, F.; Klahr, P.; and Mostow, D. (1986). Knowledge acquisition, knowledge programming, and knowledge refinement. In P.Klahr & D. Waterman, (Eds.), *Expert Systems Techniques, Tools and Applications* (pp. 310-349.) Massachusetts: Addison-Wesley Publishing Company.

Hirsch, B.E., & Thoben, K.D. (Eds.). (1992). "One-of-a-kind" production: New approaches. New York: Elsevier Science Publishing Company, Inc.

Hitch, L. (1993, October). Demystifying communications technologies. *Technological Horizons in Education*, pp. 92-95.

Hodges, M. (1993, Summer) The illusion of immersion. *Research Horizons*, pp. 2-11.

Hubbard, S. W. (1985). *CAD/CAM: Applications for business*. Phoenix: Oryx Press.

Johnson, K. M. (1982). Contemporary technology of apparel manufacturing: its effect on the designer. *Proceedings of the Association of College Professors of Textiles and Clothing*, pp. 14-17.

Kerr, R. (1991). *Knowledge Based Manufacturing Management*. Sydney: Addison-Wesley Publishing Company, Inc.

Leebaert, D. (Ed.) . (1991). *Technology 2001: The Future of computing and communications*. Cambridge, Massachusetts: The MIT Press.

Linvill, J.G. (1973). *Research and development of tactile facsimile reading aid for the blind* (The Opticon). Stanford University: Stanford Electronics Laboratory.

Majchrzak, A.; Chang, T.; Barfield, W.; Eberts, R.; Salvendy, G. (1987). *Human aspects of computer-aided design*. Philadelphia: Taylor and Francis.

Munro, T. (1956). *Toward science in aesthetics*. New York: Liberal Arts Press.

Naisbitt, J. and Aburdene, P. (1990). *Megatrends 2000*. New York: William Morrow and Co., Inc.

Of material interest. (1989, February). *Advanced Materials and Processes*, p.6.

Pannenborg, A.E. (1986). Technology push versus market pull--the designer's dilemma. In R. Roy & D. Wield (Eds.) , *Product Design and Technological Innovation* (pp. 175-181). England: Open University Press.

Petroski, H. (1993). *The evolution of useful things*. New York: Alfred A. Knopf.

Rheingold, H. (1991). *Virtual Reality*. New York: Summit.

Robinett, W. (1992). Synthetic experience: a proposed taxonomy. *Presence: Teleoperators and virtual environments*. 1,(2), 229-247.

Toffler, A. (1980). *The third wave*. New York:William Morrow and Co., Inc.

Van De Bogart, W. (1990). Using the Macintosh computer for textile and fashion design. In N.J. Rabolt (Ed.), *Association of college professors of textiles and clothing special publication number 2* (pp. 15-20). Monument, CO: ACPTC, Inc.

Watkins, S. (1984). *Clothing, the portable environment*. Iowa: The Iowa University Press.

Teaching Aesthetics In A Postmodern Environment

Betsy E. Henderson
University of Minnesota

According to history, dress has long served as an expression of the more encompassing aesthetic that prevails in a culture during a given period of time. For that reason, apparel design educators have tended to place at least some kind of emphasis on the aesthetic of that culture in planning their curricula. Up until the 1960s, the approach was on traditional cultural standards of beauty and how they could be expressed in various ways through the imagery of dress. Educators generally interpreted those standards and used them as a basis for planning classroom activities. Students, in turn, tended to emulate those standards in both creating apparel designs and planning their personal wardrobes. Despite individual variations in interpretation, there was a relatively high level of agreement among students, educators and the public about what constituted appropriate forms of dress as an expression of the prevailing aesthetic.

However, during the latter part of this century, standards of beauty have been in transition as a result of major changes in society and culture. Approaches that were once relied upon by apparel design educators no longer seem to be effective. New strategies for teaching aesthetics through the medium of dress are needed. The following discussion addresses such a problem and proposes a solution substantiated by research and theory.

Teaching Aesthetics

Because of the variety of styles worn concurrently in a given college classroom, ranging from conservative dress, preppy, grunge and hip-hop, in addition to numerous other fads that may appear, teaching design and aesthetics in relation to dress requires adaptation in each of these areas. If the discussion is on one type of aesthetic interpretation, students from other aesthetic orientations may find the information to be confusing. Traditional examples of unity, match, and coordination may be irrelevant concepts if one's perspective is that of dissonance and mismatch. Although written thirty years ago, the following statement by Brenninkmeyer (1963) is still true for some students today:

"Contemporary people are not fascinated by harmonious colors or shapes, that is old fashioned. It is more important to be startling" (p.167). Fashion acceptance in each time period brings new principles of what coordinates and matches. Aspects that break this acceptance produce the desired surprise and the beginnings of change.

When students' clothing choices are seemingly inconsistent with those of their peers as well as fashions advertised in the media and popular fashion magazines, questions may arise about their sources of inspiration and the methods used to guide their selections. As new fashions emerge, they may be initially undefined or considered distasteful to observers. This may be problematic when the trend setters are students and the persons who are providing instruction and classroom examples are orientated toward traditional views.

For this reason, alternate strategies for planning meaningful learning activities in the classroom may be called for as new fashion themes emerge in society. If educators are closed to alternative perspectives they could misunderstand and even stifle the creative urges of design and retail merchandising students. On the other hand, while students may dress according to their individual or personalized aesthetic, if their career paths involve apparel design, they may need to develop understanding and acquire experience in designing for market segments which have aesthetic preferences which are different from their own.

Fashion And Postmodernism

The term fashion is defined as being the latest mode of dress, thus involving a transition from a previously accepted style. Changes in style are often particularly observable in the current dress of contemporary youth and may result in the development of an alternate aesthetic which contributes to the postmodern environment.

The term 'postmodern' has not been clearly defined in a manner that satisfactorily describes a specific time period or is applicable to all disciplines; indeed, the general opinion is that postmodernism resists stereotypes. The architect Charles Jencks (1984) provided a visual definition by describing postmodernism in both art and architecture as the result of 'double-coding' the modern with other codes such as political and cultural pluralism, historicism and multivalence. He clarified his rationale by stating "if you want to resonate with culture as a whole, then you'd better use a wide vernacular which includes all sorts of signs and traditional motifs" (p. 4). The French philosopher Jean-Francois Lyotard (Rose, 1991) describes his viewpoint of the postmodern as the deconstruction of the meta-narratives of modernity, or an attempt to "cure" the ills of modernity. To evaluate modernity, it may be important to reconsider tradition and historicism. This deconstruction of modernity, or re-conceptualization of reality, is evident in contemporary fashion. The Tobe' Report (1993) published as a predictor of fashion, discussed deconstruction as the "postmodern idea that if reality is constructed it can be de-constructed....The deconstructivists have been breaking down the formal fashion elements" (p. 21). Referring to traditional narratives, Elizabeth Wilson's (1993) discussion of the postmodern body, supports the broad idea of postmodernism as a notion of ambivalence.

Jencks' description of 'double-coding' relates to a workable description of postmodernism provided by Andreas Huyssen (1986). Huyssen discussed postmodernism as an attempt to cross the divide between high and low art, and the high and popular culture of modernism. These contrasts relate to fashion theory and how the postmodern individual views dress and the integration of current 'high' and 'low' fashions. The work of Georg Simmel (1904) popularized the "trickle-down" concept of fashion theory. He identified fashion as a mechanism used by the upper class to separate themselves from the lower classes. Throughout history, Simmel suggested that the lower classes have tried to imitate 'high' fashions, thus encouraging fashion change. For the postmodern, this cycle is broken by the attempt to 'cross the divide.'

Margaret Grindereng's (1985) research indicates that fashion diffusion does not "trickle-down" through the social strata, but instead flows horizontally. Her statement, "all fashion leaders in all classes may be influenced by the same mass media and cultural ideals" (p. 42), pertains to the adoption of fashions by subcultures. For example, the postmodern individual takes a stance toward fashion by resisting a prescribed look illustrated in fashion magazines. The individual chooses to commodify his/her appearance by taking clothing items from upper classes and altering them in some manner or wearing the item in unexpected ways in order to maintain originality (Fiske, 1989). To negate the look of class distinction or the association with popular fashion, she/he may adopt low end knock-offs or used clothing as one tool for separation.

Fashion fads are often identified with a name that defines the look. A recent, relatively short-lived style of dressing is a segment of the broader trend of postmodern dress. For example, a desire for deliberate shabbiness and "clashing layers," or what has been labeled as "grunge" wear is an eclectic combination of clothing articles supposedly intended as a "backlash against '80s materialism" (Newsweek, p. 65). Identified by Leland and Leonard (1993) as a "return to reality after the artifice of the '80s," this shapeless fashion is not exhibited on the curvaceous supermodels, but instead on androgynous bodies described as "the gamines." This combination of flannel shirts, soft print dresses, exposed midriff and combat boots, inspired by the Seattle rock bands Pearl Jam and Soundgarden, influenced designers Marc Jacobs, Calvin Klein, Donna Karan, and Ralph Lauren to incorporate it in their work and show it as the latest style on runways. According to Peter Kobel (1993), retailers also exploited the opportunity as a merchandising tool. Window displays, designed to sell high end clothes, combined "street" clothes, or elements of grunge with more costly items such as a $985 Perry Ellis dress.

The concept of grunge wear is consistent with the postmodern notion to cross the divide between high and low fashions: to resist the stereotypes associated with a particular social strata and gender.

Indicators Of Change

It appears that the notion of naming a specific "look" is under attack. An ensemble can no longer have one description that identifies the wearer's clothes. Categories of dress formerly described by such terms as masculine, feminine, casual, formal, business or pleasure may no longer be separable, but may be worn in conjunction with one another or even in opposition to each other. Although this juxtaposition of characteristics seems incongruent, or appears as an unknown to the viewer, there may be an apparent rule of thumb for the wearer, or a motive for their chosen perspective.

The grunge look is only a recent example. It consists of combining purchased fashion items with street fashions to obtain a unique look. These combinations are not new. The trend of combining the new with the old has increased drastically since the early 1980s and became a topic of interest for the English researchers Evans and Thornton (1989) who describe the avant-garde dress of this period as postmodern.

Because the characteristics used by Evans and Thornton to describe postmodern dress clearly paralleled those seen in classrooms by this researcher, their framework was used to structure a questionnaire. The following characteristics were pursued as general themes: re-identification or de-gendering the body, visually avoiding social standing, mapping the body, and using dress to send political messages. The objective was to determine clothing clues of the new aesthetic, and identify items used by students in exhibiting those characteristics.

A Pilot Study

A questionnaire was designed to gain understanding in 3 areas: the subjects' influence for clothing selection or how their aesthetic was developed, their sources for acquiring clothing items, and what these clothing items were or how they were described by the students.[1] The questionnaires (an example is provided in the appendix) were distributed among undergraduate students in 2 classes: Draping Design and AutoCAD Applications for Apparel Design. Because a major portion of the students in these classes were apparel design students, it was assumed that their clothing choices would not only be more alternative or progressive but they would have the ability to effectively describe their dress. Thirty responses were analyzed.

The first question was designed to determine the factors that influenced clothing selection. From the seven categories provided, the students were requested to prioritize the activities which would most likely influence their clothing selection and/or clothing style change.

If factors other than those listed influenced their decisions, they were encouraged to write an additional response by the category "other." This first question was also designed to separate those who had leanings toward postmodernism from those who did not. The first four choices which could be checked by respondents were very general and/or pertained to traditional means by which women could make clothing choices. The fourth one, "looking to friends and peers," could be a traditional influence as well as a postmodern characteristic. It was used as a transitional response from the earlier ones to the last three options which were characteristic of the postmodern.

To study the respondents that indicated postmodern characteristics, the questionnaires were then divided into two groups, according to their responses in question 1. Those who selected fashion magazines, TV and movies, and retail store displays as their main sources of inspiration were identified as the control group and were separated from the study group which was characterized by electing to customize their own look, emulating the opposite sex, and integrating clothing items worn by other cultures or previous time periods.

The two groups needed to be further identified. The first group, or the control, was identified as "the visual/media-influenced" group. This name reflected characteristics similar to what Plummer (1989) suggested as tradition-directed and outer-directed groups. The visual/media-influenced group selected brand names as their first category of expression, as did Plummer's outer-directed persons who tended to be loyal to brand names because they disliked the risk of social embarrassment that a more independent choice might cause them. Plummer further defined his groups as valuing a sense of belonging and success, looking to others for what is acceptable behavior. Chowdhary (1989) suggested that consumers seek consumer-dominated sources, rather than "more informal channels" to reduce the risk factor.

The second group, consisting of those who selected to customize their own look, emulate the opposite sex, and/or integrate clothing items worn by other cultures and or previous time periods, was identified as "the inwardly-inspired group". The term was selected because of the group's individual creativity and distinct lack of interest in any commercialized visual influence. This group, which included 16 respondents, or just over 50% of the subjects questioned, ranked 'individuality' as number 1 for clothing preference.

This second group, the inwardly-inspired and the focus of the study, identified five priorities for their changing aesthetic. Each of these five priorities, as outlined below, contrasts with the traditional concept of unity and match in opposition to traditional "dress," which consists of a coordinated color palette, a consistent "look" within the historical time period, an organized combination of textures contributing to a theme, articles of clothing that identify the wearer's gender, and choices that are consistent with the wearer's culture.

Students' Aesthetic Defined

These five priorities[2] were defined as a result of analyzing and comparing the student responses in the inwardly-inspired and the visual/media groups.

1. Body-clothes Priority

This area of contrast deals with the size or fit of the garments selected. The findings of the pilot study indicated a preference for oversized clothing items among respondents in Group 2. Larger-than-body sweaters and jackets were mentioned as preferences for upper body articles. Visual mass on the lower extremities was expressed as being important and achieved by wearing "big black or unique shoes" or "shoes with thick soles or combat boots" according to two students.

This may relate to changing conceptions in the appropriate fit of clothes. In many cases the large garment is accentuated by a close-fitting garment worn next to or exposed under the oversized article. The contrast between loose or baggy and tight or too small produces a broken viewing path and alters traditional points of focus: the face, gender or sexuality. Lee Wright (Wilson, 1993) discussed the concept of too small as creating the impression that the garment is in the process of being outgrown and often directs the eye of the viewer to an area of exposed skin produced by the larger, or grown body. The body, and/or exposed flesh may emphasize waist, chest and/or biceps, as well as those areas previously exposed for sexual allure, or may focus on unexpected areas such as the lower calves or shoulders.

2. Historical Time Period

Separate mix and match articles of clothing combined according to a fashion trend makes a statement about a given time period. However, the postmodern individual prefers to combine clothing items from multiple time periods in an attempt to negate identity with any current fashion trend. This study revealed that retro styles from the 50s and 60s were preferred as an avenue of individuality or, as one respondent stated: "I think my style crosses too many generations to distinguish it from a specific group." According to the overall results, the subjects showed the use of vintage clothes[3] to express themselves and be unique. Specific comments of students were "vintage items could not be found elsewhere," it "isn't common," and it was a "break from the norm." Several comments suggested a resistance to using dress according to configurations promoted by the media. For example, in regard to adding vintage or used clothing to a customized look, some of the respondents wrote: it is "less trendy," "not the running norm," results in "unique combos," and allows the possibility of "many different choices." One specific comment was that "It's a new combination of personal style and period style - separate one from the other and this (current) time."

Jameson (1984) identified a nostalgia mode as characteristic of the postmoderns. This attempt to simulate a missing past contains a pseudo-historical depth which displaces 'real' history. The wearing of vintage, or retro styles would be defined by Eco (Davis, 1985) as "undercoding" and occurs when the absence of information necessary to form accurate interpretation of communication causes the viewer to presume or infer meanings.

The wearing of clothes from previous time periods may in itself be a political act, according to Simon-Miller (1985). He believes that the use of historical elements identify the wearer with a particular heritage or time period which the wearer views as having a preferred ideology. In another sense, dress may communicate the wearer's desire to learn from past perspectives. The attached cultural myths and the pastiche signifiers indicate a positive look to the future.

> It may turn out...that going back can be a way to go forward: that remembering the modernisms of the nineteenth century can give us the vision and courage

to create modernisms of the twenty-first. This act of remembering can help us bring modernism back to its roots, so that it can nourish and renew itself, to confront the adventures and dangers that lie ahead. (Rose, 1991, p. 100)

3. Color and Surface Structure

Unexpected color combinations and multiple surface designs are used to produce an element of surprise. Respondents in the pilot study specifically mentioned the interplay of color and pattern as important. One stated her preference as "wild colors thrown together to mix and match at will." The Tobe' Report (1993) describes this evolving trend as using an "interplay of not normally allied fabrics" (p. 5).

One way to achieve surprise is to map the body or emphasize surface pattern in unexpected areas. By slashing clothes, skin is exposed in areas selected by the wearer. In a sense, bits of fabric and exposed flesh merge to form a surface pattern. Another aspect of mapping the body is the reduction of space into a series of historical pastiche: the unifying factor is the relationship through difference. The notion of difference relates to the breakdown of the signifying chain, or expression by fragmentation.

The postmodern individual is opposed to the traditional principle of unity and "match." Jencks' notion of "disharmonious harmony" or the "improvised juxtaposition of incompatible or heterogeneous fragments, often for the ironic or parodic effect, as opposed to the principle of unity or 'match' " (Connor, 1989, p. 191), relates to Evans and Thornton's (1989) description of "bedlam" or "out of order", or as defined by Ewen (1988), "ridiculous and discordant juxtapositions abound" as do the "disembodied, decontextualized use of facades" (p. 218).

4. Gender Definition

A fourth characteristic of the current dressing style is an attempt to visually neutralize gender, or to exhibit a visual persona of the wearer's desired sex for a given time frame or day. Evans and Thornton (1989) defined one aspect of postmodern dress as a selected gender-coding, chosen and selected according to the individual's will, and not related to her/his biological orientation. Since the media tends to be gender-specific in its advertising, those individuals who respond to that sort of fashion

promotion would aspire to dress as advertised by the media. The advertising industry tends to remain patriarchal in that the female is the idealized sex or the object of the male voyeur. In this context, she supposedly 'needs' to display a beauty ideal consisting of large breasts, small waist, and to complete the infamous 'hourglass' shape, full hips to the extent that they are in proportion to her bust measurement. Clothes that exhibit these attributes, clothes that fit in a manner that detail the above physical characteristics, or clothes that contain style lines which have traditionally been characterized as focusing on these visual indicators of the female body, are rejected by the postmodern individual.

Subjects, consisting of female students only, gave interesting responses in terms of gender. Students chose to wear men's clothes because they "like the style lines" or were worn to create a "sophisticated, out-of-the-ordinary look." "You can add a whole new look to your wardrobe by taking from the 'other' gender." Plummer stated that the person with new values, or the self-actualized, values the "blurring" of sex roles (1989, p. 10). One reason for the adoption of male clothing articles, or what was described as unisex dressing, was of a practical nature. Ease of care and "mix and match" adaptability also appeared as reasons.

These characteristics are evident by multiple combinations of surface structure. The massive visual weight of combat boots or Doc Martins contrasted with small floral prints suggests a dichotomy of male/female characteristics. This results in separated viewing as described according to viewing priorities by DeLong (1987). One portion of the image describes maleness, while another illustrates femininity, causing a categorical lack of grouping. This ambivalence relates back to the body-clothes priority (p. 49), as to whether the clothes diminish to accent the female body, or whether traditional male clothing is used to accentuate the shape of the female body by comparison.

5. Multi-cultural Aspects

The students interviewed in the pilot study were questioned about their predictions for future fashion trends. Their responses suggested an International style, as opposed to fashions prescribed by large fashion centers such as Paris and New York. This rejection of culture-specific and class-specific clothing supports a dressing style that visually promotes equality within the human race. Traditional European styling or a strong Western look would not be a choice, nor would garments and accessories worn by the upper class. Instead, a peasant skirt from India, a sweater from the 60s and a dog collar worn as a neckpiece would show much more universality whereby a viewer would not be able to identify the wearer's social position. The viewer is not able to say "there goes a rich kid." If a mink stole were worn, it would accompany items of parody so as to negate the traditional connotation of white upper-class wealth.

A growing awareness of other cultures is one characteristic of postmodernism (Huyssen, 1986). Huyssen believed that non-European, non-Western cultures must be met by means other than conquest or domination. Mixing styles of dress seems to express acceptance and can be used as a tool to reach this goal.

Both the control and the focus groups indicated that future trends would reflect relevant cultural and societal issues. These clothing trends would gain popularity as they reflected environmental concerns (relating to methods of manufacture) and concerns related to the economy (U.S.-based manufacturing and the recycling of clothes). Although not specifically stated by respondents, this author would theorize that the interest in historical clothing and vintage clothing items could relate to the recycling of clothes and is popularized by a nonconsumer orientation.

Current Teaching Trends

Aesthetics applied to dress can be analyzed independently of any social standard. A technique proposed by Marilyn DeLong (1987) facilitates analyzing the dressed body through a conceptual framework referred to as the "apparel-body construct". Her four-step process of observation, analysis, interpretation, and evaluation involves a universal vocabulary and provides the viewer with a tool for potentially understanding dress in a reasoned, systematic manner. The technique is particularly useful when analyzing dress in a postmodern environment or in conjunction with an emerging aesthetic or fashion trend.

To determine a changing aesthetic, as illustrated in the pilot study, new meanings relevant to the culture need to be described by the wearers in that culture. After DeLong's framework has become familiar, lectures should be minimized and focus placed on student learning and interpretation.

In summarizing the purposes of this article, the term cooperative learning is used as the strategy for involving student groups as the learning structure.[4] The current buzzwords for "new" educational trends in the literature discuss active learning, cooperative learning, and collaborative strategies. The commonalities among these structures is that they place more emphasis on student learning through participation in comparison to the lecture experience. In this type of learning experience, students are encouraged to participate in heterogeneous groups with whom they were not acquainted. Under these conditions, the chances are likely that the student's individual aesthetic within the small group would provide material for discussion and especially if aesthetic vocabulary, concepts, and self-expression are encouraged.

DeLong's framework and the use of cooperative learning as a student focus for interpretation has the added advantage of assisting students based upon learning style, such as preference for visualization, the written word, sound-understanding, (listening) and feeling (activity). Analyzing visual images in small groups, writing interpretations, and listening to and participating in peer discussions can promote the understanding of an evolving aesthetic.

Process For Instruction

A developing aesthetic may conflict with an instructor's more conventional idea of definable fashion terminology. Teaching design and aesthetics in an undergraduate environment requires alternate choices to traditional vocabulary, instructional methods, and examples selected for illustration purposes. It is becoming apparent that illustrations or examples of color-coordinated ensembles, garments with matched seams and even hemlines are no longer priorities for some. To determine the most effective approach for teaching aesthetics to this age group, it is necessary to listen to their descriptions of preferred dress.

When designing instructional methods, consideration should be given to DeLong's framework for visual analysis as a basis for developing critical thinking skills and planning cooperative learning strategies. The purpose is to obtain a description of the emerging aesthetic according to the perceptions of the students. By identifying the viewing path, points of focus, and descriptions of the apparel-body construct, their interpretations and assigned meanings will reflect their socially constructed rules and norms as well as help to identify changing trends. DeLong's methodology can also be used as a basis for discussing the aesthetics in other market segments. By analyzing the preferences of other consumer markets, apparel design and merchandising students can develop objectivity. Through creativity, exercises can be developed that will encourage student expression. Class discussions on images that are selected by students or ensembles worn by them have the potential of facilitating their interpretation of a given aesthetic and how it emerges while providing an evolving framework for the educator and helping to build a stronger student/instructor base.

APPENDIX
Questionnaire

1. When considering a clothing purchase or a change in dressing style, which of the following activities would you be most likely to do? Indicate your favorite activity by the number 1, your second with number 2, etc.

_____Study fashion magazines

_____Observe what is being worn on TV and in the movies

_____Purchase what is displayed in retail stores

_____Look to friends/peers

_____Customize or manufacture your own look

_____Emulate clothing styles worn by the opposite sex

_____Integrate clothing styles worn by other cultures or previous time periods

_____Other

2. This question has two parts. Rate each of the following four categories as to the order of your clothing preference, with your first choice indicated by placing number 1 in the blank, number 2 for your second choice, etc. After rating the categories, circle the letter response that best describes the reason for your choice. If you select the "other" option, write in a response that describes the reason for your choice.

_____Gender-specific clothing items

    A. To define your sexuality

    B. To visually neutralize gender

    C. To add an element of the unexpected by selecting clothing items typically worn by the opposite sex

    D. Other

_____Clothes to express individuality

    A. To distinguish your personal style from popular fashion

    B. To add an element of surprise or humor

    C. To show personality or a unique style

    D. Other

_____Vintage clothes

    A. To recapture or relive the life of the period (as it being a more preferred lifestyle or environment then the present)

    B. To mix with current clothes to create a fashionable look

    C. To mix with other period clothes to customize your own look.

    D. To add an element of surprise

    E. For the purpose of economic conservation

    F. Other

_____Brand name or designer label

    A. To express fashion awareness

    B. To gain approval of others

    C. To achieve desired comfort or fit

    D. To achieve professional recognition

    E. Other

3. Which of the four areas above would society or popular culture identify as the most popular? Which would they identify as the least popular?

4. Which of the four "looks" in question 2 would mix together? Why?

5. How would you describe the social and political values of your peer group? What articles of clothing or accessories identify you with your peer group?

6. How would you define "timeless" dressing?

7. What fashion trends do you see emerging in the 1990s and why?

Endnotes

1. The research design and formulation of this study in February 1992 was well before the emergence of "grunge". The similarity of results to what was later identified as grunge provides reinforcement.

2. Priorities or categories are useful in defining, but the author realizes the danger in overgeneralization.

3. The questionnaire used the term 'vintage' but did not differentiate between vintage and used clothing. The written responses, however, discussed both terms as interchangeable.

4. Another purpose of cooperative learning is the development of student social skills such as decision-making, conflict management, and communication that it provides. Other additional advantages of this system are increased retention, critical reasoning competencies, motivation, accountability, and self-esteem.

References

Bonwel, C. & Eison, J. (1991). Active learning: Creating excitement in the classroom. *ASHE-ERIC Higher Education Report No. 1*. Washington, D.C.: The George Washington University, School of Education and Human Development.

Brenninkmeyer, I. (1963). *The sociology of fashion.* Paris: Librairie du Recueil Sirey.

Cassill, N. & Drake, M. (1987). Apparel selection criteria related to female consumers' lifestyle. *Clothing and Textiles Research Journal*, 6(1), pp. 20-27.

Conner, S. (1989). *Postmodernist culture: an introduction to theories of the contemporary.* Cambridge, Massachusetts: Basil Blackwell.

Davis, F. (1985). Clothing and fashion as communication. In M. R. Solomon (Ed.), *The Psychology of Fashion.* (pp. 15-27). Lexington, MA: D.C. Health Co.

DeLong, M. (1987). *The way we look: A framework for visual analysis of dress.* Ames, Iowa: Iowa State University Press.

Evans, C. and Thornton, M. (1989). *Women and fashion: A new look.* Great Britain: Quartet Books, Ltd.

Ewen, S. (1988). *All consuming images: The politics of style in contemporary culture.* New York: Basic Books, Inc.

Fiske, J. (1989). *Understanding popular culture.* London: Routledge.

Grindering, M. (1985). Fashion diffusion. In G. Sproles (Ed.), *Perspectives in Fashion.* (pp. 40-43). Minneapolis, MN: Burgess Pub. Co.

Huyssen, A. (1986). *After the great divide: modernism, mass culture, postmodernism.* Bloomington: Indiana University Press.

Johnson, D., Johnson, R. & Smith, K. (1991). Cooperative learning: Increasing college faculty instructional productivity. *ASHE-ERIC Higher Education Report No. 4.* Washington, D.C.: The George Washington University, School of Education and Human Development.

Jameson, F. (1984). Postmodernism, or the cultural logic of late capitalism. *New Left Review, 146,* 53-92.

Jencks, C. (1984). *The language of post-modern architecture.* London: Academy Editions.

Kobel, P. (1993, April 2). Smells like big bucks. *Entertainment Weekly,* p. 10.

Leland, J. & Leonard, E. (1993, February 1). Back to Twiggy. *Newsweek,* p. 64.

Leland, J. & Leonard, E. (1993, February 1). For gamines' gams, it's grunge wear. *Newsweek,* p. 65.

Plummer, J. (1989). Changing values: the new emphasis on self-actualization. *The Futurist,* January-February (1), pp. 8-13.

Simon-Miller, F. (1985). Signs and cycles in the fashion system. In M. R. Solomon (Ed.), *The Psychology of Fashion.* (pp. 72-81). Lexington, MA: D.C. Health Co.

Tobe' Report. (1993, June 1). *Deconstructivism.* New York: Tobe' Associates, Inc.

Rose, M. (1991). *The post-modern and the post-industrial.* New York: Cambridge University Press.

Simmel, G. (1904). Fashion. *International Quarterly, 10,* pp. 130-155.

Wilson, E. (1993). *Chic thrills: A fashion reader.* Berkeley, CA: University of California Press.

An Investigation Of The Creative Process And Application To Apparel Design Models

Sharleen L. Kato
Seattle Pacific University

Educators in the field of apparel design are in a position to encourage creative behavior as well as evaluate creative apparel products. The purpose of this paper is to provide theoretical support for apparel design process theories utilized by educators.

Creativity is an integral part of apparel design. Although educators may see creativity as a vital component of creative design, it is still relatively difficult to capture the essence of creativity. Guilford (1950) wrote that a practical definition of creativity is difficult because unquestionable and undeniable acts or products of creativity are very rare.

There are five sections in this paper: a) historical attempts to define creativity, b) major theoretical frameworks to organize creativity research, c) standards to evaluate creative products, d) creative design process, and e) applying research to two design models.

The first section will begin with a discussion on the difficulty of definition followed by evolutionary definitions throughout the century. The second section of this paper will look at the major theoretical frameworks within which creativity research is organized. This will include cognitive, personality and environmental, mental health/psychological growth, psychoanalytical, and psychedelic theories of creativity. As each theoretical body is reviewed, significant contributors will be highlighted. Although the apparel design theories reviewed later utilize the cognitive approach, it is important to understand that there are other ways to view creativity. This section will be followed by a section reviewing standards by which creative products may be analyzed as set forth by Besemer and Treffinger (1981) after reviewing over ninety research studies establishing creative versus noncreative evaluative standards.

The next section deals with the creative design process, beginning with several studies which summarize the vast creative process research and ending with several theories set

forth by organizational trainers as examples of theory put into practice.

The paper concludes by applying the creativity research theory reviewed to the apparel design model as presented by Lamb and Kallal (1992) and the apparel design process presented by Watkins (1988) with the intention of substantiating the research base for both theories.

Definitions of Creativity

In an article relating creative intelligence and personality, Barron and Harrington (1981) found that the difficulty in establishing a definition of creativity was the result of the lack of fine distinctions between referents associated with it. Differences or lack of distinction were found in the creative product's social value versus its intrinsic value, the simplicity versus complexity criteria, and the distinction between creative achievement, creative skills/abilities/talent, and creative dispositions.

In looking at the scientific concept of creativity, Pfeiffer (1979) found that no one definition proved general enough to encompass different research findings and specific enough to highlight distinction between the referents. In his review, he established four criteria with which he believed any definition of creativity should comply. These criteria include 1) the establishment of standards for distinguishing whether or not a product is creative, 2) the establishment of standards for measuring creative versus non-creative activity, 3) the synthesis for all creativity research in all disciplines to reveal commonalities and 4) few violations of accepted creativity theories and applications.

Nevertheless, many attempts have been made to define creativity. McCloy, in a 1931 study of adults and children, defined creative imagination as the ability to envision combinations and recombinations of items in a problem into unique or original products.

Fromm (1957-58) established two meanings of creativity. These included the creation of

48

something new and the creative attitude which included the ability to concentrate and envision beyond the normal mental processes. Today this might be termed "intuition."

In his work on establishing a theoretical framework for creativity, Rogers (1957-58) defined it as "the emergence in action of a novel relational product, growing out of the uniqueness of the individual on the one hand, and the materials, events, people, or circumstances of his life on the other" (p. 71). Likewise, Torrance (1962) described creativity as "becoming sensitive to problems, deficiencies, gaps in knowledge, missing elements, disharmonies . . . " (p. 8) as applied to the human process of relating to self and others.

For the purposes of this paper, a composite definition of creativity is used. Creativity is defined as the ability to develop an idea that meets the needs of the user by combining items or thoughts in a new and original way.

Theoretical Frameworks of Creativity

Several attempts have been made to organize the abundance of creativity research. Treffinger, et al. (1983) structured five theoretical frameworks within which the creativity research to date could be organized. These included 1) cognitive, rational, and semantic approaches, 2) personality and environmental approaches, 3) mental health and/or psychological growth approaches, 4) psychoanalytic approaches, and 5) psychedelic approaches. In an attempt to understand the different strands of creativity in the context of this paper, the approaches will be briefly explained.

Cognitive Approaches

The cognitive theoretical approach defines processes of creativity and the resulting products. Taylor (1975) referred to this approach as associationistic as it deals with divergent and convergent associations. Divergent thinking involves thinking in different directions or drawing from a wide range of options, whereas convergent thinking focuses on and synthesizes toward one right answer. As early as 1900, Ribot referred to these associations as the linking in the process of creative thought.

In reviewing creativity research from 1950 to 1974, Guilford (1975) formulated a model called "Structure-of-Intellect Model". In this model, intellectual processes and products and their re-

lationship to creativity are presented. The model, a three dimensional cube, incorporates the kinds of content, products of information, and intellectual operations. The kinds of content processed include visual and auditory-figural (perceptions and images of people, things, and ideas), semantic (imageless thoughts), symbolic (signs or labels attached to ideas, people, and things), and behavioral (including body language) content.

Products of information are divided first into "units" or separate elements. Then, similar units are grouped and "classes" are formed. When one class suggests or predicts another, an "implication" is the product. If the two classes have a definitive relationship, the product is called a "relation." When many classes become connected, the product is a "system." Finally, when a system causes redefinition or change, the product is a "transformation."

The intellectual operations include cognition (the coding of information), memory (the storage of information), divergent and convergent production of information, and the judging of the suitability of information. Divergent and convergent thinking both generate new information.

Guilford asserted that there is more than one way to be creative. For example, in intellectual content, visual artists such as architects specialize in visual-figural kinds of content, whereas composers and dancers specialize in the auditory-figural, teachers and scientists in the semantic, and attorneys, salesmen, and policemen in the behavioral content forms.

In the relationship of creativity to products and operations, Guilford asserted that divergent thinking and transformations have the most to do with creative thinking. The work of Guilford has been very instrumental in creative theory development. As will be discussed later, cognitive theory is seen today as an essential element in the process of creating. It is generally held, however, that the biological component or cognitive theory is but one part of the creative process picture and that a creative outcome is a result of more than the creator's experience or knowledge (Pickard, 1990).

Personality and Environmental Approaches

The personality and environmental theoretical approaches to creativity research focus on individual traits found in people who are perceived to be "creative" as compared to less creative individuals. Taylor (1975) refers to this as trait-factorial because the statistical technique of factor analysis is often employed to identify traits measured on a variety of instruments. A wide variety of traits has been cited in the research to be associated with creative individuals (Rogers, 1957; Barron, 1958; MacKinnon, 1962; Trowbridge and Charles, 1966; Gottz and Gottz, 1979).

In a comprehensive review of creativity research from 1950 to 1974, Guilford (1975) divided the personality traits of creative individuals into two areas: motivational and tempera-mental as seen in the many trait studied during this period.

Motivational traits of highly creative individuals, in comparison to less creative, groups reviewed in the individual studies are outlined by Guilford to include 1) a high energy level, 2) a high curiosity level, 3) an interest in reflective thinking, 4) a low need to work in "reality," 5) a sense of humor, 6) a high level of risk taking, 7) a high level of individuality and autonomy, 8) a high level of self-sufficiency, 9) a tendency to use themselves as a standard of evaluation (as evaluation of themselves is high), and 10) a tendency to reject conventional sex roles.

When compared to less creative individuals, temperamental traits of highly creative individuals as outlined by Guilford include a tendency to be introverted rather than extroverted and a tendency to be impulsive rather than slow and calculating.

In a more recent review of creativity research, Tardif and Sternberg (1988) synthesized the vast amount of trait research into four trait categories: 1) relatively high intelligence, 2) high originality, 3) high fluency and verbal articulateness, and 4) a good imagination. Further, cognitive abilities and the way in which people approach problems were categorized. Cognitive characteristics include the ability to think using metaphors, flexibility and decision-making skills, independence of judgment, positive response to novelty, logical thinking, and the ability to go against conventional thinking. The way in which creative people approach problems can be characterized as fluent, skewed toward nonverbal communication, original rather than adaptive, questioning, and elaborating.

Mental Health/Psychological Growth Approaches

This theoretical approach stresses human self-actualization (the desire to reach full potential) as the motivation in creative activity. Taylor (1975) referred to this as the humanistic approach, as it holds a very positive, optimistic view of people, believing creativity to be within the potential of all people.

In his treatise on creativity found in self-actualizing people, Maslow (1957-58) makes a distinction between ordinary self-actualizing creativity and creativity seen in a special or uniquely talented individual. He focused on self-actualized creativeness seen in all self-actualized people in the ordinary happenings of life. He defined this self-actualized kind of creativity as "a special kind of perceptiveness . . . can see the fresh, the raw, the concrete, the ideographic, as well as the generic, the abstract, the rubricized, the categorized, and the classified" (p. 85).

Psychoanalytic Approaches

The psychoanalytic approach traditionally viewed creativity as an unconscious, neurotic, or sometimes psychotic process (Treffinger, et al., 1983). Freud (Sprott, 1933) played a major role in this school of thought linking creativity to mental illness as he believed that creativity was a product of the tension of unsatisfied biological needs (Taylor, 1975). Jung (1958), however, took creativity from the unconscious to the preconscious state of mind. Although still viewing creativity as a need of humans, Neo-Freudians like Jung believed that creativity was closer to a conscious process (Treffinger, et al., 1983).

The basic assumption of psychoanalytic theory was described by Smolucha and Smolucha (1988) as "internalized social interactions which become higher mental functions that regulate lower biological functions" (p. 1). In a presentation at The Xth International Colloquium on Empirical Aesthetics, Smolucha and Smolucha contrasted the synergistic (psychoanalytic) approach with the cognitive approach to creativity. They assert that teaching art involves two realms. The first involves teaching the mechanics, techniques or skills involved in creative work as a formal part of the curriculum. The second involves the cognitive processes used in creating art. This part of the educational experience is usually taught in a serendipitous manner. Smolucha and Smolucha suggest that the synergistic approach to teaching art should include both the skills and cognitive processes involved in creation in the formal curriculum. This can be achieved through providing experiences which are beyond the student's skill level and require collaboration with the instructor rather than solitary, independent work.

The psychoanalytic approach focuses not only on needs, but the development of the person.

Psychedelic and Holistic Approaches

Whereas Neo-Freudian psychoanalytic approaches focus on the preconscious state, psychedelic approaches focus on the unconsciousness of the mind by utilizing dimensions of the mind which we have been taught, since childhood, to subdue (Treffinger, et al., 1983). Although the word "psychedelic" often conjures images of a drug culture, many methods, including drugs, can be used to tap the mind's vast resources that are viewed as an important step in human psychological development (Treffinger, et al., 1983).

Taylor (1975) added an additional approach to the above mentioned approaches to creativity research which he called the holistic approach. He described this approach as "a process in which a field is restructured to restore harmony and obtain equilibrium. It is not a piecemeal operation, but rather one in which each step is subsumed or affected by the whole situation" (p. 10).

The field of creativity research is naturally progressing toward a more holistic approach wherein the social system, human needs, and biological needs are integrated (Vessels, 1982). Vessels (1982) termed this approach an open-systems conceptualization which is an empirically based definition that explains why a person would be willing to take new, unfamiliar information and take it to resolution (his definition of creativity).

The holistic theory was described by Woodman and Schoenfeldt (1990) as the study of the interaction between the situation, the person, and the interaction between the person and their environment over time. The holistic theory is complex as it takes into account not only events and interactions which have occurred but also the potential for interactions and events.

Establishment of Standards for Creative Products

A difficulty in studying creativity is the disparity between societal and individual standards of establishing what is or is not considered a creative product. Besemer and Treffinger (1981) reviewed over ninety research studies from which they organized over 125 specific criteria for establishing a creative product versus a non-creative product. These were then classified into three main categories including novelty, resolution, and elaboration and synthesis.

"Novelty" refers to the "extent of newness . . . " (p. 159) of a product. This includes originality or uniqueness of the product, the product's ability to germinate or stimulate creativity in other people and other fields, and the product's transforming power or its ability to shed new light.

"Resolution" refers to the appropriateness or correctness of the product as a solution to the problem. The appropriateness of the solution can be measured by its logical nature, adequate performance, usefulness, and value to those evaluating it.

"Elaboration" and "synthesis" refer to the particular style exuded by the product. This standard of measure includes the characteristics of expressiveness, complexity, well-craftedness, and a feeling of action, life-like characteristics, and elegance or sophistication. This comprehensive study by Besemer and Treffinger serves to organize the broad research in this area.

The Creative Process

The creative process has been the topic of study for many researchers and practitioners. Several researchers have attempted to conceptualize creativity into sequential steps.

One of the earlier researchers to explore the creative process was Wallas (1926). Four stages in the formation of the problem solution were established including preparation, incubation, illumination, and verification. Preparation involves systematically analyzing the problem situation. Incubation is the "unconscious mental exploration" (p. 81) of the problem. Illumination happens when the idea first appears as a result of the preceding steps. Verification is when the adjustment and evaluation of the idea takes place in order to perfect the idea.

The process was further divided into seven stages by Osborn (1953). These include orientation to the problem, preparation or fact finding analysis of the problem, ideation, incubation, synthesis of previous steps to one or a few ideas, and finally evaluation of the problem solution.

Guilford (1950) closely paralleled Wallas (1926) in formulating four steps in the creative process. These include preparation, incubation, inspiration, and evaluation. However, Guilford added that "such an analysis is very superficial from the psychological point of view. It is more dramatic than it is suggestive of testable hypotheses. It tells us almost nothing about the mental processes that actually occur" (p. 451). He asserted that this difficulty in broad application is due to individual differences in sensitivity to problems, idea fluency, number and ease of generating novel ideas, flexibility, ability to analyze problems effectively, ability to synthesize material, and the ability to evaluate ideas effectively.

In a much quoted book on the creative process, Jones (1981) differentiated between what he termed the black box designer and the glass box designer. The black box designer works out of mystery or non-rational thought utilizing insight, whereas the glass box designer uses rational thought processing and evaluating relevant information. His focus on the glass box method reveals several common characteristics of this method including setting objectives at the beginning of the process, completion of analysis before idea and/or solution are formulated, and fixed sequential problem solving steps.

Jones outlined four types of creative problems encountered. These include 1) mass, splittable design problems, 2) smaller, unsplittable design problems, 3) circular design problems in which the problem solver must continually return to the beginning of the process in order to clarify objectives, and 4) linear problems in which all problem challenges can be foreseen at the beginning and throughout the problem solving process.

Jones asserted that problems faced today are too complicated for simple step-by-step strategies and that methods similar to artificial intelligence might best be used. The process can be broken down into three general stages which include analysis of the problem, synthe-

sis of the findings, and evaluation. These may be cycled through many times varying in degrees of generality and specificity until the design solution is determined.

Many researchers have sought practical application of creative process theory for use in schools, private industry, government training purposes, and apparel design. In an editorial article based on industry experience printed in the *General Electric Review*, Von Fange (1955) outlined the creative process for application to real-life problems encountered by readers. The nine steps included 1) defining the problem by establishing specifications and investigating possible approaches, 2) searching for problem solving methods, 3) evaluating the methods found, 4) generalizing the results from the previous steps, 5) selecting an appropriate problem solving method, 6) formulating a preliminary design, 7) testing and evaluating the design, 8) generalizing the results and 9) utilizing the best solution.

In a guide for trainers and managers of people, Van Gundy (1987) offered a similar six stage creative problem solving model. This included 1) clarifying the objective(s) 2) increasing understanding of the problem through fact finding 3) selecting a problem statement 4) generating ideas, 5) systematically analyzing potential solutions by generating specific criteria to measure them by, and 6) finding ways in which to make the chosen solution work. Van Gundy emphasized the flexibility of this process in that every step does not have to be rigidly followed nor is every step included in every problem situation. Instead, the only real necessity in this creative problem-solving model is to keep the objective(s) in view at all times. Van Gundy also suggested practical methods for divergence or expansion of the amount of data at each stage and convergence or reduction of the data at each stage.

In a well-known practical guide to increasing creative problem solving potential entitled *Synectics*, Gordon (1961) utilized a high degree of analogical and metahorical thinking strategies. He outlined nine steps for developing creativity, in which analogy and metaphor are used in each. These include 1) accepting the problem as given, 2) making the strange familiar, 3) defining the problem as understood, 4) operationalizing problem mechanisms, 5) making the familiar strange, 6) utilizing different operational states, 7) integrating different psychological states with the problem, 8) forming a viewpoint, and 9) achieving a solution or research target.

Several researchers have focused on specific aspects of the creative design process or attributes of the creative problem solver that may enhance or inhibit the creative process. Psychologist Sarnoff Mednick (1962) asserted that the creative thinking process is in essence the process of forming associations between new or seemingly unrelated elements. He believed that serendipity or accidental association of problem elements, similarity of problem elements, and mediation between common elements serve as ways to achieve a creative solution.

The importance of incubation in the creative problem solving process was set forth by Guilford (1979). He established four hypotheses concerning the nature of incubation. First is the hypothesis that fatigue plays a part as the mind needs time to rest. Second is the fresh start approach in which there is a necessary revised or renewed approach to the problem. Third is that the transformation of information takes time, and fourth is Extra Sensory Perception. He found that the further along in time a solution is found from the beginning of the problem solving task the more likely the problem solution will be of high quality. Personality traits associated with incubation include the tendency to "leave the gap open" (p. 5), persistent motivation, introversion, relaxed effort, flexibility, and the ability to modify problems, ideas and situations.

Guilford (1979) also highlighted the importance of insight and illumination in the creative problem solving process. Insight, or that "moment of inspiration" is encouraged under relaxed conditions in which there are minimal distractions and interruptions and in problem solvers who are willing to take risks.

The above review has focused on the general creative process. A few researchers have focused specifically on the visual task process within which apparel design would be included.

In an early study of the process of visual task performance in adults and children (McCloy, 1931), the researcher found a variety of ways the thirty-two subjects approached the visual task placed before them. Three of the subjects had definite concepts of how they wanted their designs to appear before proceeding. Eight subjects used trial and error initially then selected one method and followed through with it to the end. Seven subjects worked in one direction from the start with a vague, not yet determined idea where they were headed with the task. Three subjects were never able to come up with a final decision even though there was a solution at the end of the allotted time. The remaining subjects fell somewhere between these categories.

To measure intelligence, perceptions, values, and personality of 179 adult art students at the School of the Art Institute in Chicago Getzels and Csikszentmihalyi (1976) gathered data from cognitive, perceptual, and personality instruments as well as biographical questionnaires, originality and artistic potential ratings, and student grades. Through descriptive data, the researchers were able to derive indirect information about the creative process. The researchers asserted that the creative process in the fine arts is based on strong individual values and personality and may be described as somewhat existential in nature. They also found that a major factor in the approach to solving problems for the fine art student is whether the components of the problem are known or unknown.

In a practical book for developing creative visual thinking skills, McKim (1980) outlined a simple strategy: express ideas, test ideas, and cycle to an altogether different idea. This simple strategy is expanded, however, in a flow diagram of strategic choices. The flow plan begins with a definition of the problem. Then, the problem is recognized, constraints are recognized, and objectives are listed. Next, the problem solver relaxes or diverts conscious attention on the problem in order to allow incubation to occur. At this point the problem solver may choose to either stop, continue with the problem or choose another strategy (cycle). If the problem solver chooses to cycle, then a decision is made to choose one hemisphere (left or right brain) mode. McKim focuses on the right brain visual thinking strategies which include: 1) abstract (defocusing or withdrawing from details), 2) modify or clarify the problem elements, 3) manipulate or rearrange the problem elements, 4) transform or abandon attached labels and stereotypes, 5) concretize or converge thinking

53

and 6) timescan or use past and future information to add a new dimension to the problem elements.

After cycling in the right brain mode, the next step is to express, explore, and develop the idea by generating alternatives and deferring judgment after which the idea is evaluated.

In the final section of the paper, two models for apparel design as proposed by Lamb and Kallal (1992) and by Watkins (1988) will be reviewed. As appropriate, relevant creativity research covered in previous sections will be applied to these models.

Apparel Design Process Models

Watkins (1988) proposed using the creative design process model set forth by Koberg and Bagnall (1981) to teach functional apparel design (designing apparel products for specific end uses). This is a cognitive process and includes the following stages: acceptance, analysis, definition of the problem, ideation, idea selection, implementation, and evaluation. In discussing each of the following stages of functional apparel design, supporting research will be discussed as well as suggestions provided for consideration.

Acceptance Stage

This stage involves the designer "buying" in to the problem or becoming internally motivated to accept the problem. Wallas (1926) and Osborn (1953) place acceptance, analysis, and definition of the problem into a broader, defined stage termed preparation. Von Fange (1955) did not include acceptance in his proposed nine stage process.

Amabile (1983) theorized eleven societal influences that inhibit or enhance creative behavior, three of which are addressed here. These may play a part at any stage in the process and not necessarily at the acceptance stage only. Although they are external factors rather than the internal motivator that Watkins advocates, many of these do relate directly to the acceptance stage. First, individuals must be given a choice to participate. Individuals are generally more creative if they make the decision to accept the problem/task. Second, rewards can have a positive effect as the enjoyment of completing the task may be enhanced. However, solely completing the task for reward tends to negatively affect creativity. Third, free-choice

tends to motivate creative behavior as risk is allowed.

Internal motivators to acceptance could include a high curiosity level (Guilford, 1975) and a high level of self absorption which may also help enhance insight in the later stages (May, 1975).

In order to facilitate the acceptance stage for the student, more emphasis may need to be put on the individual rather than the group's interests and on the designer rather than on the user.

Analysis Stage

Watkins described this stage of the process as the point when the designer attempts to discover the nature of the problem. Torrance (1962) referred to a similar creative behavior of becoming sensitive to deficiencies.

Most creativity researchers agree on the importance of the analysis stage. Wallas (1926), Guilford (1950), Osborn (1953), and Von Fange (1955) included analysis in the preparation stage or beginning stage(s) of their proposed processes.

May (1975) established the importance of insight in creative problem solving process. Although he asserted that insight cannot be willed, dedication and self absorption into a problem can serve to make the problem solver more aware or more susceptible to insight. Other trait attributes that may be applied to this stage include a high energy level, high curiosity level, and an interest in reflective thinking (Guilford, 1975).

Definition Stage

This is the stage in which the designer sorts through an abundance of information and subsequently states the problem precisely. The definition is therefore based on a thorough analysis of the problem. Little research focuses on this stage of the process although researchers agree that the designer should fully understand the problem.

Ideation Stage

Ideation is the idea-generating stage that takes place after the problem is thoroughly understood. Watkins proposed that all students are capable of high idea generation if properly trained. Fromm (1957-58) asserts that creative idea generation is beyond normal mental processes. This may be interpreted as supporting the idea that the skill must be taught.

Many researchers have studied the ideation stage of creative problem solving. In fact, the generation of ideas, especially original or unique ideas is often the definition of creativity.

It is often discussed in terms of divergent and convergent thinking. Both types of thinking result in the generation of new ideas through combinations and recombinations of ideas.

Mednick (1962) theorized that idea generation involves serendipity and seeing similarities between unrelated items by mediating between common elements or ideas. This is often achieved through playfulness which is advocated by Watkins, especially in the idea selection stage. Analogical and metaphorical thinking strategies as proposed by Gordon (1961) may also be helpful at this stage.

Incubation is not addressed in the process applied to apparel design either by Watkins or Lamb and Kallal. Incubation, or "putting ideas on the back burner", may be an effective means to further idea generation. Guilford (1979) referred to incubation as the decision to "leave the gap open". Incubation takes time by definition and is difficult to monitor, especially in a structured classroom environment. Incubation may be encouraged by providing a relaxed and non-distracting environment.

Idea Selection Stage

Selection of the best idea from those generated in the previous stage involves both cognitive processes and intuitive responses. The cognitive approach is easier to link with the process of creative thought as it is structured and methodical. Intuitive responses, on the other hand, are generally viewed as "soft" and nonobjective. Jones (1981) referred to this stage in his discussions of both glass box and black box design. It should be noted that intuition may predominate in the idea selection stage exclusively, while cognitive process may predominate in other stages; especially in the analysis and evaluation stages.

Treffinger, et al. (1983) asserted that intuitive responses are simply using a part of the mind that many people, especially scientists, have been trained to restrict. Highly creative students may be more skilled at using intuition (Guilford, 1975). Thus, as Watkins affirmed,

students need to learn to use both cognitive and intuitive responses.

Implementation and Evaluation Stages

Little research exists on the implementation stage and most of the research on evaluation deals with evaluating the finished product, not on how the designer conducts the evaluation. Both stages are acknowledged by process theorists, however.

Evaluation criteria are established at different points in the process. For example, in the process used by Watkins, criteria are established in the analysis and definition stages. Van Gundy (1987) proposed generating evaluative criteria after idea generation. Evaluative criteria will be addressed in the following section.

The FEA Model

Lamb and Kallal (1992) presented a general framework for apparel design which includes fashion design as well as designing for special needs. The rationale for this model was to provide a model which could be used in all types of apparel design and that would not limit the designer to the functional aspects of design only. The circular model, referred to as the FEA model, combines the functional, expressive, and aesthetic needs around the user's wants and needs as well as the culture in which the interaction between the designer and client takes place. As the authors asserted, this model augments examination of the analysis and evaluation stages of the apparel design process proposed by Watkins.

In the core or inner circle of the model is located the target customer or consumer. Demographics, needs, and wants are factors that are considered by the designer. The target customer is surrounded by a wider circle denoting the culture in which the designer and the customer act. In the outer circle are located three basic design criteria which include the functional, expressive, and aesthetic criteria.

The functional criteria include factors such as how well the clothing item fits on the body, the ease allowed, mobility, comfort, and care considerations. The expressive criteria includes the communicative, symbolic and expressive nature of the clothing. The aesthetic criteria evaluates the use of the principles of design (proportion/scale, rhythm, balance, unity/variety, emphasis). These three criteria are interrelated rather than independent of each other. The design process is then combined with the FEA model in order to meet all of the three basic design criteria.

Culture, which is included in this model, is an important consideration in creative behavior. Lasswell (1957), at an interdisciplinary symposia on creativity, put forth that an effective way to examine the social context of creativity would be to identify all of the inhibitors and enhancers of creativity within a given culture. Although it would be an overwhelming task, the reward would be an understanding of the operational arrangements (eg., beliefs, faiths, loyalties, roles) of creativity within a culture. He believed that the chance for creativity to occur was heightened if the values of the individual and the collective groups meshed.

The three design criteria of functional, expressive, and aesthetics are similar to the evaluative criteria proposed by Besemer and Treffinger (1981) which included novelty, resolution, and elaboration or synthesis. Functional characteristics or meeting the needs of the user are incorporated in the resolution evaluative measure. Expressive criteria are seen in the elaboration or synthesis evaluative measure. The design criteria proposed by the FEA model are not expressed in specific terms as they are affected by culture. It should be noted that the Besemer and Treffinger study, discussed previously, summarized Western creativity research that reflects the Western value of novelty or originality as an important aesthetic factor.

Conclusions

Both the functional apparel design process proposed by Watkins and the FEA model proposed by Lamb and Kallal are supported by creativity research to date. Each could be described as cognitive approaches to apparel design. Additional research into the holistic approach to creative behavior would be beneficial in furthering our understanding of apparel design.

Future considerations might also include more emphasis on incubation as having an important function in apparel design. Subsequent research might focus on large design problems that can be isolated into smaller steps. The functional apparel design process does take into consideration smaller, unsplittable de-

signs, linear designs, and circular design problems as described by Jones (1980).

Both apparel design models are beneficial for systematically teaching apparel design. It should be noted, however, that disparities exist between creative design processes proposed by researchers and those proposed by practitioners because an accepted, standard, unchanging creative design process does not exist. Instead, it appears that the design process may vary between individuals and applications and possibly between cultures and sub-cultures. The weight or importance of one aspect (stage) of the processes may fluctuate based on the functional or fashion nature of the design problem.

The rationale given by the authors of both models support teaching a standardized process in order to help the students internalize problem solving skills. Understanding the design process is a valuable asset in any field but especially in the highly creative and expressive apparel design field. Future research will likely refine the understanding of the apparel design process. However, great care must be taken to appreciate and encourage diversity in the creative process application. We all approach the design process in a slightly different manner thus educators must be careful to not dictate one process to students. Instead, students should be encouraged to identify and manipulate the process (or combination of processes) they utilize when designing and individuality should be rewarded. Since creativity is approached differently by various individuals, these models form a framework or reference for discussion with students and provide guidance during the creative process. At the same time, however, collaboration and evaluation by others should be encouraged. Without a model process, collaboration, and evaluation by others, the design process is limited to individual experiences and prior knowledge.

References

Amabile, T. (1983). *The Social Psychology of Creativity*. New York: Springer-Verlag.

Barron, F. (1958). Psychology of imagination. *Scientific American, 199, 151-166.*

Barron, F., and Harrington, D. (1981). Creativity, intelligence, and personality. *Annual Review of Psychology, 32,* 439-476.

Besemer, S., and Treffinger, D. (1981). Analysis of creative products: Review and synthesis. *The Journal of Creative Behavior, 15*, 158-178.

Fromm, E. (1957-58). The creative attitude. *Creativity and Its Cultivation.* Interdisciplinary Symposium on Creativity, Michigan State University. New York: Harper.

Getzels, J., and Csikszentmihalyi, M. (1976). *The Creative Vision: A Longitudinal Study of Problem Finding in Art.* New York: John Wiley and Sons.

Gotz, K., and Gotz, K. (1973). Introversion-extroversion and neuroticism in gifted and ungifted art students." *Perceptual and Motor Skills, 36*, 675-678.

Gordon, W.J. (1961). *Synectics: The development of Creative Capacity.* New York: Harper and Row.

Guilford, J. (1975). Creativity: A quarter century of progress. *Perspectives in Creativity.* In Irving Taylor and J.W. Getzels (Eds.), Chicago: Aldine.

Guilford, J. (1950). On creativity. *The American Psychologist, 14*, 444-454.

Guilford, J. (1979). Some incubated thoughts on incubation. *Gifted Child Quarterly, 23*, 1-8.

Jones, C. (1981). *Design Methods: Seeds of Human Futures.* New York: John Wiley and Sons.

Jung, C. (1958). *The Undiscovered Self.* Boston: Little, Brown.

Koberg, D., and Bagnall, J. (1981). *The Universal Traveler.* Los Altos, CA: Wm. Kaufman.

Lamb, J., and Kallal, M. (1992). A conceptual framework for apparel design. *Clothing and Textiles Research Journal, 10*, 42-47.

Lasswell, H. (1957-58). The social setting of creativity. *Creativity and Its Cultivation.* Interdisciplinary Symposium on Creativity, Michigan State University. New York: Harper.

MacKinnon, D. (1962). The nature and nurture of creativity. *American Psychologist, 17*, 484-495.

Maslow, A. (1957-58). Creativity in self-actualizing people. In *Creativity and Its Cultivation.* Interdisciplinary Symposium on Creativity, Michigan State University. New York: Harper.

May, R. (1975). *Courage to Create.* New York: Norton.

McCloy, W. (1931). Creative imagination in children and adults. *Psychological Monographs, 51*, 88-101.

McKim, R. (1980). *Experiences in Visual Thinking.* Boston: Prindle, Weber, and Schmidt.

Mednick, S. (1962). The associative basis of the creative process. *Psychological Review, 69* (3), 220-232.

Osborn, A. (1953). *Applied Imagination.* New York: Scribner.

Pfeiffer, R. (1979). The scientific context of creativity. *Educational Theory, 29*, 129-137.

Pickard, E. (1990). Toward a theory of creative potential. *Journal of Creative Behavior, 24*, 1-9.

Ribot, T.S. (1900). The nature of scientific imagination. *International Quarterly, 1*, 648-675.

Rogers, C. (1957-58). Toward a Theory of Creativity. In *Creativity and Its Cultivation.* Interdisciplinary Symposia on Creativity, Michigan State University. New York: Harper.

Smolucha, L., and Smolucha, F. (1988). *Synergistic Psychology Applied to Artistic Creativity.* Presented at the Xth International Colloquium on Empirical Aesthetics, Barcelona, Sicily.

Sprott, W. (1933). *New Introductory Lectures On Psycho-analysis, by Sigmund Freud.* New York: Norton.

Tardif, T., and Sternberg, R. (1988). *The Nature of Creativity.* New York: Cambridge.

Taylor, I. (1975). A retrospective view of creative imagination. P*erspectives in Creativity.* In Irving A. Taylor and J.W. Getzels (Eds.), Chicago: Aldine.

Torrance, E. P. (1962). *Guiding Creative Talent.* Englewood Cliffs, N.J.: Prentice Hall.

Treffinger, D., et al. (1983). Theoretical perspectives on creative learning and its facilitation: An overview. *The Journal of Creative Behavior, 17*, 9-17.

Trowbridge, N., and Charles, D. (1966). Creativity in art students. *Journal of Genetic Psychology, 109*, 281-289.

Van Gundy, A. (1987). *Creative Problem Solving: A Guide for Trainers and Management.* New York: Quorum.

Vessels, G. (1982). The creative process: An open-systems conceptualization. *Journal of Creative Behavior, 16*, 185 196.

Von Fange, E. (1955). The creative process. *The General Electric Review.*

Wallas, G. (1926). *The Art of Thought.* New York: Harcourt, Brace.

Watkins, S. (1988). Using the design process to teach functional apparel design. *Clothing and Textiles Research Journal, 7*, 10-15.

Woodman, R., and Schoenfeldt, L. (1990). An interactionist model of creative behavior. *Journal of Creative Behavior, 24*, 10-20.

Design education and the creative experience: A conceptual framework

Patricia Anne Kimle
Iowa State University

How does design education help the student become a good designer? In most textiles and clothing programs, students are required to take introductory courses focused on the elements and principles of design. Why do we teach these design foundations courses, and what does the student gain from them? As an apparel design graduate, a textile designer, a design instructor, and a scholar interested in theoretical aesthetic perspectives on the creative process, I am often introspective about my own design experiences and my design education. As a practicing artist/designer, I have come to realize that courses in design foundations are vitally important to my creative process; they fund all of my experiences. Design foundations provides a conceptual framework for designers to organize and synthesize their design activities, to understand and analyze design products, and to critique and evaluate design products.

This paper will explore how the design process has been conceptualized in the literature, propose an alternative view of the design process which centers on the experience of individual designers, and finally outline a conceptual framework for the design process as it can be influenced by theory presented in introductory design foundations courses. As design foundations courses are generally part of most programs, this paper is not necessarily a call for methodological or curriculum changes, but for recognition in theoretical terms of the importance of our teaching approach. Recognition of the value of foundations courses to the students can then strengthen our courses and programs.

Through introspection upon my own design, my undergraduate education, and the aesthetic experience of "doing" design, this paper explores the impact of design education, particularly introductory design foundations courses, on the cognitive and intuitive processes in-

volved in design. It will also examine the processes involved in the development of students' skill in critical evaluation of design products. A conceptual framework of the creative experience as influenced by design theory courses will be proposed and described. This framework has implications for the theoretical discussion of creativity, and it may be useful to educators in developing educational experiences for design students. In addition to a critical examination of my own education, ideas for this paper were compared with the intended experiences as derived from a focused interview with my former undergraduate design professor.

Design Foundations and Theory

Design Foundations, alternately called Design Theory, Basic Design, or Design Principles, is a general body of concepts "which lead to or explain the visual order through which many parts are brought together in the creation of a unified whole (Gatto, Porter, & Selleck, 1978, p. 9)." Design foundations are grounded in formalist aesthetic theory which assumes that art consists of formal elements arranged in certain ways to achieve "significant form" which has the affect of arousing "aesthetic emotions" (Bell, cited in Winner, 1982). As formalist aesthetic theory is devoted to understanding the specific nature of art and design, focusing on the interactive nature of form and its influence on perception, design foundations provide the language and structure for formal analysis and discussion.

Although formalist aesthetic theory has been criticized because it depends on cyclical and incomplete definitions (art is that which has significant form, significant form is that which arouses aesthetic emotion, and aesthetic emotion remains undefined) its enduring contribution to aesthetic theory is the method and importance of analytic discussion of the formal qualities of art. For instance, most art criticism adopts some method of formal analysis as the initial phase of critical analysis, and introductory

Acknowledgment: I would like to thank Dr. Robert Hillestad for his help in developing ideas for this manuscript.

art textbooks almost always begin by stressing the importance of first reflecting on observations of form as well as our reactions to the form in an honest and systematic way (e.g., Hobbs, 1985, p. 14; Horowitz, 1985, p. 2). Formalism alone does not include analyses of cultural meaning or symbolism in art. Therefore, this paper will not attempt to address appreciation of or response to cultural meaning on a level beyond that of the individual.

Design foundations are concerned primarily with the exploration of *elements* of form in a particular visual art medium and the *principles* through which those elements interact within an object. In most texts, the elements of design generally include line, color and value, shape and form, space, and texture. The principles which are described include balance, proportion, unity, contrast, emphasis, pattern, movement and rhythm (c.f. Gatto, Porter, & Selleck, 1978; Hobbs, 1985; Horowitz, 1985). One of the most significant programs to promote the exploration of formal elements and principles of design as a teaching method was that of the Basic Course at the Bauhaus (see Itten, 1961).

Design foundations can be used as the basic structure for the development of broader theories of design. Design foundations, as a general body of concepts, can be applied to any particular field; more specific concepts can be developed for individual media or visual arts. For example, DeLong's (1987) system of visual analysis of apparel forms and their relationships to the body is an adaptation of design theory specific to textiles and clothing. Design theory goes beyond the foundations of the elements and principles of design and also encompasses other theoretical aesthetic areas including the understanding of design development issues, exploring how designed products are perceived, and analyzing the implications of design and art for our society. Therefore, I will refer primarily to design foundations as the focus of this paper, but occasionally refer to design theory as well.

My undergraduate apparel and textile design program in a mid-sized state university included a sequence of Two-Dimensional Design, and Three-Dimensional Design and Color Theory within my major department. It is the philosophy of the department that design *can* be taught and that design foundations are an integral part of the student's development as an apparel professional (R. Hillestad, personal communication, March, 1993). Design foundations are not always included in introductory art courses as one would naturally assume. Many art programs forego design foundations, believing it unnecessary and assuming their art students already understand these principles instinctively or intuitively (R. Hillestad, personal communication, March, 1993). Additionally, there is a concern that basic design theory is taught as a method of producing art rather than as a means of inquiry (Sausmarez, 1964). This concern is a matter of approach; if design foundations are conceived as an educational tool, rather than a method of practicing art, creative freedom is not limited.

Those who decry design theory offer introductory courses structured to include developmental exercises for the student, rather than directed experiences based on design foundations concepts (Rob Hillestad, personal communication, March 1993). For instance, a "developmental approach" may have students explore particular materials, such as objects collected from nature. By contrast, a design foundations exercise may begin with explanation of elements such as shape and texture; students then produce projects exploring and using those elements. Without the reflection upon or discussion of elements of design, the students are left to develop their own understanding of the design product; this can leave the students with very individual and idiosyncratic understandings, rather than general understanding of basic concepts which can be applied across many design problems and products in the future. Cumulative knowledge of design concepts are not necessarily built into the curriculum in a developmental approach. Although the developmental art approach is intended to give students the maximum creative freedom for exploration, without reflection on the formal characteristics and perceptual effects in a design product, the student does not gain many necessary and useful insights into the design activity and the product, nor does h/she gain the skills of critical evaluation.

In order to understand the designer's experiences, and how they can be influenced by design foundations, we first must place design within a context. The dominant framework currently discussed in design theory is that of "design as a process." This conception of design focuses on defining the stages and products of design activity. An alternative view of design activity which I propose focuses on *experience*. Experience is the process of learning by personally observing, encountering, testing or undergoing a phenomenon. Experience is also the cumulation of learning encounters which make up an individual's knowledge base (New American Webster, 1981). By focusing on the designer's experience, the designer's whole history of thoughts and feelings, perceptual activities, and responses to actual materials and objects becomes part of the design activity. The first perspective, the process orientation has received attention by textiles and clothing scholars, with emphasis on applications for design education and design problem solving. The second perspective will offer new insights and lead to a conceptual framework which allows the demonstration of how design foundations can influence the designer's experiences.

Design as Process versus Design as Experience

Textiles and clothing scholars have adopted various linear design process models which include several steps or stages beginning with problem identification and leading through idea development, prototype development and product evaluation (Davis, 1980; DeJonge, 1984). Watkins (1988) proposed this type of model for use in training student designers to address functional clothing design problems. According to Watkins, the designer's cognitive responses to design materials and outcomes and intuitive responses must be integrated in the pursuit of good design. The cognitive response includes conscious, analytical, and logical decisions. The intuitive response includes decisions based on feeling or intuition, subjective opinion and taste, and sensual appreciation. However, Watkin's design process model seems to consider these two response patterns as separate spheres of knowledge, with most of the emphasis placed on the cognitive processes. Although she states that idea selection must integrate cognitive and intuitive responses, the evaluation stage seems to be based only on logical comparison of design problem criteria and solutions, without consideration of intuitive responses.

Lamb and Kallal (1992) propose a framework for apparel design which specifies the dominant priorities of the ultimate consumers which must be addressed in the design solution. These priorities include the functional, expressive and aesthetic concerns of the target market. In their model, these priorities are situated within the design process model which Watkins (1988) proposed for functional design. Lamb and Kallal suggest that the incorporation of these two models "enhances previous views of the design process by expanding the considerations made in the analysis and evaluation phases" (p. 46). In other words, the value of their framework lies in defining objective criteria for problem solution and evaluation--again this perspective seems to focus on logical, cognitive processes in design activity.

Process models, with their focus on procedures, including setting goals and limitations for the problem, imply that all design decisions are both logical, conscious choices made by the designer and that those choices are externally driven by the considerations of the target market. The ideation through prototype development stages appear to be completely driven by externalities--specific problems addressed and goals for the design. This emphasis is perhaps true when the dominant concern in a design problem is functional and in "knock-off" design for lower-end, mass-market situations. However, in design priorities such as innovative fashion and fiber or wearable art, sufficient external constraints may not be identified to drive decision-making. In such design situations, a relatively unlimited array of design options may exist and the constraints which can be identified may be very ambiguous.

These models, while they may accurately portray design activity as it must produce products which fulfill certain needs within a social and cultural context, focus too closely on cognitive mental activity and do not adequately explicate other *internal* processes--physiological, psychological, affective and emotional experiences--which take place in the individual student, designer or artist. Internal processes which may have profound directive effects on what the designer produces include unconscious mental activities and the sensual, emotional, and spiritual responses of the designer to materials, objects and events (Fiore, Kimle, & Moreno, in press a). In addition, existing models treat each design problem as a separate entity, not as a moment in the cumulative history of the designer and design product.

While existing design process models are useful for teaching in that they direct development of a plan of action students can execute, they do not enhance students' self-knowledge because the designer is viewed as external to the process. The process model may not necessarily be useful for understanding the creative individual, the designer's internal processes involved, and the factors which contribute to aesthetic experience achieved through design activity. With the goal of understanding the creative individual's aesthetic experience, I suggest that we explore internal processes of creative activity, understanding that design is not only a process, but an experience; design can be a means of knowledge, self-discovery, and rewarding productive activity. Our understanding of the internal processes of creativity may then have an impact on our teaching practices, and our models of the design process may be enhanced. By taking this broader view of design as experience, design activity includes the life of the individual, as well as all phases of problem solving processes and working methods.

Design Foundations as Language Acquisition

In developing a framework for design education and its effect on individual's creative processes, I begin with a familiar metaphor that "design is a language." Many introductory art texts use such phrases as "form as a visual language" (Horowitz, 1985), "art as language" (Hobbs, 1985), "the language of art" (Fichner-Rathus, 1989), to indicate a metaphorical relationship between formal elements of art and vocabulary as the elements of language. Gatto, Porter and Selleck (1978) call the elements of form "the first simple vocabulary of the person who wants to say something visually" (p. 10). As what we say verbally is made up of units--words, what we say visually is also made up of units--elements of form.

While the art object has a communicative function which is taken up in much aesthetic analysis based in semiotics or other disciplines, it should be noted that this is not the present argument. While visual forms have communicative functions, they are not an accurate form of communication in the same manner as language, and I am not arguing for any particular system of meaning for visual forms. The degree to which visual forms communicate, and what they communicate in terms of meaning and emotion is dependent upon many cultural factors and may not be generalizable across cultures. (For a review of various perspectives on symbolism and communication in art, see Fiore, Kimle & Moreno, in press b.) In this discussion, I maintain formalism's distance from analysis of culture and meaning. It is acknowledged that symbol systems are learned at a collective level within specific cultures, however in this analysis, reflection on perceived meaning in forms is at the individual level.

In applying and extending the metaphor that design foundations provide a system of language, I will borrow from Jean Piaget's theory of cognitive development. In the Piagetian conception of children's development, language acquisition has three consequences for mental development: 1) language acquisition allows the possibility of communication with others and leads to socialization, 2) words become internalized symbol systems which are used to form thought, and 3) actions can be represented internally in the form of thought and therefore the range of possible knowledge is no longer limited to actual perceptual experiences (Wadsworth, 1971, p. 65). First, a language about design allows experiences to be shared in communication and symbol systems to be developed. Language, in the second consequence, drastically changes mental experience. Language allows thought to be structured in the mind, it provides a system for organizing experiences and relating them to each other. In the third consequence, the range of experience is expanded rapidly; one can imagine and experience mentally things which haven't actually been experienced in physical reality. I propose that design foundations provide a language, and that learning that language has similar consequences for the mental experience of the designer.

Parallel to Piaget's consequences of language, design foundations first provides a language for individuals to communicate about design with others. This communicative function of design language is vitally important. Communication about design between individuals requires a mutually understood framework to describe and discuss a problem. A suitable vocabulary must be available for individuals to compare perceptions and responses, and to consider those responses in terms of the object in question (Redfern, 1991). Greene (1991) notes that a minimal familiarity with symbol systems (language) between teacher and students is required to direct students' attention to aesthetic forms. Design foundations provides this language.

Second, as language changes the nature of thought, facilitating abstraction through symbolization in the mind, language about design changes the nature of thought about design, allowing one to think in the abstract through use of symbols for perceptual forms. And third, one can expand the range of thought about design far beyond the limits of actual experience. Greene (1991) added that having this familiarity with a vocabulary of form "may feed into the reflectiveness that deepens and extends experiences with art forms" (p. 151). Design foundations allow one to explore a myriad of possibilities in the mind without the actual physical perception or execution of a particular object. These two consequences facilitate the experiential nature of design. As earlier stated, experience is a learning encounter with a phenomenon. The abstraction of design into concepts (elements of design) which can be "thought about" allows those encounters to be explored and tested both physically and mentally. The consistent application of terms for visual phenomena facilitates the cumulation of these thoughts into a body of experience or an individual's history.

Let's explore an example: In order to discuss a simple drawing, two individuals first need a common language. Using the common vocabulary of visual elements, they can discuss the *lines* in the drawing. The word "line" becomes the abstract symbol for any number of visible (or implied) marks which have certain characteristics. All the lines in the drawing can be analyzed in terms of their thickness, weight, direction, etc. Then both individuals can mentally extend their experience of line by imagining other possible combinations of line characteristics. Although the drawing might have been sketchy with fine short lines, they may imagine the visual effects if the lines were smoother and heavier without actually seeing a drawing with the new characteristics. Finally, the meanings contained in the drawing and the responses it evokes can be analyzed in terms of visual elements which contribute to the overall effect perceived by the individuals.

The first consequence, that of communication about design with others is a vital element in the development of critical thinking about design. I will return to this theme shortly. But first, I suggest a framework for creative experience and describe how this experience is enriched as a result of language acquisition through design foundations education.

Conceptual Framework for Creative Experience and the Influence of Design Theory

Theoretical and empirical exploration of creative activity has included variables of the unconscious mind, perceptual experiences, and emotional responses of the individual creator in addition to logical, cognitive processes (Fiore, Kimle & Moreno, in press a). However, most studies examine only one component of creative activity, rather than exploring how they interact. I forward the idea that design theory, as a mode of inquiry and a system for analysis, can provide a unifying system through which a designer can unify various experiences of the mind, soul, and body. A graphic representation of this framework (see Figure 1) includes the designer, the experiential processes of perception and response to an aesthetic form, and design theory as a link between knowledge and experience with aesthetic forms.

The designer. The framework may be applied to any stage in the processes of either aesthetic appreciation or of creation. It begins with a representation of the designer in an encounter with an aesthetic form. We come to any encounter as unique individuals; within a designer are various emotions and psychological states, including attitudes, goals, and a particular outlook on life. In addition to our mental make-up, physiological states such as relaxation or tension in the body are important to consider. This physiological state affects perception of the aesthetic object or event under consideration. For instance, if one is agitated, attention to sensory aspects of form may be distracted; the subtleties within the form may be missed. And in addition to our present state, individuals each have unique personalities, with past histories and accumulated knowledge which may lead us to be more or less perceptive to various forms.

Perception. Perception is the sensation of information from the aesthetic form. It includes information gained through any of the senses which are potentially stimulated. Two-dimensional visual form may only engage vision, while a meal at a fine restaurant may engage sight, smell, taste, hearing, and touch through a combination of the food and the ambiance. Perception also has a constant role during creative activity; the designer is attuned to his/her senses during the physical manipulation of materials creating the aesthetic form. Touch and vision are particularly engaged during creative activity in the visual arts. In addition, designers may purposefully create an atmosphere where other senses are also engaged; for instance, some might use music in the studio to stimulate auditory sensation and enhance design activity as well.

Aesthetic form. The aesthetic form is any object or event upon which the individual focuses a contemplative attention. It is the object which is perceived, through appreciation and/or creative activity. The aesthetic form may be either of an object or event which the individual encounters and takes an interest in, or it may be the object of the design activity--the designer's work in progress. For instance, when beginning a creative project, the designer may seek inspiration during a walk in a park, a visit to a museum or gallery, or when reviewing past projects in a sketch diary. Aesthetic forms can include both natural and man-made objects or events.

Response. The response to the aesthetic form may include physiological, sensual, cognitive, emotional and spiritual components. Sensory stimulation may have a direct impact on physiological or emotional response. Various colors, for instance, may calm or excite an individual and may also affect one's mood. Cognitive, emotional, and spiritual responses may also be due to formal qualities of an object as well as recognition of content and meaning in the form. The response to the aesthetic form completes the circle as it may alter the initial state of the individual. For example, a designer might feel tense or excited during execution of a project. Through the sensory manipulation of form and the sensual response to that form, the designer becomes calm and relaxed.

Design Foundations/Design Theory. The experiential process of appreciating or creating a form takes place in all individuals. Often, we are not consciously aware of our perception and

response to the world around us. Thus, the cycle may be a naive or intuitive process. However, the application of design foundations concepts as a reflective mode of analysis and inquiry allows the designer to become cognizant of these processes and understand them. The understanding of formal elements and principles gained through reflecting upon the aesthetic form and its properties, applying relevant foundations principles, and critically analyzing the form enriches the designer's experiences, adding to the store of past experiences and knowledge. In addition, through reflecting upon one's own processes and response, the designer gains insight into her self and how she relates to her work and her world.

To return to the Piagetian analogy, design foundations concepts facilitate the conversion of experience to cognitive knowledge. The lower portion of the diagram in Figure 1 demonstrates the relationship between design foundations and aspects of the designer's creative activity. Experiences of perception--named, analyzed, and understood through a design theory approach--are stored and organized in the mind. Cognitive understandings of form and content in an aesthetic experience (such as recognizing fruits in a still life), emotional responses to aspects of the experience, and other responses such as spiritual or intuitive reactions can also be examined and understood as they may be associated with aspects of the form. Design foundations suggests that formal patterns must be understood in context; a pattern or texture in two objects of the same medium may lead to similar responses, while different media will change the overall perceptual effect and response to it (Gatto, Porter, & Selleck, 1978, p. 15). Through analysis of a form and one's response to it, the experience is reflected upon and becomes structured within one's thoughts. The aesthetic response becomes cognitive knowledge. All of this information which a designer stores up through applying design inquiry can lead to new knowledge about aesthetic response, the realm of design, and the self. The acquired knowledge--the experience made cognitive and understood in terms of its parts--can then become new experience, expanded through the imagination and used as source material for new design explorations.

This framework for design foundations and creative process is non-linear, and the link between experience and design foundations is multi-directional. In foundations courses, experiences are structured to begin with design concepts (elements) and explore their impact on perception, response, and cognitive knowledge. For instance, a lecture on the element of texture presents the concepts of visual and tactile texture along with many examples of visual forms with varying textural qualities for students to perceive and reflect upon their response. Applying design concepts, students are guided through an analysis of the examples in which textural characteristics and the resultant perceptual and experiential responses are described and related. The effect of the whole of the work could be understood in its component parts and as a whole. In this manner, a theory concept, texture, and its characteristics are analyzed as perceptual experiences to expand cognitive understanding of texture. Students gain an expanded vocabulary of objective descriptors for texture, mental images associated with various types of texture, and insight into how different textures can be created in different media. In addition they understand that texture influences perception of other elements such as color, light, and density or visual weight of surfaces.

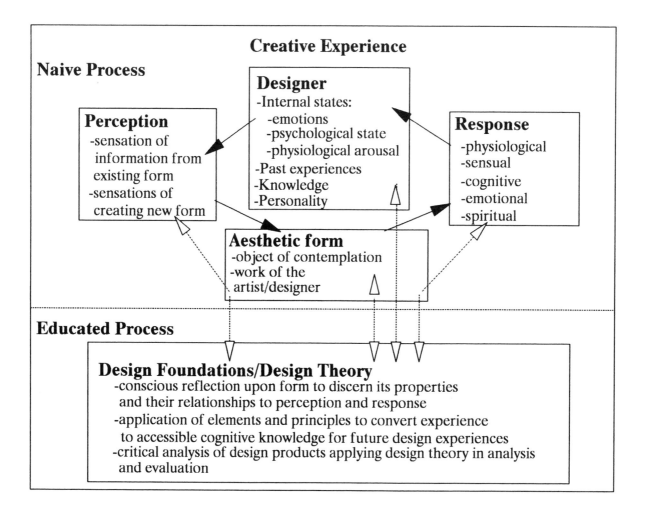

Figure 1. Conceptual framework for creative experience and the influence of design theory.

The educational experiences can also begin with theoretical propositions about design relationships, exploring the analytical principles and move to demonstration of these principles by students in perceptual, creative experiences. One of the exercises which I believe was the most valuable of my education, was an exercise exploring color theory. After lectures about color theory and color systems, students mixed paint and created "color cards." Students were to take a primary or secondary color and blend shades, tints, and tones. Actually mixing small amounts of color, seeing the differences between a color mixed with its complement or with gray or making true pastel by neutralizing the blue in white pigment, are experiences which have far greater impact on the understanding of color than numerous slide lectures. Thus the perceptual experiences of seeing and comparing various color relationships becomes conscious understanding through the application of theory. The perceptual differences in color relationships are named and explained through the use of theory, thus the sensory information is understood on both a perceptual and cognitive level. The vocabulary of color provides the framework for structuring the knowledge in the mind, and this new knowledge can be drawn upon and expanded in any future exercise in visual analysis.

In my personal exploration of design, I can begin creative activity at any point in the framework. I can collect perceptual images and response experiences, reflect on them in an analytic mode, and store the insights for later design experiences. For instance, when doing a jewelry series inspired by bird forms, I began by collecting perceptual images of birds and feathers, thinking about them in terms of line, color, and shape. These analytical musings were stored and later funded ideas for new designs. In another example, knowledge of design elements and principles were themselves the starting point for creative experience. In a series of woven fabric wall hangings, geometric elements of form and principles of pattern and color were the cognitive structures which I began to explore. In this work, I took printed and solid color fabrics, cut them into strips and plaited them to create woven surfaces. In cutting and plaiting the printed fabrics, the original print designs were shattered and fragmented by the intersection of the warp and weft. The intersection of solid-with-print and

print-with-print areas, color, size of original prints, size of fabric strips cut and plaited, and different interlacing patterns all provided different variations of the design to explore. Creating the initial images led to new perceptual experiences, each one suggesting the next possible variation in the formal structure and technique as the series continued to evolve.

Implications of design theory for creative experience. There are two general implications of design theory for the creative experience: the combination of inductive and deductive reason and the unification of aspects of the human existence--mind, body and soul. One of the models justifying the founding of home economics in the early part of this century was a model based on John Dewey's philosophy of knowledge as a process of inductive reasoning (East, 1980). Through performing ordinary concrete activities, the inquisitive mind will generate insights into the nature of things, further exploring thought and action. Cox-Bishop (1989) argued that art and aesthetics, as learning grounded in activity, is necessary and complementary to the dominant mode of deductive scientific inquiry in home economics. I would further argue that design foundations is itself a combination of both inductive and deductive knowledge, combining insight gained through perception with cognitive knowledge of a language and its theoretical principles. In his Bauhaus basic course, it was Johannes Itten's goal that study of form would cultivate for the student a unity of "experience, perception, and practical ability" (1975, p. 12). He maintained that students should "approach [the contrasts] from three directions: they had to experience them with their senses, objectivize them intellectually, and realize them synthetically" (p. 12). This synthesis is the unification of the deductive and inductive processes.

Through this conception of creative experience, barriers between forms of knowledge, types of experiences, or responses to aesthetic forms are dissolved by the conscious application of design theory. This approach allows one to feel that the entire self is involved in the work--mind, body and soul. Awareness of a unity of purpose in the mind and spirit creates a sense of peace and harmony; complete involvement of the whole self is intensely satisfying. This is an aesthetic experience which Csikszentmihalyi described as "the flow phenomenon"--an optimal state in which individuals experience an inner order or a state of psychic harmony among all aspects of the self (1975). Reflection on design theory unifies aspects of experience by making one realm of experience available or accessible to others. For example, mind and body are united when one consciously reflects on the physical sensations of manipulating materials and the ability of the body to do so. I find that not only do my perceptual skills become fine-tuned, but I am reminded as well of the wondrous creation that is a human body, therefore the sensory experience is also connected to a spiritual response. The engagement of various aspects of the self in conscious reflection on creative experience yields the sensation of "flow" and the activity becomes more satisfying than simply executing a pre-ordained plan.

Critical evaluation of design

The application of design foundations not only affect the aesthetic and cognitive experiences of design activity, it can also be an integral part of the development of critical skills for designers. DeLong asserts that a systematic approach to perception leads to a more discriminating response (1987, p. 13). She outlines a four-step approach to visual forms: observation, analysis, interpretation, and evaluation. This is the general framework applied in most critical analysis, although particular approaches may vary somewhat in method. Regardless of the methodological approach to criticism, Lankford (1991) asserted that four principles must apply: 1) a concept of art [or design] must be agreed upon; 2) a context of relevant dialogue defined; 3) goals are established for criticism; and 4) acknowledgment is made of characteristics of the participants. Lankford's principles, as well as DeLong's systematic approach can both be facilitated by design foundations and design theory. Prior to the critical analysis, one defines the design problem addressed or solved by the design product. The relevant dialogue includes both formal features of the design product and the constraints or criteria for success that it must meet. Goals for criticism vary depending on the design problem or situation; in a functional design situation, criticism may evaluate the success or failure of the outcome, while in an art situation, criticism may be directed toward increasing understanding of the work as an aesthetic experience. Finally, the level of experience and familiarity with design is taken into account in criticism, through the expectation that students employ the terms and concepts which are part of the curriculum.

So to apply DeLong's method, observation includes perceiving and describing the features of the object. One can begin by describing the object as a whole and proceed to dissect the form into its component parts and relationships, or by describing the parts and concluding with the visual effect of the whole. Design foundations provides the vocabulary to describe the parts. Analysis is the process of exploring the elements in a work, describing their character, considering their interactions, and applying relevant principles to determine or explain the relationships. Interpretation is the phase of putting the work in context and exploring what the parts mean to each other and the whole. Aspects of form have certain associations in certain contexts; in much visual art, interpretation includes recognition of things which the forms represent from the external world. And finally, in evaluation, judgments about the object are made. These can include subjective favor or preference, statements about principles of design such as unity or balance, and ratings of the success of a design based on whether it fulfills its function.

Principles of evaluation are largely dependent upon social and cultural ideals and values about art and design. Students of design learn about styles of art in conjunction with relevant standards of judgment which are appropriate to particular genre and media (Horowitz, 1985). Once students are instructed with examples of criticism which begin with these principles defined, then design foundations language and the relevant evaluative criteria can be applied. For example, when discussing a work such a Mondrian's geometric paintings, factors of color, perception of balance and space are introduced as the relevant characteristics and evaluative judgments can be made and justified by notation of the features of the work. In apparel design, features such as color, shape, texture, and interaction of clothing with body form are relevant formal features to observe; these are interpreted and evaluated based on current cultural values of fashionability, fit, construction, or novelty.

In the educational setting, critical analysis of design begins with the instructor's use of examples. Students are encouraged to become comfortable with the language of design and apply it themselves to their own work and work around them. The adoption of a critical posture toward one's own work is very difficult for students; young designers often have a great deal of personal and emotional investment in their ideas and criticism is often difficult to accept. This is why discussing and evaluating work through critical analysis based on design concepts the students have studied is very important; the language and structure of critical analysis must take evaluation out of the emotional and personal realm (R. Hillestad, personal communication, March 1993).

Without students' employment of the vocabulary which is built in the educational forum, it is impossible to know whether students are understanding and developing an aesthetic sensitivity and critical judgment (Redfern, 1991). However, this practice also takes time. Instructors may never know if they have been successful in encouraging critical judgment; the application of critical skills may not occur in the student until far beyond the time frame of a particular course (R. Hillestad, personal communication, March 1993).

Teaching students to be conscious and critical of aesthetic forms should be a primary goal for apparel programs. Osborne (1991) asserted that excellence requires of the artist not only skill and mastery of materials, but also a capacity for judgment or critical skill and sense of appropriateness in order for that work to manifestly achieve its own purpose. While this paper has focused on the experience of design within an individual (blurring distinctions between design for personal goals and for external goals), I am not suggesting that we can overlook the social and cultural context in which design takes place. To the extent that external considerations of marketing the products drive design outcomes, then the cognitive realm of experience is vital to develop and this can be encouraged through the development of critical skills. And critical judgments are grounded within an individual's experiences of her world. In a sense then, my argument has come full circle: while we have generally conceived of design as a logical, analytical process, we now must address the individual's experiences at the heart of that process to encourage the best design outcomes.

Conclusion

For undergraduate students, design foundation theory may be their first exposure to *theory* as such. Theory in science is a defined set of concepts and propositions about the relationships between those concepts which apply to a particular phenomenon. Design foundations presents design concepts and theoretical propositions about those concepts and elements. Design theory is not a single predictive theory, but a body of propositions to be explored. Sometimes a principle can be applied, sometimes not, and it is the challenge of the student to use that principle as a tool of discovery. For example, students learn that certain combinations create balance or imbalance in a visual field, but that there is no formula for creating balance.

In addition to its value in the design realm, the approach of design theory has further consequences; the application of a method of analysis and its development into critical evaluation is a skill which, once learned, can be applied to any field of knowledge, not just design. In this regard, design theory contributes to the development of the student as a thinker, not just as a designer. And just as learning about design parallels language acquisition, aesthetic principles of design theory (often conceived as metaphorical relations such as unity or harmony) often have parallel experiences in life. For instance, just as a good painting exhibits balance in composition and rhythm in repetition of elements, human social life must often exhibit balance between the repetition of daily experiences and the novelty of a change in routine for individuals to achieve an aesthetic sensitivity and satisfaction as a member of the society. At the same time, too much unity or sameness and not enough contrast between elements in the art object and in life experiences may lead an individual to become bored. The design foundations frame reference may be useful in other aspects of life, allowing individuals to become conscious of and strive toward a unity of experience and to achieve aesthetic richness in their lives.

The design foundations approach contributes not only introductory experiences for beginning design students, it provides a framework for ways of seeing, ways of doing design, and a way of being through which design activity and experience are enriched. The framework suggested allows insight into the designer, not only as a maker of products or a problem solver, but as a whole being. Application of design foundations method can make design activity more aesthetically satisfying by allowing the designer to experience a sense of "flow" and completeness of purpose. And finally, design foundations provides the seed for students to grow as discriminating, critical observers and designers. As we continually evaluate and revise our curricula, we should consider not only the content in our courses, but what the experiences we provide mean to the learning experience as well.

References

Cox-Bishop, M. (1989). Toward defining a place for research in art and aesthetics in home economics. *Revue Canadienne D'économie Familiale.* *39*(1), 18-21.

Csikszentmihalyi, M. (1975). *Beyond boredom and anxiety.* San Francisco: Jossey-Bass.

Davis, M. L. (1980). *Visual design in dress.* Englewood Cliffs, NJ: Prentice-Hall.

DeLong, M. R. (1987). *The way we look: A framework for the visual analysis of dress.* Ames: Iowa State University Press.

DeJonge, J. O. (1984). Foreword: The design process. In S. M. Watkins, *Clothing: The portable environment* (pp. vii-xi). Ames: Iowa State University Press.

East, M. (1980). *Home economics past, present and future.* Boston: Allyn & Bacon, Inc.

Fichner-Rathus, L. (1989). *Understanding art*, (2nd ed.). Englewood Cliffs, NJ: Prentice Hall.

Fiore, A. M., Kimle, P. A., & Moreno, J. (in press a). Aesthetics: A comparison of the state of the art outside and inside the field of textiles and clothing. Part one: Creator and creative process. *Clothing and Textiles Research Journal.*

Fiore, A. M., Kimle, P. A., & Moreno, J. (in press b). Aesthetics: A comparison of the state of the art outside and inside the field of textiles and cloth-ing. Part two: Object. *Clothing and Textiles Research Journal.*

Gatto, J. A., Porter, A. W., & Selleck, J. (1978). *Exploring visual design.* Worcester, MA: Davis Publications.

Greene, M. (1991). Aesthetic literacy. In R. A. Smith & A. Simpson (Eds.), *Aesthetics and arts education*, (pp. 149-161). Urbana: University of Illinois Press.

Hobbs, J. A. (1985). *Art in context*, (3rd ed.). San Diego: Harcourt Brace Jovanovich.

Horowitz, F. A. (1985). *More than you see: A guide to art.* San Diego: Harcourt Brace Jovanovich.

Itten, J. (1975). *Design and form: The basic course at the Bauhaus and later.* (revised ed.). New York: Van Nostrand Reinhold.

Lamb, J. M., & Kallal, M. J. (1992). A conceptual framework for apparel design. *Clothing and Textiles Research Journal, 10*(2), 42-47.

Lankford, E. L. (1991). Principles of critical dialogue. In R. A. Smith & A. Simpson (Eds.), *Aesthetics and arts education*, (pp. 294-300). Urbana: University of Illinois Press.

Morehead, P. D., & Morehead, A. T., (Eds.). (1981). *New American Webster Handy College Dictionary.* New York: Signet.

Sausmarez, M. (1983). *Basic design: The dynamics of visual form.* New York: Van Nostrand Reinhold.

Osborne, H. (1991). Assessment and stature. In R. A. Smith & A. Simpson (Eds.), *Aesthetics and arts education*, (pp. 93-107). Urbana: University of Illinois Press.

Redfern, H. B. (1991). Developing and checking aesthetic understanding. In R. A. Smith & A. Simpson (Eds.), *Aesthetics and arts education*, (pp. 264-273). Urbana: University of Illinois Press.

Wadsworth, B. J. (1971). *Piaget's theory of cognitive development: An introduction for students of psychology and education.* New York: David McKay.

Watkins, S. M. (1988). Using the design process to teach functional apparel design. *Clothing and Textiles Research Journal, 7*(1), 10-14.

Winner, E. (1982). *Invented worlds: The psychology of the arts.* Cambridge, MA: Harvard University Press.

Toward an Understanding of the Creative Process: An Analysis of a Knitter's Technological and Aesthetic Development

Jane E. Hegland
University of Minnesota

Patricia A. Hemmis
University of Minnesota

The purpose of this paper is to explore and begin to understand the complexities, subtleties, and even contradictions of the creative process of one knitwear designer. In the subsequent pages, an accomplished knitwear designer tells of the development of her technological and aesthetic expertise of the craft and how she works through the creative process. In the analysis section which follows the narrative text, we extract salient themes of her creative development and discuss their importance.[1]

Ghiselin (1952) stated that "the creative process is the process of change, of development, of evolution, in the organization of subjective life" (p. 12). In the creative process, the creator must develop technological expertise and foster the ability to visualize relationships to be incorporated into the object, in order to realize the desired outcome. A third component fundamental to the creative process is the creator's aesthetic response. According to Fiore, Moreno, and Kimle (in press):

> "Aesthetics" refers to both a quality of an object and a state of being. [The definition includes] the non-instrumental nature of the rewarding quality of the object or experience; an activated state of awareness of the sensual, expressive, and symbolic qualities of the object or experience; and an involvement in higher order mental events.

The creative process involves a synergetic relationship among technological expertise, visualization skills, and aesthetic responses. Entirely different outcomes may result, dependent upon the type of creativity engaged in by the creator. In order to begin to understand this synergetic relationship, we have chosen to work within the interpretive science paradigm. In a general sense, interpretive scientists search for an understanding of the ways people subjectively experience their world (van Manen, 1975). According to Jax (1984), "a research question for an interpretive scientist arises when there is a need for an experimentally meaningful, historically original, or authentically human understanding of some aspect of the interactive cultural system" (p. 10).

Within the interpretive science paradigm, the phenomenological perspective is summarized by Patton (1990) as an understanding that comes from sensory experience of a phenomenon that must be described, explicated, and interpreted:

> Phenomenologists focus on how we put together the phenomena we experience in such a way as to make sense of the world. . . . There is no separate (or objective) reality for people. There is only what they know their experience is and means. The subjective experience incorporates the objective theory and a person's reality. (p. 69)

By focusing on the experiential development of one knitter, we realize that we may challenge more traditional approaches to textiles and clothing research in three fundamental ways. In the first place, by choosing knitting, we address a craft often perceived to be of less importance than other craft forms (e.g., weaving, pottery, and needlepoint). Moreover, knitting is a traditional craft with a long history predominantly associated with women. During the past several years, methods of analysis of women's design and craft have been called into question (Buckley, 1989; Forty, 1986; Parker & Pollock, 1981). As a textile art, knitting generally has

Acknowledgment: We gratefully acknowledge the assistance of Marilyn R. DeLong, Ann Marie Fiore, and two anonymous reviewers for their insightful comments on earlier drafts of this paper.

been evaluated under paradigms set up for manufactured products. These paradigms use traditional methods which privilege products for exchange over products for domestic use, and tend to divide theoretical and methodological approaches by gender. The paradigms often conclude with a characterization that casts the work of males as the application of theory, and the work of females as the result of intuitive processes (Buckley, 1989). The outcome is the frequent silencing of the voice of the creator and her or his creative process, particularly when the process involves a craft.

In the second place, we propose that the explication, analysis, and interpretation of one knitter's creative process provides an important means of gaining insight into the workings of the creative mind. As a way of beginning to understand the creative process of one knitter, we ask that you "listen" to her voice. As researchers, we have become accustomed to a filtered rendering of the participant's/subject's/informant's words. The actual voice of the creator is seldom heard. In this paper, we include--intact--an indepth narrative through which one knitter discloses her technological and aesthetic development.

In the third place, we maintain that using a phenomenological approach to better understand one person's experience will provide valuable insights for the field of textiles and clothing. Unlike analytic-empirical methods, which generate explanations and hypotheses for human behavior, interpretive science methods aim for understanding and interpretation (Gadamer, 1975; Habermas, 1971; Heidegger, 1962; Smith, 1983). Hultgren (1989) offers a justification for such an approach when she asks:

> What then is the outcome or end of phenomenologic inquiry? In phenomenological study, one hopes to achieve awareness of different ways of thinking and acting. It is a search for new possibilities--*not* a search for laws which govern behavior. Description of experience promotes further perception of the phenomenon, uncovering it through explications of meanings in language, which allows the chance that better decisions will be made for those affected by such deep understandings. (p. 53)

And so, we look intimately at one person's journey in an attempt to understand her creative development.

A Knitter's Personal Narrative of Her Technological and Creative Development

My mother taught me to knit when I was 7 years old, confined to bed during a bout with measles. Later that year, my grandmother came to visit. I recall sitting on the sofa laboring over each stitch under her watchful eyes. I remember the sense of pride my grandmother, mother, and I shared in the completion of my first project--a long, ungainly, striped scarf which I still have in my possession. Slowly, I graduated from scarves, slippers, and dishcloths to sweaters. While in high school, I completed a Fair Isle[2] patterned vest, giving great attention to color choices which differed from suggestions in the printed pattern. Through this project, I learned the basic techniques of color stranding.[3] I didn't knit while in college; but after graduation in 1976, I resumed the craft as a result of a part-time job in a yarn and fabric specialty store. I completed a sweater from a popular pattern worked in a chunky, one-ply wool yarn. It was displayed in the store, and as a result of positive feedback toward this garment, I was offered and accepted the position of knitting instructor.

After completing several garments from printed patterns (approximately one sweater every six weeks), I decided to learn more about all aspects of the craft. To this end, I stopped knitting complete garments. Instead, I took time to knit dozens of swatches from Barbara Walker's (1968, 1970) books of knitting patterns. I chose a category, such as lace knitting or fancy ribbings, selected any pattern which caught my eye, and knit up a test swatch.

Through this exercise I came to realize that explorations of the knitting process did not always have to result in a knitted garment in order to be valuable. Furthermore, I began to understand that increasing my technological expertise was satisfying in and of itself. I liked the feeling of accomplishment--of moving to a new level of knitting. I also realized that mastering unfamiliar techniques could open up new avenues of exploration, allowing me to see possibilities that I hadn't known existed.

As my technological expertise increased, I challenged myself to become intimately aware of the intricacies of each technique. As part of this experience, I started to identify areas of knitting which held personal appeal to me, and areas which did not. For example, I discovered that I did not enjoy knitting from an entire category of pattern stitches known as cables,[4] although it is considered to be one of the most popular categories of pattern stitches.

The organization of Walker's (1968, 1970) books of knitting patterns was instrumental in my development as a knitter and designer. These books present hundreds of pattern stitches from various categories of knitting, along with clear and concise directions for their execution. However, they do not provide specific instructions for incorporation into a garment. If these volumes *had* focused on the integration of pattern stitches into garment patterns, I suspect I may have mirrored that intent. Instead, I concentrated on mastering the techniques used to create an endless variety of pattern stitches. I marveled at the fact that incredibly different surface designs were constructed from variations on two basic stitches: the knit stitch and the purl stitch.

During this period, I was acutely aware that I was thinking of the knitting craft from two perspectives: as a knitter and as a teacher. I came to perceive these two roles as inextricably connected and reciprocal. As my knitting expertise grew, I learned to analyze the underlying structure of each new technique in order to teach it to my students. Meanwhile, questions and observations raised by students allowed me to improve my own comprehension of the craft. If a student encountered difficulties with a particular technique, I had to be able to identify any problem in her or his approach before suggesting easier ways to manage the technique. Ultimately, the teaching process allowed (and forced) me to understand the complex system of knitting. I began to develop and offer classes on special knitting techniques such as cable, lace, and bead knitting, as well as color techniques.

Although I produced fewer garments during this time, I found myself visualizing sweaters with greater frequency. The visualization process initially took the form of mental additions to printed patterns, and later became mental substitutions within printed patterns. The process unfolded in two steps: First, I worked on a small swatch of a particular pattern stitch and visual-ized it as an addition or substitution within a printed garment pattern. Then, I pictured multiple ways of incorporating the pattern stitch into garments. I often made quick sketches on little slips of paper, which I stuck in the source book on top of the pattern directions. However, I did not doodle to generate ideas; I used the notation only to record the visualization process. The visualization process itself occurred while the yarn was in my hands, while I was actually forming the knitting, and while I was holding the swatch and inspecting or admiring it. This entire process took approximately one year.

Simultaneously, I was moving toward a deeper understanding of another aspect of the design process. I began to visualize a variety of garment types, and would "try on" a series of pattern stitches to the surface. With practice, I could mentally alter both the garment and the pattern stitch. For example, I worked a swatch of a complex pattern stitch called Ribbed Leaf Pattern, and pictured it incorporated into a v-neck cardigan. Then, I mentally altered the garment into a "Chanel-like" jacket, a tunic, and finally, a vest with front panels terminating in points at the waistline. I recorded my final visualization by noting it in my book of pattern stitches. As I continued to work on the swatch, I realized that I did not enjoy the knitting process. The pattern stitch contained a series of time-consuming front and back cross techniques, all too similar to those dreaded cable stitches. I began to explore other possibilities, and settled on a variation from a category of pattern stitches known as basket weave. Using this pattern stitch, I visualized a double-breasted version of the vest, but eliminated the pointed fronts because of the size of the squares created by the basket weave pattern design.

The discovery of the "Knitting a Garment" section in the *Reader's Digest Complete Guide to Needlework* (1979) was critical to my development as a knitter. This portion of the book segmented the structure of a knitted garment into categories such as shaping armholes and sleeves, shaping necklines and collars, cuffs, borders, hems, and facings. Until this point, I had not realized that certain formulas existed to achieve specific structural effects. With this awareness, I was able to read printed patterns with "new eyes" (and enthusiasm). Bolstered by this discovery, I began to depart from printed patterns. I sought out particularly attractive or unique portions of patterns to be reorganized into a series of customized garment structures. At this point, I became aware that I had developed the technological expertise necessary to manipulate basic forms in order to create new structural designs such as a deeper, wider v-neckline; a gathered sleeve cap (fashionable at the time); or even a garment shape altered to accommodate the changing physique of a pregnant woman.

As I worked through the pattern stitches, I began to understand the existence of a basic relationship between yarn color and texture. However, I did not comprehend the more complicated relationship between the yarn's color, texture, spin, and pattern stitch, until I structurally designed and knit the garments I envisioned. Yarn choice became important, as I realized that its thickness, texture, and color would influence the effect of the pattern stitch, as well as the overall garment design. I experimented with combinations of two or three yarns of varying weights and textures.

My first design venture was a jacket which incorporated a smooth, single-ply, worsted weight wool yarn in a gray-blue with a brushed, variegated mohair in various shades of blue, purple, and green. I combined the worsted weight wool and the mohair yarns for the body of the garment, and used only the wool for the borders. I included a puffed-sleeve structure from one written pattern and a polo collar from another. Simple cables of graduated length provided a visual focus along the upper portion of the back and front of the garment. A decorative ribbing was integrated into the cuffs, borders, and collar. After the successful completion of my first original creation, I felt confident to tackle a variety of design challenges.

In 1984, I traveled to London and visited a number of yarn stores. British designer, Patricia Roberts (1981, 1983) made a profound impression on me and affected my approach to creating sweaters. Roberts' cutting-edge sweater designs often used sub-cultural styles, such as punk or new-wave fashion, as source materials. A particular favorite was a short, mauve and white cardigan worked in a slip-stitch pattern[5] with vibrant patches of intarsia[6] knitting in primary colors. Roberts created different patterns on each cardigan front, and integrated the two by linking the pattern stitches of the left sleeve

with the right front, while the right sleeve and left front were constructed from another set of stitches. Roberts also played with the use of the gusset, a construction technique found in many traditional knitted garments of the British Isles. She extended the gussets from the underarm down each side of the cardigan, and worked them in a striped pattern stitch which was not repeated in the garment. In this sweater, Roberts departed from traditional knitting design in several ways. She combined texture and color pattern stitches in the same garment. She built up a layering of texture, both physical and visual. And finally, she broke with the firmly entrenched practice of creating a symmetrical structure.

Exposure to Roberts' revolutionary designs influenced me in three ways: First, she presented her work as a cohesive whole, accomplished through shrewd marketing tactics, rather than by the identifiable style of her designs. Second, she presented garments of great complexity, targeted at advanced knitters. Third, Roberts was innovative in her extensive use of intarsia knitting and appliqué techniques, in addition to color stranding, the more commonly used color knitting technique of the early 1980s.

When I was introduced to the work of another prominent knitwear designer, Kaffe Fassett, the importance of yarn in my creative process changed dramatically. I learned of Fassett's unique orientation through his first book, *Glorious Knits* (1985). This book combines Fassett's knitwear designs, written patterns, and personal philosophy of creativity, along with photographs of the designs and the sources of his inspiration. Fassett's garments are structurally simplistic, but contain complex color patterns which reflect his origins as a painter. Ultimately, Fassett is a translator of actual three-dimensional subject matter into two-dimensional abstracted patterns. For example, when designing a sweater named *Stone Patch*, the muted weathered colors of stone walls were edited and transposed onto the garment by manipulating the color and texture of the yarn.

Once Fassett determines a pattern, he experiments with various color combinations, working almost entirely in stockinette stitch which results in a smooth surface. He achieves a rich and subtle textural and color effect by choosing a category of color (such as yellow), and then composes that color of many yarns that differ in textures, tints, and shades (from pale lemon yellow to deep golds). In order to have so many different tints and shades of color in small areas, Fassett uses short lengths of yarn, "tying on" new lengths and weaving in the tails as he knits the piece. A Kaffe Fassett pattern of this period typically incorporated 20 or 30 different colors represented by 50 to 100 different yarns.

In 1987, I attended a lecture by Fassett, who spoke of the creative process he utilizes when designing both knitwear and needlework. He also displayed many of his projects, allowing the audience to touch, inspect, and put on the pieces at the conclusion of the lecture. The response to Fassett's lecture was divided; half of the audience questioned him on his creative process, while the other half asked about specific techniques or materials used in his work. I concluded that part of the audience was interested in emulating his design process in order to create their own product, and the rest were interested in duplicating his methods so they could copy his product. I found myself in the group that wanted to understand Fassett's creative process.

As a result of the lecture, I began to think about a new project designed "a la Kaffe Fassett." I struggled for several days to find compelling source materials, and finally settled on a combination of design motifs from a theater poster hanging on my wall, and from the clothing in the paintings of Gustave Klimt. I chose a variegated wool in shades of red, rust, purple, and blue, and found mohair yarns to match. I complemented these choices with two wool tweed yarns; one of red and brown, the other of blue and red. Ultimately, I gathered 10 different yarns for the project. To accurately indicate the design, I graphed my pattern onto knitter's graph paper—a grid which proportionately duplicates the horizontal rectangle of a knit stitch. I painstakingly filled in the little spaces of the grid with colored pencils, a process that took several weeks to complete.

I began knitting from the chart with great anticipation. Over three consecutive evenings, I knit approximately 24 inches of an oversized coat. To my dismay, I found the knitting process to be tedious and unpleasant. Until this point, I had not experienced such a strong negative response to knitting. After some introspection,

I realized that I disliked three specific aspects of the project: First, the time spent drafting the pattern onto graph paper had distanced me from the act of knitting, causing me to lose some of my enthusiasm for the project. Second, instead of enjoying the sensory quality of knitting, I worried about whether or not I was duplicating the paper chart. Third, I was not compelled by the process of locating two- and three-dimensional, representational forms and translating them into abstract patterning. This realization surprised me, but then it occurred to me that I enjoyed making visual connections using *yarn* as the starting point. In addition, I realized that color patterns knit in stockinette stitch seemed to "smooth-out," rather than enhance the textural nature of the yarn.

With a certain contentment that came from understanding what I did and did not like about Fassett's creative process, I ripped out the 24 inches of the coat and classified the yarn by color in my rapidly expanding yarn closet. Later, I came to understand that the marketing of Fassett's designs codified a design process which differed from his personal design philosophy and methods. Fassett's designs were presented in books with charted directions calling for a specific brand and type of yarn, or as sweater kits with pre-packaged yarn and directions. Yet, in his books, in his video, and in his lectures, he espoused a very fluid design process which encouraged the designer to collect yarns by color, to develop the pattern as it was knit, and to view mistakes as opportunities for design exploration.

With the exception of my knitting classes, I took a break from knitting for the next few months. After this brief but necessary respite, I was eager to further experiment with yarn combinations in a variety of textures and colors. In 1990, I began to conceptualize an oversized sweater to be worked in the Checked Basket Stitch, a slip-stitch color pattern. This pattern stitch creates the appearance of a series of raised, offset blocks of one color, against a smooth background of a second color. I found a variegated wool yarn which incorporated 10 saturated colors, ranging from purple to magenta, and from blue to green. I chose a companion wool which had a similar color range, but was spun to achieve an overall tweed effect. I paired these two yarns with another tweed of bright ultramarine blue accented with flecks of turquoise, hot pink, and red. I started to think about ways of combining the three different yarns into the Checked Basket Stitch pattern, which required use of only two yarns at any time.

As I played with the yarns and pattern stitch, an interesting idea took hold. I found that I was not thinking about the notion of pattern in the sense of pattern stitches; but rather, in a larger sense, as a system of color arrangements. With this thought, I decided to impose an additional "grid of color" on top of the existing system. I vertically stacked three or four blocks, which created a series of columns of varying lengths. In order to accent the columns of blocks, I chose a red mohair yarn. The red mohair functioned successfully because of its textural difference in relation to the other yarns, and because the same red was present in each of the three yarns to be used in the majority of the garment.

After extensive experimentation with color and pattern swatches, I began to knit a sweater which resulted in a cardigan jacket with an off-centered closure. A series of red blocks arranged in vertical columns are scattered throughout the garment--along the upper and lower back, on the upper left front, the lower right front, and on each sleeve.

As I was finishing the sweater described above, I began to think about the next project. Because I remained captivated by the variegated yarn used in the "block" sweater, I chose a color palette of the same yarn: from maroon through rust to gold, from purple through magenta, and from blue through green. I decided that this wool tweed yarn would dominate, and that additional yarns would be chosen to form color relationships. As I started another gathering of yarns, I looked for greater textural variety among the yarns than I had on previous occasions. I settled on gold and maroon mohair, and a wool boucle yarn of rust and purple. These yarns were complemented by a gold wool tweed with hot pink, acidic green, and purple flecks of color. Finding this tweed was particularly satisfying, because I knew the flecks of saturated color would be echoed in the predominant wool tweed yarn.

To this point, I had not yet considered a pattern stitch for this garment. While looking through pattern-stitch dictionaries for inspiration, I noticed an innovative way of knitting the stockinette stitch on the diagonal, a stitch called

entrelacs[7] or interlaces. I started to play with the yarns using this pattern stitch. I knit small 6-stitch entrelacs, and large 12-stitch entrelacs. While experimenting, I thought about ways of juxtaposing scale difference within the garment. I decided to design an oversized jacket with a v-neck front closure. I created the back of the garment by starting at the center back and working a 12-stitch version of the entrelacs out to the left edge of the garment, and a smaller 6-stitch version of the pattern stitch out to the right edge. I chose an 8-stitch version of the pattern stitch for the fronts and sleeves. Several structural problems arose due to the inherent difficulty in shaping (widening or narrowing) an entrelac pattern stitch into the v-neckline and set-in sleeves of the jacket. Consequently, it took more than one attempt to achieve the desired results.

Nearing the completion of this garment, I looked to the work of another knitwear designer. Susan Duckworth (1988) has developed innovative ways to finish knitted garments. Her attention to the details of borders, collars, and cuffs gives her designs a strong sense of integration and completeness. With this new-found knowledge, I turned my attention to the finishing elements of my own project. I decided to create tri-part borders, which included a 2-inch segment of a slip-stitch color pattern, worked in the gold wool tweed combined with gold wool mohair, followed by a stockinette stitch cording of maroon mohair, and completed by a 1/4-inch ribbing worked in the variegated wool. The results delighted me; I finally achieved a cohesiveness within my design which had previously eluded me.

Upon completion of the entrelac sweater, I started to think about other possible projects. Once again, I began to play with the yarn accumulation process, which often initiates my design activity. Over a time span of several months, I gathered yarns for three separate projects. In two of the cases, I combined a variety of colors with differing thicknesses, twists, and textures. The third collection of yarns differs from the other two, and is composed of 17 colors of the same type of yarn. Currently, I am envisioning possibilities for these yarns. I am once again "trying on" textural pattern stitches and envisioning possible garment designs. Soon, I will begin working swatches. I am toying with the idea of knitting an afghan instead of a garment. I am also playing with new ways of integrating knitting (a two-dimensional surface) with the human body (a three-dimensional form). Then, I ask myself: "Why think of pattern stitches as two-dimensional?" Why, indeed?

Analysis

A creator is an individual who conceptualizes, develops, and often executes the production of an object. Any person's journey through the creative process is complex. However, people tend to create in various and diverse ways. Hirschman (1983) suggests three types of creativity: self-oriented, peer-oriented, and commercialized. The knitwear designer who provided the preceding narration considers herself to be a self-oriented creator. Hirschman characterizes self-oriented creators in the following manner:

> Rather than seeking creative guidance from peers or the public, they follow their own inclinations and then present their creation to others--desiring to receive approval from peers and/or the public. Such self-oriented creators often hope to achieve peer and mass audience approval of their products, yet they did not start out with these audiences in mind...To follow this course of action requires a great deal of aesthetic or intellectual conviction and may leave the creator with but one satisfied consumer – the self. (p. 48)

In order to retain a sense of personal satisfaction with the craft, our knitter has instituted clear personal guidelines to confine her knitting activity to self-oriented creativity. For example, she enjoys teaching knitting classes, has made sweaters used for store samples, and has entered juried competitions. On the other hand, although she will on rare occasions sell a finished garment, she will not accept commissions for her work. She is not interested in designing sweaters for knitting publications or for yarn manufacturers. And, she has no interest in designing garments to meet special criteria for a juried competition. She feels that her brief sojourns into peer-oriented and commercialized creativity resulted in a diminished enjoyment of the craft.

In our attempt to understand the complexity of the creative process, we have extracted a number of salient themes from the narrative text. Although this knitwear designer's creative development is *not* every knitter's journey, several implications come forward about the synergetic relationship among technological expertise, visualization skills, and aesthetic response.

Over a time span of several years, this accomplished knitwear designer thoroughly explored the knitting process. She continuously acquainted herself with new techniques; sharpened her visualization skills; explored her aesthetic responses to new combinations of yarns, pattern stitches, and garment shapes; designed and produced new garments; and expanded class offerings. The narrative subtlety divides into six interrelated categories: (a) the development of technological expertise, (b) a shift in emphasis, from product to process, (c) the development and refinement of visualization skills, (d) a movement from visualization to production, (e) the influence of three knitwear designers, and (f) the yarn becomes the source of creative inspiration.Clearly, the six categories occupy different strata. Some are general, some pinpoint "steps" within the process, and one (the influence of three knitwear designers) *seems*, at first glance, to be outside the context of what might appear to be relevant steps of the process. However, all six of the interrelated categories have significantly influenced the creative process of this knitwear designer.

It is tempting to view the division of her path into six categories as something like "six steps in the creative process" or "six steps to becoming creative." However, the creative development encapsulated in the narrative is *not* a linear process of development. There was an underlying process of cycling back to previous categories, which resulted in increased expertise and creativity incorporated by the creator. For example, throughout her development as a knitwear designer, she continuously expanded her technological skills. Likewise, she improved her ability to create relationships in her head. Similarly, she developed greater awareness of, and appreciation for, the sensory aspects of the craft. Therefore, it is of critical importance that the reader recognize the synergetic relationship involved among *all* aspects of learning a craft, and of becoming and being a creative knitwear designer. With this caution to the reader, we discuss the six categories.

The Development of Technological Expertise

Learning the technological basics of any craft must precede one's ability to be creative. Even the few knitwear designers who do not actually knit, comprehend--to some degree--the properties of the stitches and the relationship between yarn, pattern stitch, and garment design. It is necessary to understand the techniques of knitting so that one is aware of how the yarn can be manipulated to make complex color and texture patterned surfaces. The technological aspects of knitting are formalized through a large body of prescriptive literature which ranges from "how to" books, to videos, to historic knitted samplers.

In the narrative, the knitter acknowledged a deep sense of personal satisfaction and accomplishment as she mastered increasingly difficult technological skills. She also understood that advancement in expertise led to greater creative opportunities. In order to gain technological expertise, she did not feel it necessary to "reinvent the wheel." She neither attempted to find new or better ways to perform knitting techniques, nor devoted time to inventing new pattern stitches. Rather, she was content to refer to published prescriptive literature. Furthermore, technological mastering awakened a greater appreciation for the sensory aspects of knitting. With this new-found knowledge, she was able to evaluate the technological aspects of knitting by posing two personal questions: First, was the knitting experience pleasurable? Second, was the outcome worth a less pleasurable knitting experience?

At several points in the narrative, the knitter spoke of unpleasurable knitting experiences. She often used terms such as "tedious" or "frustrating." Examples such as "following a color chart" a la Fassett or "turning a cable" were cited as knitting techniques which disrupted the flow of the work (in effect, its sensory aspects), and were thereby identified as unpleasurable. Moreover, she found the *process* of mastering the technological aspects of knitting rewarding in itself. Yet the aesthetic aspects of knitting, characterized by its flow, were also important. A lessening of pleasure during a tedious process was only tolerated when the outcome was considered to be worth the effort. In essence, technological expertise was considered both a means to an end and a catalyst for further design exploration.

A Shift in Emphasis, from Product to Process

At a certain point in the developmental process, the designer took a break from knitting complete garments. Instead, she concentrated on learning the intricacies of hundreds of pattern stitches. This self-generated project had two important effects. First, she began to value the *process* of knitting as well as the knitted *product*. Second, she began to *separate* the knitting process from the knitted product.

As a result of knitting hundreds of swatches, the designer began to make aesthetic evaluations of knitting processes. Her evaluations were based on the pleasure derived from the physical activity of the knitting, as often as they were grounded in the actual results of her experiments. This evaluation process resulted in the rejection of entire categories and practices of knitting (such as cables) which the designer felt were tedious or unsatisfactory. Feelings of security, born of technological expertise and experimentation, allowed the designer to comfortably contradict public perception in favor of personal preference. Ultimately, an acknowledgment of her relationship to the craft had the effect of incorporating logical, aesthetic, and technological aspects of knitting into the evaluation process, and of moving the evaluation process from the public sphere to the private sphere.

The Development and Refinement of Visualization Skills

Once the designer began to understand and value both the process and product of knitting, she started to look differently at printed sweater patterns. With practice, she developed the ability to visualize additions and substitutions in printed sweater designs. Her visualization skills had become increasingly more refined by this point, and she developed the ability to formulate sophisticated relationships between garment structure and garment surface. To this end, she had become capable of accurately predicting the outcomes of her visualized garments, a process she occasionally verified by actually knitting the altered pattern. At this relatively early point in her development, she used the accuracy of her predictions as personal confirmation of her expertise. Occurrences which were not predicted were perceived as failures or weaknesses in her expertise.

A Movement From Visualization to Production

Upon the discovery of the design segment in the *Reader's Digest's Complete Guide to Needlework* (1979), a critical change occurred in the designer's comprehension of the knitting process. She was made aware that certain clear-cut formulas exist to achieve specific structural effects of knitted garments. Following this revelation, visualization skills were further put to task, as she began to physically manipulate relationships between garment structure and garment surface. At this point, the logical, aesthetic, and technological processes interacted synergetically. Her improved visualization skills led to further explorations of the complex relationship between yarn color, texture, spin, and pattern stitch, which fostered a greater aesthetic awareness and more involvement with knitting literature in order to better understand the structural process involved.

As the knitter's logical, aesthetic, and technological skills increased in sophistication, she became less likely to view unpredicted outcomes as failures. Instead, she began to notice and even seek out the element of serendipity. For example, it was difficult to anticipate all possible color relationships when juxtaposing a variegated yarn next to a single-color yarn. Unmanipulated color relationships, which differed from controlled color relationships, were considered "eurekas" rather than unanticipated failures. These happy accidents frequently served as catalysts for new design explorations.

The Influence of Three Knitwear Designers

Three prominent knitwear designers have had a lasting effect on this designer. She used what she liked and needed, and disregarded what didn't work for her. She was initially struck by the cutting-edge designs of Patricia Roberts (1981, 1983), and appreciated the fact that Roberts departed from traditional knitting practices. Roberts combined texture and color pattern stitches within the same garment, she built up a layering of texture--both physical and visual, and she dared to play with asymmetry in her designs. Our designer has adopted these once-radical ways of Patricia Roberts.

Exposure to renowned designer Kaffe Fassett (1985) had a different effect on our designer. Although she was able to appreciate Fassett's work, she did not like drafting patterns from representational sources. As she experimented with the actual knitting of charted designs, she realized that she did not enjoy the process of knitting from a chart, regardless of the subject matter. She felt estranged from the sensory aspect of the craft, because she worried about how accurately she duplicated the paper charts in her knitting. This was caused by the constant shift between sensory engagement and logical engagement. Although the knitter experienced synergetic shifts from sensory to logical processes while designing and knitting a garment, having to adhere to a color chart required this interaction to take place in a linear (back and forth) manner. Ultimately, the flow of the knitting was lost.

She came to understand that part of her frustration was caused by her inability to differentiate the "marketed Kaffe Fassett" from his personal design process. She felt distanced from the knitting process, robbed of the sensory aspects she enjoyed about knitting. What she did take from Fassett, however, was an understanding of his painterly quality. Like Fassett's, the surfaces of her sweaters appear to be filled with thousands of tiny brush strokes. But unlike Fassett, who works exclusively in the stockinette stitch which results in a smooth surface, our designer uses pattern stitches to add physical texture to the visual texture created by color choice.

British knitwear designer, Susan Duckworth (1988) was instrumental in the creative development of our designer, in that she offered innovative alternatives for finishing garments. Duckworth's methods attend to the details of borders, collars, and cuffs. In effect, her solutions provided a framing mechanism for our designer, and gave her garments a sense of wholeness, of being finished "out to the edges."

Yarn Becomes The Source of Design Inspiration

As our designer's knitting expertise became more sophisticated, she developed an awareness of the significance of a single aspect of the knitting process; that of the yarn. It started to function as a catalyst for the visualization process, and as an inextricable element in the creation of visual and tactile forms. Throughout the learning process, the knitter began to understand and explore the various characteristics of the yarn itself; its color, texture, twist, and thickness. Through hands-on exploration, she became increasingly aware of the complexity and scope of relationships between pattern stitches and yarn. Further, she began to see how this relationship was affected when incorporated into garments to fit the human form.

At a certain point in the developmental process, the knitter came to realize that she was able to visualize many connections between the yarns, the pattern stitches, the structure of the garment, and the human form. However, she continued to physically manipulate the yarn into various pattern designs for two important reasons: First, the many sensory pleasures--the tactile experience of the yarn, the "click-click-click" of the needles as the stitches were formed, the rhythm of the repetitive motions required to make each stitch, and the smell of the fibers--were personally satisfying and even restoring to the designer. Second, she was concerned that her knitting experience not be solely confined to logical processes. She became aware that each time she moved her knitting experience from one of a combined sensory and logical process to a strictly logical process--as was the case when she attempted to create "a la Fassett"--she no longer received the same degree of pleasure from the craft.

A garment was sometimes concluded at a visualization phase and was never physically completed. The knitter would immerse herself in the technological aspects of the form until the foreseeable possibilities were exhausted. At a certain point, aesthetic pleasure was also depleted, and the knitter found herself looking for new stimuli in the form of different yarns, textures, color combinations, and technological considerations. At this stage, the desire for a tangible finished product usually (but not always) drove her to complete the garment.

Finally, the knitter enhanced her aesthetic response to the craft by acknowledging the pleasure of the "yarn accumulation" process. By formalizing the act of yarn selection as the starting point of her own creative process, she has ensured the presence of sensory aspects in her work. Currently, she views all components of the creative process as equally important and satisfying. She no longer finds it necessary to

rush through the initial accumulation and visualization phases in order to complete a project. She has come to enjoy the *process* of creating as much as the created *product*.

Implications

The purpose of this paper was to begin to understand the complexities involved in the creative process. The value in documenting and analyzing one knitter's journey has implications for the knitter herself, for researchers and teachers who attempt to comprehend the creative process, and for creators as impetus to explore their own processes.

The knitter came to a greater understanding of her own creative process by taking the time to search and document the memories of the knitting experience. At various points in her creative development, she experienced epiphanies, where she gained new insight into her experience. However, by documenting and co-analyzing her journey, she was able to achieve a new understanding of the totality of her creative process at this point in time.[8] As she continues to explore her relationship to the craft, this "episode of distancing"--when she stepped back to examine her development--will become another part of her ongoing creative engagement with the craft.

Through this process of documenting and analyzing one knitter's journey, we have come to understand that the creative process is an amalgam of sensory/aesthetic responses and logical and technological development. We also acknowledge that different motivations for creativity send creators down vastly divergent paths (Hirschman, 1983). Creators who would like to explore their own journeys, may find our knitter's path to be a useful point of departure. She spent the time necessary to develop the technological expertise of the medium. She recognized the necessity and value in separating *process* from *product*. She understood the importance in developing and refining the ability to visualize relationships of structures within the medium. She was open to the methods and ideas practiced by other creators. She realized that inspiration could come from an aesthetic response to the properties of the materials used. And finally, she knew that the path may not be linear; that there will always be a cycling back to previous categories, which may result in an increase in technological expertise and aesthetic awareness--and ultimately, creativity.

It is essential that we begin to listen to the voices of the creators. By documenting and analyzing the creative development of one accomplished knitwear designer, we have raised several issues that may challenge the reader to look at, comprehend, and experience creativity and the creative process in a new light. Working toward an understanding of the creative process is a promising, compelling, and necessary area for further research.

Endnotes

1. Both Patricia Hemmis and Jane Hegland are creative individuals. Jane has been a knitter for many years, but follows pretty closely to printed instructions. In the past few years, she has become quite sophisticated as a quilter and finds great satisfaction in playing with color and texture relationships in her quilts. Patricia is a knitter's knitter. People who do not fully understand the craft of knitting enjoy taking in her creations. However, those who comprehend the process and constraints of knitting are in for an added bonus when viewing Pat's sweaters, as she tends to "do the impossible" when creating textural, structural, and color relationships in her designs. She is an accomplished knitwear designer. It is her journey through the creative process that has been documented, analyzed, and interpreted in this coauthored paper.

2. *Fair Isle* is a traditional color pattern which originated on Fair Isle, the largest of the Shetland Isles. A Fair Isle sweater employs a visually complex color stranding pattern composed of horizontal bands of small, medium, and large motifs. Bands of medium and large motifs are further subdivided into a series of two-color stripes.

3. *Color stranding* is a color technique used to carry the unworked color across the back of the piece until it is needed again.

4. The basis of all *cable* patterns is a simple technique by which stitches are moved from one position to another in the same row. Cabling alters the order of the stitches because a number of stitches are slipped onto a cable needle and are held either at the back or the front of the piece while the next few stitches are worked. The stitches on the cable needle are then completed, creating a plaited rope-like pattern called a cable.

5. *Slip-stitch* patterns are various pattern stitches that draw strands up, across, or diagonally over the face of a knitted fabric. Many slip-stitch patterns can be worked in contrasting colors.

6. *Intarsia* is a color technique whereby a separate strand of yarn is used for each color area. The color areas are held together by twisting the two yarns at every color change without stranding or weaving on the wrong side of the fabric.

7. *Entrelacs* is a pattern stitch worked on the diagonal that gives a trellis-like effect.

8. Although Pat and Jane experience the creative process of knitting differently, our shared technological expertise and aesthetic experience were essential to the analysis and interpretation of this paper.

References

Buckley, C. (1989). Made in patriarchy: Toward a feminist analysis of women and design. In V.

Margolin (Ed.), *Design discourse: History, theory, criticism* (pp. 251-262). Chicago: University of Chicago Press.

Duckworth, S. (1988). *Susan Duckworth's knitting.* NY: Ballentine.

Fassett, K. (1985). *Glorious knits.* NY: Clarkson N. Potter.

Fiore, A. M., Moreno, J. M., & Kimle, P. A. (in press). Aesthetics: A comparison of the state of the art outside and inside the field of textiles and clothing. Part one: Creator and creative process. *Clothing and Textiles Research Journal.*

Forty, A. (1986). *Objects of desire: Design and society, 1950-1980.* London: Thames & Hudson.

Gadamer, H. G. (1975). *Truth and method.* NY: Crossroad Publishing.

Ghiselin, B. (1952). Introduction. In B. Ghiselin (Ed.), *The creative process: A symposium* (pp. 11-32). NY: Mentor Books.

Habermas, J. (1971). *Knowledge and human interests.* (J. J. Shapiro, Trans.). Boston: Beacon Press.

Heidegger, M. (1962). *Being and time.* (J. Macquarrie & E. Robinson, Trans.). NY: Harper & Row.

Hirschman, E. C. (1983). Aesthetics, ideologies and the limits of the marketing concept. *Journal of Marketing, 47,* 45-55.

Hultgren, F. H. (1989). Introduction to interpretive inquiry. In F. H. Hultgren & D. L. Coomer (Eds.), *Alternative modes of inquiry in home economics research* (pp. 37-59). Peoria: Glencoe Publishing.

Jax, J. A. (1984). Ethnography: An approach to using interpretive science in vocational education research. *Journal of Vocational Education Research, 9,* 8-19.

Parker, R., & Pollock, G. (1981). *Old mistresses: Women, art, and ideology.* London: Routledge & Kegan Paul.

Patton, M. Q. (1990). *Qualitative evaluation and research methods* (2nd Ed.). Newbury Park, CA: Sage.

Reader's Digest complete guide to needlework. (1979). Pleasantville, NY: Reader's Digest Association.

Roberts, P. (1981). *Patricia Roberts' knitting book.* London: W. H. Allen.

Roberts, P. (1983). *Patricia Roberts' second knitting book.* London: W. H. Allen.

Smith, J. K. (1983, March). Quantitative versus qualitative research: An attempt to clarify the issue. *Educational Researcher,* 6-13.

Van Manen, M. (1975). An exploration of alternative research in social education. *Theory and Research in Social Education, 3,* 1-28.

Walker, B. (1968). *A treasury of knitting patterns.* NY: Charles Scribner's Sons.

Walker, B. (1970). *A second treasury of knitting patterns.* NY: Charles Scribner's Sons.

Form In Dress And Adornment: the Shape Of Content

Robert Hillestad
University of Nebraska

Dress and adornment, like other types of artistic expression, consist of form and content. The two dimensions are so inseparable and intricately intertwined with one another that attempts at comprehending either dress or adornment on the basis of one or the other would be somewhat like formulating a conception of green on the basis of attributes of either yellow or blue (Bevlin, 1984). Despite the interrelationships between the two, a bias toward form in dress and adornment prevails in contemporary society just as it does in the form of other cultural objects. If relationships among human needs are to be validated, form and content must be consistent with one another. The objective of this essay is to make a plea for an integrated approach to form and content in dress and adornment.

FORM

Form in any type of expression, is the result when an abstract idea of an individual or group has been converted into something which can be experienced or enjoyed, expressed or communicated, used or utilized. Form is the shape that materials take after human beings have modified and transformed them through techniques to meet needs, satisfy desires, fulfill functions, or accommodate whims. Form enables meaning to be shared with others. In writing about form in art, Ben Shahn states:

> It is the visible shape of all man's growth; it is the living picture of his tribe at its most primitive, and of his civilization at its most sophisticated state. Form is the many faces of the legend--bardic, epic, sculptural, musical, pictorial, architectural, it is the infinite images of religion, it is the expression and the remnant of self. Form is the very shape of content. (Shahn, 1957)

Form consists of numerous interrelated components which cannot be isolated from one another. Any form is partially defined by the materials from which it arises. As the substance of form, materials have certain characteristics which exert themselves through ways in which they can be manipulated as well as utilized to create structure or define surfaces. The materials of form often tell a story about the resources that were at the disposal of a creator, available during a certain period of history, or that prevail in a given geographical area or region. At no other time in history has the selection of materials for garment forms been so available as it is during the present. In addition to natural materials, there is a plethora of man-made ones that have been engineered to yield special kinds of structures and surface effects.

Materials are a fundamental aspect of form in dress and adornment. Like other forms of artistic expression, interest in dress and adornment is often based on the compelling qualities of materials. Since the inherent qualities of materials vary, each type lends itself to a different kind of form. Many designers of dress and adornment have developed their expertise in relation to working with certain types of material. Just as some designers work exclusively with certain types of materials, so do some consumers exercise preferences toward materials when making selections.

Despite the impact that materials have on form, their qualities are seldom utilized without modification. Processes and techniques enable the physical and visual properties of materials to be altered, organized or refined to comply with some desired concept of form. High levels of creativity can be achieved by interrelating multiple techniques. The history of art documents the ingenuity of both individuals and peoples whose achievements in artistic form have been based on innovativeness through the use of processes and techniques. Although the recorded history of dress and adornment is relatively brief in comparison to the history of art, it documents the contributions of numerous individuals and groups who have excelled in the use of processes and techniques to create distinctive forms. Mario Fortuny and Madeleine Vionnet were designers of the past who made an impact on form through innovative techniques. Contemporary designers who are making comparable contributions include Ana Lisa Hedstrom who works with painting and discharge through the technique of shibori and Tim Harding who cuts and frays multiple layers of fabric to achieve distinctive surface effects.

Structure is the aspect of form which pertains to organization. While made possible by materials and techniques, structure is also limited by them. Structure is also influenced by the underlying intent which, in turn, impinges upon materials and techniques. In addition to all those complexities, structure is subject to certain principles of organization. Some principles are dictated by the way in which materials and techniques lend themselves to being organized whereas others are the result of notions which prevail in a culture or society about what is considered to be acceptable approaches to organization. As such, principles of organization vary in terms of the extent to which they are defined or dictated as well as the degree to which they are susceptible to being modified. Violations in established approaches to organization can become the basis for innovations in form.

Like other forms which have prevailed during a given period of history or in a certain geographical location, form in dress and adornment constitutes a visual record of cultural expression. The various garment and accessory forms make statements about which materials and techniques were used and what principles of organization were followed or not followed. When considered along with other types of cultural expression such as fine furniture or jewelry, the various forms of dress and adornment contribute knowledge about the overall preferences of a people during a given period or within a certain geographical location.

CONTENT

Just as it is difficult to separate the various aspects of form, so are there problems in isolating content from form. Content is meaning whereas form is an entity with which it is associated. Content is a complex phenomenon because it prevails at both the individual and collective levels and is susceptible to changing rapidly at each. At the individual level, content or meaning arises when a person responds to an event in his or her environment. Since various environments are made up of objects, a considerable amount of meaning is generated in relation to them. When innovative forms of dress and adornment are among the objects of an environment, they often bring about re-

sponses because of their contrasting characteristics relative to more conventional types of dress.

Content can be as minimal as a preference for certain colors or as involved as a network of interrelated concepts. Materials with unusual characteristics, the unique effects of processes or techniques, new approaches to creating structure or surface effects, and principles of organization that are highly refined or intentionally disregarded all have the potential of defining form either independently or in concert with one another. In so doing, they can serve as a basis for initiating responses and thereby result in content. Responses can lead directly to the creation of content as they do when emotional responses to certain types of stimuli, such as the exquisiteness of structure, result in appreciation for beauty, or they can also involve cognitive processes which help to facilitate meaning. Meaning associated with dress and adornment, like meaning generated in response to other types of objects, is susceptible to being modified or replaced as responses to new events are created. Designers of garments and accessories, like other designers, often control various aspects of form with the hope of bringing about a desired type of content.

The content of dress and adornment becomes part of culture through the processes of socialization and education. As individuals respond to new garment and accessory forms, they not only formulate their own meanings but share them with others through interaction. Stores and boutiques help to socialize the public to prevailing trends in dress and adornment through visual merchandising and various types of advertisement. Galleries, museums and other institutions help to socialize the public to various aspects of dress and adornment as types of cultural expression by sponsoring exhibitions and runway shows. Journalists disseminate content by providing coverage of topics pertaining to dress and adornment through the popular press and scholars, researchers and critics advance knowledge of content through discussions in professional journals, textbooks and other forms of scholarly writing.

INTERRELATIONSHIPS OF FORM AND CONTENT

In comparison to form, content is more abstract, subject to more transformations, and susceptible to being entirely lost or replaced. Although good form is a reflection of the integrity of content, noble content does not always result in purity of form. Aside from its ambiguous relationship to form, content is a slippery phenomenon because it is conceived in the minds of persons and as such not only varies from one to another but is subject to change with a person over time. Although meanings vary from person to person, their content is often similar when responses are made to common stimuli.

Content can either precede or follow the formation of form. It precedes form when it originates from some type of motivation. Motivations vary and include needs to fulfill utilitarian functions such as comfort and protection, urges for communication, desires for expression, and various combinations of all those factors. Some types of content arise in relation to a problem which can be resolved through form whereas others stem from a desire to bring about form. For example, the content or meaning that could arise from the desire, excitement or anticipated satisfaction of acquiring a whimsical garment might be strong enough to motivate the acquisition or creation of such a form. Similar motivations can arise from an appreciation or interest in the potential of certain materials or techniques for the creation of form.

Although form is brought about by some type of motivation to create meaning, the content can change or become more significant after the initial formation of form. Objects that were created to fulfill one type of purpose may be used to serve some other kind. For example, the meaning associated with containers created for carrying vegetables would change if those objects were to be used as handbags. Similar changes in meaning would occur if squares of painted fabric which were intended for decorating walls were to be used as shawls or scarves. In addition to changes in meaning which occur when an object which was intended to fulfill one type of purpose is used for another, meaning can also change as a result of circumstances. According to legend, the cuffs of men's trousers originated as a practical solution to the problem of keeping the bottoms dry. Through the years, the form continued to be used but the original meaning was no longer associated with it. Eventually, content became associated with the structural aspects of form rather than on how

form had functioned earlier in relation to solving a problem.

CULTURAL INFLUENCES ON FORM

The history of dress and adornment, like the history of art, is a story of the interrelationships of form and content. In western culture, particular emphasis has been placed on form. Form, more than content, has fit in with the scientific paradigm that has dominated western culture for more than three hundred years. Form has been more conducive than content to being analyzed through reductionist techniques to determine the merits of constituent parts. The physical and visual characteristics of form in western dress and adornment are consistent with other forms of expression that tend to emphasize materialism.

A wide range of natural materials have been available for the creation of dress and adornment forms and many man-made ones have been engineered for specific purposes. The properties of materials have been studied through the scientific method and the knowledge gained has been utilized to produce forms with desirable and often long lasting characteristics. Systems of construction have been developed for creating garment and accessory structures and various approaches have been developed for classifying them.

Creating garment and accessory forms has been a significant enterprise in contemporary western culture. Businesses and industries have competed vigorously for the opportunity to present seasonal collections of dress and adornment forms for public acceptance. In addition to manufacturing and distributing goods, organized efforts have been carried out to encourage the adoption of new forms of dress and adornment and the abandonment of old ones. Allied businesses and industries provide goods and services which support the effort of making garment and accessory forms available.

Dress and adornment, like other cultural forms, is also a medium of artistic expression. Since the body is involved, human beings experience a special relationship to garment and accessory forms. Aside from utilitarian capabilities, garment and accessory forms serve as vehicles through which the very essence of beauty and harmony can be conveyed. The traditional materials and techniques provide continuity with the past, whereas new ones help to carry the participants of a culture or society into the future. Because of the diversity with which garment and accessory forms can be created, designers have many outlets for their expression and expertise while consumers have a basis for numerous choices.

Educational programs have tended to emphasize form as opposed to content. The overall body of knowledge concerning all forms in the environment has helped to facilitate the specialized study of dress and adornment forms. The development of garment and accessory forms through history has not only been researched and written about extensively but continues to be updated and expanded. The study of textiles emphasizes the materials of garment and accessory forms according to morphology, construction, function and care. Courses are being offered in the technique of creating garment structure through methods of draping and pattern making. Experiences in sketching, selection, merchandising, and production provide additional opportunities for learning about various aspects of dress and adornment forms.

The media, too, emphasizes form. Press coverage of seasonal collections point out changes of silhouette, lengths of hemlines and characteristics of surface design such as color, pattern and texture. Both the print and electronic media have not only exposed the public to garment and accessory forms but have communicated the diversity with which they are available and the excitement which can be created by frequently changing them.

Much can be said for the emphasis on form in contemporary society. Whatever content it may be based on and regardless of the accuracy with which it might be interpreted, form makes a visual statement about human beings and where they are in time and space both individually and collectively. The form of dress and adornment depicts themes of life. It marshalls materials toward translating those themes into visual media for validation. In so doing, it is more than a vehicle for bringing about something to respond to through the senses but is, as well, an instrument or tool for enriching life. Form is more than a unit, an assemblage, an organized substance but a process which helps to trim away excessive content. It helps to eliminate unnecessary materials and structure. In this way, form is a discipline which provides more than a framework for useful objects. Through its relationship to content it can enrich life and help bring about more abundant meaning.

A PLEA FOR AN INTEGRATED APPROACH TO FORM AND CONTENT

Despite the abundance of garment and accessory forms in contemporary society and the value placed on them, there is need for greater emphasis on the refinement of content. By observing human responses to events in the environment, one can learn about meanings which occur and then analyze ways in which they are organized into ideas and concepts. Such knowledge is beneficial in formulating a conception of content which ultimately serves as a basis for the creation of form. Although this process will not eliminate the re-use of forms which have already been introduced at some time, it will validate their relationship to human needs and in essence, help to create form which is consistent with the shape of content.

REFERENCES

Bevlin, M.E. (1984). *Design through discovery (4th ed.)*. New York: Holt, Rinehart and Winston.
Shahn, B. (1957). *The shape of content*. New York: Vintage Books.

A Critical Framework For Exploring The Aesthetic Dimensions Of Wearable Art

Nancy O. Bryant
Oregon State University

Elizabeth Hoffman
University of Maine

At the 1990 national conference of the Association of College Professors of Textiles and Clothing (now International Textile & Apparel Association), a special session, "Aesthetics of Apparel: Subject, Form and Content" was convened by DeLong and Hillestad to discuss the topic of aesthetics related to apparel. Their definition of aesthetics encompasses art theory and criticism.

> Aesthetics was defined in its broadest terms, as understanding how we perceive visual forms, their characteristics and our reactions to them. Such an encompassing definition includes the study of history, philosophy, perception psychology, art theory and criticism, all pertaining to material culture. (p.33)

The need for assessing the visual experience using concepts from the fields of study mentioned by DeLong and Hillestad is important to advance scholarship in this area. For the purpose of this paper, we have addressed one of these areas, art criticism, as a means to explore the aesthetic dimensions of wearable art.

Clothing and textile researchers have studied various aspects of visual perception and the aesthetic components of apparel as perceived by the wearer or the viewer (DeLong, 1968; DeLong, 1977; DeLong, 1987; DeLong & Larntz, 1980; Hillestad, 1980; Morganosky, 1987; Rothenburg & Sobel, 1990; Workman, 1991). Some of these studies examined viewer perceptions of design based on photographs of modeled outfits. Several proposed frameworks acknowledge the importance of the human body as a significant factor in understanding the visual perception of clothing. DeLong (1968, 1977, 1987) postulated the body--costume relationship. DeLong (1977) stated, "The study of aesthetics of clothing should have as a goal the understanding of the range of visual possibilities produced by combining the materials of

dress with the human body form--the costume body form" (p. 214).

The influence of the body on appearance may include form, surface, motion, and elements of body expression. For example, a wearable art piece might include fringe or suspended ribbons that move in response to body motion. Hillestad's (1980) model of the structure of appearance includes both body and dress components.

Very little analysis has focused on the relational aspects of the aesthetic dimensions of wearable art, that is, how the creator, wearer, and viewer influence the understanding of the art object and each other. The aesthetic dimensions of wearable art include visual perception, but our intent is also to discuss the multifaceted aspects of other sensory perceptions including auditory, tactile, and kinetic perceptions of apparel. Arnheim (1974) supports the use of our senses in comprehension. He stated that "we have neglected the gift of comprehending things through our senses. Concept is divorced from percept, and thought moves among abstractions" (p. 1). Wearable art provides us with a circumstance that instantaneously engages our senses because the human body is the infrastructure that "carries" the artwork. Ostensibly, the wearer and viewer interact with the qualities that the wearable artwork has to offer that invite sensory response.

Artists who create wearable forms borrow from the traditions of both art and fashion. As "fields of study," both art education and clothing and textiles scholars are informed by theory and research from other foundation areas. Wearable art, by its very nature links the two areas of art and clothing together and invites shared discussion that explores similarities and differences in history, language, and criticism.

Because art criticism is integral to the study of art, pedagogical strategies for teaching art criticism have been a central issue for art educators. Art education publications and resources offer a wealth of methods and models to facilitate critical discussion of art objects. Current scholarship is directed toward meta-analyses of criticism methods (i.e., a discussion of the appropriateness and usefulness of criticism models). For example, Ettinger (1990) examined art criticism in terms of purpose, organization, and accessibility. She suggested that there should be "a correspondence between the art criticism format one selects to use and one's goals and purposes" (p. 34). Our framework was created to reflect the special requirements a critique of wearable art may generate.

Our objective is to look at the relationships among the visual, tactile and auditory components of perception and the involvement of the moving, body-supported wearable art object to the key players of creator, viewer, and wearer. We will discuss definitions of wearable art, compare these definitions with other art forms, and provide a brief review of the wearable art movement. This discussion will be followed by selected perspectives of art criticism that appear in art education literature.

The unique circumstances of art criticism related to wearable art and why wearable art criticism is different from the critique of other art forms is discussed. A model of the aesthetic dimensions of wearable art is developed drawing on both art criticism and the nature of wearable art. It is hoped that this framework will be used by scholars from a variety of fields of study who are interested in the aesthetic dimensions of clothing and textiles.

Wearable Art

Wearable art is a unique art form because of its dependence on the special relationships between the artwork and its creator, the wearer, and the viewer of the artwork. The obvious distinction between wearable art and other art forms such as sculpture and painting is that wearable art is worn. There is an intimate relationship between the artwork and the wearer's body. The language that we use to describe wearable art denotes the importance of the body. Words like headdress, arm band, necklace, and anklet exemplify the body interface with the object worn. When the human body enters as a variable into an aesthetic equation, the understanding of the artwork changes drastically. When the body is enveloped or used to support the art, the physical distance needed for the traditional stance to "stand back" and reflect on the balance and composition of a piece is altered. For example, the wearer's perspective is limited to viewing only certain parts of the artwork.

Additional sensory input is provided for the wearer through the feel of the garment against the skin, the way the garment affects posture and movement, and whether the garment provides auditory sensations through surface abrasion (e.g., rustling) or embellishment (e.g., bells). Clothing is truly a "second skin" (Horn & Gurel, 1981) for its proximity to our senses provides tactile, auditory, visual, and olfactory possibilities.

Because the experience of wearing clothing is common to all of us, wearable art viewers are able to project an experiential understanding of wearable art. Wearable art can be viewed like kinetic sculpture, only infinitely more familiar, because viewers can imagine themselves wearing the clothing and/or body ornament. These dimensions of projected wearing and viewing that encompass various senses provide a rich, multilayered experience.

Wearable art is generally considered clothing or accessories, therefore it serves a functional purpose. In addition to its functional purpose, apparel designated as wearable art is also imbued with visual qualities aligned more with art than with "fashion" apparel. The relationship between art and fashion has been close throughout history. Fashion designers use artists' works for inspiration for costume form and textile motif (Boodro, 1990). The quintessential example of this would be Yves Saint Laurent's dresses of the 1970s and '80s that were inspired by the paintings of Mondrian and Picasso. Artists are now borrowing from fashion designers to create performance pieces. For example, artist Cindy Sherman used the Spring 1993 ready-to-wear collection to create a series of characters that were photographed and published--interestingly enough--in a fashion magazine (Lewis, 1993).

While it would seem that a definition of wearable art is necessary, this art form may resist a concise definition. Julie Dale (1986), author of *Art to Wear*, described wearable art as

A form of body adornment that celebrates personal expression, art to wear is as richly varied and unpredictable as the individuals who create it. By its very nature, the art to wear movement defies definition. The pieces conform to no established set of aesthetic criteria. (p. 12)

The vagueness of this "definition" supports the notion that wearable art is a unique art form dependent on artist intent and viewer interpretation.

In delineating between art and apparel production the concept of the one-of-a-kind nature of art work is mentioned. Becker (1978) stated that the "uniqueness of the [art] object is prized. Artists and their publics think that no two objects produced by an artist should be alike" (p. 868). This concept of uniqueness versus limited or mass production is often used as one of the distinctions between art and craft--a common topic of discussion among artists and craftspersons (see Koplos, 1986). Dale (interviewed by Shea, 1978) also mentioned the aspect of uniqueness of the wearable art object,

> Each piece is conceived and made by the same person. These objects are not generally reproducible or made with reproduction in mind. They are made to express an idea. In a sense, these pieces are within the tradition in which art is made in our culture. (p. 22)

Another characteristic of art objects frequently mentioned in discussions among artists and craftspersons deals with the object's "utility." The aspect of utility calls into question the fact that wearable art *is* worn and thus it serves a "useful" function as well. This may be one reason why wearable art is difficult to define. In some respects, wearable art conforms to "standard" definitions of art, while in other respects it may be more closely aligned with fashion design that is influenced by market-driven considerations.

A final point of discussion of the uniqueness of wearable art deals with the purchaser (or, perhaps the wearer, in the case of wearable art). Works of art are created generally without a purchaser in mind. This is often true with those artists who create wearable art. The wearable artist who creates without a purchaser in mind forms a distinction between wearable art and "custom clothing."

Considering the attributes previously discussed, one can still offer a definition of wearable art as art composed of materials structured so they can be worn on the body and that exhibit visually exciting design elements and principles. Wearable art includes garments as well as body ornament such as headwear, jewelry, shoes, neckwear, and belts. California artist Candace Kling creates headwear (see Figure 1) that can be worn but is more frequently purchased for exhibit display. Wearable art can be one-of-a-kind, made without a specific user (wearer) in mind, and may or may not be truly "functional" as clothing or body adornment.

The Wearable Art Movement

The beginning of the wearable art movement in the United States can be traced to the 1960s. A leading specialist on the wearable art movement, Dale (1986, p. 13) wrote that the early pieces appeared in the late 1960s, in a kind of spontaneous combustion. Creativity was focused on the body as a vehicle to animate and display imagery. During that first decade, wearable artists relearned traditional crafts, such as fabric dyeing, knitting, and crochet," connecting with their heritage." This generation wanted "to

Figure 1. Church and Steeple. Headress by Candice Kling. Photo by John Bagley.

86

slow down and create objects of lasting beauty to reflect its own worth in a frenetic, throwaway society."

For some of these early wearable artists, their products were the embellishment of existing apparel--denim jeans, jackets, and vests. Their work often reflected an expressive personal nature--sometimes a message about the culture at that time. Leafing through the 1974 *Levi's Denim Art Contest Catalogue of Winners*, one sees photographs of denim clothing decorated with yo yos, bells, military insignia, flora and fauna motifs. Most of the award winners' pieces express the essence of the counter-culture movement of the time.

In the early 1970s, Julie Schafler Dale began her quest to locate wearable art and artists on the West Coast. She wrote,

> I had encountered the first full flowering of the sixties youth culture, which had been so intent on expressing itself and preaching individuality on every level, including decorated clothing. But these pieces from the early 1970s were not folk art by untrained individuals. They were the disciplined and sophisticated creations of artists. (1986, p. 10)

Dale opened Julie: Artisans' Gallery (a retail store) in Manhattan in 1973, "as a showcase for contemporary Americans creating art to be worn" (Dale, 1986, p. 10). Her retail business infused the wearable art movement with credibility, visibility, and a sales outlet. Throughout America, wearable artists experimented with new techniques in fiber and fabric manipulation, as well as dyeing, painting, printing, and embellishing. As Stabb (1988) explained, "Serious research into expanding the range of media and processes gave an added measure of depth to the work....It pushed the parameters of clothing as art toward new definitions" (p. 30).

What followed in the development of the wearable art movement might have been anticipated. Stabb continued her discussion of its evolution,

> As if burdened by the incredible complexity of the technical virtuosity they had achieved, many artists began to seek relief in simpler, lighter, less time-consuming works. Others shifted gears and sought short cuts to the very processes

they once treasured and entered the realm of limited production. (p. 30)

While some wearable artists struggled with the dilemma of meticulous one-of-a-kind pieces versus limited production to sustain their income during the 1980s, another impetus for wearable artists developed.

As the popularity of quiltmaking increased during this time, it was inevitable that piecing and quilting techniques would find their way into wearable art designs. Special design competitions offered by quiltmaking materials manufacturers encouraged this merger. The Fairfield Fashion Show is one such example. Since its beginning in 1979, the Fairfield Fashion Show has been a showcase for the approximately fifty designers who are invited annually to create one-of-a-kind garments. The show debuts in Houston at the Quilt Market, then travels throughout the U.S. during the year. In 1987, the show made its international debut. The national and international exposure of wearable art has provided another avenue for the promotion of this art form. A number of other national and international fiber and wearable art shows continue to expand and promote the field.

Some authors have expressed concern over the future of the wearable art movement. Stabb (1988) wrote,

> Like a person undergoing a midlife crises [sic], the wearable art movement has come to terms with its own mortality. Is it inevitable that the movement will die? Can it be revitalized and overcome this apparent inevitability by responding to the potential of new technologies and changing tastes in personal adornment with solutions that are creative and fresh? (p. 31)

Now, six years after Stabb wrote that there were signs that the younger generation was leading in a different direction, it appears that the wearable art movement has taken on the challenge of new technologies as artists experiment with fabric dyeing and printing, computers, photocopying, and new "high-technology" fibers and fabrics. Oregon wearable artist Elaine Spence used laser copier photo transfer technology to integrate photographs of herself and film idol James Dean in what appears to the eye to be a screen printed, commercially-produced fabric.

Rob Hillestad, a Nebraska wearable artist, experiments with fabric dyeing technology.

The wearable art movement is now a generation old, thus it should not be a surprise that the movement has changed direction. Each generation's art mirrors the spirit of the times. Talley (1988) interviewed Dale and wrote about her reaction to the wearable art movement,

> The current wearable art movement reflects the output of artists who came of age in the Sixties, but [Dale] does not believe the movement is necessarily a single generation phenomenon. In the 80s, the tools of the trade have changed, a general technological shift--a greater tendency to explore the possibilities of high technology, whereas previously artists preferred the purity of all natural fibers. People are willing to explore with things like Xerox and plastic now to make a statement. (p. 22)

For those of us actively involved in creating and exhibiting wearable art, the synergy is strong and more, rather than fewer, juried wearable art shows are publicized now than previously. While the wearable art movement may have changed directions, it does not appear to be dwindling.

Art Criticism

Art criticism has been simply defined as organized talk about art (Feldman, 1973). It differs from aesthetics which focuses on the nature of art and how and why we value it. The critical response is a discussion of the meaning and significance a particular artwork has to the viewer (Hamblen, 1991a). It involves "a direct personal encounter with a specific work of art" that usually results in a verbal or written response (Anderson, 1991, p. 18). In essence, art criticism is a concentrated effort to attend to a singular example, though generalizations directed toward the study of aesthetics may follow.

There are many art criticism instructional models that lead the viewer to critical discussion. Critical discussion involves describing, analyzing, and interpreting the viewing experience. "Organized talk" implies an organizing format or strategy. Models can take many forms such as diagrams with explanatory text (Lanier, 1968); directed, sequential, instructional proce-

dures (Feldman, 1973); flexible phases (Chapman, 1978); dialogue journals (Stout, 1993); and questioning strategies (Nadaner, 1985).

Scholars who create art criticism instructional models or write about them are informed from foundational areas such as Aesthetics, Psychology, Linguistics, Philosophy, Anthropology, and Sociology (See Hamblen, 1991b). Each model "is intended to encourage new ways of seeing, to give us new perspectives on possibilities and suggest new directions for imagining and constructing reality" (Blandy & Congdon, 1991, p. 1). Critical frameworks for viewing art can be looked at as structures to help us discover some of the subtle aspects of an artwork that may be lost to cursory viewing.

There is much healthy debate in the field of art education concerning how we look at and talk about art. Art criticism strategies have been analyzed in terms of language (Hamblen, 1984; Congdon, 1986); context (Berger, 1972; Jones, 1988); feminist thought (Garber, 1990; Hicks, 1992) and political agenda (Lippard, 1986; Nadaner, 1985). How these concerns may appear in criticism for wearable art have an impact on how we as clothing and textile specialists develop questioning strategies. For example, language used by clothing and textile specialists to critique wearable art, exhibits knowledge of fiber, fabric structure, fabric finishes, and garment structure. We have a specialized vocabulary such as "hand" or "scroop" to describe fabric texture. Our language may enrich wearable art criticism, but may also limit an outsider's understanding. If accessibility to knowledge is a goal of educators, specialized language and format should be analyzed in terms of exclusionist characteristics. Prerequisite knowledge may be necessary for the use of certain criticism strategies.

Context relates to the social milieu of the artist and viewer and the conditions under which the wearable artwork is seen. For example, the theatrical context of a runway show influences our perception of the objects shown. Runway models provide multiple perspectives for viewing as posture, gesture, movement, lighting, proximity, and setting provide variables. The static aspects of "hanger appeal" provide a different mode of appreciation than the kinetic qualities of a runway performance. Context also acknowledges the age, sex, race, class, and experience of the artist and viewer.

Hicks (1992) stated, "We need to analyze how we as viewers and critics construct meaning within the works that we investigate by drawing on the background of cultural beliefs and values through which we see the world" (p. 24).

The growing field of feminist thought may have important contributions to the development of an art criticism framework for wearable art. The cultural construction of gender, the predominantly female focus of wearable art, and the differences between the male and female "gaze" are provocative areas of interest that generate comment and questions.

Some garments are made to reflect an interest in a political agenda. Social issues may inspire the artist to communicate these concerns. For example, in response to recently proposed anti-gay legislation, Elaine Spence created "Straight Jacket" to reflect her stance on human rights. "Elephant Walk" (a wearable art coat created by the authors) was made to draw attention to the endangerment of elephants due to ivory poaching and habitat loss (see Figure 2).

Critical models evolving from formalist theory are primary and popular choices for wearable art critiques (Ettinger, 1990, p. 34). Formal models (see Feldman, 1973) rely on the description, analysis, interpretation, and judgment of art objects as isolated entities. Models such as these consider the essential, visual qualities such as the elements and principles of design central to the understanding of the artwork. In applying these models, critics may create a monologue as their critical discussion.

The proposed critical framework differs from the previous models described. It includes of a diagram that illustrates the wearable art experience as a composite of relationships. Sample questions are provided that amplify our perceptions of the essential qualities of wearable art, but also stress the relational aspects among creator, viewer, and wearer. By emphasizing the relational, interactive components of the wearable art experience we propose a criticism model that promotes dialogue rather than monologue. By identifying six relationships in the wearable art experience and presenting a model that encourages entry into critical discussion through a variety of roles (i.e., creator, wearer, and viewer) one critic can experience multiple perspectives. We also offer suggested

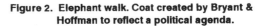

Figure 2. Elephant walk. Coat created by Bryant & Hoffman to reflect a political agenda.

sample questions that direct users to consider the possibilities of social, political and feminist perspectives. This critical framework is not meant to exclude other critical perspectives of wearable art due to its format. Instead, we invite plural approaches and encourage those with a particular viewpoint or interest to add their questions to the framework for critical discussion.

A Critical Framework for Understanding Wearable Art

By selecting, isolating, and examining six relationships among the art object, the creator, the wearer, and the viewer (see Figure 3), we intend to amplify these components of the wearable art experience. We acknowledge this arrangement has limitations because of the overlay between components and the simultaneous processing of information that may occur especially in instances where the creator is the wearer and/or viewer, etc. A description of possible expectations, influences, and satisfaction determined from the relationships is presented. This is followed by sample questions that encourage discussion of the featured relationship. These sample questions, together with Figure 3, create the framework that is our art criticism model for wearable art.

Figure 3. Model of critical framework for exploring the aesthetic dimensions of wearable art.

Creator -- Object Relationship:

The *creator <--> object* relationship is a familiar one, for much of the discussion of an art object focuses on the creator's objective, inspiration, and intended message of the object. It tends to be a self-oriented creative process rather than have a user-oriented focus. Although speaking from a marketing viewpoint, Hirschman (1983) articulated this self-oriented creativity:

> self-oriented creators create to communicate a personal vision or satisfy an inner need for self-expression. Rather than seeking creative guidance from peers or the public, they follow their own inclinations and then present their creations to others--desiring to receive approval from peers and/or the public. Such self-oriented creators often hope to achieve peer and mass audience approval of their products, yet they do not start out with these audiences in mind. Rather, they believe that by creating something that vividly expresses their values and emotions, the audience will be moved to accept their perspective. (p. 48)

Thus, the artist works to create an object that expresses first and foremost the artist's creative image, without focusing on, or being controlled by, viewer reaction to the object.

Of the six interrelationships under discussion, the *creator <--> object* relationship is the only category for which much has been written

previously. Wearable artists who have been interviewed (Bullis, 1987) often speak about the *creator <--> object* relationship. Wearable art pieces go beyond adornment for the artists who create them. Just as artists who work in other media say, the creations of wearable artists are the outpouring of their personal visual messages−from their dreams to their realities. Shea (1978) stated, "Because it is of necessity so personal−needing to be worn−clothing lends itself well to the expression of a created personal fantasy" (p. 22). Dale (1986) understands the *creator <--> object* relationship for she has worked with the artists by representing their work in her retail gallery since 1973. She stated,

> They are each distinguished by an intensity of personal content. They are about the artists who created them, unabashedly autobiographical, signaling an eruption of personal information from private spaces. They speak of vulnerability, innocence, discovery, joy, pain, sensuality, outrage, celebration--always with a vitality of emotion rarely found in adornment. These works are the physical embodiment of interior worlds and intangible ideas. (p. 12)

The creator may make choices in materials, techniques, and form due to an understanding of how a wearable art piece will be presented. A runway show, for example, may require more drama than another setting, thus reflective fabrics or embellishments in larger scale may be selected for use. Because garments will be seen in motion, those garment features that enhance gesture may be exaggerated. Because the body is seen as integral to wearable art, placement of detailing may be found near the face or hands, since those are body areas where communication is extended (i.e., where viewers generally focus for communication clues).

The vision of the artist may not be fully realized in the wearable art piece. The creator may also be restricted to placement of design elements. If it is desired that large motifs be visible, the chest or back provides the largest areas for presentation. Kimono shapes have been popular in wearable art because of their simple rectangular shapes that allow for the greatest amount of "canvas" to convey the artist's message.

Critical discussion of the relationship between the creator and the object may be prompted by the following questions. Posing questions that highlight the special qualities of the relationships presented in this paper provide a framework for critical discussion to enrich the understanding of the wearable art experience. The following sample questions are general in nature. It is expected that specific questions would be developed depending on the wearable art piece and other variables such as setting, artist's intent, viewer experience and conceptual focus of the critique. We acknowledge that some questions require projection and/or conjecture by the user of the critical framework. Since most art criticism models are from the viewer perspective, the role of wearer or creator may be more difficult to discuss.

Sample *creator* <--> *object* questions to encourage discussion may include:

1. What do you think is the artist's intent?
2. Are the choices of materials and techniques compatible with the artist's intent? Was the artist successful?
3. What questions about the artwork would you ask the artist?

Wearer <--> Object Relationship:

The wearer's body comes in direct contact with the fabric, creating a tactile experience for the wearer. The tactile sensation of fabrics against the skin, the movement of the garment when the wearer is in motion, the sound of fabrics or trims as the wearer moves, and glimpses of sleeve decoration as the wearer sees part of the clothing contribute to the wearer's appreciation of the object. Emotional and psychological benefits to the wearer may occur by wearing an object the wearer considers beautiful. Artist Marian Clayden stated,

> Garments and wall hangings are different aspects of the same idea. One sculpture moves, the other doesn't. One goes on to another life, the other carries its only life within itself. They have the same ability to move the beholder to appreciate what wasn't perceived before. But fashion can be rearranged and reinterpreted by the wearer and thus become a conversation between us. You can't do that with something on the wall. (Bullis, 1987, p. 37)

Clayden promotes the wearer as an interactive component in the wearable art experience. Since one piece can be displayed by more than one wearer, it is assumed that a variety of "conversations" can take place depending on wearer attributes (e.g., physical appearance, theatrical intent). Different wearers allow for the same piece to be reinterpreted by viewers at different times and sites. Wearers may respond to the sensual qualities of specialty fabrics such as velvet in varying degrees of appreciation. The emotional pleasure of the wearer may project to the viewer. Some art pieces especially invite wearer-object interaction. The textural qualities of Rob Hillestad's piece titled Celebration Cape IX promote interaction between wearer and object (see Figure 4).

Figure 4. Celebration Cape IX. Cape created by Hillestad illustrates the wearer interacting with garment.

Some wearable art authors discuss the concept of transformation in the *wearer* <--> *object* relationship. Porges (1989) shared some insights regarding the work of California artist Jean Williams Cacicedo,

> [Cacicedo] admits that her pieces may spend most, if not all, of their lives on display. It is essential to her, however, that they are garments because of what happens when they come off the wall and go on the body. For as much as each wearer might be changed by getting in-

side of Cacicedo's "parable," he or she transforms it as well. (p. 49)

The concept of a wearable art piece being transformed by the wearer has fascinating aspects. The wearer transforms the artwear into a kinetic sculpture integral with the wearer's body shape, size and personal coloring, but perhaps the wearer is also transformed into a different personality by wearing the art object.

Dale (1986) discussed another *wearer <--> object* aspect--that of the fantasy the wearer may want to experience by wearing an object. "Not only can I look at these pieces on a wall but I can become them. I found you can assume a role by wearing something. Wearing it becomes a form of theater" (p. 58). To exchange one's identity for another persona through appearance has been an inviting and common occurrence throughout fashion and social history. For example, people enjoy the opportunity to dress in role-playing costume on Halloween. Wearable art may allow the wearer to engage the imagination in playful exercise.

Sample *wearer <--> object* questions include:

1. How does the wearer's appearance interact with the object? Would this interaction be different in another environment?
2. What emotions is the wearer communicating? What qualities of the wearable art elicit these emotions?
3. How would the object be perceived if it were hanging on a wall rather than supported by the wearer?

Viewer <--> Object Relationship:

The wearing of apparel is an experience understood by all viewers, although they may have different expectations for garment satisfaction. The viewing experience may also be subject to varied interpretations based on one's background and experience. DeLong (1977) stated,

> Seeing is a function that is molded in the social processes by individuals in order to carry on day-to-day activities and is thus inevitably very subjective. An individual learns to perceive his world within a frame of reference based on his past experiences, expectations, and feelings. (p. 214)

One's reaction to a wearable art piece may be influenced by one's visualization of the object on one's own body. Since the wearing of clothing is common experience, an empathic projection of the wearer's experience naturally occurs. Interestingly, this projection doesn't usually involve the concern about whether the garment fits. However, one may reject a certain palette or garment style if perceived as unbecoming. We tend to personalize our reactions to wearable art by considering whether or not we would like to wear a piece. Objectivity in analyzing the creation as an art form in and of itself therefore may be difficult to achieve. In this way wearable art is a unique viewing experience as compared to viewing other art forms because the viewer (using the wearer as referent) can imagine wearing the garment while viewing it from a distance.

Frequently, one's first response to wearable art is as clothing rather than as an art form. An understanding of wearable art changes as the viewer develops greater knowledge of and experience with this art form. For those individuals who have viewed considerable wearable art objects, enjoyment may be heightened by the exposure to a wide variety of artists' visual statements. Knowing about the artist, or having some background about what an artist is communicating also can heighten the enjoyment of viewing an object.

Sample *viewer <--> object* questions include:

1. Project what it would be like to wear this garment. How would it feel to wear this garment? What are the visual, tactile, auditory, and kinetic qualities of the garment that elicit these feelings?
2. What are the salient essential qualities of the artwork that are important for its success (e.g., shape, line, color)?
3. What special language as metaphor might you use to describe the wearable art?

Creator <--> Wearer Relationship:

The creator of wearable art may take into consideration the wearer's gender, personality, emotional associations, and physical factors to achieve the highest level of physical and psychological comfort and satisfaction for the wearer. These qualities may dictate the formal aspects all artists consider (e.g., line, shape, color) depending on the relationship between the creator and wearer (e.g., provider/client, artist/model). Julie Dale has had the opportunity to wear many of the pieces from her retail gallery. She is quoted by Kaufman (1986): "The wearing of the pieces is very satisfying. I never thought I'd have the chance to participate so closely in a creative act. Wearing the clothes is a way of having the magic rub off" (p. 65). Stabb (1991) considered the importance of the wearer to the creator in the completion of the creative process, "She [Hedstrom] is intrigued by the clothing's dependency on and collaboration with the wearer, as if her work were not quite finished until worn" (p. 34).

During the creation process, the artist often is not concerned with whom the eventual wearer of the object will be, though gender and setting requirements are usually known. The artist may focus solely on the object during the creation process and may not consider the specific needs of the individual wearer when the wearer's identify is not known. Wearable artists think in generalities about how the garment will look, feel, envelope the body, and perhaps sound to the as-yet unknown wearer.

Fabrics may be selected based upon the tactile qualities of textiles that feel wonderful. Artist Marian Clayden was quoted by Talley (1988): "One has to consider the tactile qualities of the cloth--its feel against the skin, the way it drapes, and so on. When you get the wonderful garment that someone looks and feels really great in, then you feel it's all worth it" (p. 16). Some artists consider auditory elements in their designs. This could take the form of fabrics that rustle, or perhaps little bells might be attached to a Christmas jacket to provide a special sound for the wearer.

Sometimes the creator is the intended wearer. In these instances, the artist can create with great command of visual, tactile and auditory preferences, for the creator will know precisely what is to be conveyed. The wearable art object can be tried on by the creator and new ideas experimented with during the creation process. The creator may be more critical of little changes that can be made to make the piece more wearable. The creator/wearer has a vision of the piece and can decide if the object is fulfilling that vision as the process of creation unfolds.

Sample *creator <--> wearer* questions include:

1. Do you think the creator designed this garment for a specific wearer? If so, do you think the creator met the wearer's expectations?
2. What is the relationship between the wearer's body shape to the artist's design?
3. Are there variables introduced by the wearer, such as fit, that limit the creativity of the artist if it is a commission piece? Or, do these special challenges provide parameters for the artist to structure her work?

Creator <--> Viewer:

The relationship of the creator and viewer depends on the intent of the artist and the expectations of the viewer. The creator may use the art object as a vehicle to communicate to the viewer a social or political message. The viewer may or may not interpret the message as the artist intended.

Many of the early pieces of 1960s wearable art were expressions of social and cultural commentaries such as the anti-establishment youth movement. More recent examples are Gaza Bowen's shoe creations that challenge social values by using symbolic materials like sponges and kitchen scrubbers to make high heels for a piece titled "Shoes for the Little Woman" and wing tips made from shredded then woven dollar bills and titled "In God We Trust" (See Bowen, 1986). Some of these artists' visual messages are obvious, others are subtle, some not known to anyone save the creator.

One goal of the creator may be that the object make a powerful visual statement to the viewer. The viewer may be a juror selecting wearable art pieces for entry into exhibitions. If slides are the required medium for the selection process, the creator may take into consideration the juror's viewing situation. Tiny, intricate garment details are not as easily seen or appreciated when viewed as slides as they are when a garment is seen live and at close viewing range.

Perhaps the creator used the visualization of an outfit moving down a runway in a wearable art show to spark the design process. The artist may decide to add design components on the object that move with the model's motion--floating sleeve panels, or ribbon streamers for example. These details that provide movement can add to the visual excitement of a wearable art object.

When the creator becomes the viewer of her or his wearable art object, other perceptual perspectives occur. The creator can step back and observe the success of the creation when viewed on a model. From a distance, or when seen in a photograph, the wearable art object may become more or less successful in the creator's eye. Distance may be needed by the creator for more objective viewing. This distance can be physical or apparent when art objects are reproduced in other media such as camera or video. As wearable artists, we are frequently surprised at how different a wearable art piece looks to us in a photograph. On occasion, changes have been made to a piece after initial photographs have been viewed.

Sample *creator* <--> *viewer* questions include:

1. Is it apparent that the wearable art was created for a specific audience? Do you think viewer reaction would be different if the audience were predominantly male? Predominantly female?
2. Does it appear that the viewer had an influence on the creative process?
   What aspects of the object suggest this?
3. Is the creator trying to influence or persuade the viewer to act on a political or social cause through materials used or themes presented?

Wearer <--> *Viewer Relationship:*

The viewer's perception of the wearable art object is quite different from that of the wearer, for the viewer sees the entire garment, both front and back views, in motion and related to the human form wearing the apparel, and under varying conditions of light and environment. The wearer "sees" very little of the garment being worn.

The viewer and the wearer do not share the same sensory experiences. The viewer does not share the direct interaction with garment and body that the wearer experiences. During the viewing process the viewer may imagine him or herself as the wearer. Merchandisers encourage viewer projection by choosing wearers who show the garment to best advantage. Stylists may choose wearers by coloring, image, or fit

to enhance wearable art. For example, in a recent wearable art runway show, Bryant's "Beribboned and Tied" turquoise coat was shown to best advantage by a model with copper colored hair.

The wearer incites the viewer's appreciation by theatrical gesture or exaggerated stance to show off the art work. Because the wearer becomes part of the wearable art experience he or she may respond to applause or vocal kudos feeling that the audience is cheering for the wearer as well as the wearable.

Sample *wearer* <--> *viewer* questions include:

1. How does the wearer respond to the viewer's reaction to the wearable art?
2. How does viewing distance affect the perception of wearable art?
3. What special characteristics of the artwork are apparent to the viewer, but not the wearer and vice versa?

Summary and Future Direction

An understanding of the aesthetic dimensions of apparel design as wearable art requires an examination of the relationships involved. The critical framework presented in this paper consists of a diagram that illustrates six selected relationships identified by the authors as integral to the wearable art experience. This diagram is accompanied by sample questions that may be used to enrich the discussion of each selected relationship. Other configurations may elicit different discussions.

Because the relationships in the wearable art experience are very tightly interactive and the creator, viewer, wearer roles may overlap, the wearable art experience is richly complex. By isolating the relational aspects of wearable art using this critical framework, this complexity can be explored.

Creating and viewing wearable art differ from creating and viewing a painting. Critical to our discussion is the concept of the body in relation to the artwork. The human form not only inspires but also establishes the parameters within which the apparel creator must work. For example, the human form in motion defines the limits and the structure of the creation.

Future directions for discussion and research are many and varied. Possibilities for related research include examining the parameters of fashion, wearable art, and dance and theater costume. Does wearable art have closer ties to theater and dance costume than fashion? Another area of investigation concerns the relation between social cognition and wearable art. How does person/social perception influence wearable art discussion?

Building art critical models that encourage multiple perspectives and viewing stances celebrate the richness of the wearable art experience. Multiple perspectives provide interdisciplinary study. For example, this critical framework employs knowledge from the fields of art education and textiles and clothing.

References

Anderson, T. (1991). The content of art criticism. *Art Education, 44*(1), 16-24.

Arnheim, R. (1974). *Art and visual perception. A psychology of the creative eye*. Berkeley, CA: University of California Press.

Becker, H.S. (1978). Arts and crafts. *American Journal of Sociology, 83*(4), 862-889.

Berger, J. (1972). *Ways of seeing*. NY: Viking Press.

Blandy, D., & Congdon, K.G. (Eds.). (1991). *Pluralistic approaches to art criticism*. Bowling Green, OH: Bowling Green State University Press.

Boodro, M. (1990, Sept.) Art & fashion. A fine romance. *ARTnews*, 120-127.

Bowen, G. (1986, June/July). The shoemaker's art. *Threads*, pp. 56-61.

Bullis, D. (1987). *California designers*. Layton, Utah: Gibbs M. Smith.

Chapman, L. (1978). *Approaches to Art in Education*. New York: Harcourt, Brace, Javanovich.

Congdon, K.G. (1986). The meaning and use of folk speech in art criticism. *Studies in Art Education, 27*(3), 140-148.

Dale, J.S. (1986). *Art to wear*. New York: Abbeville Press.

DeLong, M.R. (1968). Analysis of costume visual form. *Journal of Home Economics, 60*(10), 784-788.

DeLong, M.R. (1977). Clothing and aesthetics: Perception of form. *Home Economics Research Journal, 5*(4), 214-224.

DeLong, M.R. (1987). *The way we look*. Ames, Iowa: Iowa State University Press.

DeLong, M.R. & Hillestad, R. (1990). Aesthetics of apparel: Subject, form and content [summary]. *ACPTC national meeting proceedings*, p. 33.

DeLong, M.R. & Larntz, K. (1980). Measuring visual response to clothing. *Home Economics Research Journal, 8*(4), 281-293.

Ettinger, L. (1990). Critique of art criticism: Problemizing practice in art education. *Controversies in Art & Culture, 3*(1), 30-41.

Feldman, E. (1973). The teacher as model critic. *Journal of Aesthetic Education, 7*(1), 50-57.

Garber, E. (1990). Implications of feminist art criticism for art education. *Studies in Art Education, 32*(1), 17-26.

Hamblen, K. A. (1984). The culture of aesthetic discourse (CAD): Origins, contradictions, and implications. *The Bulletin of the Caucus on Social Theory and Art Education, 4*, 22-34.

Hamblen, K. A. (1991a). Beyond universalism in art criticism. In D. Blandy & K.G. Congdon (Eds.), *Pluralistic approaches to art criticism* (pp. 6-14). Bowling Green, OH: Bowling Green State University Press.

Hamblen, K. A. (1991b). In the quest for art criticism equity: A tentative model. *Visual Arts Research, 17*(1), 12-22.

Hicks, L. (1992). The construction of meaning: Feminist criticism. *Art Education, 45*(2), 23-31.

Hillestad, R. (1980). The underlying structure of appearance. *Dress, 6*, 117-125.

Hirschman, E.C. (1983, Summer). Aesthetics, ideologies and the limits of the marketing concept. *Journal of Marketing, 47*, 45-55.

Horn, M.J., & Gurel, L.M. (1981). *The second skin*. Boston: Houghton Mifflin.

Jones, B. (1988). Art education in context. *Journal of Multicultural and Cross-cultural Art Education, 6*(1), 38-54.

Kaufman, J. (1986, December). Art to wear. *United Magazine*, pp. 57-65.

Koplos, J. (1986, March/April). When is fiber art "art?" *Fiberarts*, 34-35.

Lanier, V. (1968). Talking about art: An experimental course in high school art appreciation. *Studies in Art Education, 9*(3), 32-44.

Levi's denim art contest catalogue of winners. (1974). Mill Valley, CA: Baron Wolman/Squarebooks.

Lewis, J. (1993, May). The new Cindy Sherman collection. *Harper's Bazaar*, 144-149+.

Lippard, L. (1986, December). Rape show and tell. *These Times, 11*(5), 23-24.

Morganosky, M.A. (1987). Aesthetic function, and fashion consumer values: Relationships to other values and demographics. *Clothing and Textiles Research Journal, 6*(1), 15-19.

Nadaner, D. (1985). Responding to the image world: A proposal for art curricula. *Art Education, 37*(1), 9-12.

Porges, M. (1989, October/November). Coat tales. *American Craft*, 46-51.

Rothenburg, A., & Sobel, R.S. (1990). A creative process in the art of costume design. *Clothing and Textiles and Research Journal, 9*(1), 27-36.

Schafler, J. (1978, October). Style: The nontraditional wearables. *Craft Horizons with Craft World*, pp. 26-28, 58.

Shea, J. (1978, October). Style: The art of clothing. *Craft Horizons with Craft World*, pp. 22-24.

Stabb, J.C. (1988, Fall). The wearable movement: A critical look at the state of the art. *Surface Design Journal*, pp. 29-31.

Stabb, J.C. (1991, April/May). Analisa Hedstrom. Process as mentor. *American Craft*, 30-35.

Stout, C.J. (1993). The dialogue journal: A forum for critical consideration. *Studies in Art Education*, *35*(1), 34-44.

Talley, C. (1988, Fall). Art to wear: Coast to coast. *Surface Design Journal*, *13*(1), 20-24.

Workman, J.E. (1991). Searching for visual inconsistencies: A method for analyzing unity in apparel design. *Clothing and Textiles Research Journal*, *9*(2), 45-48.

Clothing and Aesthetic Experience

Joseph Kupfer
Iowa State University

Philosophers have spent little time applying aesthetic theory to everyday life and its objects. The stuff of common life such as furniture, cookware, automobiles, and computers are neglected in favor of the fine arts. It is no wonder, then, that clothing has also escaped philosophical scrutiny. To remedy this, I shall adopt the orientation found in John Dewey's aesthetic theory (Dewey, 1934). This is not only fruitful, but is squarely in the spirit of Dewey's philosophy, which aims at establishing continuity between art and everyday life.

Centering on aesthetic experience, Dewey's aesthetics can be applied to virtually any object of interest or activity--whether a frying skillet or garden hoe, whether the activity of preparing a meal or garden. I have looked at classroom education as well as violence, for example, in terms of aesthetic experience (Kupfer, 1983).

Aesthetic experience is characterized by differentiated and individualized parts, but these parts are also integrated--mutually enhancing each other's effect. The result of this mutual enhancement is an intense, growing experience which is rounded out, complete in itself. The experience is defined by a pervasive quality or mood, often an emotion or feeling. The more detailed and particularized the quality, the more aesthetic the experience.

Aesthetic experiences don't just happen to us, rather, we must take an active part. Our interaction--in the classroom, on the ballfield, driving our car--requires a balance between activity and receptivity. What we do is a response to what we take in, and what we perceive is shaped by our actions. Action includes physical behavior, thinking (such as noticing the interplay of parts), and imagining (such as anticipating what is to come).

The following discussion focuses on how clothing can enter into aesthetic experience, as the object of perception and as worn--in various situations and for various activities.

1. Clothing can be appreciated simply as designed material. This can mean viewing the clothing abstractly, apart from being worn, like a dress on a hanger or kimono on a frame. Some clothing is designed with this in mind, as wearable art, and some clothing is exhibited apart from human bodies, such as chain mail in museum cases. Its function as clothing plays little role since we attend to the textures, colors, and patterns, much as we would to wallpaper or carpet exhibited apart from a building's interior. That a particular article might not look good on someone, anyone, doesn't enter into our aesthetic perception. We are not viewing the clothing as human adornment. The material and its aesthetic features just happen to be in the recognizable shape of a dress or coat, but this defines the boundaries of the material, rather than playing an aesthetic role.

Appreciating clothing in abstraction from human form can occur even when it is being worn. All that is required is that we attend to the article of clothing apart from how it looks on the this or any person. To view it as clothing, however, requires taking into consideration how it looks on someone (Bosanquet, 1915). This level of appreciation includes the former in that we perceive color, line, texture, and the like, but adds their relation to the body. For this reason, discussion of the abstract way of perceiving clothing will be incorporated into the following examination of the aesthetics of clothing as worn.

When perceiving clothing as worn, we notice how it looks on anyone or on someone in particular. Clothing that looks good on anyone is likely to be aesthetically interesting in the abstract sense discussed above. Since its style is so versatile, its aesthetic strength must reside in its composition as designed material. But the aesthetic of much apparel would seem to vary with body type. The person's configuration is an ingredient in the clothing's aesthetic: his or her coloring, height, weight, angularity-roundedness, hairstyle, even posture or personality as expressed in body language.

We can apply Dewey's concept of aesthetic experience to clothing using the specific categories of complexity, unity, and intensity. In Monroe Beardsley's theory, these are merits, reasons for a positive evaluation; their absence makes for aesthetic weakness (Beardsley, 1958). Although Beardsley's use of these criteria of evaluation is confined to the fine arts, we can employ them in examining anything aesthetically, including clothing.

A. Among the ways complexity can be achieved is in the relationships among the articles of clothing. Contrasts among garments or the way garments set off portions of the body can generate complexity. Differences in textures, perceived weights or densities, as well as shapes and patterns shift attention and redirect perceptual energy. An ensemble's appearance can also be enriched by changes in color, depth of hue, saturation or shading.

Complexity can be created through detail in construction; stitching, buttons, folds, gathers, tucks, and eyelets can add as much complication or subtlety as can differences in color or pattern. Irregularities in material, such as silk or linen, also insinuate variation to pattern, texture, even color. Accessories like belts, gloves, and scarves can define portions of the body, breaking lines or volumes. This complexity of differentiation of spaces may be independent of whatever complexity the accessory introduces on its own, by virtue of color, shape, or texture.

Still greater complexity enters when we consider the body in motion. The change or dynamism in the appearance of a flowing gown, pleated dress, or vented jacket creates new visual, sometimes auditory perceptions. Change in shape, line, shading, or density increase complexity as the individual alters posture or gait. Perhaps it's just one area of the clad body that changes in an interesting way, such as the torso in a wind-blown rayon blouse. Perhaps it's the whole form, as when a robe is suddenly set in motion.

Complexity is valuable because it's interesting. Our senses, imagination, and thought are stimulated by variety in color or shape, texture or line. Without complexity, in clothing as in art, the experience becomes dull or monotonous. Unrelenting repetition or homogeneity in perception numbs our imagination and smothers thought. Even if what is presented is intense, as with bright colors or rich materials (leather or tweed, for instance), we are soon irritated or fatigued rather than captivated.

Another way of achieving complexity in attire is through "mixed diction." When writers pepper formal language with slang, for example, the contrast opens up new layers of suggestion. So, too, with clothing, in which a mix of styles or genres can create tension or reveal overlooked aesthetic qualities. Wearing sport coats with jeans or running shoes was once mixed diction, but now is old hat.

Complexity is compatible with simplicity in line and color. Consider a Roman style, unadorned, white dress drawn over one shoulder. Without accessories or color, differences in texture or pattern, its line is complicated only by the folds in the material. Yet it has complexity. Line and volume are modulated by the wearer's form, at rest and moving, creating an array of shapes and shadows, motions and rhythms. Like Brancusi's gleaming bronze sculpture "Bird in Flight", this garment's simplicity of means and cleanness of line harbors a host of possibilities unlocked by the play of light and movement.

B. Complementing complexity is unity. Complete aesthetic experience has both. Just as unity without complexity is tepid or empty, so complexity without unity is disorienting or overwhelming. Too much variety in color, pattern, style, texture, or volume is a hodge-podge. What is wanted is complexity with integration so that the whole "makes sense," "hangs together," "works." When appreciating an article of clothing abstracted from a person wearing it with other attire, this aesthetic constraint is absent. It's like appreciating a sofa by itself, apart from its relationship to table, chairs, carpet, drapes, or lamps.

Dewey articulates unity as interdependence of parts, "the intimacy of the relations that hold the parts together," (Dewey, p.117) and "reciprocal interpretation of parts and whole" (Dewey, p.171). For clothing, unity means that garments enhance one another's appearance instead of detracting from it or merely coexisting. Any aspect of a garment can be strengthened by its relationship to other garments. The subdued grain of a woven tie, for instance, can be accentuated in the tweed of an accompanying jacket. The beige in a print skirt can echo a blouse's color, complement a teal jacket, and soften the chocolate of a coordinated hat.

Whatever the aspect--color, texture, pattern, shape--garments and their constituents reinforce one another's effect, the way plot develops a novel's theme or rhyme meshes with a poem's meaning. Part-to-part and part-to-whole: aesthetic values build upon one another so that a garment has greater aesthetic value in this ensemble than alone, and the ensemble as a whole is better for this garment's contribution.

A tie, for example, might not be especially attractive in isolation, but could be just the highlight to bring together a shirt, jacket, pants, and hat. On the other hand, a paisley blouse might be too detailed for a particular pants suit. Are the different textures and visual weights of leather and rayon, for instance, integrated--perhaps by virtue of style or color? Do the rhythms set up by repeated lines and volumes in a skirt and jacket integrate their different styles?

Unity includes continuity, "every successive part flows freely,..without unfilled blanks, into what ensues. At the same time there is no sacrifice of the self-identity of the parts" (Dewey, p.36). In aesthetically organized clothing, our eye is drawn from one garment to the next, as in good painting it is drawn from one region to the next. Whether by blending color, repeating line, or modifying texture, unity results from part leading into part. Tensions between competing colors or patterns, changes in volume and shape, are reconciled as visual rhythm establishes continuity among the garments.

Our ordinary language indicates what is often an unreflective feel for lack of unity in clothing. We speak of an outfit being too choppy or busy; we notice a shoe style as out of place for a dress line; we find the color or sheen of an accessory overbearing for an ensemble's effect. Unity is the alternative to clothes banging up against one another, a jumble of texture and color, shape and volume. The tedious or monotonous is not so much excess of unity as lack of complexity. This is why the ideal is complexity with unity, in which diverse emphases and directions cooperate. When this succeeds, the third criterion, intensity, is realized.

C. Intensity refers to the mood, feeling, or character emerging from the interplay of clothing. The apparel's organization is intense when it yields a definite thrust. We refer to the overall effect with terms denoting this quality. We say the grouping is rugged or elegant, sleek or bold, whimsical or professional. The criterion of in-tensity speaks to the strength with which the clothing impresses us, grabs us, holds us. For an ensemble to be intense, it need not be exciting or imposing. It can be warm and yielding. Attire composed of soft fabrics in pastels could convey a calm and subdued mood intensely. Intensity lies in the strength of focus, the degree to which a singular effect is produced.

Intensity is clearly contrasted with blandness--the combination of clothes yielding no particular look or mood. It just isn't much of anything. Sometimes this happens when we sense a lack of direction, perhaps because different styles are being combined. But lack of genuine intensity can come from the opposite quarter--overt forcefulness without substance. This is where we have the garish, flashy, or cheap. Beardsley's description of the pompous in music can be translated into the idiom of clothing: "Pompousness is the outward form of grandeur and greatness--it is a long symphony with enormous crescendos--combined with an inner emptiness, lack of vitality and richness" (Beardsley, p.464).

It's the obvious attempt at intensity without real integration of tensions needed for a strong voice--splashes of bright colors, exaggerated lines, puffed up volumes of material. Other garments, other details, haven't been adapted or adjusted to the innovation, and the effect seems forced or superficial. This bespeaks a lack of real intensity, as a talk-show host's profusion of enthusiasm indicates lack of real interest.

When varied articles of clothing are integrated, a strong, distinctive character is created. "A single quality...*pervades* the entire experience in spite of the variation of its constituent parts" (Dewey, p.37). This intensity is valued just as we value art works or people with distinctive personalities. The result is a definite look, a singular, vivid quality to which each element of attire contributes.

Garments also have meaning. Colors can express attitudes, styles can connote values, and shapes or patterns can function symbolically (Hungerland, 1944; Stevenson, 1969; Weitz, 1954). When articles of clothing are combined in particular ways, meanings can be magnified or altered. Humor and criticism, for example, can emerge from a well-chosen accessory or modification in line. This area of clothing aesthetics is worth pursuing in its own right and can be taken in many directions.

It could concentrate on a particular culture or period, daily wear versus festive occasions, or take up cross-cultural themes of similarity and difference. The evolution of social, economic, political, and gender meanings of particular garments or contexts of use, for instance, has surely conditioned our aesthetic experience of clothing. In addition, the strong philosophical tradition of Expression Theory of art can be appropriated for examination of the expressive properties of clothing (Tolstoy, 1925; Casey, 1971; Benson, 1967). Because this question of meaning in clothing is so broad and deep, I just mention it here and turn my attention to how the experience of wearing clothing is aesthetic.

2. Before addressing the aesthetics of interacting with and by means of clothing, a bit needs to be said about these criteria in general. They are criteria, not formulae for arriving at judgments of aesthetic value. No rules can be laid down in advance for telling the difference between the gaudy and the lively, the bland and the subtle. Judgment or taste is needed to apply the general criteria to painting or poetry, cars or clothing. What emerges are principles specific to the various art forms (unity is achieved differently in painting and music) and their genres--complexity in a murder mystery is brought about differently than in a Greek tragedy. As we shall see with clothing, differences in context and function yield differences in the orchestrating of unity, complexity, and intensity.

Cultures may differ in these specific principles. We find greater latitude for color vibrancy and combination in Mexican fashion than in British. But in any culture, there must be a place for excess, even those championing exuberance. And even the most sedate have room for the bland or monotonous. When we add the symbolic or referential meanings assigned clothing within cultures, the range of aesthetic standards widens. The task of philosophy is not to explore these cultural variations--that's for the aesthetic branches of comparative anthropology and sociology. These descriptive enterprises explain how in fact different cultures make aesthetic appraisals. Philosophy articulates the aesthetic criteria which enable us to take into account cultural variations.

What if there were a culture for which no conglomeration of textures and colors or sizes and shapes constituted a jumble, a mess, a cacophony rather than a symphony? Would this show that there is no aesthetic criterion of unity? Not necessarily. It might show that this culture has no standards, no sense of good or bad, no taste. The existence of such a culture doesn't prove there are no criteria any more than mass murderers without remorse prove there is no moral evil. Moreover, comparative anthropology suggests that few if any cultures are without aesthetic standards of some sort. But neither does this establish the objectivity of these criteria, regardless of people's attitudes.

What we can argue for philosophically is the following conditional statement. If we wish to make aesthetic judgments which are more than our preferences, then there must be criteria of aesthetic appreciation of clothing. This leaves open the possibility of cultural or individual relativism: that good and bad is relative to what happens to please a culture or individual. The logical consequence of this is that anything goes. No ensemble can "objectively" lack in unity, complexity, or intensity. It's just a matter of cultural or personal preference. Yet even here, what are the bases for these preferences? If the culture or individual tries to defend them consistently, I suggest that we will find the criteria being discussed here. They are at work even when aesthetic judgments are relativized to cultures or individuals.

The reason is found in everyday life. Complexity, unity, and intensity characterize the experiences and activities we value most. More generally, lives that are complex, unified, and intense are more worthwhile than those barren of variety, fragmented, and lacking defined contour or personality. These lives tend to be empty, alienated, and directionless. My suggestion, then, is that the general criteria employed here to assess the aesthetics of clothing are derived from what we value in life as we ordinarily live it.

3. The aesthetic appreciation of clothing includes our interaction with it when worn. Clothing is an immediate environment, moving with and against us, like a second skin. When we wear clothing, others can appreciate the aesthetic of how we look in it better than we can. But the aesthetic of direct interaction is available only to the wearer. This interaction is above all

sensuous; seeing, hearing, smelling, and feeling the clothing adorning us has great aesthetic potential. As we raise our arm, we notice the color and texture of our sleeve; looking down, we enjoy the cut and gleam of our shoes; standing up, we appreciate the shadows created by our pants' pleats. Some fabrics stimulate us auditorily: crisp crinoline, swishy satin, whispering cotton. Still other materials have distinctive odors. An important aspect of leather's aesthetic, for example, is its thick, inundating scent.

Especially significant is the way clothing provides tactile interaction, often missing in other dimensions of daily life. Consider the aesthetic differences produced by a stiff, constraining leather coat and a soft, yielding cashmere one. Depending on other garments, context, and interests, each could enter into a rewarding aesthetic experience. The leather coat affords a sense of security in its resistance to our movement, defiance of wind, and armor-like impenetrability to rain or snow. The cashmere coat feels luxurious, caressing our neck and clinging to our legs as we stride down the street. This contrast indicates how opposite qualities can be aesthetically valuable in the appropriate context. Clothing that constrains or resists us may be as aesthetically rewarding as more pliable attire.

The same is true of weight and weightlessness. The sense of touch is compound. In addition to the surface affects on our skin are proprioceptive influence on our muscles and joints. Clothing can be heavy, weightless, and anything in between. When the experience of weight reinforces the clothing's tactile qualities, unity is increased. A dense, wool suit or coat which never lets us forget its presence can be coarse-textured so that we feel as if we are moving within a malleable shell. On the other hand, lack of pressure on our muscles can combine with gossamer surface sensations to create an easy, carefree quality, as in a lightweight silk outfit.

Forgetting what we are wearing or ever mindful of our garb--each can produce a valuable aesthetic of interaction. Still another possibility is contrast between surface tactility and proprioceptive pressure. For example, a slightly rough or scratchy cotton that is nonetheless weightless creates a disparity between surface awareness and muscle serenity.

Conversely, a heavy but smooth sweater exerts pressure but with little stimulation of the skin.

When movement is involved, proprioceptive stimulation can translate into kinesthetic sensation as the clothing's pressure deepens our awareness of movement and bodily position. In the case of the light, airy outfit mentioned above, kinesthetic awareness is provided solely by our bodies. Heavier garments can supplement our sense of bodily movement. This kinesthesia can be general or localized in a body part or region. For example, walking in heavy boots through the snow, but wearing a lightweight, insulating jacket and cap, we may feel as though our head and torso are floating above our earthbound, hard-working feet and legs. Such contrasting sensations occurring simultaneously can add complexity to the aesthetic enjoyment of interacting with our clothing.

Sometimes when we move, our clothing moves against us--a winter coat flapping against our legs as we walk. The rhythm of the repeated, regular pressure provides a steady foundation on which transitory melodies of sight, sound, and smell may play. Some people enjoy the way a voluminous blouse or robe billows and wafts about them as they move, only to envelop them gently when they sit. This alternation also sets up a unifying rhythm, and even though we may not be aware of it, such rhythms inform our aesthetic attraction for certain garments and their combination.

Think of the feel of being snugly hugged by a wool watch cap. Its mild tightness and the warmth it contains is so different from the feathery feel of a barely noticeable Panama. The Panama's brim casts a cool shadow over our face and varies its pressure on our head as the wind catches it. Tactile cues such as the feel of a crease against arm or leg, the crispness of a starched shirt, or the constriction of elasticized undergarments punctuate our aesthetic interaction with clothing.

As several of the examples discussed indicate, the experience of wearing clothing occurs within our interaction with the environment. The clothing we wear often shapes this interaction, fostering or hindering aesthetic experience.

4. From the standpoint of fashion and wardrobe selection, how clothing looks by itself and on us is paramount. But for the aesthetic of everyday life, our interaction with and by means

of our attire is more central. Where the look of clothing is what most of us think about when considering its aesthetic features, how clothing facilitates our interaction with the world probably has a more pervasive impact on our lives. To consider this, we must take into account context, activity, and function. This way of looking at the aesthetic of clothing situates us and our attire in the world: indoors and out, in rain or shine, at work and play.

We interact with the world by means of our clothing, but not the world in the abstract. Rather, we interact with a portion of it, for this or that purpose. We shouldn't expect the same aesthetic experience from an evening dress as from a bathing suit, just as we don't expect the same aesthetic delight from a night dining and dancing as a day spent at the shore. Our expectations of clothing must be tailored to the context and situation: the season and time of day, whether we are outdoors or inside, engaged in strenuous or relaxing activity.

Obviously, this subject is vast, as vast as all the possible contexts and purposes people can have. To narrow the discussion, let's consider the extremes of foot and head, each critical to whether our interaction with the environment is as aesthetically rewarding as it could be. Depending on ground surface, for instance, one kind of shoe will promote aesthetic experience and another will not. Hiking boots will probably inhibit our cutting a fancy figure at the dance, but ballroom footwear won't enable us to negotiate rocky hills or the wet forest floor.

Generalizing from this example, we see that footwear is essential to any activity in which locomotion is required. Different shoes facilitate different movements and so vary with context in their ability to promote aesthetic experience. By moving easily, at the dance or on the hike, we can enjoy the aesthetic of our bodies in motion--the rhythm of dancing, or walking and climbing. Ease in motion also enables sensory exploration of the environment which in turn frees our imagination and thinking to contribute aesthetically to our experience. Difficulty in movement, on the other hand, restricts the range of bodily aesthetic and sensory awareness. Imaginative and cognitive capacities are consequently muffled.

Wearing a broad-brimmed, beaver Stetson is ideal for walking in cool (but not frigid) weather during mild precipitation such as snow or drizzle. The material provides warmth and the brim shelters us from the precipitation. But for bicycling, the Stetson is unwieldy, its brim creating unwanted lift. In this context, a cap with protective bill enables appreciation of the bicycle's and our body's movement, as well as the environs of town or country. Not worrying about losing our hat, not being distracted by its wayward tugs, we can pay attention to the areas of experience with the greatest aesthetic potential.

What we wear on our head is important because it is the site of so much sensory input. Comfort and protection facilitate aesthetic perception. Preventing unwanted intrusions on our senses and thoughts, appropriate headgear promotes aesthetic appreciation of the environment and our movement through it.

Examples of movement underscore that aspect of aesthetic unity involving a balance between being active and receptive, what Dewey calls a synthesis of "doing" and "undergoing". "It is not just doing and undergoing in alternation, but consists of them in relationship" (Dewey, p.44). When balanced, our active doing is a response to what we perceptually undergo or take in. Similarly, our perceptual field is conditioned by what we do--the physical, mental, or imaginative effort we make. "Perception is an act of the going-out of energy in order to receive" (Dewey, p.53).

Too often our lives are characterized by excessive doing, as in performing household tasks like cleaning, or undergoing, as in passively listening to a lecture. Experience is more complete when we are both active and receptive, as in a good conversation or teamwork in a sport. On such occasions, what we say or do is a response to our perception of what others' are saying or doing; and our perception itself is governed by the possibilities of our anticipated participation.

Appropriate clothing furthers this balance of doing and undergoing in our interaction with the environment. Protective, insulating attire can enable us to explore freely what can be a forbidding winter evening. The simple activity of walking (doing) creates the audible crunch (undergoing) which in turn suggests variation in gait, pace, or direction. Because our head is protected, we are encouraged to leave the shelter of trees and look at the descending flakes sparkle in the lamplight, the perception of which leads us to seek out the moon. Perceiving its muted, milky light in turn prompts us to imagine other possibilities of movement and perception.

Clothing's capacity to further the harmonizing of our activity (doing) with receptivity (undergoing) is dramatic in sports. Goggles and bathing cap, for example, enable us to see underwater. Perceiving something of interest or danger leads to the necessary movement which consequently reveals new perceptual opportunities. Even swimming in the relatively drab environment of an indoor pool is enhanced by cap and goggles.

Undistracted by tearing eyes, blurred vision, or seaweed-like hair, how we move our arms, legs, and head can be a response to kinesthetic perception. We can pay closer attention to the sound of our breathing and the texture of the water gliding over our bodies. Changing our stroke (doing) from breast to butterfly, for example, changes our visual-auditory-kinesthetic perception (undergoing) from steady-hushed-smooth to bobbing-thumping-jerky. Perception of the new visual-auditory-kinesthetic field can then alter our tempo, pace, or subsequent stroke selection.

In the best experience, appearance and use (form and function) reinforce each other's aesthetic impact. Improving the look of a garment can enhance its aesthetic function as we interact with our environment. For example, venting a skirt or jacket adds line, movement, and shadow to the garment, thereby making it more aesthetically complex. The venting may also enable us to move more freely which can contribute to the spontaneity with which we engage our surroundings.

Designing for greater function can also contribute to the aesthetic quality of the clothing's appearance on us. A muffler or scarf provides protection and warmth in cold weather by covering up an otherwise exposed area at the throat. But its color and texture can complement or accent the color and texture of our overcoat. Woven shoes not only keep our feet cool by circulating air, they also add texture and line to the rest of an ensemble.

Of course, mutuality in the aesthetic of form and function is not always possible and one may have to be sacrificed to heighten the other's aesthetic. Too often, however, we assume this sacrifice is necessary, and give up looking for ways of promoting aesthetic partnership.

Clothing can promote or limit the complexity, unity, and intensity of our interaction with the environment. By encouraging free exploration, the opportunity for variety in sensory and imaginative experience is increased. When clothing facilitates a balance between doing and undergoing, our relationship with the world is more unified. Protected, able to move, feeling a comfortable weight and temperature, we are more likely to have an experience that fills out into a definite mood or character: an exhilarating bicycle ride; a tranquil saunter in the woods; a frivolous sprint and splash in the sea; a serious, invigorating conversation on the front porch.

Ideally, each level of aesthetic appreciation encompasses the others. Our aesthetically enriched interaction with the environment includes aesthetic interaction with our attire in which we look good and which looks good by itself! Admittedly, this might be an ideal to be striven for, rarely achieved. At which level the sacrifice should occur will depend on priorities and, again, context. When we are making a public speech, then perhaps a little discomfort is a small price for looking our best. But if we are on safari or just gardening, then how we interact with our clothes, and by means of them with our environment, might matter more than how we look.

5. The discussion has moved to increasingly larger contexts or wholes within which the aesthetic parts become more varied. In a single garment, viewed abstractly, independent of someone wearing it, its parts are pattern, texture, color, shape, style, volume, and the like. Viewed as worn, the human body, or this particular one, is an additional visual element. When we are wearing and not merely viewing clothing, sensory interaction with our attire creates a wider aesthetic field. And when we consider our interaction with clothing as part of involvement with the environment, the aesthetic whole has grown still greater. At each successive level, new elements become parts of aesthetic experience: human form, sensory interaction with clothing, interaction with environment by means of clothing.

Some cultural differences in aesthetic appreciation of clothing may be due to differences in context and activity. Instead of simply looking at a garment in isolation from use, we may have to see it in action in order to appreciate the aesthetic experience it makes possible. The plain white burnoose may be the best garment for a desert aesthetic: reflecting sun, allowing circulation of air, not restricting bodily movement. To appreciate the joys of snowmobiling, or simply shoveling a walkway, a one-piece, thermal suit is appropriate. Yet the aesthetic of burnoose and thermal suit apart from function is probably of minimal interest.

Clothing is like architecture. Both are so much a part of our daily lives that we easily miss their aesthetic impact on how we live. We tend instead to focus on how clothing and buildings look in abstraction from use. Like architecture, clothing is at its best when it aesthetically weds appearance and function. But function is here understood as including the aesthetic: functioning so as to enable and enhance our aesthetic interaction with the world.

References

Beardsely, M. (1958). *Aesthetics*. New York: Harcourt, Brace and World.

Benson, J. (1967). Emotion and Expression. *Philosophical Review*, 76.

Bosanquet, B. (1915). *Three Lectures on Aesthetics*. New York: Macmillan.

Casey, E. (1971). Expression and Communication in Art. *Journal of Aesthetics and Art Criticism*, 29.

Dewey, J. (1934). *Art as Experience*. New York: Capricorn.

Hungerland, I. (1944). *Journal of Aesthetics and Art Criticism*, 3.

Kupfer, J. (1983). *Experience as Art*. Albany, N.Y.: SUNY.

Stevenson, C. (1969). Symbolism in the Non-Representational Arts. In J. Hospers (Ed.), *Introductory Readings in Aesthetics* (pp. 185-209). New York: Free Press.

Tolstoy, L. (1925). *What is Art?* London: Oxford University Press.

Weitz, M. (1954). Symbolism and Art. *Review of Metaphysics*, 7.

From Wealth to Sensuality:
The Changing Meaning of Velvet 1910-1939

Hazel Lutz
University of Minnesota

Theoretical Background

Scholars of the history of dress have long held that clothing style expresses the spirit of an era. The discipline of material culture asserts that artifacts embed aspects of their maker's culture--beliefs, values, ideas, attitudes and assumptions--and these can be discovered through systematic study of the physical attributes of individual artifacts (Prown, 1982). The analysis of garment design requires detailed scientific observation of the interaction between garment, body of wearer, and context of use (DeLong, 1987).

Forms of dress that are cut and sewn from pre-constructed fabric constitute a complex type of material artifact. The pre-constructed fabric is itself a material artifact embedding culture. In the cut and sewn garment cultural meanings originating in past use of the particular type of fabric are viewed and manipulated in the context of the present. By creating, wearing, observing or commenting upon new garments constructed of preexisting types of fabric new meanings combine with and alter earlier meanings through the medium of the garment and are transmitted into the future.

The wearer and the observer of the wearer of garments are recognized as people who move and interact rather than remain stationary, as in a fashion plate. Additionally, the wearer and observer experience each other and the garments through several senses at a time, not through sight alone (Eicher and Roach-Higgins, 1992).[1] Consideration of the feel, sound, and sight of garments (and less frequently relevant, smell and taste) raises the issue of sensuality,

which is often misconstrued as sexuality or eroticism.

Historically changing conventions of garment forms reflect and influence a changing perception and experience of the human body (Hollander, 1978). Yet the interpretation of sexuality strictly on the basis of garment form is fraught with peril (Steele, 1989) and does not constitute the focus of this paper.[2] Following Banner (1983) I distinguish "public sensuality" from "private sexuality". A wearer's or observer's sensory experience of a garment does not necessarily imply private sexual behavior. Nevertheless in colloquial expression, garments can be conceived, perceived or described as *sexy* without implying sexual behavior by the wearer or the observer.

Discovery of the meaning of a textile occurs in several stages of systematic observation and analysis. First, the physical properties of the textile, and then its utilization in garments are examined. Next interaction of the textile in its garment forms with the wearer and observer in the context of its historical use is analyzed. Placement of textile, garment, wearer and observer within historically appropriate events requires the study of historical sources of information outside the garments themselves.

The present study of velvet garments in the costume collection of the Goldstein Gallery, University of Minnesota, adapts material culture and aesthetics of dress methodologies with a motion-oriented and multi-sensory appreciation of the experience of wearing or observing garments to understand the shift in meaning of velvet during the period 1910-1939, elucidating a chapter in the cultural history of the use of velvet.

History of Velvet

Supplementary weft and supplementary warp pile fabrics have been dated to second century BC Egypt and ninth century AD France, respectively (Harris, 1993; Wilson, 1979). The Italian Renaissance is credited with the first memorable velvets. Because its weaving re-

Preparation of this article grew out of my graduate studies in the Department of Design, Housing & Apparel at the University of Minnesota.

I gratefully acknowledge the encouragement of Dr. Marilyn DeLong, the assistance of the Director and Staff of the Goldstein Gallery, and the careful comments of two anonymous reviewers on drafts of this article.

Garment illustrations were generously provided by Holly Ryan.

quired great amounts of yarn and time, velvet production early occurred within the social context of religious and political institutions and personages. The association of this weaving technique with wealth naturally called for utilization of the yarn of the wealthy--silk.[3] Rich fabrics of extreme intricacy were woven of silk, and in combinations of silk with other fibers or precious metals and jewels, in the centers of power in southern Europe, northern Africa, Asia Minor and India through many centuries. Historical velvets are extremely complex, combining areas of ground cloth with areas of velvet pile (voided velvets), employing different cut and/or uncut pile heights (cisele and pile-on-pile), combining voided velvet with gold brocade grounds, and employing different colored yarns for different decorative motifs in ground and pile areas.[4] These rich fabrics were used to dress the bodies and homes of the aristocracy and were also used in association with religious rites and institutions (Dhamija, 1989; Harris, 1993; Latour, 1953; Smart & Gluckman, n.d.; Wilson, 1979).

The rejection of class privilege during the French Revolution led to a long abandonment of velvet for garment use, due to its undemocratic association, in French society and other Western societies strongly influenced by French fashion in clothing. Celebrations of the highest ceremonies of state and religion were the exception, as for example the dressing of heads of state and their families for public ceremonies. After the middle of the l9th century velvet sporadically reappeared in the dress of the wealthy classes but it most commonly appeared in women's dress in the form of ribbon and trim, contributing touches of luxury and importance to a garment or hair arrangement.

Mechanization of velvet production came late in the industrial revolution.[5] Industrially produced velvets nevertheless continued to utilize more time and yarn than the production of other forms of cloth, maintaining velvet's relatively expensive character. Production of complex velvets continued to employ many unmechanized production methods until well into the 20th century.

The invention and perfection of rayon technologies over several decades around the turn of the century facilitated the creation of less expensive velvets (Kauffman, 1993; Raheel, 1993; Summers et al, 1993). In the 1930s rayon yarns were being used interchangeably with silk yarns in all relevant areas of weaving (Russell, 1983).

The convergence of mechanized weaving and less expensive fibers in the early decades of the 20th century set the stage for the re-emergence of velvet as an important primary garment fabric in contrast to its familiar use as trim fabric. The wearing of ornate silk velvets played a significant role among the new American "aristocracy" in the enjoyment and display of wealth accumulated in the years before creation of the progressive income tax. With the stock market crash and onset of economic depression in the 1930s less expensive rayon facilitated the continued spread of velvet utilization in dress to a broader sector of the population.

Analysis of the Garments

I examined approximately 300 garment ensembles, many consisting of two and three pieces, and dating between 1890 and 1950. The garments included dresses, wedding dresses, slips, jackets, coats, capes, lounge wear and accessories. Many were trimmed with velvet. All garments within this period found to be constructed primarily or entirely of velvet were selected for detailed observation. They numbered seventy-nine, of which only twelve fell outside the three decades 1910-1939. Additionally I selected a few lace and other transparent fabric garments of the same three decades for close examination because they represented prevalent styles concurrent with the velvet garments; they were also trimmed with velvet ribbon. The earliest of the selected garments was dated 1890-1910 and the latest, 1940-49.

I began the garment analysis with a focus on the physical properties of the textile, garment design, and garment interface with the body both at rest and in motion. I examined the garments one at a time in approximate chronological order, treating ensembles both as integrated wholes and as separates. The garments were placed on hangers and laid and manipulated on a table to facilitate observation. Unusual garments were placed on a mannequin to aid examination. I relied upon my experience as fitter and seamstress/tailor to understand issues of body fit and textile drape in various layouts. Periodically stopping to review observations I recorded in notes, sketches and memory, I discovered repetitions and gradual shifts in design characteristics.

The interpretation of meaning of the garments rests on an understanding of their context of use gained from historical study. While mentally placing each garment in the context of use, I asked a series of questions of each garment. How did the design characteristics of the garment affect the historical wearer's experience of self and the historical observer's experience of the wearer? How did the garment relate to the situation in which it was worn? What undergarments were worn? How did the design characteristics of each garment relate to the characteristics employed elsewhere in the collection of garments? Patterns in the answers to these questions led to an understanding of the meaning of fashion eras which the garments represent.

Design Characteristics in Context

Velvet. The use of velvet itself as the fabric out of which a garment is mainly or solely constructed constitutes the central focus of this project. By means of its pile and nap velvet adds both visual and tactile texture to a garment. Texture experienced through touch was important in an era when social dancing was becoming extremely popular.

A social dance revolution was underway in the United States at the beginning of the 20th century. Buckman (1978) reports ". . . around 1914, the Maxixe was the third most popular dance after the One-Step and the Hesitation Waltz (as performed by the Castles), which just goes to show how wide was the range of dances in vogue at any one time" (pp. 170-171). The Waltz and Tango, and from the 1920s the Foxtrot, remained staples of the dance floor (Coll & Rosiere, 1922; Ballwebber, 1938; Hostetler, 1930, 1942). These were joined by a constant stream of new Latin dances. The Maxixe, various Tangos, the Rumba and the Samba succeeded each other in popularity between 1910 and 1939. They were always perceived as sensual in character, though the definition of sensual varied over time. Pictures of dancing couples in dance instruction books published in the early 1910s as well as the later 1930s depict men and women in new, sensuous dance positions (e.g., Castle and Castle, 1914; and Ray, 1932) and diagram or photograph "forbidden" dips (Malnig, 1992).

Between 1912 and 1915 dancing took the new form of afternoon teas. Professional dance team Irene and Vernon Castle promoted the afternoon format in order to counter criticisms of the debauched character of the new dances (Malnig, 1992).

Contemporary observers noted a strong relationship between the physical activity of dancing and the direction of fashion in women's clothing.

> The increased number of society dances in the United States alone during the past year, has resulted in an enormous development in the silk trade. The silk dresses required for "Tango Teas" have been responsible for many million more yards of silk than were ever before imported into that country. . . . The modern fashion in dress and hats has been largely modified and even dictated by "Tango Teas." Small close hats, and a simple compact style of hair dressing, a close-fitting skirt, and loose-fitting blouse, with conspicuously neat shoes and stockings, have become universal at those dances. (Urlin, 1914, pp. 172-173)

> Dancing has had it's influence upon the materials that have come into vogue. . . . A stiff, heavy material looks awkward and makes harsh lines about the figure in the charming measures of the dance. In consequence there has arisen a tremendous demand for soft crepes de Chine, *chiffon velvets* [italics added], delicate crepe deteors, and the softest and most supple of taffetas, which are at the moment the most fashionable of all. (Castle and Castle, 1914, p. 146)

In addition to the important tactile texture of velvet, visual texture was created by the interplay of light with the pile and nap of velvets, by the manner that light was absorbed or reflected. Alternately the ability of velvet pile to absorb light could be used, by planning for the effects of nap, to produce garments that nearly completely obliterated surface visual texture. Such garments provided a strong visual silhouette and focused attention on those uncovered parts of the wearer that reflect more light and thus become visible (see Figure 1). Black velvet garments of this design encouraged the observer to move in closer in order to better see the hidden surface detail. Possibilities for manipulating the relationships among light, pile and nap became important as the Hollywood film industry grew.

Figure 1. Black velvet ensemble of jacket, dress and scarf, Goldstein Gallery acquisition #59.002.016 a, b & c, ca. 1930-39. (This illustration and all others by Holly Ryan.) Black solid velvet scarf [not shown] and jacket are lined with *nude* fabric. Jacket: note continuous line created by circular-cut collar-cum-edge ruffles; nude lining of jacket and ruffle occasionally becomes visible with wearer's movement. Dress: note V-neck openings, front and back; gathered fit separating the two breasts; and nearly floor length skirt with train. Scarf: when worn around the neck the scarf adds to the confusion of patches of bare skin and nude lining.

Velvet also contributed physical weight to a garment. Increased physical weight altered the way garments interacted with the moving body of the wearer. The manner in which physical weight interacted with specific design characteristics will be described in subsequent sections of this paper.

The importance of velvet's historical association with wealth, luxury, royalty, the divine right of kings, ecclesiastical robes and spiritual power lent a strong presence to a garment that is aptly described as historical weight. This importance facilitated the creation of very brief garments in the 1920s "flapper" era, by justifying the radical new exposure of female limbs.

Figure 2. Navy and beige printed solid velvet dress, Goldstein Gallery acquisition #83.050.003 a & b, ca. 1920-1929. (This photograph and all others by author.) Coordinating trim of plain navy velvet and beige plain weave silk fabrics. Note pleated jabot dividing breasts. Slightly gathered emphasis on hips does not extend around the back; it focuses on the front pelvic area with beige lined velvet ties formed into a bow. Pleated velvet skirt is mid-calf length. Strong shadows against the background indicate the intensity of lighting necessary to enable viewers to see the detail of dark velvet garments.

Color and Surface Pattern. The advent of velvets in the 1910s is marked by a broad range of color and surface pattern innovations. The

Table 1. Distribution of Surface Design Characteristics of Velvet.*

| | 1910s | | | 1920s | | | 1930s | | |
	dresses		coats & capes	dresses		coats & capes	dresses		coats & capes
Textile Characteristics**									
Black Color	1	17%	0	4	27%	7	53%	10	45%	5	63%
Other Colors	5	83%	3	100%	11	73%	6	46%	12	55%	3	37%
Pattern in Pile or Color	2	33%	1	33%	6	40%	0		8	36%	0	
Voided Pile	1	17%	0	5	33%	0		6	27%	0	

*Presented in real numbers and percentages by decade.
**While Black Color and Other Colors are mutually exclusive categories, relationships with and among the remaining categories are not mutually exclusive. For example, a predominantly navy dress may also be patterned with multi-colored small voided pile flowers.

new velvets appeared in several light and bright colors as well as dark colors, in multi-colored patterns (see Figures 2 and 3), and with patterns imprinted in gold and silver (see Figure 4). This trend broadened in the 1920s and was strengthened by another innovation, the creation of voided velvet pattern on transparent ground weaves. The new weaves often also combined the pattern of voided pile with the pattern of multiple colors. Color variation in both plain and patterned velvets occurred along the three dimensions of hue, value and chroma.

The new velvets continued in popularity into the 1930s, but slowly gave way to the use of darker colored and black solid velvets in dresses as well as the long popular use of dark colors in coats and capes. The number of multi-colored velvets decreased and generally grew darker as the 1930s progressed. Patterned voided velvets also decreased in the 1930s and

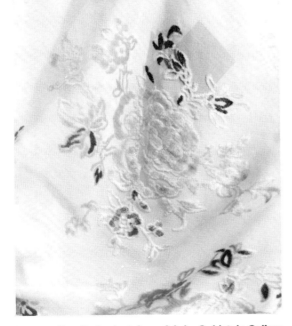

Figure 3. Detail of velvet dress fabric, Goldstein Gallery acquisition #81.014.015, ca. 1920-29. Light coral transparent ground weave with multi-colored voided pile floral pattern. The colors of the voided motifs are medium coral, yellow, beige, navy, and teal. The large blossom is four and one-quarter inches at its widest point. Note the visibility of a square piece of black paper through the transparent ground.

Figure 4. Detail of garment and fabric, Goldstein Gallery acquisition #81.003.038, ca. 1910-1920. Gold-printed pattern on muted light green solid velvet is edged with blanket stitch embroidery in teal and bears yellow glass-bead and looped-braid closures. The printed bird motif measures three and three-quarter inches high.

were replaced by plain solid velvets. (See Table 1.)

The darker velvets absorbed more light than they reflected and drew the observer's attention to the wearer's silhouette, where the body was covered, and to the exposed portions of the body when the wearer's skin color contrasted with the color of the unpatterned cloth. The focus on the curving silhouette and visible skin of arms, shoulders and back of the 1930s dresses matches well descriptions of the tenor of dances popular in that era. Of the original Cuban Rumba that inspired the American version Buckman wrote "to an insistent and arousing beat the woman performed sinuous movements of hip, trunk and shoulders, while the man did his best to respond" (1978, p. 197). Malnig described the Samba as "distinguished by its subtle undulations of the chest and lilting rising and falling motion of the body" (1992, p. 117). Appreciation of these dances was facilitated by garment designs that exposed portions of undulating torso and layout structures and fabrics that encouraged garments to cling to the surface of the covered areas of the wearer's body.

Though social dancing continued to play an important role in fashion, both through the social events themselves and their prevalent depiction in popular films of the 1920s and 1930s (Delamater, 1981; Parker & Siegel, 1978), it is the cinema itself that most affected color and pattern in velvets. The beauty of velvets patterned with voided pile or multi-colored designs did not show well through the medium of black-and-white film and could serve as obstacle to the communication of the story. Consideration for the camera's eye led to a preference for light reflecting fabrics like satin and the new rayon lingerie in which many actresses were filmed for boudoir scenes (Holt, 1988).

> It was very important that materials harmonize with the action of the scene. Often, the movement of a fabric was photographed even before the gown was made. If the director wanted the action to stand out, the dress could not be so striking that it competed with the action. If the gown was to stand out, the designer had to insure that the materials photographed to their best advantage. If the dress was to emphasize the action of a scene, it had to flow with it, or the design

had to reinforce a movement. (Bailey, 1982, p.45)

Color and pattern in many fabrics utilized in women's dress were influenced by these choices made in Hollywood.

Though velvet did not reflect as much light as satin, the nap and soft pile of plain solid velvets in combination with light or dark color and careful lighting were used to advantage by the film industry to indicate either the shapely form or curvaceous silhouette of an actress. Plain dark velvets were also used to create images of richness and importance.[6]

Red velvet was used in film costumes because it could communicate both form and silhouette through black-and-white film (Bailey, 1978, p. 50). Aside from black, of course, the viewing audience could not discern which dark color of velvet was being used in the movie costume. As a result of Hollywood's preferences, dark "jewel tones" and black displaced the lighter colors in velvet. Plain velvets also displaced patterned velvets by the end of the 1930s. Daytime use of velvet diminished and the black velvet evening dress became the predominant form in which velvet appeared in the Goldstein Gallery collection by the mid 1930s.

Ruffles and Falls. Many of the garments were characterized by ruffles or falls which hung loosely and freely from the body. They focused attention on the motions of the wearer by *echoing* and enlarging the wearer's every movement.

Four principle methods of construction were employed. Large straight-edged pieces were attached along vertical seams or edges or were attached at a single point, particularly on the sides of dresses where they fell from the hips. Pieces cut in circular shape were attached in straight lines or pieces cut in straight, on-grain shapes were attached in circular seams; both these latter methods created a bias fall of the fabric.

Narrow on-grain ruffles reacted to body movement more quickly than wide or bias ruffles. They were found only on the 1920s garments. This period was associated with the more frenetic social dances of Charleston, Black Bottom, Varsity Drag and Shimmy (Buckman, 1978, pp. 179-184). Wide ruffles appeared in the late 1920s and early 1930s. Falls in various shapes were found on garments of the late 1910s, throughout the 1920s, and into the early 1930s.

The long popularity of garment designs that magnified a wearer's movement occurred in the context of the previously described social dancing and a growing participation of women in active sports. A survey of the photographic and drawn images of women engaged in social dancing and sports pursuits in the articles and advertisements of *Vogue* magazine in the years 1910-1939 revealed a steady increase of depictions of physically active women. From a very few small images, under two inches in height, in the 1910s depictions of sports women in Vogue showed continued increase in size and number through three decades. Full-page images of physically active women and articles about actual sports women occurred in the 1930s. The inclusion of falls and ruffles on the garments that women wore indoors kept observers' attention focused on the physically active aspect of women even when they were not engaged in sports activity.

Interior Construction of Garments. The dresses were unlined and unboned. The matching or alternately *nude*-colored slips accompanying the voided velvet dresses were constructed of very light materials. Dress jackets were sometimes lined with a thin fabric, except when constructed of transparent fabric. Only one ensemble jacket from the early 1910s seemed bulky; it consisted of a blouse, jacket and skirt suitable for cold weather wear. Coats, alone, were padded and heavy, making up for the thinness of the garments underneath. Velvet linings added bulk, warmth and tactile pleasure to some of the coats.

The lack of boning and padding and the thinness of the matching slip or jacket linings of the dress ensembles allowed the outer dress fabric to lie as close to the wearer's skin as the undergarments would allow. Though undergarments were still substantial and numerous in 1910, by the early 1920s they had lightened considerably and continued to do so though the 1930s (Boehlke, in press; Cunnington and Willett, 1981). Hollywood films helped promote the new lighter underwear by setting many scenes in private areas of homes or otherwise contriving to show actresses in states of semi-dress (Holt, 1988).

A survey of advertisements and articles in *Vogue* magazines published between 1910 and 1939 showed a continued decrease in the boning and closure complexity of foundation garments. Also reduction in the number of undergarments worn together occurred through the development of simpler "combination" undergarments.

The lightening of corset bones began early in the 1910s for some individuals. In 1914 Irene Castle wrote

> but all these precautions as to the outward gowning are wasted if you continue to wear the long, stiff corsets decreed by fashion when she dismissed our hips and other curves. No amount of grace, no amount of clever training, and no amount of the knowledge of the most intricate steps will help you to dance charmingly unless your corset has "give" to it and allows you to move with supple ease and comfort. Personally I use and recommend a special corset made almost entirely of *elastic* [italics added], very flexible and conforming absolutely to the figure, which at the same time it supports. It is known as the Castle Corset, and is designed especially for dancers. Many corsets are now being brought out, however, with elastic in place of whalebone; and the late word from Paris that we may again display a waist-line and hips allows even the fairly stout woman to don shorter and more comfortable "stays." (Castle and Castle, 1914, p. 142)

Bias Cut or Placement. Utilization of velvet on the bias was repeatedly employed to create several effects. In the 1930s garment layout in women's wear became especially complex for most fabrics (Collard, 1983). This complexity is seen in velvet dresses of the Goldstein Gallery collection in which pieces of cloth were cut to curve around the body to hang on grain in some areas and on bias in others. Unconstructed areas gave an impression of naturalness and simplicity while the bias contoured the garment to the curves of the body underneath. Prevalent use of black velvet in the 1930s meant that grain and layout were often indiscernible and the observer was left only with the impression of the curving silhouette or a need to move closer to the wearer in order to better see the garment detail.

Garments cut on the bias also hugged and revealed the shape of the body underneath, especially breasts, abdomen, hips, and thighs, creating a sensual mood. The clinging nature of the bias fabric was exaggerated by the weight of velvet. It was also facilitated by the absence of outer garment boning or lining. Simplification of undergarments intervening between outer garment cloth and wearer's body enabled the velvet fabric of bias layout dresses to lie closer to and reveal the shape of the wearer's body.

Some of the ruffles, falls, gathered skirts and draped areas were also created on the bias, both in the 1920s and '30s. They moved in a more languid manner than similar designs constructed of lighter, on-grain, fabrics. The interaction of velvet pile weight with the stretch of bias draping caused fabric reaction to the wearer's movements to be delayed. It also caused the fabric's reactive movement to stretch out over a longer period of time. Together, these fabric movements created a relaxed mood, particularly in the 1930s when bias was utilized most frequently.

Exposure of Body Extremities. A slight raising of the hem in the narrow skirts of the 1910s gave increased freedom of movement when associated with openings in the bottoms of skirt seams. In the earliest versions these openings revealed undergarments rather than areas of the body, if we are to judge by Irene Castle's prescriptions.

> Therefore, while fashion decrees the narrow skirt, the really enthusiastic dancer will adopt the plaited one. A clever woman may, however, combine the two by the use of a split skirt, carefully draped to hide the split, and a plaited petticoat underneath. Thus when she dances the skirt will give and not form awkward, strained lines, and the soft petticoat, fluffing out, will lend a charming grace to the dancer's postures. The openings in a skirt of this sort can be fastened with tiny glove-snaps, so that on the street the wearer may appear to have the usual narrow costume, while at the same time she has a practical one for the daily *the dansant*. (Castle and Castle, 1914, pp. 139-140)

When hemlines reached their highest point in the garments of the 1920s, legs were covered only by stockings and arms were completely freed for evening wear by the removal of sleeves in the flapper dresses.

The new solo dances popular in the 1920s enabled women to dance whether or not they had been invited to do so and these dances made full use of the new mobility afforded arms and legs. The Charleston, in fact, appears to be a celebration of women's freedom to move extremities. The increasing physical activity of women's bodies was both facilitated and made visible by the garments. This brought women's new physical activity levels to the fore of consciousness of observers and wearers alike.

Open necklines characterized garments in the 1920s and this was expanded in the 1930s to include both front and back scoop as well as V-shaped necklines. Exposure of the back extended to the waistline in some dresses. Radical exposure of the back took some attention away from the front, but front necklines were also low. Exposure of low back and low front necklines, particularly in garments that included both features, may have slowed movement due to the manner in which such clothes made their wearers ever conscious of their clothing's potential to slip from a shoulder. One such garment in the collection was altered to prevent such a mishap; the back bias-draped scoop neckline was seamed up the middle to reduce the size of the opening. The back exposure of the garments of the 1930s works with the longer hemlines and trains to slow down the quick movements of the 1920s to a more languid pace.

Transparency. See-through fabrics were employed in two manners, both revealing the arms, neck, shoulders (down to the upper bosom in front), and back (down as far as the waist). In the 1920s and 1930s voided velvet woven on a transparent ground (see Figure 3) was used to construct entire garments. A matching under-slip completed the ensemble to cover the middle and lower torso and thighs (see Figure 5). In some cases the slips were created in nude or similar colors raising, in the case of light-skinned wearers, questions in the mind of observers regarding degree of body coverage. The same teasing occurred whenever the transparent garment and matching slip

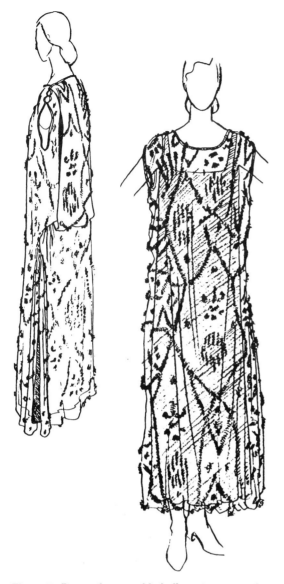

Figure 5. Dress of navy voided pile on transparent ground (two views), Goldstein Gallery acquisition #81.003.033 a & b, ca. 1920-29. Note open neckline, exposure of arms, ankle-length hem, key-hole openings on shoulder, back surplice opening from both sides, droop at dropped waistline (back only), side opening of skirt from hip to hemline, suggestion of fall, and coordinating navy slip. The pile is five-sixteenths (more than one-quarter!) inch high and forms bold patterns that are placed asymmetrically on the garment. Pattern repeat measures 26 inches in length and 11 inches in width.

color approximated that of the skin of the wearer.

In the 1930s transparent fabrics were combined with velvet in strategic locations in the garments to expose selected body parts, usu-

ally arms, shoulders or back. Though lace and netting had long been used in women's clothing in this manner, these see-through fabrics had usually revealed layers of undergarments. In the 1930s transparent fabrics revealed bare skin. One garment from the 1910s showed the transition from the earlier use of transparency by combining a deep V-shaped net inset plunging to front mid-torso with the new multi-colored velvet fabric. Fabric transparency brought consciousness of women's bodies to the fore and in association with teasing turned this awareness into an anticipatory tension akin to sexual stimulation.

Peekaboo. Several methods of construction created the effect of suddenly, quite casually revealing areas of the body and then covering them up again. In one type of design the lower portions of seams in skirts, in tiered ruffles, and in sleeves remained open and periodically exposed parts of the wearer's body as she moved. In the 1910s the garment openings were more likely to reveal undergarments than skin, but the character of these undergarments could vary considerably.

> Of course it is dancing that has made the vogue for the charming plaited petticoats of chiffon edged with lace to wear under the dance-frock or the slit skirt, because without these the foot and ankle are shown too much. It is dancing, too, that has made the vogue for the new garters, with their deep lace ruffles, and the little lace pantalets--all to hide those slender ankles that show in the dip. (Castle and Castle, 1914, p. 147)

Elsewhere the Castles decry "dark stockings showing through a filmy petticoat and a split skirt" (Castle and Castle, 1914, p. 140). Such proscription would not have been necessary unless the behavior was frequently practiced.

By the 1920s undergarments were significantly lighter and nude stockings were coming into fashion (Holt, 1988). Slips made especially for garments of revealing design or fabric were camouflaged to match either outer garment or wearer's skin color. Such underwear left observers with doubts about the extent of undergarment coverage when necklines and armholes gaped open so easily. Alternately, the new brightly colored underwear of the 1920s (Holt, 1988) would boldly announce their character even if only a momentary glimpse of them was afforded by gaping openings in outer garments. By the end of the decade undergarment coverage of the body surface had diminished considerably, just panties and brassiere sufficing (Cunnington and Willett, 1981).

Peekaboo designs over the briefer 1930s undergarments revealed a lot of bare skin. Cross-draped, deep V-shaped back closures often revealed more than they covered. Bias-cut, classic-draped scoop necklines also fulfilled a promise to reveal more of a bosom at the motion of the wearer. When deep open necklines were coupled with deep open backs, the shoulders of a dress became very unstable, potentially revealing more of the body than the wearer may have wished. However, the wearer's next movement could bring back under cover what had just been revealed.

A more sedate version of peekaboo is constructed of overlapped garment closures, most prevalent in the 1910s and early '20s, and openings in the lower portion of seams in sleeves, skirts, skirt tiers and ruffles which occurred through all three decades. Such garments were lined with coordinating under-slips. While these garments may fail to actually reveal any additional undergarment or part of the body, they presented the possibility of such revelations to the wearer and the observer.

An equally illusory, but startling, peekaboo design utilized nude colored non-velvet fabrics to line jackets or trim dresses of black velvet ensembles (see Figure 1). Working in concert with the color of a light-skinned wearer, the nude trim and lining could give a momentary impression that private areas of the body are being revealed as the jacket swung open or a ruffle with nude lining outwardly turned.

Increasingly through all three decades various forms of real and illusory openings in garments encouraged observers to become more acquainted with women's bodies. Observers were teased into a subtle anticipation that turned the tactile physical experience of velvet into a more sensual perception of the wearers of velvet garments. Whether sedate or startling, all these versions of peekaboo developed a sense of anticipation and drew attention to a woman's body. The observer was encouraged to look twice.

Droop. This characteristic was created by incorporating extra length or width of fabric into garment layout, securing the excess into relevant seams with pleats or gathers, and often providing a shorter or narrower attached lining

Figure 6. Bright Goldenrod Yellow solid velvet wedding dress, Goldstein Gallery acquisition #91.059.063 a, ca. 1916-1923. Note open neckline, classic drape, front and back surplice with overlapped openings at sides and center front, inner front bodice of cloth of gold, droop of outer folded skirt hem line, beaded medallions with bead fringe at sides of inner hem line, and gold net fall at back left hip.

114

By mimicking the muscles of the body at rest or the rolls of fat of a well-fed person, droop alluded to relaxation, indolence, abundance, and luxury. By mimicking the relaxed fall of sexual organs (breasts and testicles) droop brought to mind sexual associations.

Train. Several of the velvet garments exhibited short or long trains, a characteristic that drew upon historical associations with wealth, royalty and formal occasions. When designed into solid velvet, unlined garment trains had the effect of pulling the garment a little more taut across the abdomen, hips and thighs as the wearer walked, further revealing the body's form. Additionally the power of the body was exaggerated when bended knee and thigh distended the fabric of the skirt as the wearer walked.

The velvet train emphasized the process and direction of movement of the wearer by providing evidence of where the wearer had just been. The movement of the train provided an echo of the directional movement of the wearer. Velvet trains heightened an observer's awareness of the wearer's body form and activity.

The wearer, too, became more aware of her movement as she dealt with the cumbersome skirt. Her movement had to be calculated in order to avoid tripping on or ripping her train by any sudden change of direction. Velvet trains slowed down movement and made it more deliberate.

Unlike trains constructed of lighter fabrics, voided and solid velvet trains remained on the ground and did not float. In effect, velvet trains visually grounded wearers in their environments and associated wearers with basic and powerful things like the earth and nature.

Drape. This characteristic consisted in the gathering of extra width or length of fabric and attaching it so that it fell in loose parallel folds around or down from the body in a manner recalling classical Greek and Roman statues of important historical figures, gods, and goddesses (see Figure 6). Draped velvet called upon the power of long-standing tradition, history and religion to contribute importance to garments. It also contributed physical weight. The inclusion of drape in these garments justified the new activity levels and exposure of the female body and the generalized sensuality of

Figure 7. Bright Turquoise solid velvet coat (two views), Goldstein Gallery acquisition #77.047.003, ca. 1920-1935. Note the rich white fur collar, drooping lower sleeves and drooping dropped waist across the back.

or interior banding to hold the outer garment in a position that permitted it to fill out and droop. The attached lining or band prevented this droop from providing any extra ease of movement. Thus the droop design characteristic did not facilitate increased physical mobility; it conveyed a meaning visually. Droop was found in great exaggeration in garment areas such as a skirt hemline (see Figure 6) or cuffless sleeves of a coat (see Figure 7). It was extremely common among the garments studied in the form of subtle blousing associated with the dropped waistlines of the 1920s (see Figures 5 and 7).

the garments and their wearers. Drape was used in garments in all three decades.

Gathered Fit. This complex design characteristic consisted of areas of extra fabric simply gathered and stretched over an obtruding body part so that the fabric became tensed, drawing attention to that body part and its shape. In women's garments of the 1920s hips and the front pelvic area were the focus of this characteristic; often the extra gathered fabric that stretched over the hips ended in a tied knot or similar effect with fabric ends dangling over one hip or centrally over the lower pelvic region. In the 1930s gathered fit was used to draw attention to the breasts, notably bringing them out of the mono-bosom of preceding fashion eras and the flat chest of the 1920s to become separated into two distinct full entities (see Figure 1).

In the case of either breast or hip-and-pelvis emphasis, attention was being focused on body areas whose precise form or even location had remained hidden from public view. As the bosom became two breasts in the 1930s, bifurcated lower garments worn by women working in factories during the first World War (Ewing, 1992) and by Hollywood film actresses on and off the set in the 1930s also helped determine where a woman's crotch was located.

Overview of Garment Design Characteristics

The disparate meanings associated with the various design characteristics analyzed above, when unified within a garment or group of garments, often created a balanced tension between relaxation and the indolence of wealth on the one hand and physical activity and the stimulation associated with sensual arousal on the other. The gathered fit characteristic best exemplifies this balance by the way it conjoined opposites; relaxed, easing, gathered fabric encases active hips and stimulating full natural breasts.

The tension entailed in this concert of characteristics is one that the wearers of these garments had to live and resolve in their lives. Unencumbered by their clothes, women could become more active. They also found themselves more physically exposed. Physical and sexual boundaries that had previously been defined in part by the clothing now had to be defined and defended by the actions of the wearer.

A garment that initially seemed to have little to relate it to its contemporaries fits exceptionally well into its era when viewed in the light of the above analysis of the spirit of early 20th century fashion in women's dress, as revealed in the velvet garments in the Goldstein Gallery collection. A black, solid velvet one-piece, long-sleeved, full-length garment, soft and gathered at high neckline and waist, encouraged relaxation. Its nearly complete coverage of the body would seem to make a less overt sexual statement than its contemporaries which revealed much more of the body.

However, the bifurcated-leg design was risqué in its time and both drew attention to the wearer's crotch and associated her with the greater physical activity level of the trouser-dressed world of men. Rhinestone buttons and dangling drawstring tie front closures juggled references to both wealth and simplicity. They also boldly advertised how the garment might be opened if an observer were inclined to do so, making this a close ally of the peekaboo garments of the era. The formality of velvet and the dressiness of rhinestones also counterbalanced the leisure nature of the garment form, repeating the tension seen in garments analyzed above.

The prevalence of garments made entirely of transparent materials, contemporary to the velvet garments being analyzed herein, also makes sense in light of the above analysis of the spirit of the collection. In the late 1920s and early 1930s, for example, such transparent dresses were typically composed of yards of fabric arranged in voluminous skirts or masses of effusive ruffles which obscured the view of the body underneath promised by the transparent nature of the fabric. The skirts and ruffles exaggerated the movements of the wearer, giving her an even more active appearance than counterparts in velvet. The overall tenor of the garments remained within the meanings described for the velvet garments above and most importantly maintained a balanced tension, between the visible and the obscured body of the wearer, teasing the observer into arousal. The use of velvet and transparent fabrics together in this period, either side by side or within single garments, dramatized both the tactile pleasure of velvet and the visual excitement of viewing the female body.

The heavier velvet garments on the one hand and the busy transparent garments on the other employed different amounts of many of the same ingredients to create the same sense of wearer's presence. The transparent garments permit views of the body and greatly exaggerate the activity of the wearer so as to counterbalance the lightweight nature of the fabric. The velvet of the other garments contributes a greater weight and sensuality to garments that employ less cloth, may cover less of the body and give a more languid view of the wearer's activity.

The tension of meanings created in the velvet garments of the decades 1910-1939 occurred because new meanings were created on top of earlier meaning associated with the fabric. To a history of use by the rich, powerful, and important individuals of society, the 1910-1939 years contributed an association of velvet with women's bodies. First, as women's lives changed through participation in sports and social dancing, velvet was employed in designs that focused attention on and accentuated the rising activity levels. Then, with the increasing simplification of women's undergarments through three decades, and under the influence of the growing popularity of the black-and white film industry, plain colored solid velvet became associated with the surface, silhouette, and form of the female body. In this manner, velvet acquired a strong feminine character that was physically based and sensual. The earlier meaning of wealth and its associates--luxury, power, leisure, and indolence--interacted with the new meaning to create garment designs of sometimes exquisite tension, particularly in the 1930s as the feminine meaning grew strong. Thus sensual arousal intertwined with relaxed indolence by the 1930s in women's fashions in velvet garments.

Conclusions: A Cultural History of Velvet

The meaning of velvet, while sometimes attaching to specific physical characteristics of the fabric, such as weight and ability to absorb light, is always manipulated by the design of the garment into which the fabric is sewn or draped and interpreted in the context in which it is worn or viewed. It is not always possible when analyzing single garments to separate out the meanings of specific characteristics into physical activeness, sensual enjoyment, sexual stimulation, relaxation, indolence, wealth, and

enjoyment of luxury. The garments of the 1910s, '20s, and '30s interwove all these meanings, in varying proportions from one garment to the next, often using single design characteristics to refer to more than one meaning at a time. Moreover, there is hardly a garment in this period group that employs only a single design characteristic.

This analysis points out specifically, however, how velvet was utilized in the creation of complex meanings. Meanings that had become embedded in velvet through its history of use; its inherent physical properties of pile, nap, and weight; and applied physical characteristics of color and pattern were all utilized to design women's garments during 1910-1939.

Fashion in women's dress conversely redefined velvet as the fabric not only of wealth, luxury and power, but also the fabric of women and sensual enjoyment. The redefinition is most clearly seen in the changes through light and bright colors and complex patterned velvets to dark plain solid velvets. Velvets imprinted with gold, voided of pile to reveal textural patterns, or printed or woven in multiple colors gave way to monochromatic voided velvets, and finally to plain darker jewel tones and black solid velvets.

Redefinition was accomplished by alteration in the manner that the fabric related to the female body. Glimpses of first undergarments, later bare skin, afforded by peekaboo openings and transparent grounds of voided velvets teased and titillated both wearers and observers. Ruffles and falls in garment designs magnified the movements of women. Short-skirted, sleeveless, scoop-necked dresses afforded open views of areas of women's bodies not previously shown in public; moreover, they allowed observers to see what activity levels women's bodies could attain when unencumbered by restrictive, multi-layered clothing. Subsequent placement of plain solid velvet against the surface of women's bodies forged a closer association between body and fabric in the 1930s. Transformation in women's undergarments, popularity of social dancing and Hollywood films, and women's increasing participation in sports activities influenced velvet's redefinition.

Velvet was simultaneously feminized and sensualized. This occurred in an era when the boundary dividing public sensuality from private sexuality was shifting. Areas of women's bodies that had previously been designated as belonging to the private domain moved into the public domain where they could be enjoyed sensually. In the cultural shorthand of our contemporary era, velvet became *sexy* through association of its physically stimulating characteristics with the boundary-challenging garment designs of the 1910s, '20s and '30s. The forging of velvet's past significance with the new meaning developed by the velvet garments of these decades--an active sensuous femininity--produced a tension of meaning that has endowed these garment designs, particularly in the peak of that development in the 1930s, with a long standing power to hold the interest of observers of later generations.

Endnotes

[1] On the interplay of touch with sight in the experience of textiles, see Winakor, Chang, and Kim (1987).

[2] Analysis of sexuality in a given historical era constitutes a much broader topic than can be adequately covered in a paper about the utilization of a textile in garment design.

[3] A cheaper version of the pile fabric, woven from cotton, was developed in Europe to dress the servants of the aristocracy in the Middle Ages. This ribbed cloth was called *corde du roi*, predecessor of modern corduroy (Wilson, 1979).

[4] The velvet that is most commonly known today, a ground weave completely covered with cut pile of uniform height, is designated by the term solid velvet. Solid refers to the uniformity of pile coverage and pile height, and does not refer to color.

[5] Tortora (1992) describes three different methods of weaving velvet. The wire method employs extra warp yarn that is woven over thin wire rods at a regular interval. The rods may be removed with or without cutting these warp loops. This technique was automated in 1849. The filling pile method developed next weaves extra weft yarn floats, which are subsequently cut with a fustian knife, to create the pile. This cutting technique was still employed in 1953 for the production of some corduroy (Latour, 1953). The double cloth method weaves two parallel fabrics simultaneously employing a single extra warp yarn to create the pile of both. The two fabrics interlocked by the extra warp yarn are separated in the action that cuts and creates the pile as they come off the loom (Tortora, op cit). Though invented in 1838 this technique was not incorporated into an automated machine design until 1857. The patent was sold by the inventor for reason of financial distress in 1867 to a company that did not put such machines into production until the patent expired (Latour, op cit).

[6] "One of the most luxurious materials for cinema was velvet. It definitely added bulk to a figure, but the richness of look and feel was easily appreciated by audiences. The finest velvet was from Lyons, France, and the most popular evening color was black. . . . Velvet looked best with simple designs that used the heaviness of the fabric to outline or create attractive silhouettes. . . . the camera could not distinguish small details in a sea of black, so shapes of collars or skirts, a few large jewels, or a minimum of light accents, . . . were the maximum styling points for elegant velvet creations. Black velvet was perfect for highly dramatic scenes or to convey the rich status of a star or role" (Bailey, 1982, p. 48).

References

Bailey, M. J. (1982). *Those glorious glamour years*. Secaucus, NJ: Citadel Press.

Ballwebber, E. (1938). *Group instruction in social dancing*. New York: A. S. Barnes and Company.

Banner, L. W. (1983). *American beauty*. Chicago: University of Chicago Press.

Boehlke, H. (in press). Ruth M. Kapinas, Munsingwear's forgotten "Foundettes" designer. *Dress*.

Buckman, P. (1978). *Let's dance: Social, ballroom & folk dancing*. New York: Paddington Press.

Castle, V. & Castle, Mrs. V. (1914). *Modern dancing*. New York: World Syndicate Co. by arrangement with Harper & Brothers.

Coll, C. J. & Rosiere, G. (1922). *Dancing made easy* (New and Revised Edition). New York: Edward J. Clode.

Collard, E. (1983). *The cut and construction of women's dress in the 1930's*. Burlington, Ont.: Eileen Collard.

Cunnington, P. & Willett, C. (1981). *The history of underclothes*. (With revs. by A. D. Mansfield & V. Mansfield). Boston: Faber & Faber.

Delamater, J. (1981). *Dance in the Hollywood musical*. Ann Arbor, MI: UMI Research Press.

DeLong, M. R. (1987). *The way we look: A framework for visual analysis of dress*. Ames: Iowa State University Press.

Deschodt, A. M. (1979). *Mariano Fortuny: Un magicien de Venise*. (Photographs by Dorssen, S. Van) Editions du Regard.

Dhamijá, J. (1989). Indian Velvets. In J. Dhamijá & J. Jain (Eds.), *Handwoven fabrics of India* (pp. 52-59). Ahmedabad, India: Mapin Publishing.

Eicher, J. B. & Roach-Higgins, M. E. (1992). Definition and Classification of Dress: Implications for Analysis of Gender Roles. In R. Barnes and J. Eicher (Eds.), *Dress and gender: Making and meaning* (pp. 8-28). New York: Berg.

Ewing, E. (1992). *History of twentieth century fashion* (3rd ed.). Lanham, MD: Barnes & Noble Books.

Goldstein Gallery, University of Minnesota (Collector). Costume acquisition numbers C1385; X-26; X-89; X-185 a & b; 59.002.013; 59.002.016 a, b & c; 61.003.004; 61.003.029; 61.003.059; 61.010.023 a & b; 61.010.038; 61.013.001; 62.001.002; 64.008.001; 64.014.006 a, b & c; 64.015.012; 64.017.010; 66.008.002 a & b; 67.002.008; 68.005.002; 70.001.018; 76.025.006; 77.010.024; 77.011.001; 77.023.123 a & b; 77.031.008 a & b; 77.045.014 a & b; 77.045.016 a & b; 77.047.003; 78.012.002; 78.035.002; 79.014.002; 80.003.002 a & b; 80.003.003; 80.005.080; 80.026.001; 80.030.013; 80.030.020; 80.030.022; 80.030.026; 80.030.035; 80.119.001 a & b; 81.003.033 a & b; 81.003.038; 81.014.015; 81.033.032; 81.124.002; 81.130.002; 82.016.014;

82.069.074 a & b; 82.069.080; 82.069.089; 82.089.002; 83.013.024; 83.016.001; 83.027.001; 83.028.001; 83.028.010 a & b; 83.039.119; 83.050.003 a & b; 84.014.109; 84.014.026; 84.020.002; 84.036.003; 85.105.001; 86.003.006 a; 86.045.002; 86.045.017 b; 86.045.006; 86.045.011; 88.036.001 a & b; 89.007.001; 89.012.001; 89.019.001; 89.053.007 a & b; 90.035.001 a & b; 90.037.001 a & b; 91.006.027; 91.022.007; 91.022.017; 91.059.063 a; 92.003.003; 92.004.009 a & b; 92.016.001; 92.021.003 (Artifacts).

Harris, J. (Ed.). (1993). *Textiles 5,000 years: An international history and illustrated survey.* New York: Harry N. Abrams

Hollander, A. (1978). *Seeing through clothes.* New York: Viking Press.

Holt, K.R. (1988). *Women's undergarments of the 1920s and 1930s.* Unpublished master's thesis. University of North Carolina, Greensboro, NC.

Hostetler, L.A. (1930). *The art of social dancing: A textbook for teachers and students.* New York: A.S. Barnes & Company.

Hostetler, L.A. (1942). *Walk your way to better dancing.* New York: A.S. Barnes & Company.

Kauffman, G.B. (1993). A brief history of cuprammonium rayon. In R. B. Seymour, R.S. Porter and Dept. of Polymer Science, Univ of Southern Mississippi (Eds.), *Manmade fibers: Their origin and development* (pp. 63-71). New York: Elsevier applied Science.

Latour, A. (1953). Velvet. *Ciba Review 96.*

Malnig, J. (1992). *Dancing till dawn: A century of exhibition ballroom dance.* New York: Greenwood Press.

Osma, G. De. (1980). *Mariano Fortuny: His life and work.* New York: Rizzoli.

Parker, D.L. & Siegel, E. (1978). *Guide to dance in film.* Detroit: Gale Research Company.

Prown, J.D. (1982). Mind in matter: An introduction to material culture theory and method. *Winterthur Portfolio 17*(1). 1-19.

Raheel, M. (1993). History of cellulose acetate fibers. In R.B. Seymour, R.S. Porter & Dept. of Polymer Science, Univ. of Southern Mississippi (Eds.), *Manmade fibers: Their origin and development* (pp. 142-168). New York: Elsevier Applied Science.

Ray, L. (1932). *Modern ballroom dancing.* Chicago: Franklin.

Russell, D.A. (1983). *Costume history and style.* Englewood Cliffs, NJ: Prentice-Hall.

Smart, E.S. & Gluckman, D.C. (n.d.) Cloth of luxury: Velvet in Mughal India. *Marg 40*(3), 36-47.

Steele, V. (1989). Clothing and sexuality. In C.B. Kidwell and V. Steele (Eds.), *Men and women: Dressing the part* (pp.42-63). Washington: Smithsonian Institution Press.

Summers, T.A., Collier, B.J., Collier, J.R. & Haynes, J.L. (1993). History of viscose rayon. In R.B. Seymour, R.S. Porter & Dept. of Polymer Science, Univ. of Southern Mississippi (Eds.), *Manmade fibers: Their origin and development* (pp. 72-90). New York: Elsevier Applied Science.

Urlin, E.L. (1914). *Dancing: Ancient and modern.* New York: D. Appleton & Company.

Tortora, P.G. (1992). *Understanding Textiles.* New York: Macmillan.

Vogue (1917, Feb. 15); (1924, Sept. 15); (1928, Sept. 15); (1938, Sept. 15).

Wilson, K. (1979). *A history of textiles.* Boulder, CO: Westview.

Winakor, G., Chang, L. & Kim, C.J. (1987). Fabric Hand Descriptors Elicited by Tough Versus Touch and Sight. In *ACPTC Proceedings: Combined central, eastern, and western regional meetings* (p. 15).

The Look And The Feel:
Methods For Measuring Aesthetic Perceptions Of Textiles And Apparel

Leslie Davis Burns
Oregon State University

Sharron J. Lennon
Ohio State University

Consider the following scenario: a consumer enters an apparel store in search of a new sweater. She approaches a table stacked with sweaters and begins to feel the fabrics while visually inspecting the color and style of the sweaters. In her mind, she describes the feel of the sweaters as "soft" or "warm". She selects two of the sweaters to try on. In trying on the sweaters, she feels the fit of the sweater and again feels the fabric on her body while at the same time visually assessing the fit, color, and styling. Her mental descriptions are reassessed, "yes, the sweater feels soft and comfortable." She compares the look and the feel of the two sweaters "this sweater is softer, but I *like* the style of the other one better."

This scenario, typical of the process consumers use to evaluate aesthetic products, such as textiles and apparel, highlights the importance of the interaction of touch/feel and sight in the consumers' appreciation of the aesthetic product. Typically the consumer responds to an aesthetic product on many levels simultaneously, including sensory (tactile, visual), cognitive (identification, purpose), and aesthetic (Ripin & Lazarsfeld, 1937). Consumers' sensory perceptions of aesthetic products, such as textiles and apparel, include visual and tactile perceptions primarily, although the smell (Fiore, 1993) and sound of the product may also come into play. In addition, in the consumer decision making process, the sight and touch of the fabrics often interact with kinesthetic perceptions of garment fit and movement. Responses to visual and tactile sensations lead to affect (feelings toward a stimulus which can lead to preference or evaluation) to form the basis for

subsequent attitudes toward the textile or apparel product. These perceptions of "the expressive organization of physical and sensory aspects" of an aesthetic object, such as textiles, are sometimes defined as aesthetic perceptions (Cupchik & Heinrichs, 1981, p. 475). However, we will take a broader perspective and define aesthetic perceptions as perceptions of aesthetic objects which involve the sensory stimulation and resulting evaluative, preferential, or affective responses to the stimulus. These evaluative, preferential or affective responses might be, for example, a judgment of liking for an object, or a judgment of the degree to which an object is beautiful, or a judgment of the extent to which an object evokes pleasure in the perceiver.

> Not all stimuli evoke pleasure or displeasure. In the vast, permanent flux of inputs from the sensors to the central nervous system, the large majority elicits an indifferent sensation. For example, the sight of most objects is neither pleasurable nor displeasurable as such. If affectivity is involved, a sense of esthetics is the source of it (Cabanac, 1979, p. 2).

Thus we define aesthetic perceptions as involving both a sensory stimulation and the resulting preferential or affective interpretation of the sensations.

There has been a running debate in the psychological literature (Lazarus, 1982; 1984; Tsal, 1985; Zajonc, 1980; 1984; Zajonc & Markus, 1982) regarding research on preferences. Although this research has not focused on textile and apparel products, it has some important implications for consumer behavior and advertising. For example, a series of earlier studies has shown that positive evaluations of items can be acquired through repeated exposures (Kunst-Wilson & Zajonc, 1980; Matlin,

Acknowledgment. This report is based upon research conducted and supported as part of Western Regional Research Project W-17: Human Physiological and Perceptual Responses to the Textile-Skin interface. Participating stations are California, Colorado, Montana, New York, Ohio, Oregon, and Wyoming.

1971; Moreland & Zajonc, 1977; 1979). Similarly, DeLong and Salusso-Deonier (1983) found that repeated exposures to slides of women's business suits led to an overall preference for all costumes. It may be that repeated exposures to advertising stimuli functions in the same way.

Recognizing that the study of preferences has important marketing implications for the textiles and apparel industry, Brannon (1993) recently provided an overview of the literature dealing with the dual framework of affect and cognition and applied it to the process of apparel selection. She urged researchers to study not only the cognitive/perceptual factors, but also affective factors involved in the process. This mirrors our view of aesthetic perceptions as perceptions of aesthetic objects which contain an evaluative, preferential, or affective component.

The purpose of this paper is to describe the methods used to measure aesthetic perceptions of apparel and textile products. This body of literature comes from research conducted in a variety of disciplines including psychology, physiology, marketing, textile science, and art. Although consumers' appreciation (sensory stimulation and resulting affect/preference evaluation) of textiles and apparel is a result of multi-sensory assessments, research methods have primarily included analyses of consumers' responses to textiles and apparel based upon tactile sensations alone, visual sensations alone or combined tactile and visual sensations. However, the multi-sensory nature of the appreciation process should not be overlooked. The advantages of experimental control achieved by isolating the senses for investigation may be outweighed by the limitations in eliciting realistic (multi-dimensional) assessments from such studies. Indeed, the external validity of many studies may be questioned because senses have been isolated for investigation.

In this survey of methods used in aesthetic perception research, we do not include an exhaustive review of aesthetics literature. Instead we will cite published papers as examples of the primary measurements and procedures used in this area. In reviewing the relevant literature we searched major indexes of published work in the areas of sensory perception, tactile and visual perceptions of textiles and apparel, clothing comfort, and consumer aesthetics. We also included studies from a variety of other sources based upon our own work in this area. Abstracts were not included in our review as methodological details were often unclear in abstracts.

We will begin our survey of methodological issues surrounding the study of aesthetic perceptions of textiles and apparel with a discussion of ways in which aesthetic perceptions are measured; that is, ways in which subjects describe their perceptions. These various means of measuring aesthetic perceptions are used across procedures. We will follow with a discussion of procedures used to investigate aesthetic perceptions of textiles and apparel based upon tactile and visual sensations. In studying aesthetic perceptions of apparel and textiles researchers have used a variety of stimuli, including names of fabrics, actual fabrics which were touched and not seen, actual fabrics which were touched and seen, garment names, verbal descriptions of garments, line drawings of garments, photographs of garments, and actual garments and garment parts which were touched and seen. In many of these studies the authors did not set out to study aesthetic perceptions, but because of the nature of their dependent variables they may have collected responses which can be classified by our definition as aesthetic perceptions. In other words, they included at least one item which tapped an evaluative, preferential, or affective response. We conclude our discussion by offering some suggestions for the use of other techniques to measure aesthetic perceptions of textile and apparel products.

Descriptions of Aesthetic Perceptions

The study of aesthetic perceptions of textiles and apparel is dependent upon humans' ability to describe their perceptions. The descriptions of these multi-sensory perceptions are formulated by learning and by experience. In fact, the integration of information from eyes and hands begins when a child begins to learn language. According to Abravanel (1981),

> Once a child begins to acquire conventional language...she names or labels information that is acquired perceptually. These stored symbols are activated whenever an object is perceived by sight or by hand, and serve to link the otherwise different and disparate forms of information (p. 73).

Thus, as noted by DeLong (1987, p. 69) "a sweater may be viewed as soft because we have previously experienced its softness by touch." Ripin and Lazarsfeld (1937) found that subjects who could not see the fabrics being assessed often described their appearance based upon previous experience with similar fabrics. For example, subjects were quoted as saying, "I get the feeling it has a glossy finish" or "Distinctly gives the feeling that it's shiny."

The importance of language in research on aesthetic perceptions of textiles and apparel is reflected in the controversy in the literature over terminology used to describe the fabrics or garments studied and subsequent reliability and validity of the dependent measures used in the studies. Indeed, an underlying assumption of this research is the belief that the fabric and garment properties that lead to aesthetic perceptions can be described by individuals; and that these descriptions have meaning beyond the individual. Researchers have taken two approaches in investigating subjects' descriptions of fabrics and apparel. Some have allowed subjects to describe the fabrics as they wish. Others have attempted to define standardized terminology so that the same terms can be used across studies.

Several researchers have used open-ended measurements allowing subjects to describe fabrics. For example Wauer (1965) asked respondents to orally describe twelve different fabrics. Descriptions were tape recorded and transcribed verbatim. Through a content analysis, descriptions were found to fall in the following categories: color, design, fiber content, fabric name, texture, use, method of weave or construction, and weight.

For the most part, researchers have asked subjects to respond to specific terms with regard to their perceptions of fabrics. For example, based upon a factor analysis of subjects' descriptions of fabrics, Howarth and Oliver (1958) identified four categories of fabric hand perceptions: smoothness, stiffness, aspect of bulk or compactness, and thermal characteristics. Other researchers have subsequently used these terms in their studies (Lundgren, 1969; Paek, 1985; Paek & Mohamed, 1978). The use of researcher-provided polar adjective scales is undoubtedly the most common measurement instrument. Terms used have included fuzzy-clean, full-lean, harsh-soft, rough-smooth

(Brand, 1964); soft-hard, silky-harsh, crisp-limp, thick-thin, scratchy-slick, tight-loose, cool-warm (Chen, Barker, Smith, & Scruggs, 1992); prickly-smooth, stiff-limp, cool-warm, thick-thin (Laing & Ingham, 1983-84); coarse-fine, crisp-limp, sleazy-firm, stiff-flexible, heavy-light (Winakor, Kim, & Wolins, 1980); or evaluations of acceptability (Paek, 1975). Researcher-provided adjective checklists have also been used (Hoffman, 1965) to measure how a fabric feels (e.g., waxy, dry, bristly), how a fabric appears (e.g., matte luster, fine texture), and the fabric's aesthetic value (e.g., smart, boring, pleasing).

Some of the terms used have an evaluative or affective component whereas others are more purely descriptive in nature. For example, terms such as harsh, prickly, and scratchy possess a negative connotation; whereas terms such as thick, stiff, crisp, or heavy may possess either a positive or negative connotation depending upon the context in which the consumer is perceiving them. The terminology used in these studies has been derived in a number of ways. For example Chen, et al. (1992) developed a list of qualities of knit fabrics in consultation with expert knitters. Brand (1964) developed a list of words most often used in talking about fabric aesthetics with consumers in general.

Another methodological issue involved with aesthetic perceptions of fabrics is inclusion of the context of use for the fabric in the information given to subjects. Ripin and Lazarsfeld (1937, p. 211) noted that "many individuals were incapable of making a purely aesthetic judgment and refused to compare fabrics as such without knowing the purpose for which they were intended." When subjects were asked "How do you like it?", responses such as "It all depends what for" or "for what purpose" were not uncommon. Few studies of perceptions of fabrics have included the context of use. One exception is Paek's (1975) investigation of flame-retardant fabrics in which subjects were told the fabrics being studied were to be used for sleepwear with skin contact in their end use.

Similar methodologies as these for textiles have been used for assessments of perceptions of and preferences for clothing. In many of the clothing wear studies conducted by Hollies and his colleagues (e.g., Hollies, Custer, Morin, & Howard, 1979) subjects' responses to garments were assessed using a "subjective comfort rating scale." This scale measured the intensity of subjects' perceptions of clothing using the following descriptive terms: snug, loose, heavy, light weight, stiff, staticy, sticky, non-absorbent, cold, clammy, damp, clingy, picky, rough, scratchy. In later work Hollies (1989) developed a clothing rating chart using 37 terms obtained from interviews of users of each product type. Again, these terms may possess varying degrees of positive/negative connotations depending upon the context of perception.

In the area of consumer aesthetics researchers have typically measured aesthetic responses using verbal bipolar rating scales such as good/bad, like/dislike, or beautiful/ugly (Holbrook, 1987). However, in textiles and clothing research aesthetic responses have also been measured by having subjects freely respond to open-ended questions (DeLong, 1977; Eckman, Damhorst, & Kadolph, 1990; Lennon & Fairhurst, in press; Schutz & Phillips, 1976).

It should be noted that individual differences have been found in the number and quality of descriptions of textiles and apparel. Hollies (1989) found that after "repeated applications of comfort protocols to perception analysis of clothing... that people differ from one another not in how they evaluate garment differences, but rather in how many terms they use to describe performance" (p. 12). For example, during a wear protocol thirty subjects described the feel of the clothing using an average of nine descriptive terms, although the range was from 4 terms to 16 terms.

In addition, several researchers have found differences in descriptions made by "expert" versus "naive" judges. Wauer (1965) found that although consumers of varying educational levels gave similar descriptions of fabrics, these descriptions were different from those of experts who were more likely to describe the fabric name, weave, and weight than were consumers. Winakor, Kim, and Wolins (1980, p. 602) suggest "quantification of hand by trained judges is information that should be compared with physical measures; the assessments of consumers should be compared with consumer preferences."

Aesthetic Perceptions of Textiles and Apparel Based Upon Tactile Sensations

Fabric Hand

Methods and procedures used to study the touch and feel of fabric take into account the skin's different sensory receptors (touch/pressure, heat and cold receptors, and pain receptors) as well as the area of the body in which the fabric is felt. For several reasons, the majority of the research on the feel of fabric has focused on the touching senses of the fingers. From a physiological perspective, the fingers have a greater number of nerve receptors than other parts of the body and there are no hairs to interfere with sensing. In addition, consumers typically make initial assessments of a fabric by feeling it with their fingers. The term used to describe "the tactile sensations or impressions which arise when fabrics are touched, squeezed, rubbed, or otherwise handled" is fabric hand (AATCC, 1993, p. 353). Thus fabric hand implies the ability of the fingers to make a sensitive assessment of fabric characteristics. The constituent elements of fabric hand are "those components, qualities, attributes, dimensions, properties or impressions which make the sensation of touching one fabric different from that of touching another" (AATCC, 1993, p. 353).

Procedures Used in Studying Fabric Hand. From Binns' early studies on the touch of fabrics (1926, 1934) to more recently developed sorting methods (Lennon, Dallas, & Smitley, 1993), a variety of procedures have been used to test fabric hand. A variety of dependent measures have been used with each procedure, although, for the most part, subjects are asked to describe the test fabrics according to specific terms. Therefore, it is typical that descriptive and affective perceptions resulting from the tactile sensations are measured. These procedures include the following:

(1) subjects consider each fabric sample individually and assess the feel of the fabric on some arbitrary subjective scale (e.g., Bogaty, Hollies, & Harris, 1956; Byrne & Bennett, 1992; Paek, 1985; Schneider & Holcombe, 1991),

(2) as a refinement of the previous procedure, one fabric sample is established as a reference and subjects assess additional fabric

samples against the reference fabric (AATCC, 1993),

(3) subjects rank or place fabrics in order of the degree or magnitude of the quality being assessed (Binns, 1926, 1934; Dawes & Owen, 1971),

(4) as a refinement of the previous procedure, two extremes for the quality being assessed (such as limp to stiff) are established. The (limp) fabric is arbitrarily assigned a value of 1 and the (stiff) fabric a value of 10. Subjects place the fabric samples closer to the ends of the scale or in the middle of the scale according to the differences felt (AATCC, 1993),

(5) subjects compare two fabrics on the quality of interest and choose one fabric over another as more representative of that quality (Bogaty, Hollies, & Harris, 1956; Howorth & Oliver, 1958; Paek, 1985; Paek & Mohamed,1978; Ripin & Lazarsfeld, 1937),

(6) subjects sort fabrics into stacks according to how similar or different the fabrics feel to them (Lennon, Dallas, Smitley, 1993). Subjects responses in this procedure include written explanations as to why they grouped the fabrics as they did. Although aesthetic perceptions were not specifically elicited, subjects' explanations often included both descriptive and affective responses.

Although the relative advantages and disadvantages of all the various procedures used have not been systematically investigated, in comparisons of single fabric and paired comparison methods, both were found to be equally effective in assessing fabric hand (Bogaty, Hollies, & Harris, 1956; Paek, 1985). In their assessment of techniques to measure fabric hand, Ellis and Garnsworthy (1980, p. 231) noted "when only a few items are to be ranked, it is simple to present all samples together for comparison. However, for more than about six items the technique of comparison in pairs is to be preferred." Recently, Lennon, Dallas, & Smitley (1993) found subjects could effectively sort 60 different fabric samples based upon perceptions of similarity in fabric hand, although sorting 75 fabrics proved tedious.

Tactile Sensations and Clothing Comfort

There is limited work on assessing responses to textiles and apparel based upon tactile sensations from specific areas of the body other than the fingers/hand. Noted exceptions include work on perceptions of fabrics including fabric texture, pleasantness (Gwosdow, Stevens, Berglund, & Stolwijk, 1986) and prickle (Naylor, Veitch, Mayfield, & Kettlewell, 1992) when the fabric is systematically pulled across the forearm.

However, an extensive body of literature exists on clothing comfort, that is, the "state of satisfaction indicating physiological, social-psychological and physical balance among a person, his/her clothing, and his/her environment" (Branson & Sweeney, 1991, p. 99). Reviews of literature on clothing comfort include Markee and Pedersen (1991) and Branson and Sweeney (1991). The goal of much of the research on fabric hand and clothing comfort is to discover the relationships between the physical and mechanical properties of fabrics and the subjective assessments of fabric hand or comfort. By doing so, the development or refinement of textiles or textile products for specific end uses can be facilitated. For example, Hollies (1989) described studies designed to compare subjects' comfort responses to military combat clothing made from manufactured fibers with combat clothing made from 100% wool, to compare subjects' responses to sport shirts made from polyester/cotton blends with shirts made from 100% cotton, and to compare cotton shirts with durable press or fire-retardant finishes with those with no finishes. Thus, research on comparing subjective assessments of fabric hand and clothing comfort between fabrics or clothing has practical implications for textile and apparel producers.

Aesthetic Perceptions of Textiles and Apparel Based Upon Visual and Tactile Sensations

The perception issues surrounding the visual aspects of textiles and apparel are complex. In describing her framework for a visual analysis of dress, DeLong (1987, chapter 5) suggested that the visual components of fabrics include the surface structure (e.g., color, texture, print), layout structure (i.e., physical arrangement of the fabric on the body), and light and shadow structure (i.e., reflecting character of the fabric) of the two-dimensional fabric. She noted that these visual components interact to create appearances that may be simple or complex in nature.

Typically the visual interpretations of textiles and apparel are studied in conjunction with other sensory assessments. As noted by DeLong (1987, p. 69) "Though the visual aspects of materials and the way they can interact in viewing are primary considerations, our other senses are very much present in visual interpretation." Thus it is difficult to separate the visual and tactile bases for aesthetic perceptions of textiles and apparel. Other researchers have noted this inherent sensory interaction. For example, according to Brand (1964) "fabric aesthetic character is defined as a relationship among a minimum of six concepts: style, body, cover, surface texture, drape and resilience." Similarly, Hollies (1989, p. 16) states that "changes in textile products as seen and felt will certainly be directly related to the fibres used and the method of assembly. The perception information, however, will be organized quite naturally, in terms of the whole picture of performance and each quality in that picture."

Procedures to Study Aesthetic Perceptions Based Upon Visual and Tactile Sensations

To better understand this natural interaction between sight and touch in aesthetic perceptions of textiles and apparel, a variety of procedures have been used. These procedures can be organized around the stimuli that have been used including actual fabrics (touched only or both seen and touched), names of fabrics, names or verbal descriptions of garments, drawings of garments, photographs/slides of garments, garment sleeves, and actual garments.

Actual fabrics. Research methods have attempted to isolate the senses and compare the perceptual responses given when subjects could see *and* touch the fabrics with those given when subjects could only touch the fabrics. In a study of aesthetic perceptions of suiting fabrics, Byrne and Bennett (1992) found very little difference in the subjects' descriptions of tactile sensations and descriptions of visual and tactile sensations. In comparing touch only with sight and touch, Paek (1985) found that when subjects could see and touch a variety of fabrics that wool was rated stiffer, burlap was rated thicker, silk was rated warmer, and cotton and linen were rated cooler than when they could only touch them. Lennon, et. al (1993) found evidence of sensory interaction on how fabrics were sorted. For example, non-viewers produced categories that were more homogeneous than were those produced by viewers. Viewers seemed to sort by probable end use, while non-viewers seemed to sort by fiber content and fabric structure.

Names of fabrics. In one study women rated 46 fabric names on seven-point rating scales for their appropriateness on 48 attributes (Schutz & Phillips, 1976). Some of the attributes, which had all been generated in an earlier pilot study, were aesthetic in nature. Examples include "has an unpleasant smell" (p. 4), "enjoy wearing it" (p. 8), and "like to run my hand over it" (p. 4).

Names or verbal description of garments. Both open-ended responses and rating scales have been used to measure aesthetic responses to garment names (DeLong, Minshall, & Larntz, 1986; 1987; Lennon & Fairhurst, in press). In one of a series of three studies, DeLong, Minshall, and Larntz (1986) asked subjects to generate responses to the statement: "When I think about sweater, I think about. . ." (p. 20). A content analysis of responses revealed no evaluative properties. In the second study, the subjects rated their "schema for sweater" on 29 semantic differential word pairs which included several aesthetic perceptions; e.g., like/dislike, unpleasing/pleasing, and attractive/unattractive. Lennon and Fairhurst (in press) asked respondents to indicate what quality factors they would look for (1) in apparel items and (2) in a blouse. They were asked to write at least three sentences for each item. In describing the quality of apparel items, 26% of the responses generated were classified as aesthetic criteria. In describing the quality of a blouse, 44% of the responses generated were classified as aesthetic criteria.

Holbrook and Moore (1981) presented some of their subjects with verbal descriptions of sweaters. Descriptions contained information on pattern, fit, sleeves, neck style, and length. Subjects made evaluative judgments by rating the sweater descriptions on 20 bipolar adjectival scales. When subjects were contacted after the experiment the authors found that some of them were forming mental images of the sweater descriptions before rating them.

In these studies although subjects were not exposed to a visual stimulus which resembled an actual apparel or textile product, they were exposed to a visual stimulus of an apparel or textile name or description and aesthetic responses sometimes were affected. It is clear from these studies that people form schemata for textile and apparel items which may include an expectation of aesthetic components. Since expectations for garment appearance and quality will certainly affect consumers' satisfaction with apparel purchased through catalogs, consumers' aesthetic responses to textile and apparel words are important to study.

Drawings of garments. Holbrook and Moore (1982) presented simple black and white drawings of sweaters which were rated on 20 bipolar adjective scales. Results of a canonical correlation analysis revealed a two dimensional product space such that one of the dimensions was an evaluation dimension. In another study Holbrook (1986) presented black and white drawings of men's clothing ensembles including a shirt, tie, jacket and pants. Two levels for each of the four items were combined factorially and presented to subjects who rated the stimuli on 20 bipolar adjective-pair scales. Embedded within the 20 items was a four-item affect index which included good/bad, I like it/I dislike it, beautiful/ugly, and pleasing/displeasing. In these studies the authors cautioned readers that while black and white drawings allow for precise experimental control, they fail to reproduce other dimensions important to aesthetic responses such as color, smell, and touch. They may also fail to reproduce elements such as texture and pattern as accurately as photographs.

Photographs/slides of garments. Studies which have used photographs or slides of garments as stimuli come from work in design and apparel aesthetics. Luborsky (1988) presented subjects with 26 pictures of women's daytime dress. Pictures were selected from fashion magazines and costume history texts to represent a variety of women's fashions from the period of 1840 through 1980. Subjects rated each costume on five-point scales according to the extent to which they liked it. In a series of studies DeLong and her colleagues (DeLong & Larntz, 1980; DeLong & Salusso-Deonier, 1983; DeLong, Salusso-Deonier, & Larntz, 1983) presented subjects with slides of magazine photographs of women's dress. In each of these studies subjects rated each of the stimuli on semantic differential scales. In each case over ten of the items tapped an evaluative component; e.g., beautiful/ugly, attractive/unattractive, like/dislike.

Garment sleeves. In order to generate comfort descriptors, subjects wore 15 different pairs of fitted sleeves which differed according to fabric structure (woven, knitted), color, fiber content, fabric thickness, weave construction, and hand (Hyun, Hollies, & Spivak, 1991). Subjects were allowed to examine the sleeves in any way that would help them write about the sleeves. Forty-eight comfort descriptors were generated which were each mentioned by three or more subjects. Although aesthetic perceptions as a topic was not a focus of this pretest, one of the descriptors so generated was "feels good," which is clearly an aesthetic response.

Actual garments. In the third of a series of studies, DeLong, Minshall, and Larntz (1986) provided 10 sweaters for their subjects to assess. Subjects were able to see and touch the sweaters and rated each of the actual sweaters on 29 semantic differential word pairs. A factor analysis of responses to the sweaters revealed that an evaluative factor was the most important factor in explaining the variation in responses to the 10 sweaters. The evaluative factor included responses to word pairs such as like/dislike, like to own/not like to own, and attractive/unattractive.

Holbrook (1983) provided his subjects with 20 actual sweaters to evaluate on 34 bipolar adjectival scales. Subjects were able to both see and touch the sweaters. Results of a canonical correlation analysis revealed an evaluative dimension (e.g., good/bad and pleasing/displeasing) which was closely associated with sweaters' tactile qualities. Sweaters evaluated favorably tended to be rated as more gentle, soft, and smooth than sweaters evaluated negatively.

Aesthetic assessments are likely to occur when people purchase fashion garments. In such a setting consumers can not only touch and see the garment, but they can also assess how the body and garment interact with respect to fit. Eckman, Damhorst, and Kadolph (1990) used an open-ended format and interviewed shoppers after they had tried on a specific garment. Respondents were asked to indicate why they wanted to buy/not buy the garment and what they liked or disliked about the garment. Nearly 55% of responses to questions about specific garments related to aesthetic factors. It is also important to note that over 50% of respondents who did not purchase the garment they tried on gave aesthetic characteristics (color/pattern, styling, appearance) of the garments as attributes they disliked about the garments.

In the main part of Hyun, Hollies, and Spivak's (1991) study (a wear test), subjects rated their comfort on five-point scales. Comfort was rated using the 48 descriptors previously described which includes "feels good" as one of the descriptors. Subjects wore leotards, pantyhose, socks, and sneakers and filled out the rating forms after various lengths of time operating exercycles.

Conclusion

Aesthetic perceptions are complex and elusive. Olson (1980) described three factors that influence consumers' aesthetic responses: (a) characteristics of the aesthetic object, (b) the environment in which the aesthetic response occurs, and (c) characteristics of the consumer. The majority of research methods related to aesthetic perceptions of textiles and apparel have focused on characteristics of the aesthetic object. Although most studies have examined the effect of characteristics of the aesthetic object, the measurement of aesthetic perceptions has varied across studies. In addition, few studies have focused on either the environment or context of the aesthetic perception or characteristics of the consumer which may affect these perceptions. In this section we would like to discuss issues that have emerged from our literature review that have implications for the conceptualization of aesthetic perceptions and the external validity of studies examining aesthetic perceptions. We end with suggestions for other techniques that may be useful in this area of research.

The multi-sensory nature of aesthetic perceptions should not be overlooked when operationally defining and measuring this concept. In fact, in an early study of the relationship between tactile-kinaesthetic perception and preferences of fabrics, Ripin and Lazarsfeld (1937, p. 208) noted "we found that judgments of elements were so influenced by the totality of experience in which they occurred that a consideration of the one without the other was meaningless." Therefore, researchers should be cautioned that the external validity of studies may be questioned when isolating senses for investigation. We have reviewed methods used in examining perceptions based upon visual, tactile, and some scent sensations (Fiore, 1993); although the sound a garment makes when worn (e.g., rustling, swishing petticoats) may well affect aesthetic perceptions. Indeed, Forrest (1991) in a discussion about aesthetic perceptions of textile products (quilts) noted that quilts make "soft, crumpling, rustling" (p. 51) sounds when one moves under them. Therefore, in addition to tactile and visual sensations, scent and sound should also be investigated in terms of aesthetic perceptions of textile and apparel products.

Dialogue continues regarding the development of terminology used in dependent measures designed to describe aesthetic responses. Many of the studies included in the review were not intended to measure aesthetic perceptions, but by virtue of the fact that the researchers included at least one item in the dependent measure which tapped an affective response, the research fit within our definition of aesthetic perception. However, there are limitations to a single-item measure of this concept. For example, an item such as "I like it" does not tap all aspects of aesthetic perceptions. Personal taste or favor may strongly be influenced by contextual factors. For example, a positive aesthetic response to fabric qualities may be overridden by the fact that the consumer would not choose a garment in that fabric for him/herself. Thus, researchers need to be consider the validity of their operational definitions of aesthetic perceptions.

To create more valid and reliable operational definitions, some researchers believe standardized terms should be developed and used. Hollies (1989, p. 18) recommends that when assessing perceptions of and preferences for textiles and apparel the "most important step in perception analysis is the actual evaluation involving the use of an established language and an established evaluation protocol." However, it is assumed that the terms used in these instruments are similarly defined by subjects and that subjects would use these terms in "real life" when evaluating textile and apparel products. Because these underlying assumptions may not be true, the external validity of the measurement instruments being used may be in question.

Brannon (1993) suggests many techniques for the study of appearance product selection which might also be used to measure aesthetic perceptions. In addition, a strong case can be made for the use of an ethnographic approach to the study of aesthetic objects (Forrest, 1991). Context of use is seldom studied in terms of aesthetic perceptions of textiles and apparel. Thus it may be important to (a) evaluate aesthetic perceptions of apparel and textile products within their context of use, and (b) evaluate the effect of context of use on aesthetic perceptions in our future work.

In addition, most studies have been conducted in laboratory settings, the artificial environmental setting in which the aesthetic objects are perceived may affect the aesthetic responses obtained. Settings for further research should provide for greater realism for the consumer as they perceive and respond to the stimuli.

Finally, new sophisticated statistical techniques exist for measuring aesthetic perceptions in terms of consumer preferences which offer some exciting possibilities. Pairwise preference ratings or paired comparison consumer preferences might be analyzed by using: (a) regression analysis in combination with laddering (in-depth interviews) to get at the personal meaning of preferences (Perkins & Reynolds, 1988), (b) new stochastic multi-dimensional unfolding methods to provide a product preference space (DeSarbo, 1987), or (c) nested logit models (Moore, 1989) which have been used to examine perceptual and preference data using soft drink products. Finally, product attribute ratings and purchasing histories can be used in consumer preference structure analysis to define a hierarchy of buyer preferences (McDonald, 1993). In order to fully understand aesthetic perceptions of textiles and apparel, we challenge researchers to move beyond the traditional procedures and measurement instruments to explore social and psychological meanings consumers attribute to these aesthetic products.

References

AATCC Evaluation Procedure 5 Fabric Hand: Subjective Evaluation of. (1993). *AATCC Technical Manual*, 353-354.

Abravanel, E. (1981). Integrating the information from eyes and hands: A developmental account. In R. D. Walk and H. L. Pick (Eds.) *Intersensory Perception and Sensory Integration* (pp. 71-108). NY: Plenum Press.

Binns, H. (1926). The discrimination of wool fabrics by the sense of touch. *British Journal of Psychology, 16*, 237-247.

Binns, H. (1934). A tactile comparison of the cloth qualities of continental and noble-combed materials. *Journal of the Textile Institute, 25*, T157-T173.

Bogaty, H., Hollies, N. R. S., and Harris, M. (1956). The judgment of harshness of fabrics. *Textile Research Journal, 26*, 355-360.

Brand, R. H. (1964). Measurement of fabric aesthetics: Analysis of aesthetic components. *Textile Research Journal, 34*, 791-804.

Brannon, E. L. (1993). Affect and cognition in appearance management: A review. In S. J. Lennon and L. D. Burns (Eds.), *Social science aspects of dress: New directions* (pp. 82-92). Monument, CO: ITAA.

Branson, D. H., and Sweeney, M. (1991). Conceptualization and measurement of clothing comfort: Toward a metatheory. In S. B. Kaiser and M. L. Damhorst (Eds.), *Critical linkages in textiles and clothing subject matter: Theory, method and practice* (pp. 94-105). Monument, CO: ITAA.

Byrne, M. S., and Bennett, T. (1992). The use of repertory grid techniques in the evaluation of fabric hand. *Journal of Consumer Studies and Home Economics, 16*, 161-165.

Cabanac, M. (1979). Sensory pleasure. *The Quarterly Review of Biology, 54* (1), 1-29.

Chen, P., Barker, R. L., Smith, G. W., and Scruggs, B. (1992). Handle of weft knit fabrics. *Textile Research Journal, 62*, 200-211.

Cupchik, G. C., and Heinrichs, R. W. (1981). Toward an integrated theory of aesthetic perception in the visual arts. In H. I. Day (Ed.) *Advances in intrinsic motivation and aesthetics* (pp. 463-485). New York: Plenum Press.

Dawes, V. H., and Owen, J. D. (1971). The assessment of fabric handle, Part I: Stiffness and liveliness. *Journal of the Textile Institute, 62* (5), 233-244.

DeLong, M. R. (1977). Clothing and aesthetics: Perception of form. *Home Economics Research Journal, 5* (1), 214-224.

DeLong, M. R. (1987). *The way we look*. Ames, IA: Iowa State University Press.

DeLong, M. R., & Larntz, K. (1980). Measuring visual response to clothing. *Home Economics Research Journal, 8*, 281-293.

DeLong, M. R., Minshall, B., & Larntz, K. (1986). Use of schema for evaluating consumer response to an apparel product. *Clothing and Textiles Research Journal, 5*, 17-26.

DeLong, M. R., Minshall, B. C., & Larntz, K. (1987). Predicting consumer response to fashion apparel. *Home Economics Research Journal, 16* (2), 150-160.

DeLong, M. R., & Salusso-Deonier, C. (1983). Effect of redundancy on female observers' visual responses to clothing. *Perceptual and Motor Skills, 57*, 243-246.

DeLong, M. R., Salusso-Deonier, C., & Larntz, K. (1983). Use of perceptions of female dress as an indicator of role definition. *Home Economics Research Journal, 11*, 327-336.

DeSarbo, W. S. (1987). A new stochastic multidimensional unfolding model for the investigation of paired comparison consumer preference/choice data. *Journal of Economic Psychology, 8* (3), 357-384.

Eckman, M., Damhorst, M.L., & Kadolph, S.J. (1990). Toward a model of the in-store purchase decision process: Consumer use of criteria for evaluating women's apparel. *Clothing and Textiles Research Journal, 8* (2), 13-22.

Ellis, B. C., and Garnsworthy, R. K. (1980). A review of techniques for the assessment of hand. *Textile Research Journal, 50*, 231-238.

Fiore, A. M. (1993). Multisensory integration of visual, tactile, and olfactory aesthetic cues of appearance. *Clothing and Textiles Research Journal, 11* (2), 45-52.

Forrest, J. (1991). Visual aesthetics for five senses and four dimensions: An ethnographic approach to aesthetic objects. In R. Browne and P. Browne (Eds.), *Digging into popular culture* (pp. 48-57). Bowling Green, OH: Bowling Green State University Press.

Gwosdow, A. R., Stevens, J. C., Berglund, L. G., and Stolwijk, J. A. J. (1986). Skin friction and fabric sensations in neutral and warm environments. *Textile Research Journal, 56*, 574-580.

Hoffman, R. M. (1965). Measuring the aesthetic appeal of textiles. *Textile Research Journal, 35*, 428-434.

Holbrook, M. B. (1986). Aims, concepts, and methods for the representation of individual differences in esthetic responses to design features. *Journal of Consumer Research, 13*, 337-347.

Holbrook, M. B. (1983). On the importance of using real products in research on merchandising strategy. *Journal of Retailing, 59* (1), 4-20.

Holbrook, M. B. (1987). The study of signs in consumer esthetics: An egocentric review. In J. Umiker-Sebeok (Ed.), *Marketing and Semiotics* (pp. 73-121). Bloomington, IN: Indiana University Press.

Holbrook, M. B., & Moore, W. L. (1981). Feature interactions in consumer judgments of verbal versus pictorial presentations. *Journal of Consumer Research, 8*, 103-113.

Holbrook, M. B., & Moore, W. L. (1982). Using canonical correlation to construct product spaces for objects with known feature structures. *Journal of Marketing Research, 19*, 87-98.

Hollies, N. R. S. (1989). Visual and tactile perceptions of textile quality. *Journal of the Textile Institute, 80* (1), 1-18.

Hollies, N. R. S., Custer, A. G., Morin, C. J., and Howard, M. E. (1979). A human perception analysis approach to clothing comfort. *Textile Research Journal, 49*, 557-564.

Howarth, W. S., and Oliver, P. H. (1958). The application of multiple factor analysis to the assessment of fabric handle. *Journal of the Textile Institute, 49*(1), T540-T553.

Hyun, S. O., Hollies, S. R. S., & Spivak, S. M. (1991). Skin sensations perceived in apparel wear, Part I: Development of a new perception language. *Journal of Textile Institute, 82* (3), 389-397.

Kunst-Wilson, W. R., & Zajonc, R. B. (1980). Affective discrimination of stimuli that cannot be recognized. *Science, 207*, 557-558.

Laing, R. M., and Ingham, P. E. (1983-84). The effectiveness of specimen tactile evaluation as a predictor of garment tactile acceptability for garments as a whole and on a regional basis. *Clothing and Textiles Research Journal, 2*(1), 58-63.

Lazarus, R. S. (1982). Thoughts on the relations between emotion and cognition. *American Psychologist, 37*, 1019-1024.

Lazarus, R. S. (1984). On the primacy of cognition. *American Psychologist, 39*(2), 124-129.

Lennon, S. J., Dallas, M. J., & Smitley, R. (1993, November). *Categorization of fabrics: Tactile and visual perceptions*. Paper presented at the meeting of the International Textile and Apparel Association, White Sulphur Springs, WV.

Lennon, S. J., & Fairhurst, A. E. (1994). Categorization of the quality concept. *Home Economics Research Journal, 22*(3), 267-285.

Lundgren, H. P. (1969). New concepts in evaluating fabric hand. *Textile Chemist and Colorist, 1*(1), 35-45.

Markee, N. L., and Pedersen, E. L (1991). The conceptualization of comfort with regard to clothing. In S. B. Kaiser and M. L. Damhorst (Eds.) *Critical linkages in textiles and clothing subject matter: Theory, method and practice* (pp. 81-93). Monument, CO: ITAA.

Matlin, M. W. (1971). Response competition, recognition, and affect. *Journal of Personality and Social Psychology, 19*, 295-300.

McDonald, W. J. (1993). Consumer preference structure analysis: A managerial tool for understanding apparel catalog market competition. *Journal of Direct Marketing, 7*(1), 20-30.

Moore, W. L. (1989). A paired comparison nested logit model of individual preference structures. *Journal of Marketing Research, 26* (4), 420-428.

Moreland, R. L., & Zajonc, R. B. (1977). Is stimulus recognition a necessary condition for the occurrence of exposure effects? *Journal of Personality and Social Psychology, 35*, 191-199.

Naylor, G. R. S., Veitch, C. J., Mayfield, R. J., and Kettlewell, R. (1992). Fabric-evoked prickle. *Textile Research Journal, 62*(8), 487-493.

Olson, J. C. (1980). What is an esthetic response? In E. C. Hirschman and M. B. Holbrook (Eds.) *Symbolic Consumer Behavior: Proceedings of the Conference on Consumer Esthetics and Symbolic Consumption* (pp. 71-74). Ann Arbor: Association for Consumer Research.

Paek, S. L. (1975). Evaluation of the hand of certain flame-retardant fabrics. *Textile Research Journal, 45*, 704-711.

Paek, S. L. (1985). Effect of scaling method on perception of textiles. *Perceptual and Motor Skills, 60*, 335-338.

Paek, S. L., and Mohamed, M. H. (1978). The selected physical and hand properties of latex-bonded nonwovens. *Textile Research Journal, 48*, 281-286.

Perkins, W. S. & Reynolds, T. J. (1988). The explanatory power of values in preference judgments: Validation of the means-end perspective. In M.J. Houston (Ed.), *Advances in Consumer Research* (Vol. 15, pp. 122-126). Ann Arbor, MI: Association for Consumer Research.

Ripin, R., and Lazarsfeld, P. F. (1937). The tactile-kinaesthetic perception of fabrics with emphasis on their relative pleasantness. *Journal of Applied Psychology, 21*, 198-224.

Schneider, A. M., and Holcombe, B. V. (1991). Properties influencing coolness to the touch of fabrics. *Textile Research Journal, 61* (8), 488-494.

Schutz, H. G., & Phillips, B. A. (1976). Consumer perceptions of textiles. *Home Economics Research Journal, 5* (1), 2-14.

Tsal, Y. (1985). On the relationship between cognitive and affective processes: A critique of Zajonc and Markus. *Journal of Consumer Research, 12*, 358-362.

Wauer, M. R. (1965). Consumers' and home economists' fabric descriptions. *Journal of Home Economics, 57* (1), 33-35.

Winakor, G., Kim, C. J., and Wolins, L. (1980). Fabric hand: Tactile sensory assessment. *Textile Research Journal, 50*, 601-610.

Zajonc, R. B. (1980). Feeling and thinking: Preferences need no inferences. *American Psychologist, 35* (2), 151-175.

Zajonc, R. B. (1984). *On the primacy of affect. American Psychologist, 39* (2), 117-123.

Zajonc, R. B. & Markus, H. (1982). Affective and cognitive factors in preferences. *Journal of Consumer Research, 4*, 123-131.

Axiology, Aesthetics, And Apparel:
Some Reflections On The Old School Tie

Morris B. Holbrook
Columbia University

There are the joys of leisure
with their enriching, ordering,
revealing experiences...
the making of love...
the mystery of music...
laughter...
the religious experience....
Why explore these things?....
Why analyze ourselves?....
Because...if we don't, we speak as fools.

- Robert Osborn,
On Leisure

The business school where I teach has recently redesigned is curriculum to emphasize four themes that I refer to as "The Four E's": Environment (the global economy), Excellence (the role of quality), Ethics (the moral aspects of management), and Empathy (human relations and human resource management). All four themes bear directly on the topic for this chapter - namely, Customer Value. Yet - despite all the talk about international competition, quality, morality, and meeting human needs - something important, indeed something vital, seems to be missing from the new curriculum. I refer to the role of aesthetics, its connection to management in general, to marketing in particular, to customers especially, and to the lives of human consumers above all. With all the fuss about building better products (to compete with the Japanese) and avoiding scams or other scandals (to stay out of jail), the aesthetic aspects of the consumption experience seem to have slipped through the cracks.

Thus, during the Fall of 1992, my class on Consumer Behavior followed one on Operations Management taught by an esteemed colleague who focused primarily on his interest in quality. As I stood waiting in the wings at the close of his lectures, I heard him discuss Quality

Acknowledgment. The author gratefully acknowledges the support of the Columbia Business School's Faculty Research Fund.

Circles, the Baldridge Awards, the Total Quality Concept, and other aspects of the growing managerial obsession with functional performance and freedom from defects. Then I would enter and tease my colleague that he had just finished teaching our students about Quality, whereas I had arrived to tell them about Beauty.

Beauty - in my view - pervades the everyday consumption experiences of ordinary consumers and prompts appreciative responses that run the gamut of emotional reactions all the way from simple hedonic pleasure to profound aesthetic experience. Virtually any product - any good, service, event, or idea - can provide aspects of aesthetic value. Quite obviously, art or entertainment frequently promotes the experience of beauty. But other more mundane consumption experiences may also contain aesthetic components in general and aspects of beauty in particular. These include recreational activities, food, furniture, and - of course - apparel. The present chapter will use clothing, accessories, and related fashion products as examples; but similar points could be made by focusing on anything from peanut butter to Italian Renaissance Masterpieces.

The primary point I wish to make is that one can understand a given type of value *only* by considering its relationship to *other* types of value. One cannot understand Quality without considering Beauty or Beauty without considering Fun or Fun without considering Morality. In short, we can understand one type of value only by comparing it to other types of value with which it is closely related. Thus, we can understand Quality only by comparing it to Beauty, Convenience, and Reputation; we can understand Beauty only by comparing it to Quality, Fun, and Ecstasy.

Toward bringing these issues to bear on the topic of the Aesthetics of Apparel or the Beauty of Clothing, I shall borrow some concepts from the philosophical field of Axiology or the Theory of Value. As a field of study, Axiology has important lessons to teach marketing and consumer researchers concerned with the nature of customer value. Yet it is a perspective that has been seriously neglected in research on the consumption experience.

More specifically, I shall borrow from the literature on Axiology to address two main themes: (1) The *Nature* of Customer Value and (2) The *Types* of Customer Value. A full discussion of these themes - with what I hope will strike the reader as helpful scholarly references to the relevant literature - appears in a recent contribution to another publication (Holbrook 1993; see also, Holbrook and Corfman 1985). Here, rather than posing further philosophical conundrums - learned or pedantic, depending on one's point of view - I wish to apply the relevant concepts concerning the nature and types of customer value to the area of aesthetics in general and to the case of beauty in clothing or other wearing apparel in particular.

The Nature Of Customer Value

Since the beginning of Western Philosophy as we know it today - that is, for over two thousand years - virtually every attempt to make firm statements concerning the nature of value has prompted counterarguments and debates that have shaped this field of inquiry into a hotbed of intellectual controversy. I anticipate *no chance* that my comments on the nature of value will prompt wide or even narrow agreement among the readers of this chapter. Rather, every reader will entertain doubts and contradictory positions that she or he will wish to hold dear and to develop for herself or himself. Hence, my purpose is not so much to deliver an "answer" as to provide a framework to assist in prompting some appropriate and helpful questions. Toward that end, I propose to

define *Customer Value* as *an interactive relativistic preference experience*:

> Thus, in general, I define value as a *relativistic* (comparative, personal, situational) *preference* characterizing a subject's *experience* of *interacting* with some object. By "object," I mean any "intentional object" - that is, any possible contents of consciousness or, as some philosophers have said (rather ungrammatically), "that which consciousness is conscious of." With respect to *customer* value in particular, the "subject" of interest is a *consumer* whereas the relevant "object" may refer to any *product* (i.e., any good, service, person, place, thing, event, or idea) (Holbrook 1993, p. 6).

In what follows, I shall argue briefly for each of the four aspects of value just introduced. Whenever possible, I shall illustrate with an example based on the consumption of clothing.

Interaction

In the view presented here, value involves an *interaction* between some subject (a consumer) and some object (a product). However, throughout history, various thinkers have focused on one or the other side of the subject-object dichotomy.

Thus, *subjectivists* suggest that value occurs entirely within the subject who experiences the value (Lamont 1955; Parker 1957; Perry 1954) so that - in the words of the familiar aphorisms - "(hu)man is the measure of all things" or "beauty is in the eye of the beholder." In marketing, this view of value appears conspicuously in the argument by Levitt (1960) on behalf of customer orientation or the conviction that "if the customer says it's good, it's good" (Steenkamp 1989, p. 59). If one takes a sober look at the fashion industry, one cannot help but notice the large subjective component that underlies judgments of physical beauty. Indeed, the quixotic manner in which fashions *change* from moment to moment seems to *require* the assumption of a large degree of subjectivity. (Few besides the author can claim to have consistently maintained *grunge* in their customary style of dressing for *decades*.)

By contrast, *objectivists* claim that value resides in the object under evaluation as an inherent property (Osborne 1933; Lee 1957; Hall 1961; Loring 1966; Hartman 1967). Thus, Tuchman (1980) views quality as "inherent" (p. 39), while Osborne (1933) sees beauty as "a formal property" (p. 124) and Adler defines "admirable beauty" as "objective, not subjective" (p. 117). In marketing, the objectivist position would correspond to the product orientation (Levitt 1960) in which a manufacturer argues that some product possesses value because he or she has *put* value into it via the use of some scarce resource(s) (e.g., the classical or Marxist "labor theory" of value), via excellence in manufacturing or engineering (e.g., a low rejection rate in quality control), or via the achievement of cost efficiencies (e.g., a low price by virtue of mass production). For example, a dress designer might claim objective value because of using rare antique ivory buttons or very strong stitching or bargain-basement prices.

However plausible the extreme subjectivist or objectivist positions might appear on the surface, I believe that only an *interactionist* perspective can withstand careful scrutiny. This position claims that value always entails some *interaction* between a subject or customer and an object or product (Pepper 1958; Morris 1964; Frondizi 1971). Colloquially, in this light, recall the old philosophical puzzle about whether a tree falling in the forest makes a sound if there is no one there to hear it; the point is that, even if it does make a sound, the fact that no one hears it means that the sound can *not* have any *value*. In Frondizi's (1971) words,

> The correct assertion that nothing can be [valued] if there is no subject to appraise it, can only lead one to infer legitimately that the subject who appraises cannot be discarded when one examines the nature of value (p. 55).

Along similar lines, the economist Alfred Marshall compared value to a pair of scissors: The subject is one blade; the object is the other blade; and you need *both* blades to get any results (Fallon 1971, p. 47). Thus, a piece of clothing has value only when it is appreciated as part of a consumption experience - perhaps by someone who wears it (e.g., quality) or admires it (e.g., beauty).

Relativism

In my view, value is *relativistic* in at least three important senses. Specifically, it is (1) *comparative* (among objects), (2) *personal* (across people), and (3) *situational* (in a given context).

(1) Value Is Comparative. One cannot legitimately make utility comparisons between people. For example, it would *not* be legitimate to claim that I like Madonna's ball gown more - or less - than *you* like Madonna's ball gown. It follows that the only valid utility assessments involve comparisons among objects within the same person. That is, it *does* make sense to assert that I like Madonna's ball gown more - or less - than *I* like her dominatrix outfit. Further, the evaluative judgment may well shift if one changes one's target of comparison. I might, for example, feel that Madonna's metal-studded brassiere is bad (compared, say, to her ball gown) *or* that it is good (compared, perhaps, to her black leather dominatrix suit). This general point has been argued (somewhat more technically) by any number of philosophers (e.g., Frondizi 1971; Hilliard 1950; Laudan 1977; Lewis 1946) but was captured (more intuitively) by a *New Yorker* cartoon showing two men at a bar with the caption, "For years, I'd been saying I preferred classical music to jazz, but I suddenly realized the other day that I don't like *any* kind of music." This joke makes sense only if one completes the man's statement with the implicit phrase "compared with drinking whiskey at this bar." In other words, the man has changed his level of comparison. He used to compare one type of music with another. Now he compares all types of music with something else that he likes better - namely, getting drunk.

(2) Value Is Personal. Most philosophers agree that value is *personal* in the sense that it varies from one individual to another (Bond 1983; Frondizi 1971; Hilliard 1950; Lewis 1946; Parker 1957; Von Wright 1963). We express this principle in the old apothegm to the effect that "one man's meat is another man's poison." I suspect, for example, that - unlike the author - some readers might actually prefer Madonna's dominatrix suit to her studded bra or her ball gown; they might even feel that Madonna looks more beautiful than, say, Julie London or that she sings more pleasingly than, say, Chris Connor and Rosemary Clooney. (It is at times like this that one's ability to maintain a relativistic position is pressed to the limits.)

(3) Value Is Situational. Value also depends on the *situation* or *context* in which the evaluative judgment occurs (Frondizi 1971; Hilliard 1950; Lewis 1946; Morris 1964; Von Wright 1963). In other words, the standards on which

evaluative judgments hinge tend to be context-dependent, changing from one situation to the next (Taylor 1961). For example, a fur coat might look ravishing to audience members at a Winter Meeting of the National Rifle Association, but it would probably look pretty tacky to those attending a Summer Conference of the Animal Rights Activists.

Preference

The most fundamental point we can make about customer value is that it embodies a *preference judgment* (Morris 1964; Perry 1954). Various social scientists have supplied a wide variety of terms to cover this basic phenomenon: Positive-Negative Predisposition; Favorable-Unfavorable Attitude; Pro-Con Opinion; Approach-Avoidance Behavior; Good-Bad Judgment; Like-Dislike Evaluation. All these terms refer essentially to value (singular) as opposed to values (plural), where the latter represents the standards or criteria on which the former evaluative judgment depends. Thus - if one applies the standards of traditional styling, careful workmanship, and warmth - one might develop a strong preference for a Laura Ashley dress. Different values-based criteria (e.g., chicness, inexpensiveness, lightness) might dictate a very different value (e.g., preferring something from The Gap).

Experience

From everything said thus far, it follows that value resides *not* in the product purchased but rather in the *consumption experience* derived therefrom (Holbrook and Hirschman 1982). This claim is the fundamental tenet in my own approach to consumer behavior and receives support from any number of axiologists (e.g., Baylis 1958; Hilliard 1950; Lewis 1946; Mukerjee 1964; Parker 1957). Among economists, the importance of the consumption experience emerged clearly in the work of Abbott (1955):

> The thesis...may be stated quite simply. What people really desire are not products but satisfying *experiences*. Experiences are attained through activities. In order that activities may be carried out, physical objects or the services of human beings are usually needed. Here lies the connecting link between man's inner world and the outer world of economic activity. People want products because they want the *experience-bringing serv-

ices which they hope the products will render (p. 40, italics added).

Thus, my emphasis on experience is "radical" only in the sense that a radish is a radical vegetable: It has *roots*. It is firmly *grounded* in axiology, economic theory, and marketing thought. From the latter perspective, experience is the basis for value. Value is the basis for exchange. And exchange is the basis for marketing (Kotler 1991). When some well-heeled customer at Saks Fifth Avenue trades $700 for a fine Pucci print, she not only derives value from the shopping experience itself (the department store as theater) but also anticipates the special satisfaction gained by wearing the costume to her next cocktail party (dress for success), not to mention the sensuous pleasure of the fine silk against her skin (hedonic gratification) and the beautiful appearance of the colorful pattern imprinted on the fabric (aesthetic appreciation).

The Types Of Customer Value

Dimensions of Value

As suggested by the typology shown in Table 1, I propose that the different types of customer value vary along three key dimensions: (1) Extrinsic versus Intrinsic, (2) Self- versus Other-Oriented, and (3) Active versus Reactive. Each deserves a few words of introduction.

Dimension 1: Extrinsic Versus Intrinsic Value. Value is *extrinsic* when it pertains to a means-end relationship, when some product is prized for its functional performance, when some consumption experience is appreciated for its instrumentality in accomplishing some further purpose, or when the worth of some object is viewed as utilitarian or banausic. By contrast, *intrinsic* value occurs when some experience is appreciated as an end in itself - for its own sake - as self-justifying or autotelic, from a ludic point of view. (Helpful discussions appear in work by, among others, Baylis 1958; Brandt 1967; Brightman 1962; Deci 1975; Frankena 1962, 1967; Hilliard 1950; Lee 1957; Lewis 1946; Mukerjee 1964; Nozick 1982; Olson 1967; Osborne 1933; Perry 1954; Rokeach 1973; Taylor 1961; Von Wright 1963.) For example, in the case of apparel, money has extrinsic value as a means to the end of acquiring a new wardrobe; but wearing the clothing may have intrinsic value, as when one secretly enjoys admiring oneself in the mirror.

Dimension 2: Self- Versus Other-Oriented Value. Value is *self-oriented* when I prize a product or experience selfishly or prudentially for *my own* sake, for how *I* react to it, or for the effect it has on *me.* Conversely, *other-oriented* value looks beyond the self to some other(s) (family, friends, neighbors, colleagues) or some Other (Country, Planet, Universe, Mother Nature, Cosmos, Deity) where something is valued for *their* sake, for how *they* react to it, or for the effect it has on *them.* (See Buber 1923; Fromm 1941; Hilliard 1950; Kahle 1983; Koestler 1978; Lamont 1951; Osborne 1933; Parsons 1951; Pepper 1958; Riesman 1950; Rokeach 1973; Siegel 1981; Von Wright 1983; and especially Mukerjee 1964.) For example, one might put on comfortable underwear primarily to please oneself; but one wears black to a funeral primarily out of respect for others.

Dimension 3: Active Versus Reactive Value. Value is *active* when it entails some physical or mental manipulation of some tangible or intangible object, whereas *reactive* value results from apprehending, appreciating, or otherwise responding to some object. In the first, *I* act upon *it*; in the second, *it* acts upon *me.* (See Hall 1961; Harré and Secord 1973; Mead 1938; Mehrabian and Russell 1974; Morris 1956, 1964; Osgood, Suci, and Tannenbaum 1957; Parker 1957; Pepper 1958; Rokeach 1973). For example, one might play an active role in sewing, knitting, or tie-dying one's own dresses, sweaters, or t-shirts, whereas one might react with admiration to the haute couture displayed at an exclusive Parisian Fashion Show.

A Typology of Customer Value

By treating each of the dimensions just described as a dichotomy and combining these three dichotomies into a 2x2x2 cross-classification, we may produce the eight-celled Typology of Value in the Consumption Experience that appears in Table 1. Each cell of this taxonomy represents a logically distinct type of value (with an example shown parenthetically) and deserves a brief explanation along with an illustration drawn from the area of apparel, clothing, and fashion that pertains directly to the present context. As a challenge, I have taken all such examples from advertisements contained in the December 1992 issue of *Vogue.* The fact that we easily find pertinent illustrations in just one issue of a fashion magazine suggests that the various types of value distinguished here bear considerable relevance to the case of clothing and apparel-related consumer products.

Efficiency. As defined here, *efficiency* results from the active use of a product to achieve some selfish purpose - as measured, for example, by the ratio of outputs to inputs (Bond 1983; Diesing 1962; Hilliard 1950; Lamont 1955). When the key input of interest is time, we typically call this O/I ratio "convenience." In the case of apparel, such convenience may refer to ease of shopping, ease of washing-drying-ironing, or ease associated with some other time-saving feature.

> An ad for watches produced by *Swiss Army Brands Ltd.* shows a picture of two gleaming stainless steel chronometers and proclaims: "The two-tone Swiss Army Brand...watch reflects a bold simplicity and elegant efficiency. Easy-to-read numerals. Precision accurate Swiss quartz movement.... the main effect is functional and straight-forward. It's tooled to perfection.

Excellence. As conceived here, efficiency differs from *excellence* in that the latter entails an inherently reactive response in which one admires some object for its capacity to serve as the means to a self-oriented end in the performance of some function. Such a utilitarian emphasis on the appreciation of instrumentality appears to constitute the essence of what we mean by "quality" (Abbott 1955; Bond 1983; Juran 1988; Pettijohn 1986; Steenkamp 1989; Tuchman 1980; Zeithaml 1988).

> An ad for *Saks Fifth Avenue* presents the *Swarovski Jeweler's Collection* as the closest thing to "perfection": "A Diamond Isn't The Only Thing That's Forever.... Because of the extraordinary quality and hand craftsmanship lavished on these pieces, each one is guaranteed for a lifetime.... Swarovski crystals are regularly rated 'IF' - internally flawless."

Politics. I employ the term *politics* in a general sense to designate the active use of one's own consumption behavior toward the other-oriented end of achieving a favorable response from someone else (Nozick 1981; Perry 1954). A conspicuous example of this push toward "success" occurs when one dresses with an eye to the role of clothing and accessories in impression management.

Presumably, how one smells may determine how successfully one appeals to the targets of one's amorous inclinations. Hence, an advertisement for *Narcisse Parfums Chloé - Paris* shows a naked woman in bed with a handsome French-looking fellow and suggests a direct connection between the superimposed perfume bottle and her ability to attract this Gallic Hunk: "How I longed for him to hold me, to be in his arms...."

Esteem. The reactive counterpart to political value involves the *esteem* that may result from a somewhat passive ownership of objects whose mere possession is appreciated as a means to building one's "reputation" with others (Bond 1983; Duesenberry 1949; Scitovsky 1976; Veblen 1899). Such Veblenesque examples of conspicuous consumption might include owning clothes or hats or jewels that are too uncomfortable or impractical or expensive to wear but that can be displayed in one's home to inspire the envy of friends and neighbors.

Such signals are greatly facilitated by the use of initials to register the cachet of prestigious brand names - as in the ad for *Louis Vuitton*, which features some fine leather luggage marked with the insignia "LV" and boasts that these aristocratic objects "bear witness to the rigorous standards of the House that has given travel its stamp of nobility since 1854."

Play. As a self-oriented experience - actively pursued and enjoyed for its own sake - *play* leads to having "fun" (Berlyne 1969; Bond 1983; Dearden 1967; Huizinga 1938; Santayana 1896; Stephenson 1967). For example, one can wear one's clothes playfully (a sweat shirt with a facetious motto or humorous quote), can don apparel suitable for playing an enjoyable game (golf or tennis), or can dress appropriately for a pleasurable leisure activity (jogging or swimming).

In an advertisement for *B and B Liqueur*, a brightly smiling woman wears a wedding dress, pearls, and dark glasses; she runs through the water along the beach and holds her wedding corsage plus two glasses in one hand, a bottle of B&B in the other; the message calls our attention to her "joie de vivre": "A joyous cele-

bration of life's unexpected moments. Moments meant for B&B.... B&B excites the palate and delights the imagination.

Aesthetics. On the reactive side of play, *aesthetics* in general refers to a self-oriented appreciation of some object where this experience is valued for its own sake, for example as a potential source of "beauty" in particular. This view of aesthetic experience as involving intrinsic value can be traced back to the work of Shaftesbury in 1709 (Beardsley 1967), but owes its most influential exposition to Kant's *Critique of Judgment* in 1790: "Kant discovered the essence of beauty in design enjoyed simply for itself" (Rader 1979, p. 331). Kant's perspective found further support in Bullough's (1912) concept of "psychical distance" and has since commanded a broad consensus among aesthetic philosophers (Budd 1983; Coleman 1966; Hampshire 1982; Hilliard 1950; Hospers 1967; Iseminger 1981; Lee 1957; Lewis 1946; McGregor 1974; Olscamp 1965; Perry 1854). Thus, in short, my aesthetic appreciation for a work of art (the intrinsic value of that experience) has nothing to do with any extrinsic purpose that the artwork might serve (as the means to an end). True, one *could* use an artistic masterpiece to perform some utilitarian function. A sculpture by Jean Arp might serve as an excellent doorstop, for example; or a Picasso painting held over one's head in a rain storm might make a handy umbrella. But the moment one used such an object primarily for that kind of a purpose, the value of the consumption experience would stop being purely aesthetic and would become largely instrumental. As noted by Budd (1983):

A person can value an object that is a work of art for many different kinds of reason.... his reasons...may or may not be because he finds the experience of the work of art intrinsically rewarding. Only if he finds the experience of the work of art intrinsically rewarding does he value the work as a work of art (p. 153).

Fashion too is often prized for its aesthetic merits (e.g., on the grounds of beauty). For example, in the case of clothing, one may sometimes ignore comfort (efficiency or excellence) and even propriety (politics or esteem) in one's admiration for a style of dress that appears "stunning" or one's appreciation for an outfit that seems "smashing" (so that considerations of beauty may take precedence over those of convenience or success).

Clearly, many cosmetic products serve little useful purpose other than to beautify the faces and bodies on which they are patted and smeared. In an ad for *Cover Girl Lipcolor*, the lovely visage of Christy Brinkley beams at us - her perfectly even and brilliantly white teeth flashing brightly through lips painted with a shade called "Redwood" - while the copy describes this visual impression as "luscious lasting color like no other": "Cover Girl Lip Advance. Now more luscious, more beautiful than ever."

Morality. The active and other-oriented pursuit of *morality* aims at "virtue" sought for its own sake as its own reward (Alicke 1983; Lewis 1946; Morris 1956; Nozick 1981; Parker 1957; Pepper 1958; Von Wright 1963, 1983). Thus, deontological value entails the concept of duty or obligation to others (Bond 1983; Hilliard 1950; Perry 1954) with a heavy emphasis on the connection between ethics and intrinsic motivation (Frankena 1973; Parker 1957). Such ethical obligations often appear in the form of socially accepted rules of conduct or conventions that dictate proper behavior, as when one feels an obligation to wear a white dress at one's wedding or a tuxedo to the prom.

Unless one counts the advertisements for social causes such as *Children, Inc.* - "Serving Needy Children Since 1964" (not exactly a fashion ad) - one needs to read between the lines a bit to extract ethical implications from the ad copy found in our sample issue of *Vogue*. For example, an advertisement for *Flemington Furs* shows a model completely naked beneath her "Denim-Dyed Black Cross Mink Trench Coat"; presumably, this flagrant flouting of virtuous concerns for animal rights is morally justified by the young lady's apparent need to keep warm.

Spirituality. As a more reactive counterpart to morality, *spirituality* entails an adoption, appreciation, admiration, or adoration of the Other in which a self-motivated "faith" may propel one toward a state of "ecstasy" involving a disappearance of the Self-Other dichotomy (Frondizi 1971; Mukerjee 1964; Parker 1957; Perry 1954; Pepper 1958). Generally, we think of spirituality as attached to religious experience involving the Deity, some broad view of the Cosmos, or some profound concept of the otherwise inaccessible Inner Self. However, one should note that an ecstatic disappearance of the self-other dichotomy may also occur when one becomes so involved in the "flow" of a consumption experience that one loses all sense of one's own selfhood in the rapture of the consuming moment. Such a phenomenon may characterize some shopping behavior wherein one's search for the ideal hand bag, the most becoming shoes, or the perfectly matching scarf becomes so obsessive or fanatic that people have coined the telling phrase "Shop 'Til You Drop" to describe it.

An ad for *Safari by Ralph Lauren* appears to evoke the spiritual side of experience when it shows a young woman in various suggestive poses - astride a massive horse, walking into a vast mountainous desert terrain, and smiling foolishly in some sort of giddy rapture: "Safari by Ralph Lauren. A world without boundaries. A personal adventure and a way of life."

Aesthetics Again

I hope to have shown that the nature of aesthetics as a type of value can best be understood by placing it in the context of the other types of value that we have distinguished. Specifically, I have proposed that *aesthetic value* in general or the *experience of beauty* in particular is *self-oriented*, *reactive*, and prized *intrinsically* for its own sake as an end in itself. Of equal importance, however, are the ways in which aesthetic value resembles and differs from other closely related types of value.

For example, Beauty is often confused, collapsed, or otherwise confounded with Quality (e.g., Garvin 1988) - perhaps because both involve a reactive self-orientation. However, in the present conceptualization, the latter entails a banausic utilitarian instrumentality, whereas the former stands on its own as a self-justifying end in itself. Thus, in the typology that appears in Table 1, Beauty is to Quality as Fun is to Convenience:

137

Aesthetics/Excellence:Play/Efficiency.

Similarly, aesthetics has close connections with play in that both involve self-oriented intrinsic value - the difference being that the latter is active whereas the former is reactive in nature. In other words, Beauty is the reactive counterpart of Play, just as Quality is the reactive counterpart of Convenience and Faith is the reactive counterpart of Virtue:

Aesthetics/Play:Excellence/Efficiency:Spirituality/Morality.

Finally, this parallelism between Beauty and Faith deserves special mention in its own right. The two resemble one another in their intrinsically motivated reactivity, but differ in that the latter is other-oriented, whereas the former is oriented toward the self:

Aesthetics/Spirituality:Play/Morality.

It should be added, however, that sometimes aesthetic consumption experiences can become so powerful that they verge on ecstatic rapture (Hilliard 1950; Makkreel 1975; Straus 1981). For example, in listening to the finale of Beethoven's Ninth Symphony, gazing at the ceiling of the Sistine Chapel, reading Milton's epic poetry, watching a dramatic sunset, or even looking at a splendiferously attired fashion model or movie star, we sometimes feel almost as if we become part of the object of our admiration. We seem to lose our independent consciousness and to merge with the artistic object. At such moments, the self-object dichotomy seems to dissolve. We enter a state of ecstasy.

Conclusion

A final crucial point concerns the fact that *any* or *all* of the value types distinguished earlier may and often do *occur simultaneously* to *varying degrees* in any given consumption experience (Eisert 1983; Hilliard 1950; Lee 1957; Lewis 1946; Morris 1956; Parker 1957; Taylor 1961). This co-occurrence, commingling, or compresence of value types provides a conceptual justification for the common multidimensional representations of customer value in marketing (e.g., as an ideal point in a perceptual map or preference space). More importantly, it reminds us that one may value (say) an architectural design because of *both* its beauty (as art) *and* its quality (as shelter); a church service because of *both* its politics (as a social event)

and its spirituality (as worship); a piece of sugar-free chewing gum because of *both* its fun (blowing bubbles) *and* its virtue (avoiding cavities). In a sense, *any* consumption experience unfolds like a flower whose petals represent many different kinds of value, each contributing to the overall effect.

Hence, I might summarize everything that I have said on the subject of "Axiology, Aesthetics, and Apparel" with one final illustration that encapsulates the distinctions I have proposed within one example of clothing worn by one consumer - namely, me. In this connection, consider my Old School Tie - a navy blue rep cravat made of silk (dry clean only) with little silver-colored insignias of Hermes (the Greek God of Commerce and Patron of Thieves) that resemble the Arabic numeral "4" with two horizontal bars running across the lower stem (the official emblem of the business school where I teach). Clearly, this mythically enriched piece of attire provides every conceivable type of customer value:

Efficiency by giving me an excuse for fastening the top button of my shirt so as to keep my neck warm;

Excellence in the high-quality of the weaving and stitching;

Politics when worn to a cocktail party at the Dean's house to impress him with my loyalty to the School shortly prior to the annual salary adjustments;

Esteem when hung conspicuously in the closet of our guest room to remind visitors that I come from a "Good School";

Play in the fun-loving manner with which I speak about this object of consumption (especially my whimsically irreverent references to Hermes as the Patron of Thieves);

Aesthetics in the subtle harmonization of the tie's blue-and-silver tones with the charcoal grey of my wool suit and the white expanse of my Oxford cloth shirt;

Morality in the charitable contribution represented by paying the School approximately three times what the tie is actually worth;

Spirituality in the deep Sense of Community that fills me with School Spirit as I proudly don this Sacred Garment.

In short, without wishing to push my point too far, I might suggest that the Axiology of Apparel - so intimately intertwined with the Beauty of Clothing - pervades all aspects of consumer attire and the consumption of costumes. Figuratively, every time we get dressed and wrap ourselves with garments heavy in evaluative meanings, we put on - for better or worse - some version of our Old School Tie.

Table 1. A Typology Of Value In The Consumption Experience

Dimension 2	Dimension 3	Dimension 1	
		Extrinsic	Intrinsic
Self-Oriented	Active	Efficiency (O/I ratio or convenience)	Play (fun)
	Reactive	Excellence (quality)	Aesthetics (beauty)
Other-Oriented	Active	Politics (success)	Morality (virtue or ethical acts)
	Reactive	Esteem (reputation)	Spirituality (faith or ecstasy)

References

Abbott, Lawrence. (1955). *Quality and Competition*. New York: Columbia University Press.

Adler, Mortimer J. (1981). *Six Great Ideas*. New York: Macmillan Publishing Co.

Alicke, Mark (1983). Philosophical Investigations of Values. In Lynn R. Kahle (Ed.), *Social Values and Social Change* (pp. 3-23). New York: Praeger.

Baylis, C. A. (1958). Grading, Values, and Choice. *Mind*, *67*, 485-501.

Beardsley, Monroe, C. (1967). History of Aesthetics. In Paul Edwards (Ed.), *Encyclopedia of Philosophy Vol.1* (pp. 18-35). New York: Macmillan and Free Press.

Berlyne, Daniel E. (1969). Laughter, Humor, and Play. In Gardner Lindzey and Eliot Aronson (Eds.), *The Handbook of Social Psychology Vol.3* (pp. 795-852). Reading, MA: Addison-Wesley Publishing Company.

Bond, E. J. (1983). *Reason and Value*. Cambridge: Cambridge University Press.

Brandt, Richard B. (1967). Personal Values and the Justification f Institutions. In Sidney Hook (Ed.), *Human Values and Economic Policy* (pp. 22-40). New York: New York University Press.

Brightman, Edgar S. (1962). Axiology. In Dagobert D. Runes (Ed.), *Dictionary of Philosophy* (pp. 32-33). Totowa, NJ: Littlefield Adams & Co.

Buber, Martin. (1923). *I and Thou*. New York: Charles Scribner's Sons.

Budd, Malcolm. (1983). Belief and Sincerity in Poetry. In Eva Schaper (Ed.), *Pleasure, Preference and Value: Studies in Philosophical Aesthetics* (pp. 137-157). New York: Cambridge University Press.

Bullough, Edward. (1912). 'Psychical Distance' as a Factor in Art and an Aesthetic Principle. *British Journal of Psychology*, *5*, 87-98.

Coleman, Francis J. (1966). A Phenomenology of Aesthetic Reasoning. *Journal of Aesthetics and Art Criticism*, *25*, 197-203.

Dearden, R. F. (1967). The Concept of Play. In Richard Stanley Peters (Ed.), *The Concept of Education*. New York: The Humanities Press.

Deci, Edward L. (1975). *Intrinsic Motivation*. New York: Plenum Press.

Diesing, Paul. (1962). *Reason in Society: Five Types of Decisions and Their Social Conditions*. Urbana, IL: University of Illinois Press.

Duesenberry, James S. (1949). *Income, Saving and the Theory of Consumer Behavior.* Cambridge: Harvard University Press.

Eisert, Debra C. (1983). Marriage and Parenting. In Lynn R. Kahle (Ed.), *Social Values and Social Change* (pp.143-167). New York: Praeger.

Fallon, Carls. (1971). *Value Analysis To Improve Productivity.* New York: Wiley.

Frankena, William. (1962). Value. In Dagobert D. Runes (Ed.), *Dictionary of Philosophy* (pp. 330-331). Totowa, NJ: Littlefield, Adams & Co.

Frankena, William. (1967). Value and Valuation. In Paul Edwards (Ed.), *The Encyclopedia of Philosophy Vol. 8* (pp. 229-232). New York: The Macmillan Company.

Frankena, William K. (1973). *Ethics* (2nd ed.). Englewood Cliffs, NJ: Prentice-Hall.

Frondizi, Risieri. (1971). *What Is Value? An Introduction to Axiology* (2nd ed.). La Salle, IL: Open Court Publishing Company.

Fromm, E. (1941). *Escape from Freedom.* Oxford: Farrar.

Garvin, David A. (1988). *Managing Quality: The Strategic and Competitive Edge.* New York: The Free Press.

Hall, Everett W. (1961). *Our Knowledge of Fact and Value.* Chapel Hill, NC: The University of North Carolina Press.

Hampshire, Stuart. (1982). *Thought and Action* (2nd ed.). Notre Dame, IN: University of Notre Dame Press.

Harré, R. and P. F. Secord. (1973). *The Explanation of Social Behavior.* Totowa, NJ: Littlefield, Adams & Co.

Hartman, Robert S. (1967). *The Structure of Values: Foundations of Scientific Axiology.* Carbondale, IL: Southern Illinois University Press.

Hilliard, A. L. (1950). *The Forms of Value: The Extension of Hedonistic Axiology.* New York: Columbia University Press.

Holbrook, Morris B. (in press). The Nature of Customer Value: An Axiology of Services in the Consumption Experience. In R. Oliver and R. Rust (Eds.), *Quality in Services Marketing.* Newbury Park, CA: Sage Publications.

Holbrook, Morris B. and Kim P. Corfman. (1985). Quality and Value in the Consumption Experience: Phaedrus Rides Again. In *Perceived Quality: How Consumers View Stores and Merchandise.* Lexington, MA: D. C. Heath and Company.

Holbrook, Morris B. and Elizabeth C. Hirschman (1982, September). The Experiential Aspects of Consumption: Consumer Fantasies, Feelings, and Fun. *Journal of Consumer Research, 9,* 132-140.

Hospers, John. (1967). Problems of Aesthetics. In Paul Edwards (Ed.), *The Encyclopedia of Philosophy Vol. 1* (pp. 35-56). New York: Macmillan and Free Press.

Huizinga, Johan. (1938). *Homo Ludens.* New York: Harper & Row.

Iseminger, Gary. (1981). Aesthetic Appreciation. *Journal of Aesthetics and Art Criticism, 39,* 398-397.

Juran, J. M. (1988). *Juran on Planning for Quality.* New York: The Free Press.

Kahle, Lynn R. (1983). Dialectical Tensions in the Theory of Social Values. In Lynn R. Kahle (Ed.), *Social Values and Social Change* (pp.275-283). New York: Praeger.

Koestler, Arthur. (1978). *Janus: A Summing Up.* New York: Vintage Books.

Kotler, Philip J. (1991). *Marketing Management* (7th ed.). Englewood Cliffs, NJ: Prentice-Hall.

Lamont, W. D. (1955). *The Value Judgment.* Westport, CT: Greenwood Press.

Laudan, Larry. (1977). *Progress and Its Problems: Towards a Theory of Scientific Growth.* Berkeley, CA: University of California Press.

Lee, Harold N. (1957). The Meaning of 'Intrinsic Value'. In Ray Lepley (Ed.), *The Language of Value* (pp.178-196). New York: Columbia University Press.

Levitt, Theodore. (1960, July-August). Marketing Myopia. *Harvard Business Review, 38,* 24-47.

Lewis, C. I. (1946). *An Analysis of Knowledge and Valuation.* La Salle, IL: Open Court.

Loring, L. M. (1966). *Two Kinds of Values.* New York: The Humanities Press.

Makkreel, Rudolf A. (1975). *Dilthey: Philosopher of the Human Studies.* Princeton, NJ: Princeton University Press.

McGregor, Robert. (1974). Art and the Aesthetic. *Journal of Aesthetics and Art Criticism, 32,* 549-559.

Mead, George H. (1938). *The Philosophy of the Act.* Charles W. Morris ed. Chicago: University of Chicago Press.

Mehrabian, Albert and James A. Russell. (1974). *An Approach to Environmental Psychology.* Cambridge: The M.I.T. Press.

Morris, Charles. (1956). *Varieties of Human Value.* Chicago: The University of Chicago Press.

Morris, Charles. (1964). *Signification and Significance.* Cambridge: The M.I.T. Press.

Mukerjee, Radhakamal. (1964). *The Dimensions of Values.* London: George Allen & Unwin.

Nozick, Robert. (1981). *Philosophical Explanation.* Cambridge: Harvard University Press.

Olscamp, Paul J. (1965). Some Remarks about the Nature of Aesthetic Perception and Appreciation. *Journal of Aesthetics and Art Criticism, 24,* 251-258.

Olson, Robert G. (1967). The Good. In Paul Edwards (Ed.), *The Encyclopedia of Philosophy Vol. 3* (pp. 367-370). New York: The Macmillan Company.

Osborne, Harold. (1933). *Foundations of the Philosophy of Value.* Cambridge: Cambridge University Press.

Osgood, Charles E., George J. Suci, and Percy H. Tannenbaum. (1957). *The Measurement of Meaning*. Urbana, IL: University of Illinois Press.

Parker, Dewitt H. (1957). *The Philosophy of Value*. Ann Arbor: The University of Michigan Press.

Parsons, Talcott. (1951). *The Social System*. Glencoe, IL: The Free Press.

Pepper, Stephen C. (1958). *The Sources of Value*. Berkeley: University of California Press.

Perry, Ralph Barton. (1954). *Realms of Value*. Cambridge: Harvard University Press.

Pettijohn, Caryl L. (1986, March/April). Achieving Quality in the Development Process. *AT&T Technical Journal, 65*, 85-93.

Rader, Melvin. (Ed.). (1979). *A Modern Book of Esthetics (5th ed.)*. New York: Holt, Rinehart and Winston.

Riesman, David. (1950). *The Lonely Crowd*. New Haven: Yale University Press.

Rokeach, Milton. (1973). *The Nature of Human Values*. New York: The Free Press.

Santayana, George. (1896). *The Sense of Beauty*. New York: Dover Publications.

Scitovsky, Tibor. (1976). *The Joyless Economy*. Oxford University Press.

Siegel, Eli. (1981). *Self and World*. New York: Definition Press.

Steenkamp, Jan-Benedict E. M. (1989). *Product Quality: An Investigation into the Concept and How It is Perceived by Consumers*. Assen / Maastricht, The Netherlands: Van Gorcum.

Stephenson, William. (1967). *The Play Theory of Mass Communication*. Chicago: University of Chicago Press.

Straus, Roger A. (1981, Spring). The Social-Psychology of Religious Experience: A Naturalistic Approach. *Sociological Analysis, 42*, 57-67.

Taylor, Paul W. (1961). *Normative Discourse*. Englewood Cliffs, NJ: Prentice-Hall.

Tuchman, Barbara W. (1980, November 2). The Decline of Quality. *The New York Times Magazine*, 38-41, 104.

Veblen, Thorstein. (1899, ed. 1967). *The Theory of the Leisure Class*. Harmondsworth, England: Penguin Books.

Von Wright, Georg Henrik. (1963). *The Varieties of Goodness*. London / New York: Routledge & Kegan Paul / The Humanities Press.

Von Wright, Georg Henrik. (1983). *Practical Reason*. Ithaca, NY: Cornell University Press.

Zeithaml, Valerie A. (1988, July). Consumer Perceptions of Price, Quality, and Value: A Means-End Model and Synthesis of Evidence. *Journal of Marketing, 52*, 2-22.

Apparel Preferences: Underlying Dimensions and Measurement

Bettie C. Minshall
Kansas State University

"Aesthetics" was coined by Alexander Gottlieb Baumgarten as the name for the "science of perception" (Collinson, 1992, p. 112). According to Collinson, Baumgarten's word was a derivation of the Greek word "aesthesis" which referred to both sensation and perception, "perception by means of the senses." As Collinson stated, aesthetic response involves a full range of responses from those described as cognitive in nature to those that are more affect-based. Berlyne (1971) stated that a study of "aesthetic behavior" (human response to objects) should include the behavior of the "appreciator" (i.e., perceiver) when exposed to objects (p. 7).

An element of the individual's appreciation process regarding objects involves the development and expression of preferences. Since 1865, researchers have attempted to examine the relationship between expressed preferences and the properties of objects (Berlyne, 1971). Apparel preferences, the favoring of one apparel object over another, are therefore considered to be a behavioral phenomena; tendencies that exist not just in how an individual thinks about an apparel object, but how the individual behaves toward the object. Studies of apparel preference should, therefore, include all aspects of the product's characteristics and those of the individual engaged in response to the product.

Preferences are also thought to be derived from a series of value judgments (Pepper, 1949; Zajonc & Markus, 1982). These value judgments are frequently based on the innate approach/avoidance tendencies of human beings toward other human beings and objects. Preferences may be modified by cultural ideals and the sensory perception[1] of the arrangement or structure of apparel objects by the observer. Understanding preferences and how they are developed is of great interest to individuals involved in the design, production, and marketing of apparel. Knowing how individuals respond to and develop preferences for apparel objects would assist manufacturers in the marketing of these products. The purpose of this paper is to review preference research, both theoretical and as applied in apparel research, and to identify issues influencing the measurement of apparel preferences.

Structure of Preference

According to Mandler (1982), the act of making an evaluative judgment of an object requires the individual to process mental representations of similar objects and to search for some degree of congruity between the object and the schema. When the individual's personal expectations are congruent with the characteristics provided by the object, a positive judgment will be made. The following sections provide an overview of the formation and development of preference schemata.

Dimensions of Preference: Knowing and Liking

Preferences are believed to consist of two general dimensions: a cognitive component and an affective component. The relationship between these two dimensions has become the source of debate among attitude and preference researchers (Mandler, 1982; Mandler & Shebo, 1983; Zajonc, 1980; Zajonc & Markus, 1982). George Mandler (1982) suggests that the cognitive and affective dimensions could also be referred to as "knowing" and "liking."

In general, the cognitive dimension of preference for an object is considered to be based on information that is inherent in the object or that is considered to be "descriptive." For example, the "shirt is red." The affective dimension of preference is tied to the emotional response elicited by an object, both the experience of emotion and the expression of emotion. Two basic judgments associated with the affective dimension include measures of "beautiful/ugly" and "like/dislike." For example, the "shirt is beautiful."

Preference Acquisition

Many propositions have been set forward which attempt to identify how preferences are formed. Zajonc and Markus (1982) utilized examples of food preferences to hypothesize that preferences can be established by affective means as well as by cognitive means. For example, they cite the innate aversion of the human palate to spicy foods, yet the development of a preference for these foods on the part of Mexican children, as an example of preference developed by affective measures. In this example, spices are gradually introduced into the foods of the children so that the palate comes to like and ultimately to prefer these tastes. Factors such as parental reinforcement, social conformity pressures (neighbors and relatives eat seasoned foods), and the need for identification with the group are used by the group to influence and reinforce this preference.

Zajonc and Markus (1982) point out that many preference studies have focused on feature-based preferences. As a result, the traditional notion holds that affect is postcognitive, implying that a feeling of preference is generated once the specific properties of an object are observed, noted, and evaluated, and organized into a product that represents overall preference.

Zajonc and Markus (1982) stressed that cognitive and affective factors may interact with each other and that in some cases the cognitive factors may dominate whereas in others, the affective factors may be predominant. However, they believe that under certain conditions, affective responses and cognitive responses may be independent of each other; that it is possible for the affective response (preference) to come first with the cognitive evaluation occurring afterwards, possibly as a justification for the affective response.

An opposing view has been presented by George Mandler (1982). Mandler stated that a cognitive process always precedes an evaluative judgment. He described evaluative judgments as evaluative cognitions and considered them the basis of the experience of liking, preference, or acceptability. Mandler cited several research reports which establish the idea that people prefer the known to the unknown, the usual to the unusual, and the familiar to the strange.

Mandler and Shebo (1983) proposed that liking and disliking are not opposites on a single psychological dimension, but are, instead, evaluations derived from different cognitive associations with the object. As individuals experience or encounter similar objects, they process and store information about the objects (e.g., preferences, likes, dislikes) and are able to invoke this knowledge when evaluations of an additional similar object are needed. Under Mandler and Shebo's model, preferences are based on cognitions which appear on a continuum from feature-oriented, descriptive cognitions to evaluative cognitions based on the overall relationship of the features. For example, the "sweater is yellow" (descriptive), the "sweater is warm" (relational), the "sweater is good" (evaluative).

In an earlier work, Stephen Pepper (1949) presented a discussion of the development of likes and dislikes. Pepper stated that all humans are born with instinctive drives which lead them to develop basic preferences. He included such examples as drives stimulated by hunger, thirst, maternal instincts, and risk aversion. In Pepper's stratification of likings, objects which satisfy instinctive likings are generally considered to be universally accepted; thus explaining why some works of art appeal across cultures. The next level in Pepper's stratification would include likings influenced by family traits or social sub-groups. The most discrete level is represented by individual or idiosyncratic likings. Preferences are therefore likely to be categorized as universal, familiar, or individual.

Development of Preference Schemata

If preferences are considered to be based on a series of value judgments, some means must be available for the observer to make these judgments whether they are cognitive or evaluative in nature. The structure for these judgments is derived from schema theory (Wyer, 1980). A preference schema is considered to be a mental representation that guides observer action, perception, and thought. Schemata containing organized knowledge relevant to an object (both object attributes and relationships among attributes) are developed as a function of the experience the observer has with the object category. Individuals must be able to first identify the category to which an object belongs, and then the schematic process allows them to describe their object preferences (Fiske & Taylor, 1984). In relation to apparel products, this means that consumers will base their preferences on prior experiences with similar apparel products, and the match between the apparel product and their corresponding preference schema.

When a new object is encountered, it will be evaluated in comparison to existing preference schemata. Mandler (1982) proposed that when the structure of the object is congruent with the relevant preference schema, the observer will develop positive evaluations of familiarity, acceptability, and liking. Mandler does not insist that the "mapping" be a perfect match. He allows that deviations from the preference schema are acceptable and that a judgment of liking will occur when there is a "reasonable fit" between the object and the schema. When the object's structure is incongruent with the preference schema additional mental activity may be required to determine if the evaluation will be positive or negative.

Preference as Related to the Perceptual Process

Gibson (1971) stated that in the perception process there is a greater emphasis on the cognitive aspects of an object than there is consideration for the emotions or stimulation derived from the object.

According to Cupchik (1992), Gibson's reduction of the perceptual process to simple cognition disregards a central component of the aesthetic experience, sensory stimulation, the physiological response to an object.

Molnar (1992) adheres to the belief that the perceptual process consists of a strictly sensory part and a strictly cognitive part. According to Molnar:

> ...meaning does not yet exist at the level where aesthetic behavior begins. One can therefore speculate that "lower order" relations encompassing the retina, thalamus, and primary visual cortex might produce more information relevant to aesthetics than can the more traditional emphasis on "higher order" relations involving perception and meaning. Aesthetic pleasure seems, at least at the start, to be independent of the cognitive system. (p. 110)

Molnar defines aesthetic behavior as the sensory processing of a stimulus and aesthetic pleasure as an affective state or emotion, a response to a stimulus processed through sensory channels. Basically, the form must exist before meaning can be attached via processing in the central nervous system. As such, affective and cognitive processing of an object are considered to be complementary. During this interpretive processing, meaning is attached to an object and preference schemata are either formed or revised. The issue of which comes first in preference formation, a cognitive or an affective response, has not been resolved in the literature. A cause and effect relationship between cognitive and affective responses is difficult to establish due to the unconscious, and therefore unreportable, processing activities associated with the perceptual process (Tsal, 1985).

Role of Stimuli in Preference Measurement

Preference researchers have attempted to identify characteristics associated with a stimulus that can elicit an affective response. Berlyne's theory (1971, 1974) was based on the notion that preference for a stimulus is triggered by the object's arousal potential. Berlyne's theory was based on the notion that human beings express the greatest amount of liking for stimuli that hold only a medium amount of arousal potential. As arousal potential increases, preference will move from neutrality to maximal liking. If there are further increases in the arousal potential of an object, human beings will respond with a decline in preference and ultimate displeasure.

Berlyne (1971, 1974) stated that the potential of a stimulus to arouse response is determined by the collative, psychophysical, and ecological properties of the object. Collative properties (e.g., novelty, complexity) refer to the comparison of the stimulus with prior objects or to relationships among features of a stimulus. Psychophysical properties are the measurable physical qualities of the stimulus (intensity, hue, texture). Ecological properties refer to the meanings or values associated with the stimulus object.

According to Martindale, Moore, and Borkum (1990), preference for a stimulus can be determined from the additive effect of these three dimensions. They stated that,

> If we accept the view that semantic categories are defined in terms of prototypical stimuli, there is evidence that preference is generally related to meaningfulness in either a positive monotonic manner or in a U-shaped fashion.....In all

cases, the most prototypical stimuli are maximally preferred. (p. 56)

Martindale, Moore, and Borkum (1990) further stated that their research has not substantiated the belief that collative variables are the most important in determining preference. In a series of seven experiments, using random polygons and drawings of real objects, Martindale et al. found that when respondents were presented with stimuli with ecological variation (variation in associated meanings), meaning overshadowed the collative variables in determining preference. In four of the seven experiments, ecological variation accounted for 47% of the variation in preference, complexity accounted for 15%. "It is well known that learned meaning is more important than complexity in accounting for reactions to some stimuli" (Martindale et al., 1990, p.74).

Martindale et al. proposed that aesthetic processing of objects involves the association of stimuli with mental schemata (p. 77). In fact, they stated that Berlyne's discussion of collative properties allowed that "collative properties are not in stimuli but are products of the interaction that would now be called mental representations" (p. 77). This approach would explain why typicality, or congruence with schema, accounted for the larger variation in preference in the experiments conducted by Martindale et al. Thus an individual's preference schemata, representing all prior experiences an individual has had with a product category, can have a greater impact on determining preference than the individual object.

Change in Preference Schemata

Researchers have focused not only on identifying preferences, but have also been interested in examining how preferences change, or if preferences can be forcefully changed. Pepper (1949) discussed preference change as a function of "mechanized habit mutation." Out of habit, individuals tend to develop preferences that, over time, tend toward neutrality in the amount of pleasure or pain derived from an object. As a result, through repeated exposure, objects which are originally disliked come to be much liked, and vice versa.

Zajonc and Markus (1982) discussed the difficulties encountered when trying to initiate preference changes. Their research indicates that if a preference is affect-based, the method used to change the preference should aim directly at the affective component. An appeal to the emotions would need to be made with little emphasis on cognitive components. To change preferences developed on a cognitive basis, however, generally requires persuasive communications that stress the "features" of the object.

As individuals acquire more information about, or experience with, an object's category, the associated preference schema will change. The ability of others to force a change in preference will therefore require an understanding of the formation of the schemata. Depending upon the nature of the schemata (was it developed on a cognitive basis, or was it affect-based), a variety of appeals or learning activities may need to be provided to elicit a preference change.

Preference for Apparel Objects

Behavior, as related to the selection of apparel objects, is an area that provides an opportunity to study the formation and influence of preference schemata (Miller, McIntyre, & Mantrala, 1993). Zajonc and Markus (1982) highlighted the importance of including a study of preference schemata in any field in which preferences are considered to be a subjective measure of an object's utility or value. Preference schemata will have an impact on what forms of apparel individuals choose. The following sections highlight the impact of (a) symbolic meanings in a cultural context, (b) experience, and (c) fashion on preference measurement in apparel-based research.

Influence of Symbolic Meanings in a Cultural Context

The existence of different symbolic meanings associated with apparel objects has led to varying preferences among cultural subgroups. Miller, McIntyre, and Mantrala (1993) have stated that:

Though most products, product attributes, services, and actions have utilitarian value to the consumer, the symbolic meaning attached to them provides additional value. When items are similar in their utilitarian value, their symbolic value may become a major determinant of choice. In many examples, the symbolic meaning can overcome seemingly large utilitarian deficiencies, as in the cases of tightly laced corsets, high-heeled shoes, and Elizabethan wigs. (p. 143)

Miller, McIntyre, and Mantrala further illustrated this concept with a comparison of a "black leather jacket" to a "brown leather jacket." The two jackets, while functionally equivalent, differ in symbolic associations. As the authors stated, "Because symbolic meanings, in general, evolve only in the context of social interaction, preferences between functionally equivalent styles exist only within a specific context and do not exist prior to the consideration of that context" (p. 146).

Ericksen and Sirgy (1992) examined the relationship between self-congruity, ideal congruity, and the clothing preferences of employed women. Employed females were found to prefer to wear outfits congruent with their actual and ideal self-image. This suggests that respondents preferred outfits that match the schema for their position of employment; outfits that matched the context of their ideal self-image.

Worth, Smith, and Mackie (1992) examined the relationship between subjects' masculine or feminine self-schemas and preference for gender-typed products. Female subjects were asked to evaluate a gender-neutral apparel product (blue jeans); however, some subjects were provided a distinctly masculine product description, others a feminine description, or one combining elements of both. They found that,

> Regardless of the traditional image of the described product itself, and regardless of the actual gender of the perceiver, subjects preferred a product described in terms that matched the gender attributes that they perceived as both characteristic of and important to themselves. (p. 28)

These studies support the contextual relationship between symbolic meanings and preference for apparel. Within a given subcultural context (based on occupation, social group, gender, or other recognized grouping), individuals will seek congruency between their context-based schema and the stimulus object. A positive evaluation, or preference for an apparel object, will be obtained when there is a perceived match between the object and the relevant schema.

Influence of Experience

Sugan (1985) noted that expert consumers (i.e., consumers who had experience with the product) were more likely than nonexperts to complete an in-depth analysis of object attributes when they were presented with objects which differed from their stored schema. Nonexperts were more likely to continue to utilize their prototypic schema representations. This suggests that experience with the stimuli will result in differing processing strategies when attributes in the object description vary in congruence with the schema.

DeLong, Kim, and Larntz (1993), hypothesized that a lack of experience with proportionally-sized garments would leave consumers less sensitive to proportional differences in part-to-whole relationships within garments. The assumption being that the existing schema for jacket would have been based on greater experience with non-proportional jackets. After providing respondents with information on proportion associations, DeLong, Kim, and Larntz found that their respondents preferred the stimuli representing jackets that were length-proportioned or totally-proportioned to their stimulus control. The control stimulus was a similar jacket with Misses-sized details. As a result of the training they had received, their respondents were better able to focus on object attributes and to discern subtle differences in proportion.

Influence of Fashion

Minshall, Winakor, and Swinney (1982) noted in a study of fashion preference that current and classic styles were preferred by both sexes over newly-introduced and outdated styles. Current or classic styles are more likely to match, or represent "typicality" in fashion, than are newly-introduced or outdated styles. The acceptability of styles currently in fashion or considered to be classic is a form of acceptance of prototypicality. DeLong, Minshall, and Larntz (1986) found that when real products (sweaters) were measured against respondents' schema for sweater, the products that were closer to matching the schema were evaluated more favorably than the sweaters that were judged as atypical.

There is also evidence to suggest that the preference schema for "fashionable" garments will change over time. DeLong, Salusso-Deonier, and Larntz (1981) compared responses to visual stimuli at two different points in time. A set of stimuli were presented to respondents with a 12-week gap between the first presentation and the second. This gap corresponded to a change from Winter to Spring in fashion. The researchers noted differences in the perceptions of the garments during the two time periods. An assumption underlying the study was that by Spring the fashion image would be different enough to change the observers' schema for suits. DeLong, Salusso-Deonier, and Larntz observed that when their Spring subjects responded to suits that varied in correspondence to the images, the response pattern did indicate a difference from the schema used by Winter observers.

In an additional study, DeLong and Salusso-Deonier (1983) noted that when repeatedly exposed to the same apparel stimuli there was an over-all shift in preference. This change was more pronounced for the evaluative measures utilized than for informational measures relative to the stimuli; thus supporting the belief that apparel preferences can be changed by repeated exposure.

Noting that "fashionable" reflects a societal influence, which in turn influences the development of the schema prototype and its revision over time, careful selection of stimuli for apparel preference research becomes an important consideration. When respondents are presented with stimuli that are congruent with the schema for "fashionable," a positive evaluation is obtained. As stated earlier, typicality can be shown to account for the largest variation in apparel preference. These studies also illustrate that, as Pepper (1949) suggested, there is the potential for a shift in preference to occur over time through repeated exposure.

Methodological Issues in the Measurement of Apparel Preference

Research focused on apparel products has included elements of both the cognitive and affective dimensions of preference; however, most of the research has been focused on the cognitive aspect of preference. Studies have focused on the relationship between preference, experience, and collative properties such as preferred colors, styles, fit, and other characteristics inherent in the stimulus object (DeLong, Kim, & Larntz, 1993). Efforts have been made to examine the relationship between the schema prototype for a given product category

(sweaters) and subsequent evaluations of real apparel products (DeLong, Minshall, & Larntz, 1986). In addition, other studies have addressed the relationship between preference and the symbolic meanings (ecological variation) attached to apparel products in varying subcultural contexts (Erickson & Sirgy, 1992; Worth, Smith, & Mackie, 1992).

The complexity and multidimensionality of preference raises certain methodological issues that need to be addressed by future researchers. In particular, issues influencing the selection of stimuli and measurement scales are discussed in the next section.

Selection of Stimuli

Selection of appropriate stimuli for use in preference studies is crucial to the question itself. As shown in the previous studies, the congruency between the stimuli presented and the schema prototype held by individuals can have an impact on the processing strategies utilized by respondents during preference measurement.

Use of artificial versus real apparel products. Holbrook (1983) discussed two contrasting methodological approaches to the selection of stimuli for preference measurement: (a) the manipulation of artificial stimuli (such as pictures or verbal descriptions); and (b) the use of real products (or prototypes) to obtain affective responses. Holbrook noted that when presented with real apparel products as stimuli, respondents appear to base their evaluation less on the visual factors and more on the tactile aspects of the object. Presentation of real products as stimuli allowed respondents to consider a variety of multisensory cues all relevant to the preference decision. The use of actual products may allow the respondents to consider aspects of the apparel which may be more obscure in artificial stimuli.

DeLong and Larntz (1980) found that a collective response to clothing as a whole form does exist. They noted that, "In this age of mass produced, ready-to-wear clothing, there is an obvious value in studying the collective response to clothing in a state close to what an observer would actually experience" (p. 293).

Use of typical versus atypical stimuli. When selecting apparel products for preference studies it is important to distinguish between typical and atypical stimuli. According to the perspective offered by Berlyne (1974), typical objects may be evaluated on the basis of extrinsic motivations (e.g., practicality), while atypical stimuli may be evaluated on the basis of intrinsic motivations (e.g., beauty). It may be possible that preference schemata for everyday dress are based on exposure to typical or prototypic examples, the variations that the individuals are likely to encounter in their daily lives. Atypical dress would include variations of items of dress that are not encountered in daily life.

In apparel studies focusing on everyday dress, it is therefore important to select stimuli relevant to the respondents' schema for everyday dress. This would allow the researcher to concentrate on the relationship between the collative properties of the objects and preference. If studying dress for purely affective response, stimuli which deviate from the schema for everyday dress (e.g., special occasion dress), and which are more atypical, may prove more beneficial in eliciting affective responses. For example, if examining preferences for apparel for the mass market consumer, the researcher would need to select apparel consistent with that available in the mass market. If a more affective response was desired, the researcher could select examples of "everyday dress" as presented by the haute couture.

Cupchik (1992) reiterates the notion that the processing of objects for aesthetic purposes differs from the processing strategies utilized with stimuli as everyday objects. According to Cupchik, aesthetic theorists characterize 'diversity' in objects by examining (a) the physical/sensory aspects of an object, and (b) the semantic aspects. Each of these are considered to be "multilayered, with each layer possessing its own 'qualitatively' distinct principles of organization" (p. 91). Cupchik stated that the physical/sensory level of an object can be examined in psychophysical terms (e.g., hue or tone) or in terms of "grouping" principles (e.g., symmetry or rules of organization). The semantic level includes the measurement of implicit or inferred meanings associated with the object.

The diversity in stimulus objects coupled with their congruency with schema prototypes can influence the researcher's ability to measure preference. Attention should be given to whether or not the selected stimuli elicit cognitive or affective responses. Preference will be more completely measured when the stimulus

objects and scales used by researchers elicit both the cognitive and affective dimensions of preference.

Selection of Measurement Scales

Russell and Gray (1991) have questioned the equivalency of evaluative scales used in studies of aesthetics. It has been common practice to assume that preferability, likability and pleasingness scales "are simply interpretable and essentially equivalent" (p. 76). In studies conducted by Russell and Gray, findings have indicated that the preferability scale contains more heterogeneity than previously thought. Russell and Gray suggest that "the question of what people 'prefer,' therefore, may not be simply answerable, and closer attention needs to be paid to the nature of this and other scales" (p. 76).

Most studies have used only one type of response scale (Russell & Gray, 1991) from a larger set of possibilities including "preferability," "likability," "pleasingness," "pleasantness," and "interestingness." (This has also been the approach used in apparel-based preference studies.) These "evaluative" scales (Berlyne, 1974), are used to measure the perceiver's degree of positive or negative response, to both the affective (e.g., like) and aesthetic (e.g., pleasant) qualities of stimuli. According to Russell and Gray, however, why a researcher has selected a certain scale is rarely explained in research studies. Russell and Gray (1991) stated that the assumption that these various scales are measuring the same construct can lead researchers to erroneous conclusions:

> To treat terms as synonymous in this way is to imply that the various scales all measure the same underlying psychological variable. To rank (or to rate) stimuli on, say, preferability, is assumed to be equivalent to ranking them on pleasingness, likability or any of several other properties. The main justification for this assumption comes from correlational and factor analytic studies. (pp. 76-77)

Russell and Gray concluded that the use of single item scales for preferability (e.g., most preferred to least preferred) or likability (e.g., like to dislike) may result in an incomplete or inaccurate measurement of aesthetic and affective response. For example, in some cases, the most "preferred" object may not be rated the most "pleasing." Likewise, the most "preferred" may not be the most "interesting."

The use of what appears to be a relatively homogeneous, unidimensional preferability scale may be masking the underlying basis for preference among sub-groups of respondents. In a study conducted by Russell and Gray (1991), they found that "some subjects base their preferability judgments on the degree to which the stimuli 'please' them, whereas others base their judgments on the degree to which they find the stimuli 'interesting'" (p. 77). On this basis, they proposed that pleasingness and interestingness may be regarded as causally prior to, or as determinants of preferability. Due to its high correlation with preferability, likability may share similar characteristics.

In three studies on the relationship between fashion preference and perceived risk, Lubner-Rupert and Winakor (1985), and Minshall, Winakor, and Swinney (1982) found that evaluative word pairs were closely related to preference rankings of the stimuli. Minshall, Winakor, and Swinney found that preference rankings for stimuli appeared to be related to the position of each stimulus relative to the least-liked style in the group. Preferability in this instance may actually have been determined by the degree to which the stimuli "pleased" them. Winakor and Goings (1973) were unable to establish a correspondence between style preferability and purchase behavior. The relationships between the dimensions of preferability, likelihood of owning, and actual buyer behavior have not been clearly established in apparel research.

The varying results obtained by apparel preference researchers indicate that the limited nature of the evaluative measures utilized may not be capturing all dimensions of apparel preference. According to Russell and Gray (1991), "studies that seek to link preferability to such stimulus properties as style, content, familiarity and complexity" (p. 83) should incorporate a variety of evaluative measures to examine in greater depth the content of preference judgments.

Summary and Recommendations for Future Research

Most of the research on preferences has focused on the cognitive dimension, the intellectual awareness and comprehension of the visual object by an observer. More recently, the affective or evaluative dimension, which is closely related to the emotional response of an observer to an object, has become important in preference research. Apparel, as a product category, allows observers to respond both cognitively and affectively. Therefore, a more complete study of apparel preferences should include both the affective and cognitive components of preference, as well as their interaction. Apparel preference researchers may find it useful to examine whether or not there are particular categories of apparel which evoke strong affective response while other items yield more cognitive responses. For example, how do viewers' responses to lingerie items (which are worn close to the body) differ from responses to raincoats (which are worn at a relative distance from the body). Greater attention should be given to the relationship between the research question to be addressed, the physical nature of the stimulus objects and their relationship to the category schema, and the varying influences affecting the preference schemata utilized by respondents.

Researchers generally accept the idea that preferences for apparel objects may change while the properties of the objects remain constant; that preferences will change with aspects of the perceiver's characteristics. When these preference changes are likely to occur, how they occur, and whether or not they can be induced by external forces is of great interest to individuals involved in timing the availability of products to coincide with the preferences of consumers. Questions here might include: What degree of product saturation, or length of exposure, leads to preference neutrality?; Should an apparel advertising campaign focus on the cognitive or affective dimensions of preference?

Preferences are not static and can be quite complex. Apparel preference research should combine the feature-oriented cognitive dimension and the affective, or evaluative, dimension, and should be constantly re-evaluated to determine whether the methodology used actually measures preference for apparel objects. For example, attention should be given to the use of stimuli that are at the appropriate level of detail (ranging from line drawings, to photographs, to real products) to evoke the desired responses. The mere presence of a stimulus can force a differing processing strategy than what would occur in the absence of stimuli, when individuals are more dependent on their mental representations of a given category of apparel.

In addition, studies in the area of aesthetics should incorporate a variety of scales to measure evaluative response. While a single scale may be useful in establishing rank order, it may not provide sufficient information for the subgrouping of respondents to examine more subtle variations in preference rankings. If respondents are asked to rank stimuli that they do not like their responses may reflect their preferences for particular items, but may not indicate where these preferences fit in their individual stratification of likings. Greater use of forced-choice, paired comparisons may yield more information on preference rankings than can be obtained from a single item scale.

As stated by Russell and Gray (1991), "future research may well benefit from becoming more 'multivariate' in character, allowing especially for the essentially multifactorial nature of dependent variables such as preferability" (p. 83). The complexity of apparel preferences make them difficult to measure and interpret, but also make them an interesting and challenging area of study.

Endnotes

[1]Sensory perception includes a variety of responses such as those derived through visual, tactile, olfactory, and auditory senses.

References

Berlyne, D. E. (1971). *Aesthetics and psychobiology*. New York: Meredith Corporation.

Berlyne, D. E. (Ed.). (1974). *Studies in the new experimental aesthetics*. Washington, D. C.: Hemisphere.

Collinson, D. (1992). Essay four: Aesthetic experience. In O. Hanfling (Ed.), *Philosophical aesthetics: An introduction* (pp. 111-178). Oxford, UK: Blackwell Publishers.

Cupchik, G. C. (1992). From perception to production: A multilevel analysis of the aesthetic process. In G. C. Cupchik and J. Laszlo (Eds.), *Emerging visions of the aesthetic process: Psychology, semiology, and philosophy* (pp. 83-99). New York: Cambridge University Press.

DeLong, M. R., & Larntz, K. (1980). Measuring visual response to clothing. *Home Economics Research Journal, 8*, 281-293.

DeLong, M., Kim S., & Larntz, K. (1993). Perceptions of garment proportions by female observers. *Perceptual and Motor Skills, 76*, 811-819.

DeLong, M. R., & Minshall, B. C. (1988). Categorization of forms of dress. *Clothing and Textiles Research Journal, 6*(4), 13-19.

DeLong, M. R., Minshall, B., & Larntz, K. (1986). Use of schema for evaluating consumer response to an apparel product. *Clothing and Textiles Research Journal, 5*(1), 17-26.

DeLong, M. R., & Salusso-Deonier, C. (1983). Effect of redundancy on female observers' visual responses to clothing. *Perceptual and Motor Skills, 57*, 243-246.

DeLong, M. R., Salusso-Deonier, C., & Larntz, K. (1981). Comparison of visual responses of female observers to clothing over time. *Perceptual and Motor Skills, 53*, 299-309.

Ericksen, M. K., & Sirgy, M. J. (1992). Employed females' clothing preferences, self-image congruence, and career anchorage. *Journal of Applied Social Psychology, 22*, 408-422.

Fiske, S. T., & Taylor, S. E. (1984). *Social cognition*. New York: Addison-Wesley Publishing Company, Inc.

Gibson, J. J. (1971). The information available in pictures. *Leonardo, 4*, 27-35.

Holbrook, M. B. (1983). On the importance of using real products in research on merchandising strategy. *Journal of Retailing, 59*(Spring), 4-20.

Lubner-Rupert, J. A., & Winakor, G. (1985). Male and female style preference and perceived fashion risk. *Home Economics Research Journal, 13*, 256-266.

Mandler, G. (1982). The structure of value: Accounting for taste. In M. S. Clark and S. T. Fiske (Eds.), *Affect and cognition* (pp. 3-36). New York: Academic Press.

Mandler, G., & Shebo, B. J. (1983). Knowing and liking. *Motivation and Emotion, 7*, 125-144.

Martindale, C., Moore, K., & Borkum, J. (1990). Aesthetic preference: Anomalous findings for Berlyne's psychobiological theory. *American Journal of Psychology, 103*, 53-80.

Miller, C. M., McIntyre, S. H., & Mantrala, M. K. (1993). Toward formalizing fashion theory. *Journal of Marketing Research, 30*, 142-157.

Minshall, B., Winakor, G., & Swinney, J. L. (1982). Fashion preferences of males and females, risks perceived, and temporal quality of styles. *Home Economics Research Journal, 10*, 369-379.

Molnar, F. (1992). A science of vision for visual art. In G. C. Cupchik and J. Laszlo (Eds.), *Emerging visions of the aesthetic process: Psychology, semiology, and philosophy* (pp. 100-117). New York: Cambridge University Press.

Pepper, S. C. (1949). *Principles of art appreciation*. New York: Harcourt, Brace and Company.

Russell, P. A., & Gray, C. D. (1991). The heterogeneity of the preferability scale in aesthetic judgments of paintings. *Visual Arts Research, 17*(1), 76-84.

Sugan, M. (1985). Consumer knowledge: Effects of evaluation strategies mediating consumer judgments. *Journal of Consumer Research, 12,* 31-46.

Tsal, Y. (1985). On the relationship between cognitive and affective processes: A critique of Zajonc and Markus. *Journal of Consumer Research, 12,* 358-362.

Winakor, G., & Goings, B. D. (1973). Fashion preference: Measurement of change. *Home Economics Research Journal, 1,* 195-209.

Worth, L. T., Smith, J., & Mackie, D. M. (1992). Gender schematicity and preference for gender-typed products. *Psychology and Marketing, 9*(1), 17-30.

Wyer, R. S. (1980). The acquisition and use of social knowledge: Basic postulates and representative research. *Personality and Social Psychology Bulletin, 6,* 558-573.

Zajonc, R. B. (1980). Feeling and thinking: Preferences need no inferences. *American Psychologist, 35,* 151-175.

Zajonc, R. B., & Markus, H. (1982). Affective and cognitive factors in preferences. *Journal of Consumer Research, 9,* 123-131.

Cultural Foundations of Aesthetic Appreciation:
Use of Trope in Structuring Quiltmaking Sentiment

Catherine A. Cerny
Virginia Polytechnic Institute and State University

Today we recognize that social life in the United States is culturally diverse. While we share common values as Americans, we are also individuals whose social lives reflect a vital mix of subcultural influences, including age, gender, ethnicity, and lifestyle. The post modern perspective, according to Best and Kellner (1991), encourages exploration of the dynamic interplay of these social forces on people's lives by favoring a world characterized by "multiplicity, plurality, fragmentation, and indeterminacy"; it acknowledges a relativist world in which individual knowledge is "historically and linguistically mediated" (p. 4). Correspondingly, aesthetic appreciation, as positioned within this perspective, combines both individual and collective viewpoints, integrating the unique experience of an individual and the particular sociocultural circumstances that frame the experience.

Fiore, Moreno, and Kimle (in press) have defined aesthetics as the study of human response to products, specifically internal processes, the product's multi-sensory characteristics, and the psychological and socio-cultural factors of the individual that affect response to the non-instrumental quality of the product.

The focus of this analysis is on the appreciation process, what is qualified as "the internal processes that take place during the aesthetic response" to a quilt (Fiore, Moreno, and Kimle, in press). However, the nature of this appreciation is not to be considered in isolation as simply an emotion, feeling, or thought but must be understood by examining of the circumstances that frame the viewer's knowledge of and reaction to the object. If we are to formulate a critical, comprehensive aesthetic theory about the textile/apparel object, we must recognize how psychological, social, and cultural factors interrelate to constitute the aesthetic experience Wheter during the creative process or in the object's appreciation.

This paper yields insight into the nature of aesthetic appreciation by suggesting how a cultural ideology may shape sentiments toward the aesthetic form. Sentiment, "an attitude, thought, or judgment permeated or prompted by feeling; a complex of emotion and idea" (*Webster's Third New International Dictionary*, 1981, p. 2069), arises when personal reactions are informed by culturally based meanings and reflects individual emotions mediated by cultural obligations. By embodying the complexity and creativity of ideological thought, the play of tropes enriches an individual's emotional experience of an aesthetic object by offering potential meanings. Tropes include figurative devices, such as metaphor, metonymy, synecdoche, and irony, and refer to "the use of a word or expression in a different sense from that which properly belongs to it for giving life or emphasis to an idea" (*Webster's Third New International Dictionary*, 1981, p. 2542). The correspondence and interaction of several tropes (i.e., play of tropes) within a specific event or text potentially integrates each person's experience around the unifying cultural theme(s).

In developing this perspective on aesthetic theory, the researcher must acknowledge the individual's cultural viewpoint. A semiotic orientation to the nature of culture, the role of language, and their importance in structuring individual knowledge can expand understanding of aesthetic appreciation. In this case, I draw upon the concept of cultural bricolage to characterize the creative role of tradition in shaping contemporary quiltmaking and the concept of play of tropes to describe the influence of ideology in structuring quiltmakers' sentiments.

Interpretive Perspective

Post modern assumptions shape the interpretive perspective: A person's knowledge of the world and his/her subsequent perception of and reaction to the aesthetic object are seen as historically and linguistically mediated. The mediation that links the person to the social circumstance, can be defined conceptually through understanding ideology as cultural bricolage. Aesthetic appreciation responds to a dialectic that juxtaposes individual and cultural attempts to resolve the paradoxes extant in social life. Attention to the play of tropes embedded in the subcultural traditions can reveal the complex juxtapositions of meaning that bind a person to the culture and lend significance to individual action.

Cultural Bricolage

Susan Kaiser (1990a, 1990b) urged apparel scholars to acknowledge the post modern conditions influencing apparel use in late twentieth century American society. She observed that people react to mass culture in favor of more individualistic styles and use clothing selectively in managing appearances and in on-going processes of creating the self. Kaiser (1990b) characterized this individualistic expression as bricolage:

> a French word referring to the idea of "do-it-yourself"--of finding solutions to problems by examining, using, and combining cultural signs in ways in which they were not initially intended. (p. 468)

A re-examination of Levi-Strauss' discussion of bricolage suggests that we must look more closely at the mythological context of cultural discourse to understand the impact of its meaning. In making Levi-Strauss' discussion pertinent to American subcultures, I expand his conception of bricolage to include the ideological context of a culture: Ideology is comparable to mythological thought. Both serve as logical models, or explanatory systems, which structure understanding of reality; ideology "tries to solve social contradictions," while mythology "tries to solve contradictions with nature" (Larrain in Noth, 1990, p. 378). Both underlie quilt tradition to the extent that the quiltmaker positions a genetically determined body within a culturally defined space.

Levi-Strauss (1966) referred to mythological thought as a form of "intellectual bricolage." Like science, it represents knowledge that has been systematically observed and ordered. But unlike science, mythological (and by extension, ideological) explanations of reality may appear random, irrational, and without basis in fact. These explanations are preconstrained yet enriched by the limited, heterogeneous bricolage

that is a culture's history: While new meanings about an event or object are shaped by its place within this history and by the significance of its features within the semiotic system, they need not replicate historic patterns or relationships. The signs themselves are permutable: Although signs draw from a rich and extensive repertoire of knowledge that is continually generated within social life, the new meanings are the consequence of random explanations, appropriate for their potential in accounting for current contradictions, ambiguities, and ambivalence, rather than representing a logical evolution of form or ideas over time.

Levi-Strauss' notion of bricolage can be applied to post modern social life. Understanding of the contemporary American quilt subculture can be expanded by acknowledging that women's involvement in quiltmaking involves reference to traditional conceptions of female identity and social roles. Lasansky (1988) positioned contemporary quiltmaking as recent manifestation of the colonial revival movement; she noted that the colonial past was valued "to educate us, to console us, to distract us, and to lend credibility ..." (p. 97). Gunn (1993) commented on the persistence of quilt myths throughout the twentieth century even as quilt historians became more rigorous in their documentation. Williams (1992), in her study of an Indiana guild, demonstrated that quilters can clearly relate the concept of tradition to contemporary quiltmaking; the utility of the quilt links "lives and sentiments" and recalls "traditional images of womanhood and women's work" (p. 137). At the same time Langellier (1991), in her study of a Maine quilt guild, found that quiltmaking empowers a feminine identity, one that "refashions, but does not reject, dominant meanings for femininity" in light of "the changing roles of women in society and the changing culture of quiltmaking" (p. 49). Embedded in the literature of contemporary quiltmaking (i.e., popular quilt books and magazines) and in the activities of a quilt guild (i.e., show-and-tell and programming) lie both the ideological foundations of quilt tradition and the infusion of new ideas, techniques, meanings, and opportunities that reflect changing society (see also, Langellier, 1993; Williams, 1992).

Play of Tropes

The orientation to culture as a complex meaning system used by people to make sense of themselves and the surrounding world (Geertz, 1973; Spradley, 1979) has challenged researchers to examine the semiotic constituents of society, especially language. However as suggested by Levi-Strauss' view of culture, the access gained to a person's conceptual world through language will not yield straight forward relationships or simple explanations of meaning. James Fernandez (1991) noted that

> we are living at a time when the referential value of language, its ability to provide us with an accurate, transparent view through to and mapping of the reality of things--an "immaculate perception," as it is called--is profoundly questioned, and we have become acutely aware of the figurative devices that lie at the very heart of discourse, defining situations and grounding our sense of what is to be taken as real and objective and, therefore, entitled (by means of the figurative entitlements we employ) to have real consequences. (p. 1)

The words of a language can be described as signs, arbitrary relations between sound images (i.e., signifier) and concepts (i.e., signified) (Saussure, 1916/1983). But meaning, as suggested in the discussion of cultural bricolage, is a far more complex formulation.

Attention to tropes, or figurative devices such as metaphor, helps sort out the complex associations and permutations of signs evidenced in the discourse, behaviors, and objects of social life. Lakoff and Johnson (1980) (see also, Johnson, 1987; Lakoff, 1987) demonstrated the pervasive nature of metaphoric processes as metaphors frame a person's understanding of reality. Anthropologists and art historians (Adams, 1975; Neich, 1982; Nunley, 1981; Schwarz, 1979; Turner, 1980) have applied metaphor to define the significance of textiles and dress in culture. They noted that parallels between object form and social order underlie the object's significance. Levi-Strauss (1966) suggested that the correspondence between social life and ideology evidenced by the object involves the individual in its appreciation:

> aesthetic emotion is the result of this union between the structural order and the order of events, which is brought about within a thing created by man and so also in effect by the observer who

discovers the possibility of such a union through the work of art. (p. 25)

An observer's understanding of reality, as constituted by culture, not only informs the making and use of the object, but shapes its appreciation.

Noth (1990) found that the definition of metaphor in *Webster's Third New International Dictionary*, combined key criteria evidenced in its conventional applications. Metaphor is:

> a figure of speech in which a word or a phrase denoting one kind of object or action is used in place of another to suggest a likeness or analogy between them. (p. 128)

For example, the metaphoric association of the quilt as a history draws upon the similarity between the quilt pieced with diverse, colorful fabrics and a history composed of diverse stories of women's lives. Debates among scholars about the semiotic implication of metaphor have been extensive (see Fernandez, 1974; Johnson, 1981; Ricoeur, 1981). Recognizing analogies between society and the individual, we expand our understanding of metaphor. Building upon the work of Bicchieri (1988), Terence Turner (1991) argued that metaphors "take on more, and deeper, 'life,' that is, deeper and more central meanings for the system in which they arise" (p. 129). The implications of this view are that metaphor is not a unique cognitive faculty or a privileged construct; rather, that metaphor, as well as other tropic and nontropic forms, "can shade or change into one another in response to changes [i.e., diachronic or synchronic] in context" (p. 129). Responsive to the changing social dynamics of post modern society, metaphor can reflect the immediate significance of an event and provide a path that involves participants in the social action.

Metaphor functions in coincidence with other tropic forms, including metonymy and synecdoche. Together they constitute an play of tropes that, through the juxtaposition and interrelationship of imagery, defines personal experience and involves individuals in social life. Metonymy indicates that the significance of an object is defined through a substitution based on its contiguity with other phenomena (i.e., objects, activities) with which it has a customary association (Eco, 1979, p. 280-1); this may include "substituting for the name of a thing, the name of an attribute of it or of something closely related to it" (*Oxford English Dictionary*, 1989, vol. XVII, p. 696). For example, attributes of the body (i.e., hand, heart) are used to represent specific qualities of personhood (i.e., craftsmanship, affection). Body and personhood are distinctive concepts, yet they exist in customary proximity to each other. Closely related to metonymy, synecdoche indicates that the significance of an object is defined through substitution with other phenomena that share conceptual content (Eco, 1979, p. 280-1); this may include substituting "a more comprehensive term ... for a less comprehensive term or vice versa; as whole for part or part for whole, genus for species or species for genus ..." (*Oxford English Dictionary*, 1989, vol. IX, p. 478). For example, hearth is substituted for home, implying through more specific imagery (i.e., glowing hearth) the warmth of family, those who reside in the home and gather around the hearth. Turner (1991) characterized how synecdoche may contribute to the play of trope; synecdoche represents "a specific relationship between metaphor and metonymy, as when a part of a whole (a metonymic relation) also replicates the form of the whole (a metaphoric relation)" (p. 148). The significance of the above example is contingent on the broader metaphoric imagery, which relates the making of the warm quilt, also found within the home, to women's contribution to the comfort and unity of family life.

Metaphor, metonymy, and synecdoche are interconnected in substantiating ideological thought. Turner (1991) noted that

> both tropes and cultural structures are constructed through a "play of tropes," a dialectical process in which meaningful wholes are simultaneously integrated as parts of larger wholes and differentiated into new patterns of relationships among their own parts. Not only is meaning constructed in such a process through the interplay of distinct tropes, but the same symbolic elements ... figure in different tropic capacities at different levels of the structure of the same ritual, myth, or other type of meaning construct. (p. 150)

Identifying the interplay of metaphor, metonymy, and synecdoche in quiltmaking literature

offers the opportunity of deconstructing quilt tradition and isolating persistent mythic themes.

The Play of Tropes in Quilt Sentiment

The analysis draws from the texts of nineteen quilt books, published between 1915 and 1980.[1] The literature was initially reviewed in 1985-6 with the purpose of identifying the role of tradition in characterizing twentieth century quilt revivals (Cerny, 1986). I examined how twentieth century literature drew upon the art and experiences of historic quiltmakers to define contemporary values and practices. As orientations toward the purpose of quiltmaking in women's lives changed, a romanticism about the evocative power of quilts and quiltmaking appeared to be defined, integrated, and perpetuated (see also, Gunn, 1993).

A more recent interpretation of these passages, presented in this paper, suggests that tropes may be influential in relating the values embedded in quilt tradition to the social experiences of contemporary quiltmakers. The play of tropes draws upon an immediate experience of the quilt (i.e., the perception of a quilt's warmth and the bodily sensations accompanying quiltmaking) to mark the emotional intensity of social connectedness and personal empowerment. Initially I located occurrences of tropes in the texts, recognizing that a metaphor, metonym, or synecdoche would not be limited to a single word but would encompass a phrase or longer passage of text. It was necessary to cite enough of the passage to understand how the imagery was used to structure meaning. Secondly, I sorted the tropic passages according to dominant themes (i.e., warmth/social connectedness and body/personal empowerment) and then organized them according to sensory, personal, and sociocultural domains of expression. At this stage of the textual analysis I was concerned with identifying persistent cultural themes that unified the body of literature and then with understanding how tropic imagery might be used in relating the themes to the reader. These domains were defined from careful and repeated readings of the passages.

Critical perspective of the correspondence of this imagery with contemporary quiltmaking comes from the study of a Minnesota quilt guild during the mid 1980s (Cerny 1992a & 1992b; Cerny, Eicher, & DeLong, 1993), subsequent involvement in the Rhode Island quilt documentation project in the 1990s (Welters, Cerny, Ordonez, & Kaye, 1994), and research on contemporary quilt guilds (Langellier, 1991 & 1993; Williams, 1992) and historic needlework (Parker, 1986). The ideological stance that quilts and quiltmaking empower women's identity within the family and community is replicated by meanings quiltmakers and quilt owners attach to their quilts.

Experiential Domains of Quiltmaking

The textual analysis illustrates how the play of trope communicates the ideological/mythological thought of quilt tradition. Moving from sensory to personal and community contexts, sentiments involve the women in a structuring of reality that connects individual priorities with values of the larger social world and provide her with a comprehension of her connectedness in social life.

The experience of quilt tradition can be understood on an immediate sensory level. Kinesthetic sensations occur as the quiltmaker designs, cuts the fabric, assembles the quilt top, and quilts the fabric layers. The physiological sensation of warmth may come from use of the quilt as a bedcover or garment.

Second, quilt tradition can be understood on a personal level, in part stimulated by the sensory experience of making or using a quilt. The completion of a quilt can lead to a sense of pride in one's accomplishment. Simultaneously, the comfort of a quilt's warmth, transformed, can be experienced as psychological comfort: of well-being with one's self and of security in one's circumstances (e.g., family). The sensory experience (i.e., of making or using) suggests a contiguity of domains (i.e., of quilt and person) that facilitates the transfer of meaning.

Finally, quilt tradition can be experienced on a social level as a person integrated within a community, albeit as quiltmaker or woman. The quiltmaker's appreciation of her quilt may be structured by her experiences within a quilt guild and/or through her knowledge of quiltmaking history. The individual woman sees herself as quiltmaker, one of many who in a nation of great diversity, shares common experiences and values. Quiltmaking and hence quilt appreciation can lead to the experience of communitas, a sense of oneness among members of an otherwise diverse community. Victor

Turner (1969) referred to communitas as that moment

> in and out of secular social structure, which reveals, however fleetingly, some recognition (in symbol if not always in language) of a generalized social bond that has ceased to be and has simultaneously yet to be fragmented into a multiplicity of structural ties. (p. 96)

Together these experiences, whether they be immediate or drawn from memory, have the effect of reflecting the wholeness of one's being. This coming together of the person as part of a community and a tradition, first as a quiltmaker and then as a woman and citizen of the United States, is parallel to the piecing together of fabric pieces that constitute the completed quilt. In both cases, it is the woman who is worthy recognition.

As we see, two distinctive yet interconnected, patterns of tropic play are evidenced in the quilt literature. The first pattern is grounded in the experience of the warm quilt. Warmth becomes a metaphor that elaborates on personal relationships and social connectedness. In the discourse of quilt tradition evidenced in the literature, successive permutations of warmth juxtapose differing levels of experience to facilitate an integration of the reader's experiences within the broader context of a women's history in America. The second pattern is grounded in the activity of quiltmaking. In this case, metonymic markers that reflect the physical and psychological body, juxtapose the action of assembling the quilt with the symbolic implications of quiltmaking. As the quilt becomes coincidental with the quiltmaker, qualities of femininity are highlighted. Although metaphor stands out in the first pattern and metonym in the second, each evidences the influence of synecdoche in unifying and strengthening the impact of communicating the significance of quilts and quiltmaking to the contemporary quiltmaker.

The Comfort of a Warm Quilt. Warmth describes a person's perception of the quilt in two ways: On the one hand, warmth is concrete and familiar--a bedcover that protects against the cold. On the other hand, warmth is a more abstract concept--the affection between individuals that defines their relatedness. In social life, physical and emotional warmth may be experienced simultaneously. Ickis (1949) evoked such experience in the following memory: "the cold frosty mornings on the farm at Grandmother's when the gay homemade quilt on her four-poster felt cozy and warm" (p. 253). The experience of the quilt and its warmth enhances understanding about more abstract qualities of psychological and social life. In the phrase "cozy and warm," there is a physical comfort concomitant with a psychological comfort, the well being of a self secure in family and home (i.e., "cozy"). Finley (1929) broadened the symbolic implications of the quilt beyond the family context by commenting that quilts are the "most popular form of feminine hospitality" (p. 33).

Both Ickis' and Finley's statements must be read in light of other commentary. Not only do quilts represent the home as a pleasant and comfortable retreat to family and visitors, but both quiltmaking and home fall within the domestic responsibilities of women. Webster (1928)[2] noted that "the comfort of the family depended upon the thrift, energy, and thoughtfulness of the woman" (p. 80). Chief among these domestic responsibilities is providing a social context that unifies the efforts and objectives of family members and preserves solidarity. Quiltmaking not only provides good practice in developing skills necessary in managing a household, but provides an opportunity for the woman to involve the cooperation of family members. Ickis (1949) noted:

> The quilting craft, which is so deeply rooted in the home, offers a binder to hold its conflicting interests together. Father and the boys will find pleasure in making the quilting frame and its supporting stands, and in keeping them in topnotch condition. The girls can easily join in making the quilt blocks and will enjoy stories about the pieces and patterns (p. vii)

Women who meet their responsibilities gain the affection of family members. Both accomplishments reinforce self concept. Webster (1928) noted that "the selection of design, the care in piecing, the patience in quilting; all make for feminine contentment and domestic happiness" (p. xvi). The association of woman with the quilt and then with home highlights the implications of society's expectation that women are primar-

ily responsible for enhancing the connectedness of individuals within a family.

Quiltmaking might occupy many hours of piecing and stitching but it broke the monotonous routine of daily life and allowed the woman to reflect on the joys of her life. Peto (1939) emphasized the centrality of women's duty to the family, but acknowledged some reward for the individual creativity:

> quilts were born of urgent necessity, to fulfill a basic need ... added to the utilitarian purpose of the quilt was the desperate need women felt to keep their hands busy during so called leisure hours, for feminine minds and hearts were occupied with stern and sorrowful things ... Still, their patchwork contrived to be gay. (p. xiv)

More recently, Bacon (1975) found a balance between familial duty and personal needs:

> A strange blending of the twin goals of practicality and artistry, it served two purposes: the very physical necessity of keeping warm in rudely constructed, mud-daubed houses, and equally important, the creating of a quilt met a psychological need--serving as an outlet for the pioneer woman's artistic and aesthetic longings. (p. 26)

In providing for the comfort for the family, the quiltmaker also gains a comfort from personal hardships through her expression. In part, quiltmaking was seen as therapy through which a woman could work out psychological conflicts. Radka Donnell, in forward to Chase and Dolbier (1978), pointed out that "quilts, as fabric arts, speak of warmth, closeness, contact, and union among persons ..." (p. 7) and in a subsequent paragraph defined the tropic nature of the quilt, "by its closeness to a person's body the quilt can become an icon of personal feeling and hope" (p. 7). The quilt metaphorically stands for the woman and embodies her life experiences. The quilt has evolved as a vehicle by which the quiltmaker can give voice to her unique experiences.

From the experience of warmth, an individual is comfortable and comforted; s/he gains a sense of well-being from the security one gains from a family. This same security is transferred to the country as a whole through the imagery of warmth. Quilts are about American history; McKim (1962)[3] described this history in terms of quilt patterns "kindled" by the creativity of women:

> And the story of their wanderings, their few possessions, their accumulations, the friendships formed, their abiding faith and the home established, is the story of the patchwork quilts. Study the names of patterns and again you will know they were so christened by young ladies of imagination, sometimes devout, sometimes droll but always kindled by that divine spark of originality. Listen to this for a less-than-500-word history, all quilt names stitched in bed coverlets, which are more comforting, if not more enduring, than words graven in stone. (p. 3)

As the authors manipulated the reader's sentimental attachment toward the quiltmaker, they likewise revealed images of empowered women. Finley (1929), in her characterization of a key moment in quiltmaker/women's history, noted the importance of the past and focused on a women's history:

> Eighteen-eighty is an important date in the progress of American womankind; for it was only after 1880 that woman's economic and political status really began to change. Freed in the end from psychological as well as material restraints, women closed the gate at the end of many a road. Her journey of more than two and a half centuries along the trail of her patchwork was finished. The story of her heart, as written in this particular work of her hands, was done. (p. 198)

Quilt histories principally talked about women in generalities. The lives of individual quilt makers were largely unrecorded. What remained of their lives were their quilts. Quilt historians, such as Ickis (1949), pointed out how these extant quilts can stimulate memories of ancestors and unify family over time. "Quilts were the family records of good days and bad--pictures of the past for younger generations to cherish...They made real stories to tell around the glowing hearth on winter evenings" (p. 266-267). For Webster (1928), quiltmakers could be just as crucial to the connectedness of a family as they could be to a nation: "be a source of

much satisfaction to all patriotic Americans who believe that the true source of our nation's strength lies in keeping the family hearth flame bright" (p. xvi). Quiltmakers, as guardians of home and social life, have worked in partnership with men to establish "civilization" in rural America.

Hand, Heart, Mind, Voice. Central to understanding the experience of quiltmaking is the metonymic use of parts of the body to stand for the whole body and, by virtue of its contiguity to self, to stand for the person. Through the use of metonymic references to the body, the authors linked the history of quilts to individual quiltmakers. At the foundation of this dialectic are the act of quiltmaking and the activity of the quiltmaker's hands. Hall (Hall & Kretsinger, 1936), in speaking to contemporary quiltmakers, pointed out the psychological and social implications of handwork:

> Quiltmaking is the ideal prescription for high-tension nerves. It is soothing and there is no exercise can equal that of really creating something with the hands. And later the product of these hands may be handed down as a treasured heirloom. (p. 46)

Newman (1974) placed this labor in the context of quilt history:

> Working with fabric is a flexible, fluent, exciting experience, leading to endless invention made possible by the plethora of fabrics, threads, and inventive stitches that have multiplied over time. It is no wonder that new expressions are still emerging from the stitches of so many hands. (preface)

But contiguous to the labor of quiltmaking is the expression of a quiltmaker's emotion and ideas. Robertson (1948) summarized this creative process. "They cut bits of cotton cloth into shapes of familiar objects or into shapes which somehow best expressed their thoughts and feelings for the moment" (p. 39). The quilt is valued for "its universal use and intimate connection with our lives" (Webster, 1928, p. xv). Ickis (1949) provided a intimate picture of one woman's experience:

> My whole life is in that quilt. ... All my joys and all my sorrows are stitched into those little pieces. ... And John too. He was

stitched into that quilt and all the thirty years we were married. Sometimes I loved him and sometimes I sat there hating him as I pieced the patches together. So they are all in that quilt, my hopes and fears, my joys and sorrows, my loves and hates. I tremble sometimes when I remember what that quilt know about me. (p. 270)

As we saw in the discussion on the metaphor permutations of warm, the quilt represents the woman. However in this case, the reader observes the woman actively involved not only in making the quilt but in formulating the expression.

References to hands and hearts, albeit implied through descriptions of quiltmaking, are elaborated in characterizing the implications of extant quilts. Finley (1929) was explicit in her use of the metonym. "Her journey of more than two and a half centuries along the trail of her patchwork was finished. The story of her heart, as written in this particular work of her hands, was done" (p. 198). Later authors, more subtle in expressing this contiguity more specifically between the quiltmaker (rather than more generally as woman) and social history, relied on the readers' understanding of the lexicon of quilt tradition. Ickis (1949) noted that "life histories are tightly stitched within the gay covers--tales of individuals and communities filled with failure and triumphs" (p. 253). Newman (1974) noted: "Stitch by stitch, the story of humanity describing the fabric of everyday life has been sewn into countless examples of quilting, patchwork, and applique" (p. 1). Each life history is like the fabric scrap that comprises the completed quilt. Just as the pieces are stitched together to form the quilt so too do individual lives interrelate to constitute the social life of a family, community, or nation.

The history of quilts is a story about women. Yet in accomplishing this task, the authors drew upon the inherent nature of the quilt. Just as the completed quilt is comprised of many fragments of fabric; so too is history comprised of individual stories. The fragments once composed within the quilt contribute to the overall beauty of the whole; so too does each woman contribute to the viability of contemporary American social life. The pragmatic and artistic choices that mark the process of making a quilt become opportunities for the quiltmaker to speak out about her experiences as a woman. These choices account for the unique design and expression of the quilt. For example, Webster (1928) noted:

A distinct individuality is worked into every quilt by its maker, which in most instances makes it worthy of a name. The many days spent in creating even a simple quilt give the maker ample time in which to ponder over a name for the design, so that the one selected generally reflects some peculiarity in her personality. (p. 115)

Quilt names tell about the "inner and outer life" of generations of American women (Finley, 1929, p. 8). Choices about the design and name of a quilt are parallel to the use of words in speech; the quilt itself is the medium of expression, not unlike that of the voice. Ickis (1949) used this trope:

Some seem to speak in soft voices and reveal decorous manners, while others are bold in design depicting the rigors of pioneer days, of war between the states, or...are the special ones for weddings, winter and summer use, expressions of friendships and many others ... (p. 207)

More recently, Gutcheon (Gutcheon & Gutcheon, 1976) questioned the extent to which the contemporary quiltmaker could assume women's contribution to this dialogue:

I came to feel that American quilts are not just a series of artifacts but an important part of the history of American women. That their beauty, their ingenuity, and also the vast amount of repetition, the great number of cautious variations on familiar themes, in some important way constitutes a record of what life has been like for American women. Not the least important is the fact that while the quilts contain a great deal of testimony, almost all of it is mute. American women have long had hearts and minds, but only a very few have had voices. (p. 6-7)

The Orlofskys (1974) noted that women "have created works of great evocative power as part of an endless struggle for expression" (p. 73). Perhaps the contemporary quiltmaker sees herself as part of this struggle, albeit as the history of women or the history of the United States.

The quilt historians drew upon the evocative power of the quilt to envelop the quiltmaker in a cultural and historical tradition. Likewise, their attention to the features of the quilt points to the individuality possible in quiltmaking and, more importantly to a recognition of personal contributions to American history. Hechtlinger (1974) noted:

> While the immediate charm of a quilt comes from its color, its design, and its fabric, that appeal is augmented by its history, which may be personal in its association but which also may recollect important aspects of our national history. (p. 287)

A quilter gains not just the moment--"the pleasure of doing" or "the joy of possession" (Webster, 1928, p. 149), but with reflection upon the past--"remind[ing] us of the simple pleasures of our grandmothers" (p. 136) and a look to the future--"the reward of her work ... can be passed on even to future generations, for a well-made quilt is a lasting treasure" (p. 149).

Referential Nature of Quiltmaking

These early books on quilts and quiltmaking do not take the conventional orientation in documenting a history of quilts. Rather, the extant quilt must stand in place of specific people and events as evidence of a past. Collectively in their discussion about the significance of the quilt and the value of quiltmaking, the authors capture an ideology upon which quilt tradition is founded and perpetuated. The play of tropes juxtaposes the historic tradition with contemporary practice in such of way as to empower quiltmaker as women in society. The modern quiltmaker faces a different world from that of her predecessor. Yet, quiltmaking can still serve as an outlet for her coping with life's adversities and celebrating its joys. Through their discourse, the quilt authors suggest to the contemporary quiltmaker that the complex feelings and ideas she has about herself can be worked out through her quiltmaking, just as past quiltmakers. Furthermore, in the process of, and as a consequence, of her quiltmaking the woman can mark the totality of her self--her individuality, her familial ties (both generational and immediate), her community affiliations, and her identity as a woman.

The discourse of quilt literature elaborates a play of tropes by which quiltmakers can interpret perceptions of social life within a common mythic structure that juxtaposes quiltmaking and domestic domains of experience. In its reconstruction of quilt tradition, quilt literature situates the history of quilts within a history of quiltmakers. In turn, these women--wives, mothers, grandmothers have been crucial players in American history. In this juxtaposition of domains, intricately described through the play of tropes, the contemporary quiltmaker/woman can readily place herself, via her own quiltmaking, within a woman's history and consequently in an American history. A crucial feature in this re-creation is the literature's characterization of social life. The coincidence that in the latter twentieth century women are faced with challenges and conflicts similar to women of the past involves them in the discourse.

The ideology embedded in the quilt books, likewise, structures aesthetic appreciation. As the quiltmaker is integrated into the subculture, she appropriates understanding of quilt culture. Culturally defined meanings influence personal reactions. Yet the consistency of these sentiments among a group of quiltmakers can be evidenced, for example, in women's remarks about quilts in the show-and-tell of guild meetings and in written comments by quilt owners and makers on exhibited quilts (Cerny, 1988; Cerny, Eicher, & DeLong, 1993). The quilts are to be appreciated not only for the design features, but for the circumstance of their making--for their power in speaking about women's lives.

Importance of Cultural Analysis to Aesthetic Theory

The multiplicity of late twentieth century social life requires understanding the cultural forces that shape subcultural society. Likewise a cultural orientation to aesthetics necessitates thorough knowledge of the traditions that mediate the thought and actions of a people. In each case ethnography provides the methods for documenting social events and for interpreting their relevance from the perspective of the participant. The persistent ideological/mythological themes of a culture are apparent in its traditions, but traditions change over time. Equating ideological/mythological thought as cultural bricolage allows the researcher to address the creative forces that allow culture to accommodate the ambiguities of social life precipitated by change.

When focusing on the significance of an aesthetic object, scholars must reference their conclusions through careful analysis of the meanings that circumscribe its making and appreciation. Such meanings, although not always explicit and straight-forward, are integral to a person's knowledge and appreciation of the object. Attention to the play of tropes in the oral and written traditions of a people provides one means of linking individual experiences to unifying cultural values. In this study I described how the play of tropes relates the warmth of a quilt and the act of quiltmaking to values of social connectedness and female empowerment. The mythic tradition of quiltmaking, evidenced in part by the popular literature, evokes images of female struggle and accomplishment, which in turn may be personalized through the varied expressions of contemporary quiltmakers. In this instance I suggest that meanings, articulated in the creation of the quilt form, are mediated by an correspondence between quilt tradition (including patterns and techniques) and personal experience.

By questioning the basis for the sentiments that quiltmakers have for their work, I suggest that the internal processes occurring during an aesthetic response involve a dynamic interplay of psychological and cultural factors. Cultural mythology/ideology when manifest as tradition in written discourse of quiltmaking, utilizes tropic imagery to relate collective values to the individual. These meanings can be conceptualized as sentiment. The quiltmaker's appropriation of this sentiment is contingent on the nature of her experiences both within the subculture and broader reaches of social life. This paper has addressed the presence of tropic imagery in quilt literature. Studies of contemporary quilt guilds evince a communication of quilt sentiment in group activities. Further research, which draws upon intensive interviews and life histories of quiltmakers, is needed to detail the impact of individual sentiments in the aesthetic appreciation of a quilt.

Endnotes

1.Four additional books, published prior to 1980, were examined and found not to contain passages in which tropes were used to characterize historic quiltmaking traditions. Their elimination from this analysis does not preclude the presence of metaphor, metonymy, or synecdoche in the texts. While these twenty-three books are not exhaustive of all publications prior of all publications prior to 1980, they do represent the more widely recognized works (Finley, 1929; Holstein, 1973; Ickis, 1949; McKim, 1962; Orlofsky and Orlofsky, 1974; Peto, 1939; Webster, 1928). The books range in focus from the how-to books, with information on technique, design approaches, patchwork and quilting patterns, contemporary use, and/or historic overviews, to historic surveys.

2.Webster was originally published in 1915 by Doubleday, Page and Company in New York.

3.McKim was originally published in 1931 by McKim Studios in Independence, MO.

References

Adams, M. J. (1975). Structural aspects of a village art. *American Anthropologist, 75*, 265-279.

Bacon, L. I. (1980). *American patchwork quilts.* New York: Bonanza Books.

Bicchieri, C. (1988). Should a scientist abstain from metaphor. In A. Klammer, D. McCloskey, & R. Solow (Eds.), *The consequences of economic rhetoric* (pp. 100-114). Cambridge: Cambridge University Press.

Best, S. & Kellner, D. (1991). *Postmodern theory: Critical interrogations.* New York: The Guilford Press.

Cerny, C. (1986). Quilt tradition. Unpublished manuscript.

Cerny, C. (1988). Quilted apparel: A case study of a cultural vehicle. (Doctoral dissertation, University of Minnesota 1987). *Dissertation Abstracts International, 48*, 3545B. (University Microfilms No. DA 8802390).

Cerny, C. (1992a). Quilted apparel and gender identity: An American case study. In R. Barnes & J. B. Eicher (Eds.), *The anthropology of dress and gender: Making and meaning* (pp. 106-120). Oxford: Berg Publishers.

Cerny, C. (1992b). A quilt guild: Its role in the elaboration of female identity. In L. Horton (Ed.), *Uncoverings 1991* (pp. 32-49). San Francisco: American Quilt Study Group.

Cerny, C., Eicher, J. B., & DeLong, M. R. (1993). Quiltmaking and the modern guild: A cultural idiom. *Clothing and Textile Research Journal, 12*, 16-25.

Chase, P. & Dolbier M. (1978). *The contemporary quilt: New American quilts and fabric art.* New York: E. P. Dutton.

Eco, U. (1979). *A theory of semiotics.* Bloomington: Indiana University Press.

Fernandez, J. W. (1974). The mission of metaphor in expressive culture. *Current Anthropology, 15*(2), 119-145.

Fernandez, J. W. (1991). Introduction: Confluents of inquiry. In J. W. Fernandez (Ed.), *Beyond metaphor: The theory of tropes in anthropology* (pp. 1-13). Stanford, CA: Stanford University Press.

Finley, R. E. (1929). *Old patchwork quilts and the women who made them.* Philadelphia: J. B. Lippincott Co.

Fiore, A. M., Kimle, P. A. & Moreno, J. M., (in press). Aesthetics: A comparison of the art outside and inside the field of textiles and clothing, Part 1. *Clothing and textiles Research Journal.*

Funk and Wagnall's Standard Dictionary. (1980). New York: Signet/The New American Library, Inc.

Geertz, C. (1973). *The interpretation of cultures.* New York: Basic Books, Inc.

Gunn, V. (1993). From myth to maturity: The evolution of quilt scholarship. In L. Horton (Ed.), *Uncoverings 1993* (pp. 192-205). San Francisco: American Quilt Study Group.

Gutcheon, B. & Gutcheon J. (1976). *The quilt design workbook.* New York: The Alchemy Press.

Hall, C. A. & Kretsinger, R. G. (1936). *The romance of the patchwork quilt in America.* Caldwell, Idaho: The Calton Printers. Ltd.

Hechtlinger, A. (1974). *American quilts, quilting, and patchwork.* New York: Galahad Books.

Ickis, M. (1949). *The standard book of quilt making and collecting.* New York: The Greystone Press.

Johnson, M. (Ed.). (1981). *Philosophical perspectives on metaphor.* Minneapolis, MN: University of Minnesota Press.

Johnson, M. (1987). *The body in the mind: The bodily basis of meaning, imagination and reason.* Chicago: University of Chicago Press.

Kaiser, S. (1990a, July). Fashion as popular culture: The postmodern self in the global fashion marketplace. *The World & I,* 521-529.

Kaiser, S. (1990). *The social psychology of clothing: Symbolic appearances in context.* New York: Macmillan Publishing Co.

Lakoff, G. (1987). *Women, fire, and dangerous things: What categories reveal about the mind.* Chicago: The University of Chicago Press.

Lakoff, G. & Johnson, M. (1980). *Metaphors we live by.* Chicago: The University of Chicago Press.

Langellier, K. M. (1991). Contemporary quiltmaking in Maine: Re-fashioning femininity. In L. Horton (Ed.), *Uncoverings 1990* (pp. 29-55). San Francisco: American Quilt Study Group.

Langellier, K. M. (1993). Show-and-tell as a performance event: Oppositional practice in contemporary quiltmaking culture. In L. Horton (Ed.), *Uncoverings 1992* (pp. 127-147). San Francisco: American Quilt Study Group.

Larrain, Jorge. (1980). *The concept of ideology.* Athens: University of Georgia Press.

Lasansky, J. (1988). The colonial revival and quilts: 1864-1976. In J. Lasansky (Ed.), *Pieced by mother: Symposium papers* (pp. 97-105). Lewisburg, PA: Oral Traditions Project of the Union County Historical Society.

Levi-Strauss, C. (1966). *The savage mind.* Chicago: The University of Chicago Press.

McKim, R. S. (1962). *One hundred and one patchwork patterns.* New York: Dover Publications Inc.

Neich, R. (1982). A semiological analysis of self-decoration in Mount Hagen, New Guinea. In I. Rossi (Ed.), *The logic of culture: Advances in structural theory and method* (pp. 214-231). South Hadley, MA: J. F. Bergen Publishers, Inc.

Newman, T. R. (1974). *Quilting, patchwork, applique, and trapunto.* New York: Crown Publishers, Inc.

Noth, W. (1990). *Handbook of semiotics.* Bloomington: Indiana University Press.

Nunley, J. (1981). The fancy and the fierce. *African Arts, 14*(2), 52-58, 87.

Orlofsky, P. & Orlofsky, M. (1974). *Quilts in America.* New York: McGraw-Hill.

Oxford English dictionary. (1989). (Vols. 1-20). Oxford: Clarendon Press.

Parker, R. (1986). *The subversive stitch: Embroidery and the making of the feminine.* London: The Women's Press.

Peto, F. (1939). *Historic quilts.* New York: The American Historical Company.

Richards, I. A. (1950). *The philosophy of rhetoric.* New York: Oxford University Press.

Ricoeur, P. (1981). *The rule of metaphor: Multidisciplinary studies of the creation of meaning in language.* Toronto: University of Toronto Press.

Robertson, E. W. (1948). *American quilts.* New York: The Studio Publications Inc.

Saussure, Ferdinand de. (1983). *Course in general linguistics.* (R. Harris, Trans.). London: Duckworth. (Original work published in 1916)

Schwarz, R. A. (1979). Uncovering the secret vice: Toward an anthropology of clothing and adornment. In J. M. Cordwell & R. A. Schwarz (Eds.), *The fabrics of culture* (pp. 23-45). The Hague: Mouton Publishers.

Spradley, J. P. (1979). *The ethnographic interview.* New York: Holt, Rinehart and Winston.

Turner, T. (1980). The second skin. In J. Cherfas & R. Lewin (Eds.), *Not work alone: A cross-cultural view of activities superfluous to society* (pp. 112-140). London: Temple Smith.

Turner, T. (1991). "We are parrots," "Twins are birds": Play of tropes as operational structures. In J. W. Fernandez (Ed.), *Beyond metaphor: The theory of tropes in anthropology* (pp. 121-158). Stanford, CA: Stanford University Press.

Turner, V. W. (1969). *The ritual process: Structure and anti-structure.* Chicago: Aldine Publishing Company.

Webster, M. D. (1928). *Quilts: Their story and how to make them.* New York: Doubleday, Doran and Co., Inc.

Webster's third new international dictionary. (1981). Springfield, MA: G. and C. Merrian Co.

Welters, L., Cerny, C. A., Ordonez, M, & Kaye, A. (1994). *The Rhode Island Quilt Documentation Project* [machine-readable data file]. Kingston, RI: University of Rhode Island, Department of Textiles, Fashion Merchandising & Design (Producer).

Williams, C. N. (1992). Tradition and art: Two layers of meaning in Bloomington Quilters Guild. In L. Horton (Ed.), *Uncoverings 1991* (pp. 118-141). San Francisco: American Quilt Study Group.

Aesthetics of the Body[1] and Social Identity

Nancy Ann Rudd
Ohio State University

Sharron J. Lennon
Ohio State University

In the American culture of the late 20th Century, the body is a very important component of personal appearance and contributes significantly to judgments of attractiveness. Attractiveness is a cultural construction whose aesthetic parameters change with respect to strength, duration, and sanctions. According to scholarly writers (e.g., Banner, 1983; Beuf, 1990; Freedman, 1986), the contemporary standard of ideal female beauty is based primarily on facial attractiveness and body attractiveness in terms of size/weight[2] (e.g., Alicke, Smith, & Klotz, 1986; Douty & Brannon, 1984; Lennon, 1988). Women, then, quickly learn to monitor their appearances in an attempt to approximate the cultural ideal perhaps to reach what they believe is their full attractiveness quotient. Through such physical manifestations of appearance as body form and size, cosmetics and grooming procedures, and apparel and accessory selection, we actively create our appearances in response to a cultural ideal. Although we focus on the U.S. culture in the late 20th Century, we believe that the same process occurs in many other cultures and time periods.

In this paper we offer a model to explain individual response to the cultural ideal as it relates to appearance. This model builds upon two previous models (DeLong, 1987; Hillestad, 1980) which provide strong justification for focusing on the body as a major component of appearance. In Hillestad's taxonomy of appearance, the body is a key unit in the structure of appearance. The body is the vehicle for carrying and giving aesthetic and social expression to articles of dress. Aspects of the body such as form, surface, and motion may each contribute uniquely to the total structure of appearance.[3]

Body form refers to size, shape, or "packaging" of various body parts. While a genetic predisposition accounts for many variations in form (e.g., rounded shoulders, tiny rib cage, height, facial and body proportions), cultural body ideals may account for achieved variation in body form (e.g., sculpted muscles, tucked tummy, or anorexic thinness). Wide variation also exists in body surfaces, both in natural features, textures, and colors, and in their achieved modifications. Body motions continually change the landscape of personal appearances through posture, facial expressions, and mannerisms, each of which may be influenced by time and culture. The other key unit in Hillestad's taxonomy is dress, including all articles of clothing and adornment. The unit of dress is also comprised of innumerable combinations of sub-units, including materials, processes, and techniques of production. These likewise vary over time and culture, and are strongly influenced by changing ideals. Hillestad's taxonomy is applicable to an understanding of how appearances are constructed within social and cultural boundaries. Aesthetic codes continue to affect constructions and presentations of the body and of dress, thereby altering the interrelationship of these elements of appearance.

DeLong's (1987) apparel/body construct concentrates on perceptual organization and comprehension of visible cues of the clothed body. The body (its structure and proportions, surfaces, parts, and movements) is critical to the aesthetic perception of a clothed appearance and the impact of that appearance on others. A critical visual analysis of apparel in relation to the wearer and to the surrounding space is influenced by simultaneous responses to the visual form, responses to the context (physical, social, cultural) in which the form is viewed, and responses of the viewer based on personal traits and experiences. As such DeLong's model is cognitive in orientation and is particularly useful in examining the complex ways an appearance is visually created by the individual and perceived or evaluated by others. Although both Hillestad (1980) and DeLong (1987) acknowledge the importance of dress and the body in their models, in this paper we will focus on aesthetics of the body. This is not to say, however, that dress is not important in our model, but simply that its significance will not be addressed in this paper.

Both DeLong's (1987) and Hillestad's (1980) models of appearance, as well as social identity theory (Tajfel & Turner, 1979) form the foundation of the model we propose. Social identity theory has evolved from categorization theory (e.g., Medin & Barsalou, 1987; Rosch, 1973; Rosch, Mervis, Gray, Johnson, & Boyes-Braem, 1976) and social comparison theory (Festinger, 1954). As part of our daily lives we perceive and organize our stimulus worlds through the process of categorization. According to the categorization literature, we tend to exaggerate differences between groups and minimize differences within groups (Linville, 1982). When these groups are culturally relevant and serve to classify and distinguish people based on differences, they become cultural categories. In our culture, attractiveness is a cultural category. Cultural categories have a daily impact on people's lives and are often intricately connected with appearance, clothing, and fashion (Kaiser, 1990). In many cultures individuals are distinguished as a function of these cultural categories such that the discriminations often result in unequal access to prestige, privileges, and power. One process through which individuals can distinguish themselves from others is through social comparison.

Social comparison theory was developed by Festinger (1954), who posited that people have a drive to evaluate themselves. As conceived by Festinger, social comparison theory applied to ability and opinion evaluation. However, more recently it has been applied to the evaluation of appearance (Richins, 1991; Tesser, 1980). Although Festinger did not mention self-esteem as an outcome of social comparison, researchers have linked the two constructs. Social comparison occurs when people evaluate themselves in relation to others (Festinger, 1954), which may result in increased or decreased feelings of self-esteem (Morse & Gergen, 1970). Specifically, in terms of appearance this means that if an individual compares herself with someone of lesser attractiveness (downward comparison) her own self-esteem will increase (Morse & Gergen, 1970; Tesser, 1980). When comparing to someone who is more attractive (upward comparison), one's self-esteem will decrease (Morse & Gergen, 1970;

Tesser, 1980). Social comparison appears to affect: (a) specific appearance management behaviors employed as an individual creates her appearance and (b) the internalization of appearance evaluations. Self-esteem is an important focus in our model because it seems to motivate appearance management behaviors to approximate the cultural aesthetic ideal.

Social comparison and cultural categories are integrated under social identity theory. Social identity theory (Tajfel; 1981; Tajfel & Turner, 1979) makes a fundamental claim that when people are grouped into a category, they immediately and automatically evaluate people within the group as better than people outside the group. Two major axioms of the theory are: (a) people attempt to achieve and maintain a positive self-image and (b) self-image is made up of two components, a personal identity and a social identity. *Identity* is a concept which has not been defined precisely (Brown, 1985, p. 551). However, social identity may be thought of as arising from group memberships (e.g., ethnicity, religion, or sex), while personal identity may be thought of as arising from individual achievements or acknowledgements; e.g., a fulfilling personal relationship, a rewarding career, Miss America Pageant winner, valedictorian. It is thought that any improvement in personal identity or social identity will lead to an improvement in self-image. The evaluation of both personal identity and social identity involves social comparison, often on the basis of appearance. Appearance is also often the basis for the formation of cultural categories[4]; e.g., race, attractiveness, age, or sexual orientation.

Research shows that certain appearance characteristics which are distinctive in comparison to others are centrally featured in our thoughts regarding the self (Fiske & Cox, 1979; McGuire & Padawer-Singer, 1976; Morse & Gergen, 1970). Although, as originally conceptualized, a theme of social comparison research was predicting who would be selected for comparison (e.g., Castore & DeNinno, 1977; Festinger, 1954; Jellison & Arkin, 1977; Myers, 1978), other scholars have suggested that some social comparison might occur automatically (Fiske & Cox, 1979; Goethals, 1986; McGuire & Padawer-Singer, 1976; Morse & Gergen, 1970). Automatic comparison might occur when one is confronted with an especially handsome/beautiful individual while going about daily activities.

Media images also provide comparisons which intrude or are imposed upon us. Such imposed comparisons are likely to be pervasive in our daily lives and, therefore, powerful. Young women, in particular, compare themselves to idealized advertising images (i.e., the cultural aesthetic ideal) and such comparisons both elevate their standards for personal attractiveness and lower satisfaction with their own attractiveness (Richins, 1991).

Through a variety of appearance management behaviors an individual constructs her personal appearance and in so doing may experience aesthetic pleasure. Thus, not only can the created appearance enhance self-esteem, which has many social ramifications, but it can also serve a non-instrumental function and provide aesthetic pleasure to the individual who is constructing her appearance. It can be argued that both functions (e.g., self-esteem enhancement and aesthetic pleasure) can and probably should be achieved at the same time, but in reality the instrumental side of constructing one's appearance may take priority over the non-instrumental side.

Part I: Model

The model (see Figure 1) we propose extends social identity theory to explain the active creation of appearances in response to the cultural aesthetic ideal. Our model is predicated on the belief that the predominant appearance ideal of any culture, but particularly the American culture, becomes the internal aesthetic standard which individuals use to create their appearances and against which individuals compare themselves. The central premise of the model is that we use the process of social comparison to continually assess the personal aesthetic value of ourselves and others. If one's evaluations come close to the appearance ideal, self-esteem is elevated, leading to stronger personal and social identity, both of which contribute to a strong self-image. If one's appearance does not come close to approximating the appearance ideal, one may engage in one of four coping strategies to create and re-create appearances in an attempt to closely approximate the aesthetic ideal. Evaluations of our appearances by others also factor into our perceptions of proximity to the aesthetic ideal. The degree to which we internalize these evaluations may also affect the coping strategies which prompt us to create and re-create our appearances.

As a result of social comparison, then, we engage in a variety of appearance management behaviors as we create our appearances; we

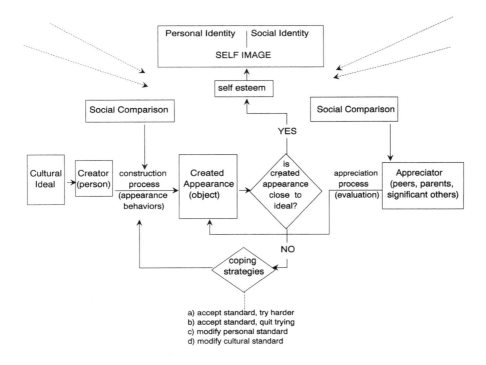

Figure 1. Model of the effects of social comparison on the construction and evaluation of appearance.

present the appearance to others, and we internalize their evaluations of our presented appearances. Whereas positively, but not negatively, perceived assessments may lead to a strong self-image, negatively perceived assessments will always lead to a feedback loop in the model. Positively perceived assessments can also lead to a feedback loop: (a) when we attempt to justify our effort in creating and recreating our appearances and (b) when we are reinforced in the creation of our appearances. In general, we attempt to make more valuable those things we must work hard to achieve, in order to make the effort appear worthwhile (Aronson & Mills, 1959). In the feedback loop, we employ one or another coping strategy, engage in appearance management behaviors to create new appearances which are presented to others, and then continue to assess how we are evaluated by others in relation to the aesthetic ideal. We believe that the aesthetic appearance standard will affect people throughout their lives. Since our society does value attractive appearances (e.g., Fallon, 1990; Hatfield & Sprecher, 1986; Jackson, Sullivan, & Rostker, 1988), people who fear the consequences of an "unattractive" appearance are, in fact, reacting to a very real situation. Thus, concern with appearance and attempts to recreate one's appearance are not only common, but may be mentally healthy responses.

The potential difficulty is that some individuals may never exit the feedback loop, perceiving that they do not measure up and perhaps employing hazardous practices in a re-attempt to meet the cultural aesthetic standard. In extreme cases, such as cosmetic surgery "addicts" (Healy, 1993; Pruzinsky & Edgerton, 1990), these individuals may have such distorted perceptions (Fallon & Rozin, 1985) that, if their personal worth is tied primarily to how they look, they may never achieve a strong self-image. As a result of low self-assessed attractiveness, self-image may continue to decline. Commenting on this extreme type of preoccupation with appearance, a social historian says

> If beauty is in the eye of the beholder, those who rely on beauty are ultimately controlled by others. Their sense of satisfaction will always depend on the compliments and approval they win, rather than an authentic sense of personal effi-

cacy and worth (Brumberg, 1989, p. 276).

Phases of the model will be discussed further, along with substantiating evidence from literature in psychology, sociology, and aesthetics. This model examines the social ramifications of approximating a cultural aesthetic ideal of appearance, while acknowledging the role of the aesthetic experience in this process. In Part II, Cultural Aesthetic Ideal, we discuss how individuals are motivated by the cultural ideal as a function of the extent to which it is internalized. In Part III, Factors Affecting the Internalization of Aesthetic Standards, we examine the factors affecting appreciation via social comparison, as well as the effects of comments by familiar and unfamiliar others. In Part IV, Methods of Attaining the Aesthetic Ideal, we explore the creation of personal appearance and subsequent appearance management behaviors, as well as the created appearance. In Part V, When Attempts to Attain the Aesthetic Ideal Fail, we consider the effects of the aesthetic experience and the appreciation process on the individual. Certain strategies enable the aesthetic experience, while others may be more limiting.

Part II: Cultural Aesthetic Ideal

In the U.S. the cultural appearance ideal in the late 20th Century is rather narrowly and arbitrarily defined. By conducting content analyses of a variety of media over long periods of time researchers have documented the existence of an ideal body type (e.g., Garner, Garfinkel, Schwartz, & Thompson, 1980; Morris, Cooper, & Cooper, 1989; Silverstein, Perdue, Peterson, & Kelly, 1986). An examination of the heights and weights of Miss America beauty contestants over a 20 year period found (a) winners were thinner than the average contestant and (b) a trend for a thinner shape over that period (Garner, Garfinkel, Schwartz, & Thompson, 1980). In an examination of the extent to which the mass media may play a role in promoting a thin ideal standard of attractiveness, researchers (Silverstein, Perdue, Peterson, & Kelly, 1986) found that: (a) female television characters are much more likely to be thin than male television characters, (b) popular actresses have become thinner, (c) women are bombarded with more messages from magazines to keep their bodies thin and shapely than are men, and (d) since 1965 the models in two women's magazines have become progressively thinner. This American standard of ideal female beauty has been adapted from Europe, and in addition to attractiveness and thinness, encompasses such criteria as large breasts, small waist and hips, long legs, and a narrow range of attractive facial features including narrow noses, high cheekbones, and large eyes (Morris, Cooper, & Cooper, 1989; Rudolph, 1991).

These characteristics are perpetuated by the media. Media images tend to be idealized, and are thought to be largely responsible for reinforcing the cultural ideal (Rudolph, 1991; "The body game", 1993). Although people are bombarded with a highly mixed, diverse set of visual images, there still exists remarkable lack of diversity with which women are depicted with respect to body size and shape, facial coloring and features, hair texture, and age (Gilday, 1992). Umiker-Sebeok (1981) in her analysis of women's images in advertising feels that a primary motivation of cosmetic ads and beauty commercials is to encourage young women to transform themselves into objects of beauty. However, if what they see in ads and hear in commercials is very narrowly depicted, and if women compare themselves to these depictions, such comparison may lead to feelings of dissatisfaction with themselves (Richins, 1991).

Such aesthetic standards are internalized by individuals (Fallon, 1990). For example, college women are known to evaluate themselves against such standards (Richins, 1991). To the extent that the ideal reflects Euro-American beauty standards, its realization may be impossible for many women, particularly for women of color (Neal & Wilson, 1987) and women whose body forms do not match the thin ideal. Thus, this aesthetic ideal of beauty is exclusive rather than inclusive of many women. In addition, the definitions of particular physical characteristics as desirable, attractive, or ideal are culturally bound and validated through group consensus.

We can see culture setting the standards (a thin ideal), individual biology providing the backdrop for inadequacy or falling short (e.g., a heavier body), culture providing the acceptable avenue for alteration (dieting), and one's membership status (i.e., being female and having one's self-worth be dependent on one's physical attributes) within the cultural group influencing the vigor with which

one pursues the avenue for alteration (Fallon, 1990, p. 81).

Part III: Factors Affecting the Internalization of Aesthetic Standards

The cultural expectation of attractiveness and thinness may be more powerful for women than for men, and may strongly affect feelings of self-esteem, as well as resulting appearance management behaviors (Hueston, Dennerstein, & Gotts, 1985). Fallon and Rozin (1985) report that 95% of adult women overestimate their body size; such inaccurate perceptions may undermine self-esteem (Freedman, 1988). Women are also more critical of their bodies than men in evaluations of weight (Levison, Powell, & Steelman, 1986) and evaluations of appearance, fitness, health, and sexuality (Cash, Winstead, & Janda, 1986). It has been suggested (Freedman, 1984) that as traditional gender roles are replaced by more non-traditional overlapping roles, people may be less likely to define "femininity" by beauty. Yet there is remarkable evidence that women are much more likely to be defined primarily by their aesthetic value than are men, and by aesthetic value over other personal and social values (Freedman, 1986; Hatfield & Sprecher, 1986). Consequently, women who hold this traditional societal view are thought to pay a great deal of attention to self-presentation through appearance (Brownmiller, 1984; Freedman, 1988; Wolf, 1991). In fact, for many of these women beauty may become a duty (Paoletti & Kregloh, 1989).

Therefore, one factor which may influence the extent of a woman's participation in the production of her appearance is her gender ideology. An individual's gender ideology may also affect the degree to which one is influenced by the cultural aesthetic ideal. Gender ideology consists of cultural expectations for male and female roles; it may be represented on a continuum from traditional to non-traditional. Traditional gender ideology for women is thought to promote a narrowly defined concept of beauty associated with being attractive and thin (Wolf, 1991), with emphasis on social rewards for appearance as opposed to actions or accomplishments (Freedman, 1986; Lips, 1981). Research provides some support for this relationship. As compared to a control group of women who did not elect surgery, women who elected breast augmentation surgery were more likely to ascribe to a traditional gender ideology (Shipley, O'Donnell, & Bader, 1977).

Another factor which affects the internalization of an aesthetic appearance standard is evaluation by others. Social comparison operates after the individual publicly presents the created appearance to others who evaluate that appearance, often unconsciously, within the context of given social and cultural parameters. Such evaluations may be either positive or negative and are usually made known to the individual, either reflected through behavioral responses or through direct comments. How such evaluations are internalized by the individual may affect her understanding of how close her created appearance comes to the cultural ideal. Two groups of individuals who are especially susceptible to such evaluations are performers and children. Performers are concerned with evaluations of their appearances because they are on display and must maintain their audiences. Children are vulnerable because of their life stage and because people feel free to comment on their appearances. Ann Beuf, a medical sociologist who has worked with "appearance-impaired" children for over 20 years relates several instances in her book in which children's appearances were evaluated by others.

> Carrie . . . is a white child of six, from a working class family. . . She has spots of depigmented skin on her legs and thighs. . . [Because of this] the children at school call her names "like Spot" and "they hit on her all the time." At school, she must stay close to the teacher to protect herself from these experiences. While, Martha, a plump pre-teen, was not subjected to such extreme treatment, this daughter of a New York lawyer told us about two types of incidents which bothered her: the teasing remarks of family members and the wolf whistles of Manhattan construction workers (Beuf, 1990, p. 51).

The aesthetic appearance standard is learned through socialization. Children learn at an early age that "what is beautiful is good" (Kaiser, 1990, p. 129), in such diverse arenas as peer relations (Adams & Crane, 1980), perceived control over their lives (Dion & Berscheid, 1974), and friendships (Dion, 1973). Positive assessments of children by significant others may operate on the basis of attractiveness. For example, teachers have been found to perceive attractive children as more intelligent and interested in school than unattractive children (Clifford & Walster, 1973) and have consequently given them more attention in the classroom (Adams & Cohen, 1974). As compared to unattractive children, attractive children are viewed as more honest (Dion, 1972) and are thus punished less severely (Berkowitz & Frodi, 1979). Physical attractiveness takes on more importance during adolescence, particularly with respect to social advantages (Kaiser, 1990). For female adolescents, attractiveness is more important than effectiveness in determining self-feelings (Lerner, Orlos, & Knapp, 1976). One explanation may be that, during this life-cycle stage, worth or status may be more dependent on physical appearance than on other avenues of success that may not yet be open to adolescents (Levinson, Powell, & Steelman, 1986). Articles in the popular press address the distressing effects of peer evaluation of appearance on teenagers and how it can influence them to undergo cosmetic surgery (Rosen & Sheff-Cahan, 1993; Rosen, Lynn, Jenkins, & Sandler, 1993). Teens and pre-teens are especially susceptible to such evaluation (Beuf, 1990).

Sometimes parents' views can be critical and harmful to children with appearance impairments. For example, mothers who hold a traditional gender ideology tend to place greater value on appearance than non-traditional mothers (Beuf, 1990, p. 96). Fathers' evaluations also affect their children. One man, a physician, watched his daughter lose 70 pounds (half of her body weight) in three months and held her up as a good example to his patients (Beuf, 1990, p. 38). In this manner the opinions of significant others have an important effect on the development of one's aesthetic standard.

Evaluations by unfamiliar others also play a part in the development of an aesthetic standard. Appearance may be the stigmatizing factor for people who are obese, bald, or who have disfiguring scars[5] (Beuf, 1990). Stigmatization may be verbal, in the form of rude questions, unsolicited judgments, and ridicule about the individual's appearance. For example, a young girl with vitiligo was lunching with her mother when another patron offered the unsolicited evaluation, "Oh, she would be pretty if she didn't have *that*" (Beuf, 1990, p. 48). Stigmatization may also be nonverbal, as evidenced by stares, avoidance behavior, finger-pointing, laughing, and even physical abuse (Beuf, 1990). The observations and evaluations rendered by unfamiliar others are felt so strongly that such "appearance impaired" individuals have often turned to physicians or to psychologists trained in body image therapy interventions (Beuf, 1990; Cash & Pruzinsky, 1992). However, even medical personnel sometimes trivialize appearance impairments, which to the individual may seem overwhelming (Beuf, 1990).

Part IV: Methods of Attaining the Aesthetic Ideal

The process of social comparison may operate both before and after the individual creates an appearance. Through social comparison, one observes the standards of appearance among one's immediate reference group, and learns to engage in associated appearance management behaviors. Such behaviors include dieting, exercising, weight training, cosmetic use, and selection of apparel to enhance one's appearance. Use of such products or procedures may be a means of increasing attractiveness and obtaining accompanying social benefits which may result in both aesthetic pleasure (Wilson, 1985) and increased self-esteem (Bloch & Richins, 1992).

According to Fallon (1990) some of these behaviors may be impractical (e.g., wearing constricting clothing), painful (e.g., body piercings, teeth straightening), or even life-threatening (e.g., anorexia, cosmetic surgery). Several popular teen and women's magazines offer routine suggestions for impractical and even painful appearance management behaviors that can alter physical characteristics and enhance attractiveness (Umiker-Sebeok, 1981). In general, the time and effort involved in altering one's appearance may reflect the extent to which one strives to create an ideal appearance (McCrea, Summerfield, & Rosen, 1982) or wishes to approximate the cultural aesthetic.

The Hillestad model (1980) provides a rich framework for discussing the diversity of products and procedures that may be used to achieve modifications in body form, surfaces, and motion. For example, dieting, weight training, and cosmetic surgery[6] could be employed to alter body form. In addition, articles of dress and their constituent materials can also modify body form[7] (e.g., temperature sensitive fabric that changes color as one sweats, pump-up bikini tops, and control top pantyhose). Body surfaces are often modified through cosmetic application, tanning, shaving, plucking, or filing.[8] Body motion may be influenced by constrictive undergarments, certain shoes, and even hairstyles.

Clothing may be used as a means of attaining the aesthetic ideal, making some characteristics of the body salient, while masking other less desirable characteristics. In a recent study (Markee, Carey, & Pedersen, 1990) body satisfaction was higher when subjects were asked to consider a clothed appearance for themselves than when asked to consider an unclothed appearance. Many body characteristics as well as general appearance were rated significantly higher in the clothed, as compared to the unclothed, condition. The researchers concluded that clothing is more than a body covering and may create a better self-perception of the body.

Part V: When Attempts to Attain the Aesthetic Ideal Fail

If the created appearance is perceived by the individual to be too far from the cultural aesthetic ideal, the individual may engage in one of several coping strategies. Some of these strategies encourage or validate the individual creative pleasure that can come from constructing one's appearance, while other strategies discourage or invalidate that creative pleasure if they are not valued within the larger culture. Our exposition of coping strategies has been influenced by Brown (1985). He says there are three possible outcomes of a *negative* social identity (i.e., not matching the aesthetic ideal in our model), which we call coping strategies. Two of these strategies, *exit* and *pass* operate at a personal level and are focused on achieving a positive social identity and increased self-esteem. *Exit* occurs, according to Brown, when an individual moves out of a group with a negative social identity. *Pass* occurs when an individual is categorized by others as belonging to a higher status group, while being self-categorized as a member of a lower status group. We have combined these two outcomes in our first coping strategy.

In this *first* strategy, an individual may continue to accept the aesthetic standard of appearance and work harder than before to attain it. Such a strategy might be used by someone trying to tame unruly hair via different hair styles. The problem with this strategy is that for many women attainment of the aesthetic ideal may be impossible. For example, women of color will never be white; therefore this strategy is not a realistic option for them, although such products as *Porcelana* and *Esoterica* fade creams persist in the marketplace. Furthermore, women who are large-sized may never achieve the thin ideal for any sustained period because of certain biological characteristics (Allen & Beck, 1986; Grady, 1988; Roberts, Savage, Coward, Chew, & Lucas, 1988). However, such women may continue for years with yo-yo dieting in the mistaken belief, reinforced by the media, that a little more will-power and dedication will allow them to attain the ideal body size. Thus, while a woman may derive pleasure from her rounded form, she may be constantly reminded that this feeling is unacceptable. At least socially, it may be more important for her to alter her attitudes and appearance management behaviors than it is to derive aesthetic pleasure for the way she comes packaged. Similarly, while a woman may love to see natural curls frame her face or enjoy the spring of her hair as she brushes it, that truly aesthetic experience is diminished when she is given tips on ironing or straightening her hair by well-meaning friends or beauty practitioners.

Women with body image disorders may use this type of strategy. Body image refers to the mental image we have of our bodies (Schilder, 1950, p. 11). Anorexics may incorrectly perceive themselves to be fat and may limit their food intake and/or engage in rigorous exercise, often to the point of death or serious debilitation; e.g., heart arrhythmia, neural dysfunction, or cessation of menses. They are thought to suffer two types of body image disturbance that may function separately or together: (a) a perceptual disturbance which causes them to incorrectly evaluate their body size, and (b) extreme emotional reaction of dissatisfaction (Garner & Garfinkel, 1981). Recently body image has received much-needed attention in the scholarly press (e.g., Cash & Pruzinsky, 1990; Freedman, 1986; 1988; Rodin, 1992). The approach these therapists have taken in working with women who have body image disorders is to build their self-esteem by learning to be more accepting of their appearances, rather than trying to re-create new appearances to be congruent with the cultural aesthetic ideal. Thus, this first coping

strategy can be very restrictive to the individual's aesthetic experience because she is actually submerging or sacrificing her personal aesthetic experience for what is valued by society.

According to Brown (1985) another outcome of a negative social identity is stagnant acceptance. Thus, in our model, individuals may react to a negative social identity (i.e., not matching the aesthetic ideal) by accepting the appearance standard, but ceasing to try to approximate it. This is the basis of our *second* strategy. Such a strategy may avoid the dire risks of the first strategy, yet may result in a blow to self-esteem. Endorsing the cultural aesthetic ideal affirms it as a standard, yet a decision to stop trying to approximate the ideal is incongruent with acceptance of that standard. When an individual holds such cognitively inconsistent attitudes or beliefs there is a tension to change one of the beliefs or attitudes (Festinger, 1957). In this instance the person can either devalue the cultural ideal or derogate her own appearance. Typically, however, a woman or girl raised in our culture and exposed to the media will derogate her own appearance (Beuf, 1990; Wolf, 1991). This strategy permits a woman to derive little aesthetic pleasure from creating her appearance. In fact, BDD (body dysmorphic disorder) is an extreme example of this lack of aesthetic pleasure in that the individual has an extreme aversion to a particular body part, often associated with the face, that is objectively normal-looking (Pruzinsky, 1990). This aversion may be translated into behaviors such as avoiding mirrors or ceasing to go out in public.

Such self derogation is thought to lead to lower self-esteem (Freedman, 1986, 1988; Wolf, 1991). For example, Clark and Clark (1947) studied young children's doll preferences as a function of the doll's appearance (e.g., African-American or Caucasian). The Caucasian-looking doll was preferred over the doll with the African-American appearance by both African-American and Caucasian children. This research demonstrates in-group derogation which has been found in other cultures for minority or subordinate groups (e.g., Milner, 1975; Giles & Powesland, 1976). This is significant because in at least one doll study replication (Ward & Braun, 1972) African-American children who preferred the doll with the Caucasian appearance had significantly lower self-esteem than those children who preferred the doll with the African-American appearance. To summarize, self-derogation based on appearance standards can lead to lower self-esteem; therefore, this strategy is the poorest of all the coping strategies because the others have the potential for raising self-esteem.

A *third* strategy involves modifying one's personal standard of devotion to a cultural aesthetic ideal, a strategy which may be very empowering to the individual. This strategy has no parallel in Brown (1985). It is possible that when an individual realizes how subjective and exclusionary a cultural appearance ideal can be, or how time-consuming and demeaning some efforts to this end can be, the individual may relinquish strict adherence to the standard. Such a step might allow her the freedom to experience aesthetic pleasure from her own physical appearance. This step might also allow her to focus on achievements and relationships in her life that bring about feelings of self-esteem. Carole Shaw, editor of *Big Beautiful Woman* magazine encourages her readers to adopt such a strategy. In the magazine's statement of policy, she questions the value of the cultural aesthetic ideal and urges women to become more self-accepting.

> This is where you STOP FEELING GUILTY about being a large-size woman and concentrate on being the beautiful and attractive PERSON you are, regardless of size. Are you any smarter if you wear a size 8 dress? Is your basic character any more worthwhile if you're 120 lbs., rather than 220-plus. . . The point is you are who and what you are, and your dress size has nothing to do with your success or failure as a person. You are neither smarter, better educated nor, for that matter, jollier than a person of smaller physical dimensions. The fact is that many of us have treated ourselves as second-class citizens, and therefore we have attracted that kind of treatment from the fashion industry in general . . . We are 30% of the population. . . It's time we start respecting ourselves . . . (Shaw, 1991, p. 4).

Our *fourth* strategy is based on Tajfel's (1981) interpretation of *voice*. Social action, called voice, aims to raise social identity by changing societal norms, such as a cultural aesthetic of appearance, so the group's characteristics will be more valued. To implement our fourth strategy, an individual may join with others or personally attempt to modify the prevailing cultural aesthetic ideal in order to make a diversity of appearances aesthetically valued. While such a strategy may require a thick skin to withstand insensitive comments and even social ostracism (Chapkis, 1986), groups may eventually achieve a sense of aesthetic satisfaction and give "permission" to other groups to set and follow their own aesthetic standards of appearance. Tajfel and Turner (1979) have identified ways to successfully implement this strategy. The most important way is a re-evaluation of group attributes. A distinctive appearance may be a key factor in such re-evaluation. It is important for group members to value their own appearances and cease to accept the aesthetic standards of the majority group. Brown (1985) suggests that striking good looks in the minority group may help. "A broader historical and geographic perspective on beauty can [also] help . . . If enough people say that a certain kind of appearance is good . . . then . . . [it is] good, because the only reality is social" (Brown, 1985, p. 565-566).

Through this *last* and probably most uncommon coping strategy, women of all colors, shapes, and sizes can move from the constraints of a cultural aesthetic ideal of beauty that may socially mark them (hooks, 1992) to an unmarked status in which a diverse grouping of physical characteristics is celebrated as attractive. Thus, this strategy is the most positive with respect to building self-esteem and most liberating in terms of the potential to derive pleasure from one's appearance. For example, "the slogan, 'Black is Beautiful' has had some success in causing the re-evaluation of black appearance. It has put a halt to extreme self-defeating efforts to bleach the skin and straighten the hair. . ." (Brown, 1985, p. 566.)[9]

Regardless of which alternative coping strategy is employed, the individual continues to create and re-create her appearance in relation to the cultural aesthetic through various appearance management behaviors. The result is that either more or less satisfactory or healthy behaviors may be practiced. For example, if the strategy is to try harder, appearance management behaviors may well become more demanding, costly (in time or money), and impractical or even hazardous. On the other hand, if the strategy is to modify one's personal standard of devotion to approximating the cultural ideal, then the appearance management behaviors one practices may become less impractical or hazardous and more gentle and affirming, thereby enhancing perceived quality of life.

Summary

This model was developed to depict the complex relationship between the cultural aesthetic ideal and the creation and evaluation of personal appearances. Aesthetic codes, which vary over time and culture, affect both the appearance ideal and appearance management behaviors that are practiced toward achieving the ideal. Attractiveness is a cultural category which is used by individuals to award prestige, privileges, and power. Social comparison is the process through which people evaluate themselves in relation to others (Festinger, 1954). Social comparison operates in both the creation of appearances and the internalization of appearance evaluations as we continually assess the personal aesthetic value of ourselves and others. Social comparison and cultural categories work together in social identity theory (Tajfel, 1981), which posits that we try to achieve a positive self-image through both personal identity and social identity. If we perceive that our presented appearances are evaluated positively by others, then self-esteem is often strengthened, leading to a strong self-image. However, if we perceive that our presented appearances are evaluated negatively, or devalued through social stigma, self-esteem may decline. When negative evaluation occurs, the individual can resort to one of four coping strategies, leading to the re-creation of appearances and subsequent differences in self-esteem and aesthetic pleasure, and ultimately self-image.

In this model, we discuss both aesthetic factors and socio-cultural factors that work in tandem in each component. Suggestions for studying the aesthetics of appearance are plentiful in relation to each component of the model. We hope that this model may facilitate an interdisciplinary perspective in studying appearance as a cultural construction. Aspects of body image, appearance impairments and social stigma, the functioning of social comparison as it relates to appearance, advertising and social comparison, gender ideology, appearance

management behaviors, and therapies to treat body image disorders are all pertinent possibilities which can best be addressed via subject-matter perspectives from sociology, psychology, medicine, aesthetics, and textiles and clothing. We also encourage historians and anthropologists to apply this model to other time periods and other cultures.

Since the factors which contribute to self-esteem and quality of life are complex and multifaceted, we think an interdisciplinary research focus is warranted. The categorization, portrayal, valuation, and internalization of aesthetic ideals of appearance within the U.S. culture result in a wide range appearance management behaviors, which may be employed as part of a coping strategy. These factors have a significant impact on social identity and self-esteem, both of which contribute to perceived quality of life. By studying the cultural construction and internalization of aesthetic appearance ideals, researchers will be better able to assess quality of life and develop resources to improve it.

Endnotes

1. Although this model focuses on women, there is no reason to assume that it doesn't apply to men as well. It is based on research literature, which is focused primarily on women in the late 20th century.
2. Other variables which not been examined in the research literature, but which we believe mat influence judgments of body and facial attractiveness, are skin color, skin texture, and hirsuteness.
3. Indeed, on a practical level, visual merchandisers are aware of the contribution of the body form to an aesthetically pleasing display of apparel; they will "stuff" jacket sleeves or pants to suggest human form.
4. However, how one smells or how one sounds (e.g., accent or dialect) may also be a basis for cultural categorization.
5. Other examples include birthmarks, paralysis, or body spasticity.
6. Other examples include liposuction, implants, and facelifts.
7. Other examples include Lycra, sequins, and shrink-to-fit jeans.
8. Other, less common, examples include skin bleaching, dermabrasion, electrolysis, painting or coloring, and perming or straightening.
9. However, we do need to be aware that such products still are advertised and are found in the marketplace.

References

Adams, G. & Cohen, A. (1974). Children's physical and interpersonal characteristics that affect student-teacher interactions. *Journal of Experimental Education, 43*, 1-5.

Adams, G. & Crane, P. (1980). An assumption of parents' and teachers' expectations of preschool children's social preference for attractive or unattractive children or adults. *Child Development, 41*, 224-231.

Alicke, M., Smith, R., & Klotz, M. (1986). Judgments of physical attractiveness: The role of faces and bodies. *Personality and Social Psychology Bulletin, 12*, 381-389.

Allen, D. O., & Beck, R. R. (1986). The role of calcium ion in hormone-stimulated lipolysis. *Biochemical Pharmacology, 35*, 767-772.

Aronson, E., & Mills, J. (1959). The effect of severity of initiation on liking for a group. *Journal of Abnormal and Social Psychology, 59*, 177-181.

Banner, L. W. (1983). *American beauty*. Chicago: The University of Chicago Press.

Berkowitz, L. & Frodi, A. (1979). Reactions to a child's mistakes as affected by his/her looks and speech. *Social Psychology Quarterly, 42*(4),420-425.

Beuf, A. (1990). *Beauty is the beast*. Philadelphia: University of Pennsylvania Press.

Bloch, P. H., & Richins, M. L. (1992). You look "Mahvelous": The pursuit of beauty and the marketing concept. *Psychology and Marketing, 9*, 3-15.

Brown, R. (1985). *Social psychology* (2nd Ed.). New York: The Free Press.

Brownmiller, S. (1984). *Femininity*. New York: Linden Press.

Brumberg, J. J. (1989). *Fasting girls: The history of anorexia nervosa*. New York: Plume.

Cash, T. & Pruzinsky, T. (Eds.) (1990). *Body images: Development, deviance, and change*. New York: The Guilford Press.

Cash, T., Winstead, B., & Janda, L. (1986). The great American shape-up: Body image survey report. *Psychology Today, 20*(4), 30-37.

Castore, C. H., & DeNinno, J. A. (1977). Investigations in the social comparison of attitudes. In J. M. Suls and R. L. Miller (Eds.), *Social Comparison Processes* (pp. 125-148). Washington, D. C.: Hemisphere/John Wiley & Sons.

Chapkis, W. (1986). *Beauty secrets: Women and the politics of appearance*. Boston: South End Press.

Clark, K. B., & Clark, M. P. (1947). Racial identification and preference in Negro children. In T. Newcomb and E. L. Hartley (Eds.), *Readings in social psychology* (pp. 169-178). New York: Holt.

Clifford, M., & Walster, E. (1973). Research note: The effect of physical attractiveness on teacher expectations. *Sociology of Education, 46*, 248-258.

DeLong, M. R. (1987). *The way we look: A framework for visual analysis of dress*. Ames, IA: Iowa State Press.

Dion, K. (1972). Physical attractiveness and evaluation of children's trangressions. *Journal of Personality and Social Psychology, 24*, 207-213.

Dion, K. (1973). Young children's stereotyping of facial attractiveness. *Developmental Psychology, 9* (2), 183-188.

Dion, K., & Berscheid, E. (1974). Physical attractiveness and peer evaluation among children. *Sociometry, 37*, 1-12.

Douty, H. I., & Brannon, E. L. (1984). Figure attractiveness: Male and female preferences. *Home Economics Research Journal, 13* (2), 122-137.

Fallon, A. (1990). Culture in the mirror: Sociocultural determinants of body image. In T. F. Cash and T. Pruzinsky (Eds.), *Body images: Development, deviance, and change* (pp. 80-109). New York: The Guilford Press.

Fallon, A., & Rozin, P. (1985). Sex differences in perceptions of desirable body shape. *Journal of Abnormal Psychology, 94* (1), 102-105.

Festinger, L. (1957). *A theory of cognitive dissonance*. Stanford, CA: Stanford University Press.

Festinger, L. (1954). A theory of social comparison processes. *Human Relations, 7*, 117-140.

Fiske, S. T., & Cox, M. G. (1979). Person concepts: The effects of target familiarity and descriptive purpose on the process of describing others. *Journal of Personality, 47*, 136-161.

Freedman, R. J. (1986). *Beauty bound*. Lexington, MA: Lexington Books.

Freedman, R. J. (1988). *Bodylove*. New York: Harper & Row, Publishers.

Freedman, R. J. (1984). Reflections on beauty as it relates to health in adolescent females. *Women and Health, 9* (2/3), 29-45.

Garner, D., & Garfinkel, P. (1981). Body image in anorexia nervosa: Measurement, theory, and clinical implications. *International of Psychiatry in Medicine, 11*, 263-284.

Garner, D., Garfinkel, P., Schwartz, D., & Thompson, M. (1980). Cultural expectations of thinness in women. *Psychological Reports, 47*, 483-491.

Gilday, K. (1992). *The famine within*. TV Ontario: Kandor Productions, Ltd.

Giles, H., & Powesland, P. F. (1976). Speech style and social evaluation. *European monographs in social psychology* (No. 9). London: Academic Press.

Goethals, G. R. (1986). Social comparison theory: Psychology from the lost and found. *Personality and Social Psychology Bulletin, 12*, 261-278.

Grady, D. (1988, March 7). Is losing weight a losing battle? *Time*, p. 59.

Hatfield, E., & Sprecher, S. (1986). *Mirror mirror: The importance of looks in everyday life*. Albany, NY: State University of New York Press.

Healy, K. (1993, April). Plastic surgery addicts. *Allure*, pp. 80, 83,

Hillestad, R. (1980). The underlying structure of appearance. *Dress, 5*, 117-125.

hooks, b. (1992). *Black looks: Race and representation*. Boston, MA: South End Press.

Hueston, J., Dennerstein, L., & Gotts, G. (1985). Psychological aspects of cosmetic surgery. *Journal of Psychosomatic Obstetrics and Gynaecology, 4*, 335-346.

Jackson, L. A., Sullivan, L. A., & Rostker, R. (1988). Gender, gender role, and body image. *Sex Roles, 19*, 429-443.

Jellison, J., & Arkin, R. (1977). The social comparison of abilities. In J. M. Suls and R. L. Miller (Eds.), *Social Comparison Processes* (pp. 235-257). Washington, D. C.: Hemisphere/John Wiley & Sons.

Kaiser, S. B. (1990). *The social psychology of clothing: Symbolic appearances in context.* New York: Macmillan Publishing Co.

Kato, D. (1993, April 1). A love-hate relationship: Women's magazines elicit ambivalent feeling among readers. *The Columbus Dispatch*, p. E1.

Lennon, S. J. (1988). Physical attractiveness, age, and body type. *Home Economics Research Journal, 16*, 195-204.

Lerner, R. M., Orlos, J., & Knapp, J. (1976). Physical attractiveness, physical effectiveness, and self-concept in late adolescents. *Adolescence, 11*, 313-325.

Levinson, R., Powell, B., & Steelman, L. (1986). Social location, significant others, and body image among adolescents. *Social Psychology Quarterly, 49* (4), 330-337.

Linville, P. W. (1982). The complexity-extremity effect and age-based stereotyping. *Journal of Personality and Social Psychology, 42*, 193-211.

Lips, H. (1981). *Women, men, and the psychology of power.* Englewood Cliffs, NJ: Prentice Hall.

Markee, N., Carey, I., & Pedersen, E. (1990). Body cathexis and clothed body cathexis: Is there a difference? *Perceptual and Motor Skills, 70*, 1239-1244.

McCrea, C. W., Summerfield, A. B., & Rosen, B. (1982). Body image: A selective review of existing measurement techniques. *British Journal of Medical Psychology, 55*, 225-233.

McGuire, W. J., & Padawer-Singer, A. (1976). Trait salience in the spontaneous self-concept. *Journal of Personality and Social Psychology, 33*, 743-754.

Medin, D. L., & Barsalou, L. W. (1987). Categorization processes and categorical perception. In S. Harnad (Ed.), *Categorical perception: The groundwork of cognition.* Cambridge: Cambridge University Press.

Mervis, C. B., & Rosch, E. (1981). Categorization of natural objects. In M. R. Rosenzweig & L. W. Porter (Eds.), *Annual review of psychology* (Vol. 32, pp. 89-115). Palo Alto, CA: Annual Reviews.

Milner, D. (1975). *Children and race.* Harmondsworth, Middlesex: Penguin.

Morris, A., Cooper, T., & Cooper, P. (1989). The changing shape of female fashion models. *International Journal of Eating Disorders, 8*, 593-596.

Morse, S., & Gergen, K. J. (1970). Social comparison, self-consistency, and the concept of self. *Journal of Personality and Social Psychology, 16*, 148-156.

Myers, D. G. (1978). Polarizing effects of social comparison. *Journal of Experimental Social Psychology, 14*, 554-563.

Neal, A. M., & Wilson, M. L. (1989). The role of skin color and features in the black community: Implications for black women and therapy. *Clinical Psychology Review, 9*, 323-333.

Paoletti, J. B., & Kregloh, C. L. (1989). The children's department. In C. B. Kidwell & V. Steele (Eds.), *Men and women: Dressing the part* (pp. 22-41). Washington: Smithsonian University Press.

Pruzinsky, T. (1990). Psychopathology of body experience. In T. F. Cash and T. Pruzinsky (Eds.), *Body images: Development, deviance, and change* (pp. 170-189). New York: The Guilford Press.

Pruzinsky, T., & Edgerton, M. (1990). Body image change in cosmetic plastic surgery. In T. F. Cash and T. Pruzinsky (Eds.), *Body images: Development, deviance, and change* (pp. 237-252). New York: The Guilford Press.

Richins, M. L. (1991). Social comparison and the idealized images of advertising. *Journal of Consumer Research, 18*, 71-83.

Roberts, S. B., Savage, J., Coward, W. A., Chew, B., & Lucas, A. (1988). Energy expenditure and intake in infants born to lean and overweight mothers. *New England of Medicine, 318*, 461-466.

Rodin, J. (1992). *Body traps.* New York: William Morrow & Co., Inc.

Rosch, E. (1973). Natural categories. *Cognitive Psychology, 4*, 328-350.

Rosch, E., Mervis, C., Gray, W., Johnson, D., & Boyes-Braem, P. (1976). Basic objects in natural categories. *Cognitive Psychology, 8*, 382-439.

Rosen, M., & Sheff-Cahan, V. (1993, April 26). Now I can be free. *People Weekly*, pp. 83-84, 87.

Rosen, M., Lynn, A., Jenkins, J., & Sandler, B. (1993, April 26). New face, new body, new self. *People Weekly*, pp. 88-90, 92.

Rudolph, B. (1991, October 7). Beauty and the bucks. *Time*, pp. 38-40.

Schilder, P. (1950). *The image and appearance of the human body.* New York: International Universities Press.

Shaw, C. (1991, November). BBW statement of policy. *Big Beautiful Woman*, p. 4.

Shipley, R. H., O'Donnell, J. M., & Bader, K. F. (1977). Personality characteristics of women seeking breast augmentation. *Plastic Reconstructive Surgery, 60*, 369-371.

Silverstein, B., Perdue, L., Peterson, B., & Kelly, E. (1986). The role of the mass media in promoting a thin standard of bodily attractiveness for women. *Sex Roles, 14*, (9/10), 519-532.

Tajfel, H. (1981). *Human groups and social categories.* Cambridge, England: Cambridge University Press.

Tajfel, H., & Turner, J. C. (1979). An integrative theory of social conflict. In W. Austin and S. Worchel (Eds.), *The social psychology of inter-*

group relations (pp. 33-47). Monterey, CA: Brooks/Cole.

Tesser, A. (1980). Self-esteem maintenance in family dynamics. *Journal of Personality and Social Psychology, 39,* 77-91.

"The body game." (1993, January 11). *People Weekly,* pp. 80-85.

Umiker-Sebeok, J. (1981). The seven ages of women: A view from American magazine advertisements. In C. Mayo & N. Henley (Eds.), *Gen-*

der and Non-verbal Behavior (pp. 209-252). New York: Springer-Verlag.

Ward, S., & Braun, J. (1972). Self-esteem and racial preferences in black children. *American Journal of Orthopsychiatry, 42,* 664-667.

Wilson, E. (1985). *Adorned in dreams: Fashion and modernity.* Berkeley, CA: University of California Press.

Wolf, N. (1991). *The beauty myth: How images of beauty are used against women.* New York: William Morrow and Company, Inc.

Application of an Aesthetic Framework to Compare the Appearances of Male and Female Adolescents

Catherine Rutherford-Black
Texas Tech University

Marilyn Revell DeLong
University of Minnesota

There are many instances when people follow similar patterns in the way they dress. Such patterns may be analyzed to determine similarities and differences in subgroups as well as changes over time in what people wear in a constant situation. Such an instance is one that links individuals to posterity, as when high school seniors are photographed for their yearbook.

The present research was a continuation of a larger study of adolescent dress conducted at a public senior high school serving a small suburban city on the edge of a major metropolitan area in the Midwest (Michelman, Eicher, & Michelman, 1991; Eicher, Baizerman, & Michelman, 1991). The present portion of this larger study not only utilized a framework of DeLong (1987) but also Roach-Higgins and Eichers's (1992) system for classifying types of dress and their properties.

The purpose of this portion of the research was to analyze similarities and differences in adolescent appearances through an application of DeLong's (1987) systematic framework involving visual priorities. These visual priorities are a part of a framework to analyze the aesthetic aspects of images. Finding a means to systematically analyze male and female appearances in this school yearbook provided the data about the student population. The method reported in this paper was necessary to proceed with the investigation and was developed to quantify data that previously had been considered more qualitative in nature.

The importance adolescents place on yearbook photographs is indicated in the preparation time, money spent, and high percentage of students who submit their photographs for inclusion in the yearbook. By this age it was thought that aesthetic preferences in clothing would be formed and expressed in the yearbook photographs. Though students may claim to be individual in their choices, they may appear very similar and conforming in their patterns of dress. To conform is to choose the shared ideas and expectations about how members of the senior class should dress. Analyzing shared aesthetic aspects of their presentations within a cultural context is an important step in understanding adolescents.

Theoretical Framework

In *The Presentation of Self in Everyday Life*, Erving Goffman (1959) focused upon the importance of everyday life and individuals' behaviors with one another. His perspective has been called dramaturgy, because of the analogies between human behavior and the stage. He frequently dealt with the topic of dress, using clothing and appearance examples to support his ideas, especially the manner in which individuals use clothing and appearance to present themselves positively to others. Appearance cues represent the nonverbal part of communication. In exploring impression management, he referred to an individual's "identity kit" of symbols associated with appearance in various social roles. Clothing represents a form of appearance that is readily changeable and may enable individuals to move from one role to another.

Stone (1962) defined the uniform as dress that is standardized within a peer group, the representing of self, and reminding the wearer and others of an appropriate identity (Stone, 1962). Adolescents presenting similar visual images would be presenting a uniform, indicating the desire and necessity to conform to dress established by peers, and indicate peer group affiliation. Conformity can be a subtle dimension of daily life that can include similarities in hair length and cut, body positioning, as well as clothing characteristics. Eicher, et al. (1991) found that hairdos distinguished males from females more than did clothing.

Some studies show that patterns of conformity differ between males and females. Hambleton, Roach, and Ehle (1972) found a greater tendency for males to be high conformers whereas females showed medium or low levels of conformity. Brown (1982) reported that females experience significantly stronger pressure to conform to dress and grooming standards. Fuhrmann (1990) also indicated that females seem to feel pressure to conform. However the findings of a study of cheerleaders by Littrell, Damhorst, and Littrell (1990) indicated that the majority of these adolescent girls were somewhat comfortable dressing differently from their friends.

In a study by Hethorn (1987) male and female adolescents ranked eight images of other adolescents photographed in a public mall. Though gender was not mentioned in the questionnaire, the images did include four each of male and female. Results indicated that neither gender of the images nor that of subjects totally altered the rankings according to "like/dislike and "would wear/would not wear." This implies that gender was not a differentiating attribute to this group of subjects.

In previous studies adolescents have been questioned in order to provide data, but in this study the data used were adolescent images. Development of a method of analysis of these images was necessary as one step in a process to determine conforming patterns in the visual presentations of male and female adolescents.

Visual images presented in the high school yearbook represent only a partial, but public image of an adolescent's body. Such photographs of adolescents were used as a data base to focus upon a particular event and point in time. High school graduation in the United States is a rite of passage that includes a gradual separation from school, as well as passage into adulthood for many students. The purpose of this study as to compare adolescents' visual presentation within yearbook photographs to understand conformity and deviation in the type of dress generally worn by members of a peer group.

This paper focused on an application of a systematic framework to examine visual cues in dress. DeLong (1987)[1] developed this theoretical framework of visual analysis to provide the terminology and method for the systematic observation of interactions that occur between the body, dress, and surrounding environment. The term apparel-body-construct (ABC) is used to mean the entire visual form presented by the interaction of apparel based upon sense data. Through aesthetic awareness this system allows the viewer to become sensitive to the interactions that occur.

The framework for the visual analysis of dress as presented in *The Way We Look* (DeLong, 1987) provides a basis for understanding the visual images presented by the adolescents. Yearbook photographs are not total ABCs but partial figures of head and shoulder and thus some accommodation was necessary. The basis for a visual analysis of adolescent males' and females' appearance in yearbook photographs included closed-to-open, part-to-whole, planar separation-to-planar integration, and determinate-to-indeterminate (Table 1). These concepts adapted from DeLong were used with the exception of one visual priority, flat-to-rounded, which because it referred to the appearance of whole body surfaces was not

Table 1. Visual properties of the Apparel-Body-Construct

considered appropriate.

CLOSED	OPEN
CLOSED: The form is self-contained, with the silhouette acting as a visual boundary between the ABC and the surrounding environment. OPEN: The form does not appear self-contained since it interacts visually with the surround.	

WHOLE-TO-PART	PART-TO-WHOLE
WHOLE-TO-PART: The form is distinguished by emphasis on the whole ABC, and defined silhouette, and overall surface design. PART-TO-WHOLE: The form is distinguished by distinct parts within the whole.	

PLANAR SEPARATION	PLANAR INTEGRATION
PLANAR SEPARATION: The figure is seen on a plane some distance from its ground. PLANAR INTEGRATION: There is figure-ground ambiguity as the figure appears on a plane very close to the ground.	

DETERMINATE	INDETERMINATE
DETERMINATE: Surfaces appear definite, sharp, regular, and clear cut; if shapes are present they are few and simple or overall repetitious; minimal light and shadow effect creating little visual texture. INDETERMINATE: Surfaces often appear blurred or soft or with indefinite levels or ambiguity of figure-ground; shapes are irregular; much light and shadow effect creating much visual texture.	

Method

Continuums provided by DeLong for the visual priorities were modified for this study through the identification of discrete categories assigned between each pair of polar extremes.

Though polar extremes presented no problems when analyzing images quantitatively using DeLong's system, images that were not extreme could not be quantified. For example, images totally open to the surround, thus representing an extreme, would be placed along the continuum at the same end point regardless of the number of images analyzed. However images that would be placed between the two polar extremes required more discrete categories. During pretesting it was determined that two yearbook photographs that did not represent extremes could be identified as having equal amounts of open or closed areas to the surround and could include clothing closed/hair open to the surround or hair closed/clothing open to the surround. Both images could be identified at the same point along the continuum, yet provide different visual presentations that would not be discriminating enough for this study.

Discrete categories emerged as researchers viewed images in previous yearbooks. A preliminary investigation revealed specific areas of the photographs that could be determined as either open or closed to the surround. The areas included hair, skin, and clothing. Once specific areas were identified, possible combinations of open-to-closed were then considered. These combinations later became categories along the continuums. Categories were developed, pretested, and then refined in order to obtain an accurate reflection of the students' images. The categories identified were mutually exclusive and exhaustive of the content relating to the classification system and the visual images.

Sample

The senior high school used in this study was the only public senior high located within the city of 48,000 people. At the time of the study in 1991, 2200 students attended the school with approximately 550 students in grade twelve. The student body was fairly homogeneous as the majority of students came from Euro-American, middle and upper-middle income families.

Students chose from one of four photographic studio's to have their pictures taken. Students were responsible for selecting the items worn at their photo session. Photographers indicated that students brought from one to ten changes of clothing for their session.

Since the photo sessions occurred off school property, the school had little control over the type of clothing students wore. The only reason for excluding a photograph from the yearbook was if the student's back rather than face was forward. Students were responsible for submitting their picture for inclusion into the yearbook.

Procedure

Simple random selection, in which every student's photograph had an equal opportunity of being selected from the entire population, was used through the aid of a random numbers table (Babbie, 1989). Each senior student who attended the midwestern suburban public high school and had his/her photograph included in the 1991 yearbook was assigned a number. Three hundred black and white photographs were randomly selected from a total population of 554 12th-grade student photographs. An equal number of males and females were included in this study to allow gender comparisons.

Each photograph contained a frontal view of a student, including the student's head, hair, and chest area. In each photograph, the surrounding environment was medium grey in value. Color value was measured using Liquitex^R value finder.

Content Analysis of Visual Representation

The author and a research associate used content analysis to code and measure visual priorities. These two coders who were familiar with the classification system analyzed each selected photograph. Analysis of the images focused on the silhouette and visual parts within the ABC, figure-ground spatial relationships, and determinacy or indeterminacy of the surfaces.

Kappa coefficient (Kraemer, 1982), a measure of association testing the degree of reliability between the coders showed high agreement (K.90) for the four visual priorities measured. An average score was calculated from the individually coded scores for each visual priority, and the average score was reported. Frequency counts and percentage distributions were used for descriptive purposes. Log-linear models were used to analyze relationships among the visual priorities through pairwise association.

178

Results

The findings indicated a significant difference between photographs of males and females for the visual priorities of silhouette, visual parts, figure-ground spatial relationships, and determinacy or indeterminacy of the surfaces (p.001). Log-linear analysis was used to investigate significant interactions of independence among the four visual priorities. The log-linear model identified three significant (alpha .05) pairwise visual priorities: 1) whole-to-part by open-to-closed silhouette; 2) whole-to-part by figure-ground; and 3) whole-to-part by determinate-to-indeterminate.

The relationships among the visual priorities created partial ABC's for male students which are significantly different from those of the female students (p .001). Male photographs, more than female, were more open to the surround, and had more visual parts, more spatial planes, and more determinate hair and indeterminate clothing.

Table 2. Visual Presentations of Male and Female Subjects[3]

	1	2	3	4	5
CLOSED					OPEN
Males	15	54	60	6	11
	1		3		
Females	75	10	47	4	11
		2		1	

	1	2	3	4	5
WHOLE-TO-PART					PART-TO-WHOLE
Males	08	20	28	54	33
				3	4
Females	11	63	46	13	12
	1	2		1	1

	1	2	3	4	5
PLANAR SEPARATION					PLANAR INTEGRATION
Males	58	36	24	15	08
	9				
Females	14	14	44	60	15
		2		1	

	1	2	3	4	5	6
DETERMINATE						INDETERMINATE
Males	56	51	23	03	04	02
	7	3			1	
Females	27	07	00	75	17	15
		2		7		

males n=150
females n=150

Visual Priorities for Males and Females

Open-Closed. "Closed-Open" describes how the ABC occupies space and whether it is distinct or independent of the surround or inter-

Figure 1. Yearbook photograph illustrating visual priority, Closed/Open

Figure 2. Yearbook photograph illustrating visual priorities, Closed/Open; Determinate/Indeterminate

dependent with the grey surround of the photographs. More than half the students presented images that portrayed silhouettes closed or mainly closed to the surround with hair and clothing acting as a boundary to the surround or with only the collar or neck area open to the surround (n=157; 52.3%) (Table 2, figure 1, #1 & #2)[2]. Silhouettes identified as having equal amounts of open and closed areas, that is, with the clothing open, with the hair closed to the surround, occurred second most frequently (n=107; 36%) (figure 2, #3). Only a small percentage of students presented images which were viewed as totally open to the surround (n=22; 7.3%, #5).

There was a significant difference between males and females as to the openness of the silhouettes presented (p.001). More females than males presented completely closed silhouettes, 50% of the females (n=75) whereas only 10% of the males (n=15) presented completely closed silhouettes where the head and/or hair and the clothing act as a boundary to the surrounding environment (#1). For females, the second most common silhouette occurred when the head and/or hair remained closed to the surround whereas the clothing remained open to the surround (n=47; 31.3%) (figure 2, #3). That is, the head and/or hair area appeared self-contained from the surround, whereas the open areas' of the shoulder and chest

Figure 4. Yearbook photograph illustrating visual priorities, Closed/ Open; Whole/ Part; Planar separation/integration; Determinate/Indeterminate

Figure 3. Yearbook photograph illustrating visual priority, Closed/ Open

Figure 5. Yearbook photograph illustrating visual priorities, Closed/ Open; Whole/ Part; Planar separation/integration; Determinate/Indeterminate.

interact with the surround and do not appear self-contained. The strong line created around the silhouette of the hair draws the viewer's focus towards the head prior to viewing the shoulder and chest area.

Two silhouettes representing a major portion of male images were: 1) the hair is closed with the clothing and/or head open to the surround (n=60, 40%) (figure 3, #3); and 2) the hair and/or head along with the clothing remained closed to the surround, with the facial skin and neck open to the surround (n=54; 36%) (figure 4, #2). The least frequent silhouette for males and females was the hair was open to the surround with clothing closed to the surround, only six males and four females were viewed as

presenting this image (n=10; 3.3%) (figure 5; #4).

Whole or Part. Whole or part describes the organizing means of perceiving or taking in the ABC by some visual path. A preliminary investigation revealed students' images on a continuum from those viewed as whole or a single part to those viewed as having many parts.

There was a significant difference between males and females in the whole-to-part relationships presented (p.001). The majority of the female images were viewed as having two distinct areas of interdependent parts. The most common ABC presented by females occurred when the face was distinct from the rest of the ABC (n=63; 42%) (figure 1, #2). The second

180

most common ABC for females was characterized with hair and/or face as one distinct part, while the clothing was a second visual part ($n=43$; 30.7%) (figure 5, #3).

Male ABC's were characterized by more visual parts than were the female. Fifty-four males were identified as having some distinct independent parts within the ABC, while 33 males were identified as having many distinct parts (22%) (figure 7, #5). Within the male ABC's, visually distinct parts included hair, face, shirt, tie, blazer, sweater or any combination (figure 4, #4). Distinct parts for males were also created through surface designs such as sweaters or blazers with patterns and shirts with stripes (figure 7), whereas this was rarely the case for females. Overall, female ABCs were identified as whole or containing one distinct part, whereas male ABCs generally contained more independent parts.

Planar Separation or Integration. Figure-ground expresses the forward-backward spatial relationship of the parts to the whole. Some photographs were identified as having only one plane with no separation, whereas others had three or more planes. There was a significant difference in figure-ground relationships between males and females ($p.001$).

The type of planar separation presented by males was different then the planar separation presented by the females. The most common presentation by females was the face on a plane separate from the hair and clothing which appear to recede due to the dark color values ($n=60$; 40%) (figure 1, #4). The second highest number of females presented the head on one plane with the clothing on a second plane ($n=44$; 29.3%) (figure 5, #3), essentially dividing the images in half. Planar separation for females was created by the variations among skin, hair, and their garments. Males, on the other hand, used numerous garment pieces and/or color value combinations within a single garment piece to create planar separation. Fifty-eight males were viewed as having three or more planes (figure 4, #1), while only 14 females were viewed as having more than two planes of separation. An example of three planes was when the outer garment and hair were on one plane, while the shirt and face appeared on other planes.

Determinate or Indeterminate. Determinate or indeterminate refers to the apparent thickness of the surfaces of the ABC and their distance from the observer (DeLong, 1987). Hair and clothing were significant when analyzing figure-ground relationships. Hair was identified as either determinate or indeterminate while clothing was identified as determinate, midpoint between determinate and indeterminate, or indeterminate. The combinations of hair and clothing created six categories rather that five as in the previous priorities. Categories one to three have determinate hair with changes in clothing from determinate-to-indeterminate (#1,#2,#3), while categories four to six have

Figure 6. Yearbook photograph illustrating visual priority, Determinate/Indeterminate

Figure 7. Yearbook photograph illustrating visual priorities, Whole/Part; Determinate/Indeterminate.

indeterminate hair with clothing from determinate-to-indeterminate (#4,#5,#6).

There was a significant difference between males and females in their determinate-indeterminate surface relationships (p.001). One hundred and forty males presented images with determinate hair (figure 4), whereas one hundred and fourteen female presented images with indeterminate hair (figure 2). The determinacy of hair was significantly different between males and females (p.001). Males had hair that was shorter and smoother, whereas females had hair that was longer, curlier, with more volume.

Clothing of males was seen as determinate with little or no surface texture (n=59; 39.3%) (figure 4) or somewhat indeterminate (n=55; 36.7%) (figure 6), and their clothing was rarely identified as indeterminate (n=25; 16.7%) (figure 7). One hundred and two females were identified as having determinate clothing with determinate or indeterminate hair (68%) (figure 5). In terms of the total sample, both males' and females' clothing viewed as determinate was presented by 53.6% (n=161), somewhat determinate by 34.3% (n=103), and indeterminate by 18.3% (n=55) of the students.

Interaction of the Visual Priorities for Males and Females

DeLong's (1987) terminology and methods allow for the systematic analysis of apparel as it interacts with the body and the surrounding environment. Examination of the interactions among the visual priorities of dress aids in a clearer understanding of the visual images presented by the adolescents. Log-linear analysis was used to investigate interactions of independence among the four visual priorities.

Log-linear analysis uncovered significant pairwise associations existing between specific visual priorities (p.001). The log-linear model identified three significant visual priorities: 1) whole-to-part by closed-to-open; 2) whole-to-part by figure-ground; and 3) whole-to-part by determinate-indeterminate. These visual priorities were independent except through whole-to-part priority. The following section describes the significant pairwise associations for various levels within each visual priority as identified through five by five contingency tables for males and females.

Whole-to-Part by Closed-to-Open. Fifty-five females were identified as having silhouettes closed to the surround, and were characterized as whole, with only their face a distinct visual part. Thirty-two males were identified as having a silhouette closed to the surround, except the neck or collar area of the body. This group of males were also viewed as having some distinct parts, prior to viewing the whole. The men in this group usually wore ensembles which included a blazer, shirt, and tie or a sweater, shirt, and tie. Distinct visual parts included not only blazers, sweaters, shirts, and ties, but also hair and face. Sixty-one students were identified as having hair closed to the surrounding environment, whereas their clothing was open to the

Table 3. Log-linear Model for Interaction of Open-to-Closed by Whole-to-Part for Male and Female Subjects[4]

Open-to-Closed		Whole-to-Part	Observed	Expected	Std.Res.
Females					
(1)	by	(2)	55	32.0	4.1
(3)	by	(3)	39	15.0	6.2
Males					
(2)	by	(4)	32	22.8	1.9
(3)	by	(3)	22	11.0	3.3
(1)	by	(2)	09	2.0	4.9
(5)	by	(1)	06	0.6	7.1

surround. This presented an image with two distinct parts: 1) head/hair and 2) clothing. This association was identified for 39 females and 22 males. Log-linear analysis indicated that the number of observed was higher than would expected by random chance, indicating there was more than a chance association between these two visual priorities (Table 3).

Whole-to-Part by Figure-Ground. Sixty-one females were characterized as whole with only the distinct facial coloring is viewed as figure and the person's clothing and hair as ground. Fifteen males were also viewed in this way. In total, this combination of part-to-whole with figure-ground separation accounted for one-quarter of the students. Forty-three females and 21 males presented images with the head one visual part and the clothing a second part. This formed images with two distinct planes, with the hair and head viewed as closer than the person's clothing. Thirty-five males were characterized by the coders as having some distinct parts, prior to considering the whole silhouette, which were seen as having figure-ground rela-

Table 4. Log-linear Model for Interaction of Whole-to-Part by Figure-Ground for Male and Female Subjects

Whole-to-Part		Figure-Ground	Observed	Expected	Std.Res.
Females					
(2)	by	(4)	61	26.5	6.7
(3)	by	(3)	43	14.4	7.6
(5)	by	(1)	09	1.2	7.1
(4)	by	(2)	07	1.3	5.0
Males					
(4)	by	(1)	35	25.2	2.4
(4)	by	(2)	24	16.4	1.9
(5)	by	(1)	24	14.7	2.4
(3)	by	(3)	21	4.1	8.3
(2)	by	(4)	15	2.0	9.2

tionships with three or more planes. An example of a figure-ground relationship with three or more planes was when a blazer or sweater, hair, and tie (if present) are on one plane, and the shirt and face appear on other planes. Surface designs on a blazer or sweater also increased the number of visual planes. Twenty-four males were characterized as having some distinct parts, prior to considering the whole silhouette, which were viewed as creating figure-ground relationships with two planes. Seven females were also identified as having the same whole-to-part by figure-ground association. In both cases, the observed was significantly higher than would be expected. Thirty-three students, including 24 males and 9 females were characterized by many parts, with figure-ground relationship forming three or more planes. Only two pairwise associations were considered significant, that is, with an observed greater than would be expected through random chance (Table 4).

Whole-to-Part by Determinate-Indeterminate. Nine females (O=9, E=1.8, Std.Res=5.3), who were identified as presenting an ABC as a whole, were also seen as having indeterminate hair with somewhat indeterminate clothing. The only significant association for males was characterized by viewing many parts with indeterminate hair and somewhat indeterminate clothing (O=13, E=5.6, Std.Res=3.1).

Discussion

There was a significant difference in the visual patterns between males and females as to the openness of silhouettes, with females presenting silhouettes more closed than males. Females were viewed as more whole-to-part, whereas males were more part-to-whole. There was also a significant difference between males and females in planar separation and integration. Finally, when examining determinate-to-indeterminate, there was a significant difference, between males who had determinate hair and females who had indeterminate hair. Female's clothing was also perceived to be more determinate than males.

Conformity within the social environment of the high school can be viewed at various levels and within various groups. The framework for visual analysis of dress can be used to distinguish between males and females, as well as identify differences among each group. Females presented images which were more conforming than were male images. The findings of this study support the same general patterns of conformity identified by Hamilton, Roach, and Ehle (1972) in that conformity differed between males and females. Brown (1982) and Fuhrmann (1990) indicated that females experience significantly stronger pressure to conform to dress. Females in this study did present images that were viewed as more conforming than males.

Eicher, Baizerman, and Michelman (1991) found that "some differentiation in hairdos distinguished male from female more than apparel" (p. 684). While the finding in the Eicher et al. study was based on qualitative observations, statistical data from the present study also supports the finding that hair was a distinguishing factor between genders.

"Visual literacy goes beyond merely seeing. It means understanding how we see visual forms and being able to share their meaning at some level of universality" (DeLong, 1987, p.1). This includes taking complex visual forms and systematically analyzing them in some meaningful way. Professionals need a clearer understanding of the relevance of dress for adolescents, including both the form and meanings associated with dress in a given subculture.

This paper presents a method to quantify a visual analysis of adolescent appearances and the results using a theoretical framework proposed by DeLong (1987). In order to quantify visual priorities discrete categories were developed and tested. This was necessary since two images placed along a continuum at the same point could have different visual presentations. When using DeLong's framework for visual analysis of dress to analyze quantitatively it is necessary to identify points along a continuum in order to interpret what is being viewed.

Endnotes

[1] This is not the intent of this paper to describe the DeLong method of systematic analysis. For a complete description refer to *the way we look* (DeLong, 1987).

[2] The numbers in brackets refer to the discrete category or placement of the visual images along the related continuum. See Table 2 for number placement along the specific continuums.

[3] The numbers represent the mean between the two coders. The numbers listed below the line represent discrepancy between the coders.

[4] The single bracketed numbers refer to the same number presented along the continuums in Table 2.

References

Babbie, E. (1989). *The practice of social research* (5th ed.). Belmont, CA: Wadsworth.

Brown, B. B. (1982). The extent and effects of peer pressure among high school students: A retrospective analysis. *Journal of Youth and Adolescence, 11,* 121-133.

DeLong, M. R. (1987). *The way we look: A framework for visual analysis.* Ames: Iowa State University.

Eicher, J. B., Baizerman, S., & Michelman, J. D. (1991). Adolescent dress, part II: A qualitative study of suburban high school students. *Adolescence, 26,* 679-686.

Fuhrmann, B. S. (1990). *Adolescence, adolescents.* Glenview, IL: Scott, Foresman.

Goffman, E. (1959). *The presentation of self in everyday life.* Garden City, New York: Doubleday Anchor.

Hambleton, K. B., Roach, M. E., & Ehle, K. (1972). Teenage appearance: Conformity, preferences, and self-concepts. *Journal of Home Economics, 64,* 29-33.

Hethorn, J. L. (1987). *Adolescent appearance: Some issues impacting changes in acceptability.* Unpublished doctoral dissertation, University of Minnesota, St. Paul, MN.

Kraemer, H. C. (1982). Kappa coefficient. In S. Kotz and N. L. Johnson (Eds.), *Encyclopedia of Statistical Sciences: Vol. 4. Icing the tails to limit theorems* (pp. 352-354). New York: John Wiley & Sons.

Littrell, M. A., Damhorst, M. L., & Littrell, J. M. (1990). Clothing interests, body satisfaction, and eating behavior of adolescent females: Related or independent dimensions? *Adolescence, 25,* 77-95.

Michelman, J. D., Eicher, J. B., & Michelman, S. O. (1991). Adolescent dress, part I: Dress and body markings of psychiatric outpatients and inpatients. *Adolescence, 26,* 375-385.

Roach-Higgins, M. E., & Eicher, J. B. (1992). Dress and identity. *Clothing and Textiles Research Journal, 10* (4), 1-8.

Rutherford-Black, C. (1993a). Conformity Adolescent in dress: A Analysis of visual analysis. *Proceeding of the American Home Economics Association,* p.85.

Rutherford-Black, C. (1993b). *Conformity in dress: Analysis of visual representation in high school yearbook portraits.* Unpublished doctoral dissertation, University of Minnesota, St. Paul.

Stone, G. P. (1962). Appearance and the self. In A. M. Rose (Ed.), *Human behavior and social process* (pp.86-118). Boston: Houghton Mifflin Company.

The Aesthetics of Men's Dress of the Kalabari of Nigeria

Tonye V. Erekosima
University of Port Harcourt

Joanne B. Eicher
University of Minnesota

Kalabari Dress As Ensemble

Asante uses the term African aesthetics to mean "the conscious aesthetics of people of African descent who are aware of participating in some African tradition" (1993, p. 54). Our previous analysis of Kalabari dress and the social order (Eicher and Erekosima, 1993) sets the stage for analyzing Kalabari men's dress and textiles as one example of African aesthetics. Our Kalabari data provide an in-depth analysis of the aesthetics of one group of Africans who exhibit a rich dress and textile heritage that contradicts much stereotyping of Africans. For example, Ghanaian dress and textiles are seen and used by many African Americans as representing "typical" African dress. The Kalabari data illustrate only one of many African traditions of dress that exist, for Africa is a large and complex continent.

The Kalabari case of African aesthetics in men's dress to be described here typifies a distinctive clothing tradition, that of cut-and-sewn fabrics. Other outstanding examples of distinctive African dress from cut-and-sewn fabrics for men include the Yoruba handwoven materials in stylistic varieties of ensembles (Wass, 1975), and the Hausa dyed and embroidered ensembles (Perani, 1992). Similar Ghanaian hand-woven textiles are not made into tailored garments but worn in toga-style (Picton, 1992). Other men's outfits include those of the Oba of the Benin kingdom who wears ensembles of heavy coral beading with wrappers and skirts, and the Mande hunters' shirts with leather charms (McNaughton, 1982). These West African examples have not, however, been studied principally from the aesthetic perspective of the wearers themselves, the perspective we take in our following analysis of the Kalabari.

Within Kalabari society both male and female dress have been analyzed as indicating respectively sociopolitical and sociophysical placement of individuals in regard to their basic styles of dress (Daly, 1984; Daly, Eicher, and Erekosima, 1986; Michelman, 1987; Michelman

and Erekosima, 1992; Eicher and Erekosima, 1993). In this paper, we focus on adult male dress and draw from the interviews and fieldwork of Erekosima and Eicher since 1979 (see Eicher and Erekosima, 1993 for an extensive bibliography), as well as Erekosima's (1989) focused research on Kalabari male dress which followed a preliminary analysis by Erekosima and Eicher (1981).[1] We briefly summarize the types of dress in relationship to sociopolitical meaning and elaborate on the aesthetics, etiquette and nuances understood by the Kalabari as necessary for a man's proper appearance in public.

Kalabari men, living on islands in the Niger delta of Nigeria, engaged in trade with Africans and non-Africans for centuries and treasured a variety of imported textiles that they incorporated into their daily and ceremonial lives. One of the unique aspects of their aesthetics of dress was and is their creativity in taking materials from elsewhere and subjecting them to rigorous, indigenous standards to make new ensembles that convey their own ethnic identity and concerns of societal organization.

The art of ensemble for Kalabari men characterizes most of their forms of dress with subtle distinctions and aesthetic elaborations. These distinctions and elaborations constitute efficient vises that glue together discrete and foreign-made items into a montage of Kalabari dress. We will describe and provide illustrations of the ensembles peculiar to Kalabari men, discuss their use, and analyze the expressive aspects the ensembles convey. An elaborate set of aesthetic rules about cloth and dress among the Kalabari with appropriate local nomenclature provides evidence of a sophisticated taste. Stylistic differentiation plays a key role in communicating men's roles within the social order, and a clear-cut set of aesthetic standards accompanies the practiced style differences.

The conversion of borrowed artifacts to indigenous, cultural usages, we have termed the

Cultural Authentication Process (CAP). It has been postulated as a construct entailing four main steps of SCIT: Selection, Characterization, Incorporation, and Transformation (Erekosima and Eicher, 1981). The process of cultural authentication begins when a new item is introduced into a culture unfamiliar with it and becomes an item of meaningful transaction or legitimate cultural currency in the second culture.

Initially, the specific artifact is singled out from a variety of possibilities, or, in other words becomes selected. The artifact also becomes named, or characterized symbolically by members of the receiving community who acquire a shared reference in regard to it. As the object becomes associated with a definite function in the social order to solve a problem or aid in enhancing the well-being of individuals or in enriching life, it is, thereby, incorporated into the social order. Finally, when the object is transformed through creative responses to modify it so that it no longer is perceived as simply borrowed, it is then culturally authenticated. The process of cultural authentication is found throughout Kalabari life, not only in men's dress ensembles, but also in funeral display, the production of pelete bite (cut-thread cloth), and female dress. Our focus in this paper is to elaborate the examples of cultural authentication as found in the aesthetic expressions of Kalabari men's dress.

What the Kalabari of Nigeria regard as their men's traditional dress consists largely of textiles used as wrappers, garments, accessories and ornaments imported from overseas or fabricated outside their culture. The dress items include familiar Western clothing like shirts (in some modified form), trousers, accessories like hats, shoes, handkerchiefs and walking sticks as well as ornaments like gold and silver chains or studs. Some ensembles include "wrappers" and gowns of Indian textiles in combination with Western garments. Superficially, a man in such attire is not visibly wearing indigenous Nigerian dress. However, they represent to the Kalabari, objects of considerable economic value and aesthetic worth and the sociopolitical status of Kalabari males is represented by specific types of dress for age and social position.[2] Aesthetics reflect the tension between conformity and differentiation, or matter and form in cultural life. Aesthetic standards are explicitly evident within Kalabari society as specific acceptable general rules of expressive or appreciative representation. These standards include subtleties of taste that pervade the process of aesthetics and allow idiosyncratic (individual) or segmental (subgroup) emphases. Aesthetics of dress among the Kalabari also include a knowledge of the stylistic forms of dress appropriate to specific categories of people or events as well as knowledge of the transitory fashions of a specific time and place.

Kalabari aesthetics of dress exemplify African aesthetics in other realms. Practical utility merges with meaning and use. Kalabari dress is neither mere commodity or pure art.[3] This merger is the context within which we view Kalabari dress. Hence Kalabari aesthetics simultaneously encompass the pairing of sentiment and substance. African aesthetics resonates as the vantage point or basic perspective from which objects and events of reality obtain interpretation or assignments of meaningfulness in the setting of cultural lifeways.

Kalabari Men's Traditional Dress

The peculiar ensembles and the characteristic use of the imported items of dress together define Kalabari men's traditional dress. As one informant put it, Kalabari dress for men means: "to tie *injiri* cloth, wear a garment over it, put on a hat, and pick up a walking stick" (Erekosima, 1989:337). Two major components make up the classic styles of Kalabari men's traditional dress ensembles. One is the sewn garment that covers the upper torso. The other is a length of cloth called a wrapper. When tied on the wearer, it covers the lower torso from waist to feet. The most frequently used and preferred textile for a man's wrapper is injiri, the Kalabari name for Indian madras, the plaid cotton cloth, that for centuries has been imported from India through European merchants to West Africa.

Who are the Kalabari of Nigeria whose rigid dress code for men has a strong aesthetic component? This sub-unit of the Ijo ethnic group, estimated at slightly more than one percent of the 90 million population of Nigeria, was important in the development of Nigeria: early on as fishermen, but who centuries ago turned principally into traders of salt, slaves, and palm oil. They live and have lived on a series of islands in the delta of River Niger, 4 degrees above the equator. Their overland trade with other West Africans (Alagoa, 1970) has been indicated as predating their European trading contacts with the Portuguese who came by sea in the 1400s. Later, the Dutch, French and British also arrived by sea for trade and sporadic attempts at missionary work. The 1700s and 1800s were the heyday for the Kalabari as superb traders and middlemen (for men did the trading) with the Europeans, dealing first in slaves and then in palm oil (Adams, 1823; Dike, 1956; Jones, 1963). The fortunes of the Kalabari shifted markedly after the British took political control of the geographical area that became known as Nigeria in the early 1900s. Instead of the king and chiefs being in complete control of their own political and economic affairs, they fell subject to the machinations of the British. By 1960, when independence was won for Nigeria, the Kalabari maintained pride in their ethnic heritage, but many rose to the challenge of seeing themselves as part of the larger political, economic, and geographical unit of the Nigerian polity.

Varieties of Sewn Dress and their Patterns of Use

The Kalabari word *kapa* which stands for sewn garments, has been identified by a linguist (Jenewari, 1976) as a word in Portuguese which means dress. There is, therefore, a likely correspondence between the emergence of this sewn variant of Kalabari men's dress (in contrast to the handwoven lengths of cloth used as "wrappers") and Portuguese influence among the Kalabari starting from the early 16th century.

These Europeans clearly introduced a whole range of items of dress to the Kalabari which were both Western and non-Western (Vogt, 1975). This introduction tremendously enlarged the Kalabari wardrobe, with the Portuguese term for dress being borrowed and used in a generic way to reflect the new major development. The injiri cloth from India has already been cited as one such item brought in by the Portuguese (Evenson, 1991; 1993).

The records show, for instance, a documentation by Pereira in 1514 of Portuguese trade in clothing items with Benin (Ryder, 1965). A trade report by Antonio de Coyra in 1516 and then by Alvaro Frade in 1519 also attest to the same activity. Similarly, Blake (1942) describes trade with the Casa da Guinea in Lagos as reported in 1498 by Joham de Avellar and in another Casa da Guinea document of 1533. Even with-

out the Kalabari having direct link to the Portuguese, both of these towns of Benin and Lagos were thriving market centers to which they had access at the time, as already indicated. The Kalabari trade with these ports only subsequently expanded, especially when direct trade contacts began. And the extent of the growing commerce in clothing can be inferred from the report by Davis (1954) that clothing constituted approximately 70 percent of British imports to West Africa in the 1700s.

Regarding commerce to the Niger Delta hinterland, Alagoa remarked (1970, p. 322) that:

> By the beginning of the sixteenth century ... north-south trade was already far advanced, and carried on with huge canoes on a large scale over a long distance.

Thus was the channel kept open that led to the indirect reference about Portuguese presence in the Niger Delta hinterland by the 1600s. One European traveler (Ogilvy, 1970, p. 480) noted that there was a nobleman of Owerri, Don Antonio De Mingo, whose father had married a Portuguese woman that he had met while in Portugal and whom he brought back with him to Africa.

A more direct reference to the impact of Portuguese fashions on Kalabari society occurs in the following remarks of the British colonial administrator, Amaury Talbot, who did an ethnographic survey of the cultures of southern Nigeria in the early decades of the 20th century. In describing one of the revered deities of Kalabari society he noted (Talbot, 1932, p. 38) as follows:

> When one remembers the number of Portuguese mariners who, in old days, made their way to this part of the coast, it is not difficult to understand why the carved figure of *adumu* is here shown with the pointed mustache and beard, the ruff and feather-trimmed hat of a don of the period when these bold seafarers first penetrated to the lower regions of the Santa Barbara [river].

The Kalabari were not merely passive recipients of borrowed forms of dress. They did not just retain or copy the Portuguese garments or treat dress as artifacts of purely material import. Their response was unlike the current unimaginative and almost passive use of Western dress by contemporary Nigerians. Among many Nigerians, over a century of adoption of modern European dress is known (Wass, 1975). Many items such as the men's suit ensemble continue to be worn with little change or modification. In addition these items are not given local names, nor modified in form or function, for they are not used in an indigenous way. In contrast, the Kalabari reacted differently to the items of dress borrowed from outside. They introduced their own words for innovations that they made, while adjusting the innovations in a practical way to fit their own perspectives of life. The result was a genuine learning situation such as Piaget and Inhelder (1969) stipulate, by which the Kalabari effected a significant adaptation of the received artifact to their deeply challenged and versatile culture. In creative response, they altered and accommodated new inputs, or adjusted their preexisting frame of reference, and brought both to an adaptive equilibrium.

This approach, earlier defined as the Cultural Authentication Process, guides our analysis of Kalabari dress. The Kalabari used a series of modified upper garments to be worn with wrapped cloth for the lower garments and added a variety of imported accessories to create a complete ensemble.

The traditional ensembles worn by Kalabari men in public are indicated by the names of the sewn garment for the upper torso that is knee-length, calf-length, or ankle-length. Kalabari traditional dress ensembles representing four ranks of the sociopolitical order are listed below in descending order of importance (Figure 1). The gown known as _attigra_ is outside the ranking system and is described afterwards:

1. Ebu
2. Doni
3. Woko
4. Etibo

i) Describing the Ebu

The _ebu_ is an ankle-length gown worn by the king (Amanyanabo) and his paramount chiefs, made of an imported plaid cotton fabric from India known as injiri. The style is specifically characterized by a broad, "V-shaped" front for the collar that reaches to mid-chest but is square across the back, reminiscent of the uniform of sailors. The latter were the crew of the visiting ships who rowed their smaller vessels ashore, and wore uniforms with this type of collar (Figure 2). Kalabari contact with Euro-

Figure 1. Kalabari men's dress from the left: _etibo, woko, doni, ebu, attigra_

pean sailors and traders may have provided this key symbol of new developments in Kalabari society that resulted from stimulation from Western mercantile activity. To counter the danger to their community from the demand for slaves made by the Europeans, the Kalabari had to restructure their society radically. A monarchy coordinating expanded family trading and defense corporations emerged. The traditional extended families assimilated thousands of "strangers" from hinterland societies to evolve these new "War-Canoe Houses," and allowed the most enterprising of even these former aliens to rule over these units. Kalabari men's dress emerged to symbolize and communicate functions within such a new order.[4]

Figure 2. Front and back view of the e͟bu͟

The gown is worn only with a matching piece of injiri wrapper (*bite͟ wari͟*). Its decor is one of simplicity, since no loud or rich accessories normally accompany it. A bowler hat or top hat is appropriate headgear, along with simple jewelry such as one solid piece of coral bead stretched across the stud-fastened mini-collar of the white shirt worn underneath. The long sleeves of the ebu must be folded to slightly above the wrist, to expose the cuffs of the white shirt underneath which are usually secured with gold or silver links. A few gold rings may be worn on one or two fingers of both hands and a simple cane or walking stick held.

The ebu is regarded as most fitting for the very elderly chiefs of eminent status who no longer need to assert high public visibility through ornate habiliment. They leave such projection of the image of a chief actively exercising power to those who are younger and for whom the *doni͟* is a more appropriate attire than the ebu.

The simple style of the e͟bu͟ matches the status of the elder statesman who gracefully stays in the background as he offers words of wisdom and tactfully guides the strategies of the active community leaders who serve as public representatives. This perspective led to the uncontrived situation of the King (Ama͟ny͟ana͟bo͟) of Kalabari appearing among his Council of Chiefs at a cabinet session in 1966 as the only one amongst them wearing ebu.[5] Traditionally only the king and his handful of leading statesmen wore the e͟bu͟.

Also close discriminations are made about the quality of Indian madras, which the Kalabari call injiri, that may be obtained or used. The top of the class is called "Real India" cloth, recognizable by textural qualities as well as perforation markings at the sides of the cloth. A less refined quality of injiri is called "mandras or madras," and an even less durable brand of the cloth which sold rather cheaply was called Pinion. Its texture was inferior or rougher, and its colors faded readily with laundering.

ii) Describing the D͟oni͟

The doni is an ankle-length robe worn by Kalabari notables who are chiefs (*a͟lapu͟*). Made like an elongated shirt, from thick and colorful woolen material, its collar is narrow at the back with two flaps at the front (Figure 1). Four button-holes are centered in a front placket for display of good-sized gold or silver studs. A chain connects the studs to a brooch pinned on the left side pocket. The placket is often fashioned in a pattern called fish-gill (*sa͟ngolo*), ladder, or such other designs, with a large tab at the bottom (*do͟ni͟ be͟le*) that apparently enables the wearer to pull down the garment while walking, to straighten it out.

The sleeves of the doni are slightly folded back when worn, to expose the cuffs of the white shirt that must be worn underneath it. The collar band of the shirt is fastened with a big, matching gold or silver stud, and the shirt cuffs fastened with matching links. The doni is ankle-length or sometimes slightly shorter, and it must have an injiri wrapper of good quality tied underneath that shows an appropriate "volume" relative to the "big" fit of the doni on its wearer. The gown should not fit too closely or be too tight around the ankles.

Use of a walking stick is almost always mandatory for a man wearing the doni; shoes are optional. The hat need not be elaborate except during ceremonial occasions, perhaps a top hat or bowler hat. Wearing gold rings is expected. Each side of the doni is slit from the hem to below the armscye, to allow for easy movement by the wearer.

Informants did not agree on the origin of the doni. Some insisted that it initially came from the Portuguese in its present form. These informants claimed that it was being worn by the Portuguese merchants, who gave away some in token of friendship to their leading trading partners. This item of clothing was presented as what is worn by the dons in Portugal. *Don* was the title for a nobleman in Portuguese, as is shown by examples like the legendary Don Juan, or Don Quixote of literary fame, and of names like Don Pedro that are given to Portuguese and Spanish notables and also taken up by some Kalabari families. Some suggested that the outstanding Kalabari traders of the period who received this gift of clothing which they called doni in their own dialect - were thereby being recognized as members of the league of successful entrepreneurs.

Other informants contended, however, that the word doni came into use only during the period of English dominance and presence in the Niger Delta, which was some time in the early eighteenth century. They insisted that the English introduced a knee-length, woolen shirt (somewhat like the later "boiled" army shirt). The Kalabari chiefs, only then emerging as a force in the internal political scene, needed to be distinguished by adopting some highly visible symbol of their status. They instructed the Sierra Leone and other repatriated black tailors on the ships at the time, to sew these for them by making them reach "down." These tailors were black men who had been repatriated from America to Africa and who had acquired artisan skills. Some became itinerant craftsmen plying the Atlantic coast and sharing their modern ways as missionaries and artisans or tradesman. Communication in any common language at the time was difficult, so the story is told that the chiefs said in a halting English: "doni", "doni" for, "down." These accounts argue that the ankle-length gown emerged as an elongated shirt that became the doni and the exclusive garb of Kalabari chiefs.

In examining the credibility of the first version, we found that a search through books illustrating European period dress (Evelyn, 1968) does not show anything like the doni being worn by the Portuguese, or any European peoples at all, from the sixteenth through to the twentieth century. The idea of an indigenous adaptive thrust using dress as a symbol of the new order, therefore, becomes more plausible or reinforced.

Whether the garment was adopted or adapted, however, the doni remains a Kalabari dress on account of the ensemble that forms it, and rules of etiquette associated with wearing it. Apparently such an ensemble never existed in Europe, and even differs markedly from a similar outfit worn by neighbors of the Kalabari in terms of its associated aesthetics (Erekosima, 1989).

iii) Describing the Woko

This garment, worn by Kalabari men in the rank of Opu A̱sawo̱, or the Gentlemen of Substance, also differs from similar garments called the *jompa̱* that are worn by other Niger Delta neighbors in the riverine city-states and other areas outside the Delta (as among the hinterland Igbos). This word derives from the English "jumper" but does not designate clothing that fits the same description. Among the Kalabari, however, it is called wo̱ko̱. and is made of plain-colored fabric in contrast to the figured cloths members of the other Eastern Nigerian communities use.

This form of dress probably originated from somewhere other than in Kalabari society. Bonny is a possible dispersal source for the jompa or wo̱ko̱, but Kalabari informants remained quite vague when discussing its origin. The Kalabari may have, again, simply devised their own unique version of the already existing outfit in order to serve some pressing internal need of status demarcation.

The Kalabari make the wo̱ko̱ out of white or khaki drill and, generally today, plain terylene, wool, or serge. The colors used are yellow or beige, off-brown, or other neutral hue. This contrasts with the bright red, black, green or crimson colors criss-crossed with animal or bird motifs that characterize the *blangidi̱* or woolen material out of which the non-Kalabari peoples make their own equivalent of the wo̱ko̱. With the Kalabari, it is generally boorish and an anathema to wear this latter type of designed textile in the wo̱ko̱ style.

The woko is simply-cut, hangs from the shoulders of the wearer, with front placket and no collar band. The front placket of the Kalabari woko or jompa is plain in contrast to the elaborate gill-pattern or ladder-design motif on the plackets of the non-Kalabari jompa, and the Kalabari doni. The sleeves are wide and elbow length; the garment itself is knee length. A band of the same cloth is sewn full-length at the back center of the Kalabari woko "to give it character," according to informants. The bottom hem is straight with side slits which are largely only stylistic. The earlier, older version of the woko had two front pockets and was not as long as contemporary ones. The term woko, which appears to have come from the Kalabari usage wokoro-wokoro, meaning "loose-fitting," seems an apt description for the garment.

The woko placket has buttonholes for three studs of gold or silver, attached to each other by a chain. A wide pocket on the left, usually sports a fluffy matching handkerchief. A walking stick is considered a necessary accessory and a straw hat or other informal head-gear like the embroidered one called "smoking cap" will be worn which is an embroidered round hat, flat on the top but decorated with tassels or metallic thread trimmings.

The woko is frequently worn with an injiri wrapper, but can also be worn with trousers, as it has been for many years. A photograph of Chief Ikiriko of Buguma said to be taken in 1917 shows him dressed with woko and trousers. Wearing trousers supposedly reflects a need for convenience, as when the wearer is bustling about at the beach front handling commerce and does not want to worry about the breeze lifting up his wrapper.

The Kalabari do not sew their woko with the cloth called blangidi like their neighbors use for the jompa. They agree in their judgment that the use of this fabric for woko shows poor taste. Nearer to the truth, however, may be the fact that heavily patterned and brightly colored fabrics had generally been assigned to the sewing of doni, to add to the full view colorfulness and commanding presence of chiefs. By sticking to only the blandly-colored fabrics for their woko, a clear-cut and highly distinguishable collective identity was also established for the Kalabari. A general sense of disdain for use of the supposedly garish blangidi to tailor a woko therefore sets the Kalabari apart, even though this disdain is an insular appraisal by the Kalabari about others.

A singular appreciation of this fabric is, however, in evidence for Kalabari men also have a clear ranking of blangidi. At the bottom of this hierarchy is a very inferior type of printed woolen cloth called *fuun* that is used only to make children's clothes. Then there are the various kinds that Kalabari women tie, like *feni, ologboin-gboin, nama-sibi,* which are largely the type used for sewing jompa among their neighboring peoples. Finally there are other kinds of blangidi the men consider to be heavy enough and which they will use in sewing the doni, such as *ojugbe, aru pike, okolobi torungbo, igbe biri and mene bite.*

iv) Describing the Etibo

The name *etibo* is an elision of the words "eight bob" or eight shillings which represented the cost of such a shirt brought for sale during the English period of dominance on the coast. Etibo is at the bottom of the hierarchy of Kalabari men's dress in the valuation of traditional dress and is associated with the bottom rank, the sociopolitical status of Asawo or the Young Men That Matter. The garment, simply a large white, long-sleeved shirt, is made of cotton. The bottom of the etibo has a rounded shirttail, in contrast to the straight hem of the woko, and the cotton material is comparatively much lighter and cheaper than the heavier woolen cloth of earlier versions. Respondents said the early examples were not usually white but colored, thick flannel material, and shorter than the current style called etibo. The version of the 1980s and 1990s reaches to about mid-calf, whereas the original etibo was knee-length.

The original, imported etibo appears to have simply disappeared from the market, just like several other European imported dresses that were formerly popular. One was the "Bush Shirt," which had fur-padded parts on the shoulders and back and was made of thick wool so that it served well in keeping the cold away. Another was the Formal Dinner Shirt, with the buttonholes inserted in the wide front placket (ekpe kuro).

The contemporary etibo appears to have emerged from being the undershirt (*sheti*) that chiefs wore beneath their doni and ebu. Some of these Kalabari chiefs of the recent past were very big and tall people whom the European shirt ill-fitted. These men, such as Chiefs Jim George (died 1943), Inko-Tariah (died 1943), Graham Douglas (died 1949), Walter Okorosa (died 1958) as well as Okoma Tom George (died in 1950s), therefore, ordered their own shirts to be sewn to size locally. Before long, such "trendy" shirts went on to become the single, outside garb of the lower status young men and took on the name etibo. Its use specifically enjoyed a boost after the Nigerian Civil War of 1967-1970.

The sheti worn underneath other garments by chiefs had a detached collar as well as one buttonhole for a stud and for cuff links, and was not the regular shirt worn by Europeans. Some informants called it the imported English "Crown Shirt," for which the local terminology "Krama Sheti" appears to have been substituted.

The new etibo took closely after its forerunner in not having a collar, and in always having a cloth loop at the center of the back yoke. Its sleeves have buttons, not buttonholes for links; this change accommodates the decreased concern for prestige among younger men, although a shirt pocket was added to permit display of colorful handkerchiefs. Etibo is worn only with a single stud, as opposed to three worn with the woko and four with the doni. It can also be worn with any pair of trousers, although an injiri wrapper is the only correct accompaniment to the garment when one is dressing formally as Kalabari (Figure 1).

The etibo has become the focus of connoisseurship of injiri-tying styles because it allows more of the wrapper to be seen. Skill is required to manipulate the slim gingham piece (injiri ikiba), two yards long and one yard wide. Tying the cloth around the waist must be carefully done in order that the wrapper does not appear to be tied carelessly and too loosely, thus inviting a comment about careless appearance (biri ayi sima). Normally the bottom edge of the injiri wrapper should be at least 2 inches above the instep (buo ikara). However, this general rule is offset by the opportunity to display a variety of cloth tying styles that modify the rule, indicating the wearer as one thoroughly at home with cultural knowledge and etiquette of men's dress as discussed later.

v. Describing the Attigra

The attigra ensemble does not fit into the set of four which we have described that marks the Kalabari political hierarchy, but derives its great importance simply as the foremost ceremonial or dancing garb of the Kalabari as leisure-loving people. The attigra also attests to the primacy the Kalabari give to culture over politics, for cultural events have continued to be important and resilient in Kalabari life even as their political structure has become subordinated to that of the larger polity of Nigeria. The contrived dazzle of an attigra outfit is, therefore, another Kalabari original, along with its companion ajibulu hat that produces an effect of a balance in bulk. One informant described the wearer of this hat as holding forth like a masquerade, and amply filling the vista with his dazzle upon appearing (Erekosima, 1989:339).

Attigra is the Kalabari designation for a Northern Nigerian, handwoven cotton robe with Arab-influenced embellishments of embroidery that came into Kalabari hands before the country of Nigeria came into being. The Kalabari word "attigra" is formed as an elision of the usage "Atta Igarra," which derives from the words "Attah of Igalla." This king of an ancient kingdom at the northern limits of the Niger Delta (Miles, 1936) with which the Kalabari chiefs carried on their early trade, was described by informants as the donor of the outfit to his contemporary Kalabari nobility, and the dress was then named after him. A more fashionable contemporary version is made from velvet material that is imported from India, usually embroidered with gold or silver threads. The attigra is primarily distinguished by having open sleeves that are about one third the length of the garment. The rich fabrics used are cut amply to give bulk to the wearer and to provide an image of the wearer as munificent. Matching velvet material is tied as a wrapper beneath the velvet attigra and shows below its hem, where it reaches to the lower calf or ankle. If the homespun variety of attigra from Northern Nigeria is chosen, then a matching wrapper of gingham plaid cloth called injiri is worn.

To wear the early form of attigra, for instance, a man must have either an English top-hat or the imposing indigenous creation of the ajibulu hat. A circlet of tiger's teeth (siri aka) or of cowry shells around the neck is a required accessory to accentuate the ajibulu hat. The contemporary velvet version is usually worn with an ajibulu and layers of coral beads bedecking the neck, imported mainly from Italy. Underneath either gown, the man must wear a European-style long-sleeved shirt and underneath that, a singlet (cotton u-neck, knit undershirt). It is normal to wear heavy gold rings on several fingers with this outfit.

Because shoes are viewed as restrictive of dance steps, being barefoot is preferred; but if shoes are worn, socks are generally not worn. To complete this outfit, a decorated fan (ye biri efenge) should be held in the right hand, and an elephant tusk (oworowo) or other material of tusk shape, made of glass or cowry shells, must be held in the left hand. Walking sticks and canes are not used when wearing attigra.

Cloth Tying Techniques

Each of the above ensembles includes a wrapper as part of the outfit. Two distinct classifications of cloth-tying methods for men's wrappers are recognized by the Kalabari. One is biri oki or biri olo which means to hold the cloth on to the waist, and within which such techniques as akinda, ikpukpu kpo, pele suka and tingili are practiced. Akinda involves making a loop over the private parts and passing the tips of a handwoven cloth known as akwamiri or other strip of cloth through a band of the same cloth tied around the waist. This is generally practiced today only in relation to the practice of preparation of corpses for burial. Wrestlers would also resort to a variant of this form in a bid

to secure themselves adequately from exposure. Injiri or any other domestic cloth can be used to tie ikpukpu kpo which entails making a firm knot so that the rest of the cloth can be gathered, especially around the knees, to permit strenuous work or vigorous movements. A picture of the war-party of Chief Will-Braide of Bakana presumably taken in 1879, shows some soldiers in this style, a common injiri-tying method for young people at the time.

Pele-suka entails laying over one side of the upper end of a cloth on the other and tucking it in, without actually tying either tip. The thick tawulu or beach towel is normally worn this way, for situations like going to the river for an early morning dip. Tingili is another way of wearing the tawulu but is better suited to the lighter and more voluminous wax-prints. It entails wrapping the crossed-over tips of the cloth's upper section over and over on itself at about the level of the navel till the length of the cloth has been reduced to just above the feet, and it has been firmly secured on the waist through the multiple rolling turns (Figure 3).

The second main method of cloth-tying for Kalabari men is that of actually wrapping the cloth (inwain) around the waist. A variety of styles or techniques have been developed (See Table 1)including eremoni or kiri pele, alaate or amatubonye, inturu and otobiri and are de-

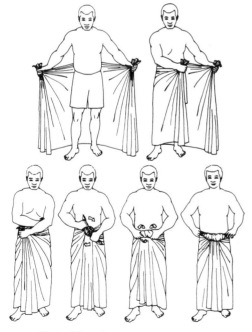

Figure 3. Method for tying a wrapper in tingili style, most often used with tawulu or wax print cloth

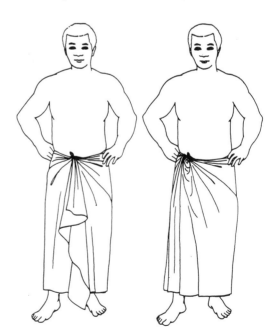

Figure 4. Method for tying a wrapper in inturu style (left) and eremoni style (right)

193

Table 1: Styles of Cloth-tying (bite inwain) in Kalabari Men's Traditional Dress.

Style Name	Description
1. Eremoni or Kiri pele	The cloth is wrapped fully to the ankle; the bottom tips are even, with one overlapping the other. This is tied like Kalabari women tie their cloth (except that women tie to the left, not the right), hence the name eremoni or "fit for women's envy." This method of tying assumes slow, dignified movements in walking, because the manner of wrapping around the body does not allow a long stride. The name kiri pele depicts the precision of "roundedness" at the bottom of the wrapper in encircling the body from waist to feet.
2. Alaate or Amatubonye	One tip of the cloth points down in front on the right side, with this tip longer than the rest of the bottom of the cloth. The names alaate (meaning "I have made good") and amatubonye (meaning "Who owns the town anyway?") are suggestive of its "dare-me" casualness.
3. Inturu	The cloth is wrapped so that the hem is parallel to the ground with the two ends open on the left side. As the wearer strides along, the wrapper opening shows off white underpants (knickers) underneath trimmed with lace at the knee (buo sua kapa). The cotton plaid textile called injiri, usually selected for this style, often has a pair of white shirting strips sewn at the waist for ease of tying the style.
4. Otobiri	The wrapper length is tied shorter than the inturu; the hem is equal and round, with the tying occurring at both ends of the waist. The word otobiri is suggestive of "sweet experience." This is a relatively new style which a leading men's club in Buguma is teaching all its members to tie as a presumably proprietary discovery.

scribed below. Figure 4 illustrates *eremoni* and *inturu*.

Men's cloth is always tied to the right of the waist, while women always tie theirs to the left. Any man who consistently ties his cloth to the left risks being accused of wizardry, and that is for so audaciously flouting a key rule or practice involving gender differentiation.

The Kalabari invested much creative energy in tying wrappers as one aspect of the total ensemble of men's traditional dress. So elaborate has this become that clearly more than just the use of dress in basic or ordinary socialization is involved. These style options for men, their range of skill, the particular occasions of use, verbal designations and specific shared meanings constitute an important dimension of Kalabari aesthetics in dress for men.

Additional evidence gives us further insight into the subtleties and the mystique built around the cloth tying style called inturu that enthralls members of the Kalabari public. One middle-

aged informant told Erekosima that when a man ties inturu:

o bu ke bu sin te,

(he has laid hold on his dignity)

o Kalabari bo bara sime te

(he has taken on the true image of being Kalabari).

To convey the way most informants felt about tying inturu, we might say that it gives a Kalabari man the feeling that is as luxurious as getting to tool around town in a prestigious car, even if for only an evening. For among the array of styles that Kalabari men may display in cloth manipulations, the inturu is the "Mercedes Benz" of them all.

Another informant, forty-two years old, a Young Man (Asawo) by Kalabari classification, rhapsodized as follows on the pleasures of tying inturu:

"When the wind blows, the injiri has to open up and the underpant (*drosi*) just shines forth, the white underpant is just beaming (*saniari*). The dancer or wearer is mounting an underpant display declaring that he is neat down to the pin, for it [the underpant] is just as immaculate as his etibo [outer garment] is immaculate."

An elderly informant explained that: "For the Kalabari man, the style of tying injiri which exposes his long underpants, is treasured." (Erekosima, 1989:376).

One of the informants went so far as to point out that the original name of this style was *intuku* (whose meaning relates to uprightness), but which has colloquially become *inturu*. Thus the ensemble is linked to the portrayal of moral integrity and character as the Kalabari define these. This reference to character is one that reflects an apparent demeanor of nonchalant leisureliness (*asa ti*) while remaining fully alert to one's responsibilities (*bu nimi*). Horton (1966) has given similar depictions of the ideal Kalabari man in masquerade portrayals.

The wearer of the *inturu* wrapper exudes subtlety of character, or sophistication, for he is "surprised" by the breeze lifting his wrapper (but actually his gait does it) to expose, ever-so-inadvertently, his immaculate underpants to onlookers, until he adjusts his wrapper once more to feign modesty by covering it. Indeed, because of its one-upmanship intricacies, the inturu was initially a style of wrapper-tying reserved exclusively for chiefs amongst the Kalabari.

The Rules and Etiquette of Kalabari Men's Dress

In expressions such as *orattigra bulo warari* (he is donning an attigra), or *osime bara bu gbem* (his turnout is befitting), *osuakapa ogbeaa* (his dress does not fit him), Kalabari people convey an evaluation of a man's attire which combines items on various parts of the body in forming a single unit of accouterment. The assessment of a Kalabari man's appearance does not end simply with the mix of appropriate items on the head, neck, body, and waist or in the hands, pockets, and plackets, that make up each of the ensembles of the attigra, ebu, doni, woko and etibo. It also extends to details of color, fit and proper accessorizing.

A stringent adherence to aesthetic standards demands that white material must retain its whiteness; that cloth be tied so that its tip is only about one and a half inches above the ankle and not way up away from it (*fekepu*) or awkwardly below it; that allowances for body fit be made in the design and sewing of clothing, so that it neither appears too short nor too long, too loose or too tight; that rich and heavy material for sewn garments not be worn with lightweight or cheap cloth for the wrapper; that studs be worn in specific ways when dressing is casual, as against when it is formal; and that ornaments like gold or silver match the colors of dress and shoes that are worn. Therefore, silver, for example, is matched to black and blue shades, while gold picks up beige or brown colors of dress.

These examples illustrate subtler physical attributes and standards of Kalabari men's dress than do the mere ensembling process of specific items put together from different parts of the world. Instead, explicitly recognized lengths, textures, amount of bulk, positioning and color choices all contribute to a configuration that only the practiced eye will catch, and on which the Kalabari instruct their youth. The fact that each Kalabari ensemble combines materials from different cultures and not from a single source, and that the Kalabari also apply their own indigenous aesthetic standards of proper dress, indicates that they have not copied another society's styles or aesthetics.

Among the rules of dress, tradition decrees that no man should wear the ensemble of a rank higher than his. An Asawo or Young Man that Matters, for instance, is not supposed to wear a woko or jompa, for they belong to the Opu Asawo or Gentleman of Substance category. Nor should anyone who is not a chief put on the doni, for he invites being fined, beaten and stripped.

Through observation of this regulation, orderly relations are maintained by all members of the social system; aspiration to the next functional level is sustained for all who still may climb higher; and authority operates undiminished from the higher levels to the lower without recourse to use of sanctions.

"Stepping Down," " Stepping Up," and "Stepping Out" Practices in Kalabari Men's Dressing.

Among the understood rules, however, there is a generally permitted pattern that a member of a higher rank may wear the outfit of any of the ranks below him, in a context of dressing in an informal way. For example, chiefs wear the woko in black for attending the funeral of a person who is not a chief, but will wear only a black doni to the funeral of a fellow chief. A chief could also wear the etibo to receive visitors at home, but must wear at least the woko in going out for a meeting that is of his War-Canoe House and not a formal state affair. The latter he can only attend in doni or ebu. He may also informally walk about town by "stepping out" only in the innovative kala doni or woko but not in a straight etibo.

A chief who informally wears the woko that is allocated to "Gentlemen" and strolls out on the street, however, may show his actual status by wearing his woko with only one stud. This is different from the three that an Opu Asawo, or Gentleman, would need to have, all in place, while wearing this outfit of his rank. The Opu Asawo may, himself, show informality by wearing the etibo out on the street, but ensuring that he has a felt hat on along with his walking stick. The Asawo, in turn, gets informal by wearing his etibo without buttoning the stud, and if possible wearing a pair of trousers with it instead of tying an injiri wrapper. In either case, he does not need a hat nor a walking stick.

The above practice of "stepping down" from one's proper outfit, has its "stepping up" counterpart in Kalabari society also. The occasion of funeral obsequies which mark a transition in families, provides for temporary suspension of the strict code of dressing by one's rank only. At this time events are introduced, like the Amabro (funeral parade) and Dinkrama ti (obsequies-completion dance) during which younger men will wear the woko and even the doni or ebu in a public display.

If the death were that of a chief or very old person, there is even a complete loosening of clothing regulations in the accompanying event of igira sara (storming out with a stomp). Here women join in too, sporting leaves and rags with the youth of the affected community and trotting about in martial and other uncomely or sexually explicit gait.

A return to normal dress also marks the end of the disequilibrating episode of death on which attention has been briefly lavished. Thereafter only persons close to the deceased may enter into a period of seclusion and of mourning in black, which somehow takes them out of the mainstream of the visual communication setting for public conduct.

Political Change and Its Influence on Kalabari Men's Dress

As the power of the king and the chiefs as Heads of the Canoe-Houses began to wane under the impact of British colonialism, their control over those under them became lessened. Subordinates of the actual Heads of War-Canoe Houses got to be appointed by the British administrator in certain cases to exercise power over everyone following an administrative change in the 1920's. The move spelt a death-knell to Kalabari traditional authority and initiated a marked era of individualism. The rule of the previous indigenous political regime collapsed accordingly, and along with it went strict adherence to some of the practices it had sustained, including those related to dress as a visible expression of sociopolitical rank. Not only were Kalabari men generally relieved of their previous allegiance but they had an opportunity to pursue broader identities and affinities when they were ushered into a new framework of an independent Nigerian state in 1960. Consequently changes, not only in aspects of the clothing that constitute Kalabari men's dress ensembles, but also in their patterns of use, have occurred. The old order has changed and its significant symbols have been diminished. We have identified six changes in the aesthetic standards as follows:

1. The attigra, for instance, has been shown to have changed from a traditional handwoven cotton material with stitched-on designs to richly embroidered, factory-produced velvets worn with heavy coral beads. This style, which was introduced from about 1914, also came with a distinctive, Indian-Sikh type of headgear having a streamer running down the back. This form of dress may not be strictly considered contemporary given the time of its introduction by people like Chief Charles Inko-Tariah, but it is not traditional. It may be labeled simply as a modern response to current industrial life in contrast to the life of the trader during the mercantile era. It particularly reflected the incidence of personal style as a result of pronounced individuation in Kalabari society.

2. The ebu as it is used today by chiefs shows the impact of modern trends. Partly because its cotton material is lighter than that of the woolen doni and is more suited to the tropi-

cal conditions of the delta climate, and also because it is less demanding to wear in terms of required accompanying accessories, virtually any chief wears it on choice today with little adherence to established protocol.

3. The doni, too, is more regularly worn with shoes today as all chiefs are not expected to be expert dancers as they were in the past, and showing off the feet for dancing has not retained its importance. The several long gold chains that were frequently found worn with the doni in pictures of earlier chiefs seem to have, in turn, disappeared. There is a greater orientation toward economy and practical personal considerations, and less involvement with group norms and display.

A new form of dress is appearing on Kalabari users, called *kala doni* (the mini-doni). It is virtually like the doni or sometimes the contemporary etibo, except that it is often made of light woolen material instead of white cotton. It has the characteristic Kalabari decorations for a doni put on it. These are, in particular, the decorated chest in the form of *sangolo* (fish-gill) or *lada* (ladder) frills on both sides of the strip marking the button-holes. Then there is the flap (*bele*) sewn on underneath the strip. This outfit dispenses, however, with requirements like being worn with a shirt underneath it.

Kalabari chiefs are increasingly found wearing this dress as semi-formal out-door gear instead of the woko. A few chiefs, of course, condemn the use of the newfangled kala-doni that has neither place nor fit.

4. The woko is innovatively worn today with trousers that are made of the same material as the top garment. Previously a white or khaki woko or one made with some plain woolen material would be preferably worn with injiri, or else trousers of serge or wool that only color-matched the upper apparel.

The woko is also being worn now by Kalabari young men (rather than being seen as the outfit suitable only for their elders) with a lace inner shirt (similar to the Yoruba men's buba that is topped by an agbada upper garment). This innovation is apparently reflective of fairly comfortable financial standing, and may be a contemporary Nigerian fashion. The neighboring Ikwerre people appear to be the ones introducing this fashion.

Another aspect of this trend toward greater fancifulness among Kalabari young men is the increasing introduction of decorative chest designs on their woko. This was clearly unacceptable earlier to the Kalabari, and was more characteristic of their neighbors like the Okrika.

An even more forbidden practice that middle class Kalabari young men are beginning to adopt is the wearing of woko sewn with blangidi of feni or namasibi. This is the fashion that has been popularized by men in the Bonny, Opobo, and Nembe societies. The Kalabari men adopting this form of dress still use these only in the townships, and wear them because they are more expensive (showing them to be well-off) and are colorful, unlike the generally drab type preferred traditionally by Kalabari etiquette.

5. The contemporary etibo, as shown earlier, is a rather recent innovation starting around the 1950s, which got its latest boost since the 1970s. In addition to its adoption, the younger generation of Kalabari males who are about the age of new secondary-school graduates are avid consumers of this etibo as well as other fashions that are emerging as Nigerian forms.

6. Adoptions have arisen from other Nigerian traditional forms of dress, such as those of the Yoruba or Hausa. One case is the danshiki or short, embroidered or tie-dyed garment that is worn with trousers. Other examples are the loose-fitting buba or bariga gowns derived from Yoruba and Hausa sources respectively worn with tight trousers that hug the legs closely, usually made of the same material as the upper garment. New fashionable versions of such male dress which appear in silk or other modern fabrics, cut to contemporary taste by Nigerian fashion designers, are quite frequently seen being worn by Kalabari young men on the streets of Buguma.

Thus Kalabari young men have rapidly adopted some of the styles and current fashions from their various neighbors. Male members of Kalabari society appear committed to explore new options of identity as represented through dress, no doubt as a continuation of their willingness to combine cultural development with a political focus.

In the setting of contemporary Nigeria, however, it is not only the Kalabari who are responding to change and adopting the forms of dress of their neighbors. Kalabari men's dress is also being widely adopted by new users outside its traditional cultural circles. Many young men from the communities of Ahoada, Abua, Engenni, Ikwerre and several other places of the Rivers State have been seen wearing the etibo to go to work in government offices, or stroll about on the streets of Port Harcourt, the state capital in the 1980s and 1990s. Similarly, the "traditional dress" claimed by the bulk of hinterland Igbos today, of a wọkọ (jompa) made with blangidi, feni, or namasibi design and worn with regular European trousers, comes from the societies of the Niger Delta city-states. Contemporary Igbo chiefs have also shown a penchant for adornment in the doni worn with Benin or Yoruba-derived headgear especially, and beads, when passing off as royalty.

Our research indicates not only Kalabari responsiveness but also their aesthetic creativity as a result of their interaction with members of Western society and exposure to items of dress from Western culture. The Kalabari also interacted extensively with members of other African cultures and were exposed to other African items of dress. Systematic, aesthetic rules of dress developed. These were clearly understood and practiced within Kalabari society, for the dress codes paralleled the social order. However, there has been a recent loosening of attachment to the protocols of Kalabari appearance. As our data suggest, even the chiefs or community leaders have not been conservative custodians of the "good, old ways." However, there is no suggestion that the Kalabari, as purveyors of an African aesthetic in men's dress have diminished interest. Vigorous interest and animated discussion continues among them concerning the "rights" and "wrongs" of dress and the appropriateness of new styles and fashions.

We have added another dimension to the aesthetic knowledge relating to dress as cultural heritage in the diverse continent that is Africa. We caution against oversimplified or glib references to and descriptions about "Africa" through profiles that are too limited and narrow. In addition, with the concept of the Cultural Authentication Process, we have demonstrated that the use of materials and artifacts from other cultures is a dynamic and creative process that indicates strong aesthetic commitments and choices.

Endnotes

[1] Our data were collected during eight field trips by Eicher, three of which overlapped with Erekosima who is Kalabari. He collected data as participant observer over a number of years. In addition, his dissertation research included an eight week, detailed pedestrian survey, 20 formally structured interviews, 10 informal interviews as well as conversation and discussion about men's dress. Eicher's research included taped interviews, informal discussion recorded in written field notes, and slides documenting daily and ceremonial dress for all eight trips.

[2] Elsewhere (Eicher and Erekosima, 1993), in the context of African cultural continuity and change with the Nigerian Kalabari as a case study, we analyzed Kalabari use of textiles and dress to communicate social order in four main dimensions: 1) The order of sociopolitical ranks as assigned to a predominately male gender, 2) The reproductive and socialization order that is predominately female, 3) The ritual order of funerals, and 4) The ceremonial order of masquerades and dance.

[3] A parallel example is given by Ingold, Riches, and Woodburn (1991) who claim that for the Kalahari Bushmen of southern Africa, the two perspectives of utility and art merge in regard to the animals they hunt for food and also depict in their exquisite cave paintings.

[4] For details see Erekosima, 1989

[5] This was during Eicher's first visit to the island of Buguma. She took a photograph of the King and his Council of Chiefs at that time that documents this statement.

References

Adams, Capt. J.. (1823). *Remarks on the country extending from Cape Palmas to the River Congo*. London.

Alagoa, E. J. (1970). Long distance trade and states in the Niger Delta. *Journal of African History*, 2(3), 405-419.

Asante, M. K. (1993). Location theory and African aesthetics, in Welsh-Asante, K, Ed., *The African aesthetic: Keeper of the tradition*. Westport, CN: Greenwood Press.

Blake, J. H. (1942) Ed. *Europeans in West Africa, 1450-1560*. London: Hakluyt Society.

Daly, M. C. (1984). *Kalabari female appearance and the tradition of Iria*. Unpublished doctoral dissertation, University of Minnesota, Minneapolis.

Daly, M. C., Eicher, J. B., and Erekosima, T. V. Male and female artistry in Kalabari dress. *African Arts*, 19(3), 48-51, 83.

Davis, R. (1954). English foreign trade, 1600-1700. *Economic History Review*, 7, 150-166.

Dike, O. (1956). *Trade and politics in the Niger Delta 1830-1885: An introduction to the economics and political history of Nigeria* (1962 ed.). London: Oxford University Press.

Eicher, J. B. and Erekosima, T. V. (1993, April). *Taste and 19th Century patterns of textile use among the Kalabari of Nigeria*. Paper presented at Dartmouth College conference "Cloth, the World Economy, and the Artisan: Textile Manufacturing and Marketing in South Asia and Africa, 1780-1950", Hanover, New Hampshire.

Erekosima, T. V. (1989). *Analysis of a learning resource for political integration applicable to Nigerian secondary school social studies: The case of Kalabari men's traditional dress.* Unpublished doctoral dissertation, Catholic University of America, Washington, D.C.

Erekosima, T. V. and Eicher, J. B. (1981, February). Kalabari cut-thread and pulled-thread cloth: An example of cultural authentication. *African Arts, 14*(2), 8-51, 81.

Evelyn, H. (1968). *History of Costume: Tracing Spanish, Dutch, English and French costumes from peasant to court attire from the 15th century to the 20th century.* Vols. 1 - 3.

Evenson, S. (1991). *The manufacture of madras in South India and its export to West Africa: A case study.* Unpublished Master's thesis, University of Minnesota, Minneapolis.

Evenson, S. (1993, April). *The export of Indian madras plaids: Shifting patterns of exchange.* Paper presented at Dartmouth College Conference "Cloth, the World Economy, and the Artisan: Textile Manufacturing and Marketing in South Asia and Africa, 1780-1950," Hanover, New Hampshire.

Horton, R. (1966, September). Igbo: An ordeal for aristocrats. *Nigeria Magazine, 90,* 168-183.

Ingold, T., Riches, D., and Woodburn, J., (1991). *Hunters and Gatherers,* New York: Berg Publishers.

Jenewari, C. E. (1976). The identification of ethnolinguistic units in early European records: The case of Kalabari. *Journal of Niger Delta Studies, 1,* 9-18.

Jones, G. I. (1963). *The trading states of the Oil Rivers: A study of political development in eastern Nigeria.* London: Oxford University Press.

McNaughton, P. R. (1982, May). The shirts that Mande hunters wear. *African Arts, 15* (3), 54-58, 91.

Michelman, S. O. (1987). *Kalabari female and male aesthetics: A comparative visual analysis.* Unpublished Master's thesis, University of Minnesota, Minneapolis.

Michelman, S. O. and Erekosima, T. V. (1992). Kalabari dress in Nigeria: Visual analysis and gender implications. In R. Barnes and J. B. Eicher (Eds.), *Dress and gender: Making and meaning in cultural context.* Oxford and Providence: Berg Publishers.

Miles, C, (1936). A Nigerian kingdom: Some notes on the Igalla Tribe in Nigeria and their divine king. *Journal of the Royal Anthropological Institute of Great Britain and Ireland, 66,* 393-435.

Ogilvy, J. (1970). *Africa, being an accurate description.* London: Translation of Dapper.

Pereira, D. P. (1937). *Esmeraldo de situo orbis.* London: Hakluyt Society.

Piaget, J. and Inhelder, B. (1969). *The psychology of the child.* New York: Basic Books.

Perani, J. (1992). The cloth connection: Patrons and Producers of Hausa and Nupe Prestige Strip-Weave in *History, Design, and Craft in West African Strip-Woven Cloth: Papers Presented at the Symposium organized by the National Museum of African Art, Smithonian Institution, February 18, 1988.* National Museum of African Art: Washington D.C., 95-112.

Picton, J. (1992). Tradition, Technology, and Lurex: Some Comments on Textile History and Design in West Africa in *History, Design, and Craft in West African Strip-Woven Cloth: Papers Presented at the Symposium organized by the National Museum of African Art, Smithonian Institution, February 18, 1988.* National Museum of African Art: Washington D.C. 13-52.

Ryder, A. F. C. (1965). Dutch trade on the Nigerian coast during the 17th century. *Journal of the Historical Society of Nigeria, 3,* 195-210.

Talbot, P. A. (1932). *Tribes of the Niger Delta: Their religion and customs* (1967 ed.). New York: Barnes and Noble.

Vogt, J. (1975). Notes on the Portuguese cloth trade in West Africa, 1480-1540. *International Journal of African Historical Studies, 8*(4), 623-651.

Wass, B. M. (1975). *Yoruba dress: A systematic case study of five generations of Lagos family.* Unpublished doctoral dissertation, Michigan State University, East Lansing.

Welsh-Asante, K. (Ed.). (1993). *The African aesthetic: Keeper of the tradition.* Westport, CN: Greenwood Press.

Male Appearance Aesthetics: Evidence to Target a Homosexual Market?

Nancy A. Rudd
Ohio State University

Louann S. Tedrick
CompuServe, Inc.

Research into segmentation of the male apparel market has typically dealt with fashion innovators and fashion opinion leaders, with each group important in the marketing sense because they hold influence over other consumers in fashion adoption and purchase decisions. Innovators and fashion opinion leaders differ in certain lifestyle characteristics, yet both groups have been studied as specific market segments to (a) help retailers determine the fashion adoption potential of particular items or general style features, and (b) understand how certain consumers legitimize items or style features for their reference groups. However, research is limited in relation to other segmenting characteristics of age, income, occupation, social status, education, and sexual orientation. In 1980, Stabiner suggested that the male homosexual population is an untapped market segment with great buying power. Reasons for targeting this segment include size, amount of discretionary income, lifestyle characteristics, and extensive use of apparel and grooming aids when socializing. While a few designers, manufacturers, and marketers have indeed targeted the male homosexual market over the past several years (Ash, 1989; Triggs, 1992), the size and psychographics of this market might warrant much greater attention. For these reasons, in addition to changing attitudes regarding advertising targeted to a gay market, the time is ripe to address the question of whether or not there is sufficient aesthetic evidence to encourage fashion marketers to further consider targeting strategies. Aesthetic evidence, in this case, is defined as significant differences in preferences and usage of apparel and grooming products.

To this end, this paper will provide (1) a comparison of male homosexual and heterosexual aesthetic responses to selected apparel style categories and fragrance categories, and (2) a discussion of characteristics and behavior of male homosexuals as appreciators of fashion and appearance products. More specifically, we will examine some socio-cultural factors that may contribute to aesthetic sensitivity and to the valuing of dress, defined herein as "an assemblage of modifications of the body and/or supplements to the body" (Roach-Higgins & Eicher, 1992, p. 1). Furthermore, we will consider targeting implications based on aesthetic responses.

The male homosexual market is slowly coming to be viewed as a viable market segment to be targeted. Recent literature (Johnson, 1993; Levin, 1993; Miller, 1992b; Rodkin, 1990; Schwartz, 1992) attests to a changing openness on the part of some marketers to advertise their products in gay publications, particularly those that are less political and more lifestyle oriented, thereby courting an audience that is often considered to have high disposable incomes (Miller, 1990), to be brand loyal (Rodkin, 1990), and to be conscious of image particularly with respect to fashion and luxury products (Levin, 1993; Miller, 1990). Products advertised to the homosexual market include categories such as liquor, beer, compact discs, travel and vacation plans, tobacco products, greeting cards, fragrances and apparel (Elliott, 1990; Miller, 1990; Miller, 1992a). Among those fashion marketers who have recently entered into such advertising are Banana Republic (Levin, 1993), Benetton[1] (Levin, 1993; Miller, 1992b), Calvin Klein (Levin, 1993; Miller, 1992b), and Perry Ellis (Levin, 1993), all of whom may be considered to be well-known, mainstream apparel marketers. While some advertising analysts believe these marketers will create a domino effect whereby more mainstream marketers will follow suit (Levin, 1993; Johnson, 1993), other analysts believe that there will be few marketers making the cautious foray into such advertising due to their general homophobia as well as a lack of specific demographic data (Miller, 1990).

However, several market research firms have collected data to substantiate particular characteristics of the homosexual population. Based on a readership study of eight gay newspapers in 1988, Simmons Market Research Bureau reported that the average household income of readers was $55,430, compared to a national average of $32,114. Those households earning over $100,000 annually comprised 12% of their readership, compared to 2.5% of the households in the total population reported by the Census Bureau; average household size was 1.96, with 13% of the members below the age of 18 (Miller, 1990). Thus, high income and few dependents suggest a relatively high amount of discretionary income. Overlooked Opinions, a gay market research firm, provides further data (Schwartz, 1992), including demographics, psychographics, and purchase behavior of homosexual consumers in the U.S., citing a higher median level of education (15.7 years versus 12.7 for the general population), and a sizable number (20%) who go to a fitness club 10 or more times monthly. Another characteristic noted by this market research firm is the greater percentage of homosexual travelers who vacation abroad, 60% versus 14% of the general population (Davis, 1993).

Figures concerning the actual size of the male homosexual population are much more difficult to come by, however. Kinsey et al (1948) established the incidence of homosexuality at 10% of the male population and 4-6% of the female population (Kinsey et al, 1954). Current estimates of the incidence of homosexuality vary from 14 million (Johnson, 1993) to 25 million (Miller, 1992b), of which approximately 2/3 would be male. In major cities like New York, San Francisco, Los Angeles, and Washington D.C., the estimates run from 15% to 22% of the population (Stabiner, 1982). Estimates are unlikely to become more specific in the near future, even given the fact that the 1990 census form had a question concerning co-habitating same sex partners; many homosexual individuals are understandably reluctant to answer such a question, fearing reprisal or believing that living arrangements are private matters.

Socio-cultural Factors Contributing To Aesthetic Sensitivity

Stabiner (1982) reported that homosexual men spent more time and money on clothing per year than heterosexual men, and were well aware of creating an image through appearance. Appearance has been important in homosexual socialization (Marmor, 1980), serving both attraction and communication purposes. Homosexual men have been found to place comparably greater importance than heterosexual men on aspects of physical appearance such as body build, grooming, attractiveness, and dress (Kleinberg, 1980; Lakoff & Scherr, 1984). Hatfield & Sprecher (1986) suggest that gay men understand how important physical attractiveness is in attracting potential partners, due in part to the emphasis men place on appearance in sexual encounters (Hagen, 1979; Symons, 1979).

> Unlike other men, gay men may have discovered how important beauty is in attracting men; thus, they become as concerned as women have always been about "measuring up" (Hatfield & Sprecher, 1986, p. 29).

Perhaps as Clark (1977) believes, homosexual men are socially conditioned to be attracted to a narrow range of body types and to focus on physical attractiveness over other personal characteristics. Sergios & Cody (1986) found that physical attractiveness, rather than social assertiveness skills, was the primary indicator of partner liking and future dating intentions among homosexual couples. The researchers comment that limited group settings (bars, discos) and limited time periods for partner selection may be the significant factors explaining the importance of attractiveness. Another reason why attractiveness may be so important is that men have been socialized to be very competitive; a homosexual man may "compete" for a man more attractive than himself (Clark, 1977) and he may feel rejected if he does not measure up to some socialized standard of attractiveness himself (Sergios & Cody, 1986). Indeed, homosexual men have indicated greater discrepancies between their actual body shapes and their ideal body shapes, and greater dissatisfaction for certain body parts, than did heterosexual men (Mishkind, Rodin, Silberstein, & Streigel-Moore, 1986).

References to clothing and appearance signifiers within the male homosexual community are virtually non-existent in the literature, yet popular opinion or myth seems to suggest that dress is very high quality, distinctive, and often trendy. This notion may perhaps stem from an assumed high discretionary income, or perhaps be attributed to a need for disenfranchised or stigmatized people to draw some attention to themselves if they are overlooked by the predominant culture. Fischer (1977) undertook a photographic study of appearance signifiers in one San Francisco neighborhood. In it he described a sign system that signaled sexual orientation and availability through such items as handkerchiefs, keys and earrings; color and placement of these symbols were other variables that suggested meaning. In addition, Fischer photographed and discussed five "archetypal media images" of homosexual men that he believed have been adopted to some degree as fashion and which formed a "style" within the culture. These images include the following: classical - a beautiful model in a dramatic or artistic pose; natural - no particular physical appearance, but posed in outdoor or wilderness environments; Western - a rugged, masculine-looking model wearing cowboy attire; urbane - a stylish, confident-looking model who functions within the mainstream culture; leather - an unconventional, defiant-looking model wearing black leather items, pictured with chains and motorcycles. Fischer believed that the Western, urbane, and leather images exist to a significant extent in real gay culture, but that the classical and natural images apply to a much lesser degree in contemporary dress and appearance.

Homosexuals are seen as a trend-setting subgroup that is influential with other consumers (Elliott, 1990). Fads that begin in the gay community, such as style of dance and designer jeans and earrings, may gain wider acceptance in the general population. Gay and lesbian imagery has become a part of mainstream imagery (Martin, 1993; Wilson, 1993). Use of clothing and grooming aids is more extensive for homosexual men than heterosexual men (Stabiner, 1980). According to Jeff Vitale (cited in Moore, 1992), who is president of the gay-market research firm Overlooked Opinions, "dressing well and buying expensive clothes has been a hallmark of gay men and gay women" (p. 2B). These characteristics may serve to distinguish homosexual subcultures from heterosexual subcultures. One of the core characteristics of any subculture is that it has both a distinctive vocabulary and a manner of expression that may exist together, with differ-

ences in "style, dress, and folkways" from those in the general culture (Humphreys & Miller, 1980, p. 146). This by no means suggests that homosexuals are easily recognized through appearance, speech, or mannerisms, which is a widespread stereotype (Marmor, 1980; Voeller, 1980). However, some research is presently underway which examines clothing and posturing among homosexuals (Wiens & Johnson, 1993). The homosexual community, particularly in large urban settings, may in fact encompass several subcultures, each of which may have distinctive modes of expression.

In a study that explored the appearance sign system within the male homosexual community, Rudd (1992) found that to a small degree there is an appearance code that constitutes meaning among homosexual men. Stimulus models representing six distinct typologies in appearance were derived from several schemes of expression through dress (Fischer, 1977; Kron, 1986; McJimsey, 1973; Von Furstenburg, 1978). These six typologies included 1) Dramatic - bold, contemporary and sophisticated, 2) Natural - casual, relaxed, earthy, 3) Classic - conservative, simple, traditional, 4) Romantic - elegant, luxurious, soft, 5) Gamin - carefree, mischievous, trendy, and 6) Ingenue - faddish, detailed, naive. Subjects rated slides of each unnamed stimulus model on fifteen bi-polar adjectives, and in addition, completed a psychographic measure of sexual and political attitudes, personality attributes, and homosexual identity. The ingenue appearance was perceived as the most liberal, homosexual, sociable, extroverted, impulsive, lively, and artistic of all the appearances. Classic and natural appearances received the most neutral ratings overall, with respondents expressing more interest in social interaction with the classic stimulus model. Even though the sample (N=40) was relatively small, considerable agreement was found among subjects in perceptions of meaning based on appearances. This research does not support any stereotypical public opinion of male homosexual appearance, nor does it support the media images Fischer (1977) found in San Francisco. However, distinct differences may well exist in person perception and attribution of meaning between homosexual and heterosexual men.

In light of findings from these few studies and recent advertising advances into the gay market, a study was warranted which could further examine clothing as a signifier within the male homosexual community. Dress is a communicator of identity in social situations (Roach-Higgins & Eicher, 1992). An individual holds several identities, some of which are ascribed at birth and others which are socially acquired throughout the life cycle. All of one's identities together constitute a unique collection that are incorporated into a person's self-concept. The self, as defined by Roach-Higgins & Eicher (1992, p. 1), is "a composite of an individual's identity communicated by dress, bodily aspects of appearance, and discourse, as well as the material and social objects (other people) that contribute meaning to situations for interaction." These identities may be continually reviewed in social interactions with others, or whenever one presents "the self" to others.

Scholarly efforts since 1985, according to Escoffier (1992), have extended the social construction of identity for homosexuals to include interpretation of texts, cultural codes, signifying practices, and social attitudes toward homosexuality. It is the signifying practices and cultural codes surrounding those practices that are most relevant to a study of male homosexuals as appreciators of appearance products. The purpose of this study was to determine the extent to which differences exist between male homosexuals and heterosexuals in aesthetic responses to selected apparel style categories and to fragrance categories. Since homosexuals may communicate to each other based on dress cues (Voeller, 1980) and since they are likely to appeal to new partners through appearance (Sergios & Cody, 1985/86), the following hypotheses were formulated:

H1) Homosexual male college students will differ from heterosexual male college students in their clothing shopping behavior.

H2) Homosexual male college students will differ from heterosexual male college students in their preferences for trendy and innovative apparel styles.

H3) Homosexual male college students will differ from heterosexual male college students in their preferences for floral/sweet and Oriental/spicy fragrances, and in their cologne usage.

Method

A descriptive-survey research design was employed for the study. Data were collected through a questionnaire developed by the investigators. The independent variable was sexual orientation, while the dependent variables were clothing shopping behavior, clothing style preferences, and cologne preference and usage.

A purposive sample, consisting of male college students attending a large midwestern university, was selected. The age range of 18-28 was targeted because, according to Kinsey (1948), men between the ages of 18 and 28 are usually sexually active and fairly secure with their sexuality. Fifty homosexual and 50 heterosexual respondents were surveyed; usable responses were received from 47 homosexual and 48 heterosexual respondents. The homosexual sample consisted of student patrons of a local gay bar, and the heterosexual sample consisted of members of three campus fraternities. The sampling procedure was approved by the behavioral and social science human subjects review committee at the university. Respondents self-reported their sexual orientation.

A review of literature yielded no suitable instrument that measured the variables under consideration; therefore, a 97-item questionnaire was developed consisting of Likert scale statements, multiple choice questions, true/false questions, and checklists. The clothing shopping behavior section consisted of 31 statements, adapted from an instrument measuring female lifestyle, shopping orientation and store patronage developed by Gutman and Mills (1982). Items were reworded to suit male consumers, and were evaluated for face validity by 6 female graduate students in Textiles and Clothing. Resulting categories in this section of the instrument included shopping enjoyment, time and effort spent shopping, reasons for shopping, store patronage, cologne shopping behavior, and amount of money spent on clothing purchases.

The clothing style preference section contained 22 items. Eight statements dealt with aesthetic styles generally preferred by the respondent (e.g., "I prefer trendy, upscale styles", and "I prefer tight, body conscious styles") which were evaluated on a 5 point scale of agreement. Fourteen statements measured specific aesthetic preferences for innovative/trendy, classic/traditional, or casual/relaxed apparel styles as shown through line drawings in 14 style categories representing 3 aesthetic types each. Respondents circled which style they preferred or circled "don't wear" or "none of the above" as appropriate. Style categories included sweaters, jeans, dress shirts, dress pants, sports coats, casual shirts, casual pants, jackets, underwear, dress shoes, outercoats, socks, ties, and casual shoes. These categories were based on combined works of Kron (1986), McJimsey (1973), and Von Furstenburg (1978). The three aesthetic styles (innovative/trendy; classic/traditional; and casual/relaxed) were not identified by those names to subjects. Instead, each drawing was described very simply using style feature terminology (e.g., "bomber", "pea jacket", and "safari" in the casual jacket category). A 6-member panel of graduate students was given 83 photographs of men's fashion, representing the 14 style categories under investigation, taken from several issues of *GQ* (formerly *Gentleman's Quarterly*). Each person sorted the photographs by the Q-sort method into innovative/trendy styles, classic/traditional styles, and casual/relaxed styles. The most consistently sorted photographs for each of the 3 variations in each of the 14 style categories were identified, resulting in a total of 42 photographs. These photographs were reproduced in line drawings using the same male figure in an effort to keep subjects from responding to color of garment or size and stance of model in the photograph. This methodology is substantiated by Whisney, Winakor, & Wolins (1982) who found no significant difference between the use of photographs and fashion drawings in media for clothing research. Texture was not controlled in the drawings because, in many instances, texture and style were inseparable.

The section of the questionnaire that measured fragrance scent preference, usage, and brand preference consisted of 29 items. Twelve items measured extent of cologne usage which subjects evaluated on a 5 point scale of agreement. One item concerned brand name usage, in which subjects were asked to rank order their top three fragrance preferences by brand name. The last 15 items measured fragrance preferences via a scent test. Subjects responded on a 5 point scale of strongly agree to strongly disagree to the statement "I would like to wear

this cologne" after sniffing a card of scented blotter paper saturated with each of 15 fragrances. Each card was stored in a glassine envelope to keep the scents from blending. Cologne samples were given to subjects in 3 sets of 5 cologne samples each; the 3 sets were evaluated at different points throughout the questionnaire in order to avoid scent fatigue. The 15 colognes represented all of the 5 fragrance "families" identified in the *M. Edwards' Fragrance Manual* (1993) -- floral, spicy, woody, fresh, and fougere -- and the 5 fragrance "concepts" identified for men by the *H&R Fragrance Guide* (1991) -- lavender, oriental, chypre (mossy), citrus, and fougere. Because even these industry fragrance guides differ somewhat in their classification systems, fragrance buyers and sales staff were consulted for clarification. Apparently, fragrance buyers may classify their lines in loose approximation to industry guides depending in part on how accurately *they* can distinguish scents. Thus, floral fragrances for men may be categorized as floral, oriental sweet, fougere floral, or citrus floral. And so forth. Therefore, a men's fragrance buyer from a local major retailer assisted in the selection and categorization of colognes, resulting in 3 categories based on agreement within the industry guides. These were: (a) woody, green; (b) Oriental, spicy; and (c) floral, sweet.

Demographic information was also collected with regard to age, year in college, major, employment status, income, and sexual orientation. The Kinsey continuum of sexual behavior (The Alfred C. Kinsey Institute of Sex Research, 1974) was used, ranging from 0 (exclusively heterosexual) to 6 (exclusively homosexual), so that subjects could self-report their orientation. Because extremes were to be compared in this study, 5 subjects who marked responses other than 0, 1, 5, or 6 were eliminated from the analysis of data.

A pretest of the instrument was administered to 5 homosexual and 5 heterosexual male college students to determine content validity (Snezek, 1986). Innovative/trendy, classic/traditional, and casual/ relaxed aesthetic styles were readily distinguished within each of the 14 style categories. Fragrances were distinguishable too, but the pretest identified that scent fatigue occurred when all scents were evaluated in sequence.

Results

Analysis of data included descriptive statistics, t-tests, chi-square tests, analysis of variance, and Fisher's Exact tests. The average age of homosexuals was 24; for heterosexuals it was 21. The majority of homosexuals were seniors or graduate students; the majority of heterosexuals were sophomores or seniors. Majors were similar for both groups; business administration was the most common, followed by arts and sciences, and engineering/architecture. More homosexuals (81%) worked while attending school than heterosexuals (52%). Average reported monthly income was higher by about four times for homosexuals.

Shopping Behavior

Homosexual respondents were more likely to view shopping as a means of gathering fashion information without necessarily intending to purchase ($t=2.27$; $p=.026$). They also reported spending more time shopping ($t=2.75$, $p=.0072$) and enjoying shopping more ($t=5.29$, $p=.0001$) than heterosexual respondents. Homosexual respondents spent significantly more on apparel expenditures annually than heterosexual respondents (chi square $=23.21$, $df=3$, $p=.0001$). Homosexual subjects shopped in a broader mix of retail establishments than heterosexual subjects, but the difference was not significant as far as overall patronage was concerned. Overall, the hypothesis on differences in shopping behavior was accepted.

Apparel Aesthetics

Responses to eight statements and fourteen style categories were evaluated to assess differences in aesthetic style preferences between self-identified homosexual and heterosexual male college students. Chi square analyses revealed that sexual orientation and preferences for innovative/trendy styles were not independent. Homosexual respondents were more likely to prefer innovative/trendy styles ($M=3.62$) than heterosexual respondents ($M=2.19$), which was a significant difference (chi square$=15.54$, $df=4$, $p=.0004$). Responses were more varied for heterosexual respondents than for homosexual respondents on questions regarding classic styles, casual styles, loose versus tight fitting styles, wearing clothing to stand out in a crowd, wearing different styles of clothing for work/school and social situations, and styles of clothing that make them feel most attractive. While descriptive statistics

Table 1. Clothing Style Preferences of Homosexual and Heterosexual Men

Style	Group	Trendy N	Trendy %	Traditional N	Traditional %	Casual N	Casual %
Sweaters	Ho (N=47)	18	38.3	11	23.4	13	27.7**
	He (N=48)	11	22.9	21	44.7	13	27.1
Jeans	Ho	6	12.7	28	59.6	8	17.0
	He	8	16.6	32	66.6	5	10.4
Dress Shirts	Ho	18	8.3	6	12.7	19	40.4
	He	5	10.4	12	25.0	30	62.5
Dress Pants	Ho	25	53.2	8	17.0	13	27.7
	He	11	22.9	18	37.5	12	25.0
Sport Coats	Ho	16	4.0	14	29.8	13	27.7
	He	8	16.6	21	43.8	16	33.3
Casual Shirts	Ho	17	36.2	21	44.7	4	8.5
	He	6	12.5	31	64.6	5	10.4
Outer Jackets	Ho	32	68.1	7	14.8	2	4.2
	He	15	31.3	18	37.5	5	10.4
Casual Pants	Ho	6	12.7	20	42.5	13	27.7
	He	0	0	24	50.0	16	33.3
Undergarments	Ho	14	29.8	28	59.6	3	6.3
	He	7	14.5	21	43.8	11	22.9
Dress Shoes	Ho	14	29.8	8	17.0	21	44.7
	He	15	31.3	6	12.5	24	50.0
Coats	Ho	8	17.0	29	61.7	5	10.6
	He	6	12.5	35	72.9	4	8.3
Socks	Ho (N=47)	14	29.8	12	25.5	19	40.4**
	He	1	2.1	21	43.8	19	39.6
Neckties	Ho	24	51.1	9	19.1	11	23.4
	He	9	18.8	19	39.6	13	27.1
Casual Shoes	Ho	10	21.3	17	36.2**	18	38.3
	He	1	2.1	17	35.4	26	54.2

* Does not include "don't wear" and "none of the above" responses.
**Differing percentages are due to differences in Ns in two samples.

reflected this variation, chi square values indicated that sexual orientation was independent of preferences.

With respect to the illustrations of three aesthetic styles in each of 14 garment style categories (innovative/trendy; classic/traditional; or casual/relaxed), there was no clear-cut preference for any one aesthetic style by either homosexual or heterosexual respondents (Table 1). Both groups preferred the classic/traditional aesthetic variations of the style categories that typically constitute a basic campus wardrobe (jeans, casual pants, casual shirts, underwear, and coats), with insignificant chi square values found in jeans and coats. However, three of these style categories (casual pants, casual shirts, underwear) had significant chi square values due to disagreements in the trendy aesthetic variation which homosexual respondents tended to prefer more than heterosexual respondents. Fisher's Exact tests of probability were computed as a confirmation of chi square probability if any cells had expected counts less than 5. Thus, homosexual respondents differed in their preferences for trendy aesthetic variations in casual pants (*chi square*=6.66, df=2, *p*=.036, Fisher's Exact *p*=.036), casual shirts (*chi square*=7.295, df=2, *p*=.026, Fisher's Exact *p*=.027), and underwear (*chi square*=7.52, df=2, *p*=.023, Fisher's Exact *p*=.024).

However, sexual orientation and style preferences were not independent in style categories in which personal preference is more easily displayed (dress pants, dress shirts, outerwear jackets, neckties, socks, and casual shoes). In these six categories, the biggest disagreements were found in the innovative/trendy aesthetic variations (preferred by homosexual respondents) and casual aesthetic variations (preferred by heterosexual respondents). Significant differences by sexual orientation were evidenced in

- dress pants (*chi square*=9.07, df=2, *p*=.011, Fisher's Exact *p*=.011),
- dress shirts (*chi square*=11.66, df=2, *p*=.003, Fishers Exact *p*=.003),
- jackets (*chi square*= 12.18, df=2, *p*=.002, Fisher's Exact *p*=.001),
- neckties (*chi square*=10.46, df=2, *p*=.005, Fisher's Exact *p*=.0046),
- socks (*chi square*=13.57, df=2, *p*=.001, Fisher's Exact *p*=.0007),
- casual shoes (*chi square*=8.81, df=2, *p*=.012, Fisher's Exact *p*=.011).

Preferences in the style categories of dress shoes, sport coats, and sweaters were found across all three aesthetic variations for both homosexual and heterosexual respondents, with no significant chi square values.

Hypothesis two, which stated that homosexual males would differ from heterosexual males in their preferences for innovative/trendy aesthetic styles, was therefore accepted due to the fact that different aesthetic preferences were found in 9 out of 14 style categories.

Fragrance Aesthetics

Responses to statements regarding fragrance usage, a list of brand name fragrances worn, and 15 scented cards, were evaluated to assess differences in fragrance aesthetics between homosexual and heterosexual male college students. Of the statements related to fragrance usage, significant differences were found between homosexual and heterosexual respondents on daily fragrance use (*chi square*=8.97, df=4, *p*.05) and occasional use (*chi square*=17.51, df=4, *p*.05). Homosexual respondents used cologne daily, while heterosexual respondents used it occasionally. Significant differences were also found in response to the categories of fragrance in which respondents felt most attractive and sexually appealing (*chi square*=11.56, df=2, *p*.05), Fisher's exact *p*.01); homosexual men felt most attractive and appealing when wearing floral/sweet and Oriental/spicy fragrances, while heterosexual men felt so while wearing woody/green fragrances. Number of colognes worn by all men ranged from 1 to 21 per person. Homosexual respondents wore an average of 5 fragrances each (*M*=4.98), while heterosexual respondents wore an average of 4 (*M*=3.98), a difference that was not statistically significant.

Scent preference tests of 15 cologne samples yielded significant differences in response between homosexual and heterosexual respondents. Using straight frequencies for responses of strongly agree and agree, the most preferred fragrances were determined for each group of subjects. While we intended to report the top 5 fragrances preferred, ties resulted in a total of 8 fragrances for homosexual respondents and 7 fragrances for heterosexual respondents. Of the 8 fragrances preferred by homosexual men, 5 were in the floral/sweet category (Drakkar Noir, Perry Ellis, Giorgio for Men, Aramis 900, and Grey Flannel), 2 were in the Oriental/spicy category (Royal Copenhagen Musk, and JHL), and 1 was in the woody/green category (Oscar). Of the 7 fragrances preferred by heterosexual men, 5 were woody/green (Halston, Polo, Paul Sebastian, Devin, and Jacomo), 2 were floral/sweet (Drakkar Noir, Giorgio for Men), and none was Oriental/spicy. Distinct preferences emerged, in that homosexual subjects overwhelmingly preferred the floral/sweet and Oriental/spicy categories, while heterosexual subjects preferred the woody/green fragrances (*chi square*=114.65, df=2, *p*.05).

Based on the results of the statements regarding fragrance usage and results of the scent tests, the third hypothesis was accepted; that is, homosexual and heterosexual men differed in fragrance preference and usage.

Discussion

Results from this study indicate that there is at least some evidence of a preferred appearance aesthetic for homosexual men, although perhaps not as obvious as may be commonly thought. The homosexual men in this study enjoyed shopping more, spent more time shopping, had different reasons for shopping, and patronized a different mix of retail establishments (including vintage/antique clothing stores and trendy boutiques) than heterosexual men. Homosexual men also reported spending more money on apparel than heterosexual men. As far as a significant aesthetic preference in apparel, there was no *one* aesthetic variation (innovative/trendy, classic/traditional, casual/relaxed) that was consistently preferred by one sexual orientation or the other across all apparel style categories. Yet, homosexual men did prefer innovative/trendy styles more than heterosexual men, who almost never preferred trendy styles. There were clear differences within categories. Few differences were found in responses from homosexual and heterosexual men for styles of jeans, casual pants, casual shirts, underwear, and coats; for these items, classic/traditional styles were overwhelmingly preferred by both groups. These are perhaps items that constitute a basic campus wardrobe or "uniform"; because everyone wears them, they do not offer room for creative appearance management or identity formation. The classic/traditional items selected were Levi's 501 jeans, a striped oxford shirt, chino trousers, white briefs, and a classic wool coat. Given that these items may be viewed by many men as more utilitarian than expressive, perhaps the innovative/trendy and casual/relaxed aesthetic variations were not considered appropriate or worth investing in for this social setting. Yet, there were some significant chi square values for casual pants, casual shirts, and underwear due to some preferences expressed by homosexual men for innovative/trendy styles.

For garment categories that would not constitute a basic campus "uniform", there were clear differences in aesthetic preferences between homosexual and heterosexual men. Innovative/trendy aesthetic variations in dress pants, dress shirts, outerwear jackets, neckties, socks, and casual shoes were preferred by homosexual subjects nearly twice as often or more

than by heterosexual subjects. Heterosexual subjects preferred the classic/traditional and casual/relaxed aesthetic variations in each of these style categories. These are all items which might allow a person to experiment with appearances in perhaps different social settings. In categories of sport coats, sweaters, and dress shoes, preferences were found across all three aesthetic variations regardless of sexual orientation.

Homosexual men seemed to hold a distinctly different fragrance aesthetic than heterosexual men. They wore cologne more frequently, felt more attractive and appealing when wearing floral/sweet or Oriental/spicy colognes, and preferred different categories of cologne (floral/sweet and Oriental/spicy) than heterosexual men. In fact, in scent tests, most colognes preferred by homosexual respondents were not preferred by heterosexual respondents, with exceptions being the fragrances Drakkar Noir and Giorgio for Men.

Thus, the findings of this study substantiate opinions presented in the literature, that homosexual men may tend toward a more image-sensitive, fashionable, distinctive presentation of themselves to others (Marmor, 1980; Stabiner, 1986; Levin, 1993; Johnson, 1993). There is little in the way of consumer behavior or aesthetic research to date which lends credence to *how* such images are operationalized, if they are. Clear preferences for one apparel aesthetic throughout several categories of dress implies that some homosexual men do in fact prefer more novel, trendy ways in which to present themselves than do heterosexual men. Clear differences in a fragrance aesthetic for homosexual and heterosexual men, both in cologne usage and preference, also indicates differences in manner of self-presentation. It is also possible that, due to social stigma experienced by many homosexual men, two different appearance styles may be required -- one to present themselves in a fairly ambiguous, blending-in way on a large college campus where sexual orientation has little to do with the learning environment, and a second to present themselves in a clear, unambiguous way in social settings such as clubs or bars in which one's sexual orientation may be signaled. The results lend support to this difference, since all men preferred the campus "uniform". Homosexual men, however, stated a preference for trendy styles of apparel which would likely be worn in social settings, while heterosexual men were more apt to prefer traditional or casual styles for these apparel categories.

It is a critical time to examine representations that are socially constructed through appearance that may encourage binary thinking about good and bad (hooks, 1992).

> Frequently, personal style constitutes one of the few avenues of identity expression available to disenfranchised groups and subcultures. Thus, style and fashioning of self become mechanisms for re-enfranchisement and collective participation. Historically, clothing and apparel styles have provided means for self-actualization and theatricalization among individuals who otherwise have little visibility in the cultural landscape. (Kaiser, 1993, p.7)

Self-presentation through clothing and fragrance may allow men with a homosexual orientation to proclaim both personal and social identity, and thus achieve a strong sense of identity within a larger culture that often stigmatizes and disenfranchises them. It appears that aesthetic codes can be somewhat empowering.

Aesthetic codes in personal appearance may express collective participation in re-enfranchisement. The existence of several "looks" that fit within the aesthetic code offer not only the opportunity for individual expression (making of the self), but also for the construction and reinforcement of group identity. Within the individual context, appearance may provide assistance in individual strategies for stigma management, a concept discussed by Troiden (1989) as a means to achieve identity synthesis. While he does not specifically consider the implications of appearance to the strategies discussed, we believe the results from the present study provide a logical connection to strategies employed by homosexual individuals as they formulate their sexual identity.

Conclusions and Implications

From the findings of this study, it would appear that images can be both liberating and entrapping. The difference would seem to exist in how images are used both by the presenters and the perceivers. Much remains to be studied about the social construction of appearance

among homosexuals, both from a semiotics perspective and from the socio-cultural perspective of formation and reinforcement of identity. According to Hamilton & Hamilton (1989):

> Dress, as a pan-human expression of culture and, therefore, of being human, is often much more profound than is generally supposed. It can be an extremely powerful, symbolic, ritualized way of expressing and reinforcing subtle values, relationships, and meanings in human cultures. It may be that the social, ritual, and symbolic significance of human deserves rethinking in the context of cultural systems. (p. 22)

The topic of the social construction of appearance among homosexuals is a scholarly endeavor that is fraught with political overtones and precious little in the literature, but if one ignores these barriers, it seems there is a contribution to be made to the understanding of all consumer cultures. Issues of self-feelings and self-perceptions, social participation and empowerment, can be examined through the medium of constructed appearances. Aesthetic codes may operate in a meaningful way in the social construction of appearances, yet one must be careful not to over-generalize or make light of many nuances in such codes.

Marketing implications from this study do exist, yet the authors would be the first to caution against viewing such a market segment from a profit perspective only. A broader, psychographic approach that contributes to quality of life seems more desirable. Because the homosexual respondents as compared to heterosexual respondents in the study indicated greater enjoyment and time spent in shopping, and shopped in some stores that required time and effort to find (i.e., vintage/antique clothing stores and trendy boutiques), it is likely that they were more interested in shopping overall. Davis (1987) found that subjects who scored high on fashion opinion leadership were more interested in shopping than subjects who scored low on these characteristics. Thus, it is possible that homosexual men may be more likely to be fashion opinion leaders and fashion innovators than heterosexual men based upon the findings of the present study. Baumgarten (1975) found that innovative communicators, the term coined to describe consumers who are both fashion innovators and fashion opinion leaders, have been found to spend more on clothing and own more styles of apparel and more cosmetics. Homosexual respondents in the present study reported spending more money on clothing purchases annually and owned more colognes than heterosexual respondents; therefore, if homosexual men are more likely to be fashion innovators and fashion opinion leaders, they may well serve this function for both the homosexual population and the heterosexual population. Even though such a link has been suggested or even assumed (Elliott, 1990; Martin, 1993), substantiation of a widespread influence is necessary. We suggest comparing fashion innovation and fashion opinion leadership characteristics, venturesomeness (Robertson & Kennedy, 1968), or sensation seeking (Zuckerman, 1979) of homosexual and heterosexual men. In addition, tracking an array of specific apparel and grooming products and practices within homosexual and heterosexual populations could substantiate the extent to which homosexual fashion change agents may be influential in fashion adoption and diffusion in both homosexual and heterosexual populations.

Johnson (1993) cautions that targeting the male homosexual population as one narrow segment rather than as a broad, diverse segment would not be prudent, any more than targeting all heterosexual men as one market segment. We concur. It makes sense that marketers may be most attracted to the subset of the gay market that is more fashion innovative, urban, and has above-average disposable income. However, the diversity within this population could be appealed to through specific marketing strategies. If homosexual men spend more time shopping and enjoy it more than heterosexual men, as our findings suggest, then directly involving the consumer through such strategies as self-improvement seminars (that focus on wardrobe planning, grooming, and use of grooming products) may result in even more time and money spent in the store. Another marketing strategy might be to mix product style categories together in departments according to like aesthetic variation (trendy, classic, or casual) instead of separating products by style categories (shirts, pants, ties, etc.). Grouping innovative/trendy styles of dress shirts, dress pants, suits, sportcoats, ties, and socks together in one department might be more appealing to the consumer because he

doesn't have to spend time going from department to department just to find similar aesthetic expression.

Because homosexual men reported stronger preferences for and usage of cologne, a novel idea might be the product positioning of fragrance and apparel together in various departments. Cologne could be displayed as an actual accessory of apparel, with samples representing specific cologne categories shown next to specific apparel styles. For example, a trendy, high quality suit could be displayed with an innovative silk tie and one or more Oriental/spicy colognes. Closeby, a traditional navy blazer and classic repeat pattern tie could be positioned along with a woody/green fragrance. The ultimate marketing strategy might be that sales staff would advise the consumer in the purchase of multiple colognes to coordinate with his various tie, suit, or sweater purchases. These kinds of images are presently promoted through clever print advertising of men's fragrances, so the next step would be to follow through on some of these images in store displays and selling strategies.

Print images presented in the media are strongly influenced by the photographer's vision or "eye". For example, Bruce Weber has become an arbiter of standards of appeal to men in presenting fragrance and apparel products (Triggs, 1992). He has established some new ground by giving permission for images of men to appear sensual, attractive, and even ethereal. His photographs for Calvin Klein and Benetton, among others, may have done much to position their products within the gay community. Investigation of the creation, nature, and appeal of such advertising images in publications targeted to homosexual and heterosexual audiences would provide valuable insight into marketing strategies.

Further research into different appearance aesthetics for male homosexual and heterosexual consumers should focus on the characteristics of color, texture, and specific style features, each of which may play a role in determining various consumer aesthetics. It may well be that a perceptual interaction of such characteristics, in addition to fragrance, could further define consumers with differing appearance aesthetics, much in the way that Fiore (1993) found that a multisensory organization of appearance cues functions in impression formation. Her study suggests that visual, tactile, and olfactory cues work together in a complex relationship to produce meaning when observing appearance. Thus, it would seem worthwhile to investigate to what extent this relationship operates when expressive variables of aesthetic style and fragrance are presented in personal appearance. Given the variety of aesthetic cues present in style categories of innovative/trendy, classic/traditional, and casual/relaxed and the variety of qualities present in floral/sweet, oriental/spicy, and woody/green fragrances, many associations are possible.

Findings of the present study are not sufficient to establish a distinct male homosexual appearance aesthetic, yet they do suggest that clear preferences exist regarding apparel style categories and fragrance categories. These findings, therefore, provide support for viewing the homosexual market as a unique, diverse, and viable market segment often with different shopping behaviors, preferences, and motivations than the heterosexual market segment. The aesthetic response to apparel and appearance products may well underscore the importance of appearance in socialization (Marmor, 1980) and the construction of identity (Troiden, 1989). By more completely understanding aesthetic response to apparel and appearance products, as well as examining how such products are used in the social construction of identity, we may arrive at a richer understanding of the social and symbolic meaning of dress within the male homosexual culture.

Endnotes

1. These marketers/manufacturers have broadened their advertising scope from mainstream upper-class, white youth to include appeals to audiences that are diverse in age, ethnicity, and sexual orientation.
2 No comparable statistics were found for patronage among the general population.
3 It is true that Levis has some very expresive advertising campaigns for their products, yet the products themselves may be viewed as utilitarian ("jeans go with everything").

References

Ash, J. (1989). Tarting up menswear: Menswear and gender dynamics. In J. Attfield & P. Kirkham (Eds.), *A view from the interior: Feminism, women and design* (pp. 29-38). London: The Women's Press.

Baumgarten, S. (1975). The innovative communicator in the diffusion process. *Journal of Marketing Research, 7,* 12-18.

Cass, V. C. (1983/84). Homosexual identity: A concept in need of definition. *Journal of Homosexuality, 9,* 105-126.

Cass, V. C. (1984). Homosexual identity formation: Testing a theoretical model. *The Journal of Sex Research, 20,* 143-167.

Clark, D. (1977). *Loving someone gay.* Milbrae, CA: Celestial Arts.

Davis, L. (1987). Fashion innovativeness, fashion opinion leadership and purchasing involvement. In Ruth Marshall (Ed.), *ACPTC combined proceedings* (p. 128). Monument, CO: Association of College Professors of Textiles and Clothing.

Davis, R. (1993, January 18). Sky's the limit for tour operators. *Advertising Age, 34,* p. 36-37.

Edwards, M. (1993). *The Michael Edwards fragrance manual.* New York: Beauty Fashion, Inc.

Elliott, S. (1990, July 17). Advertisers bypass gay market. *USA Today,* Sec.B, p. 1-2.

Escoffier, J. (1992). Generations and paradigms: Mainstreams in gay and lesbian studies. *Journal of Homosexuality, 24* (1-2), 7-26.

Fiore, A.M. (1993). Multisensory integration of visual, tactile, and olfactory aesthetic cues of appearance. *Clothing and Textiles Research Journal, 11* (2), 45-52.

Fischer, H. (1977). Gay semiotics: A photographic study of visual coding among homosexual men. San Francisco: NFS Press.

Gutman, J. & Mills, M. K. (1982). Fashion life-style, self-concept, shopping orientation, and store patronage: An integrative analysis. *Journal of Retailing, 58,* 64-68.

H & R fragrance guide to feminine and masculine notes: Fragrances on the international market, 2nd ed. (1991). Hamburg, Germany: Gloss Verlag.

Hagan, R. (1979). *The bio-sexual factor.* New York: Doubleday.

Hamilton, J. A. & Hamilton, J. W. (1989). Dress as a reflection and sustainer of social reality: A cross-cultural perspective. *Clothing and Textiles Research Journal, 7* (2),16-22.

Hatfield, E. & Sprecher, S. (1986). *Mirror, Mirror . . . The importance of looks in everyday life.* Albany, NY: State University of New York Press.

hooks, b. (1992). *Black looks: Race and representation.* Boston: South End Press.

Humphreys, L. (1972). *Out of the closets: The sociology of homosexual liberation.* Englewood Cliffs, NJ: Prentice-Hall.

Humphreys, L. & Miller, B. (1980). Identities in the emerging gay culture. In Judd Marmor (Ed.), *Homosexual Behavior: A modern reappraisal.* (pp. 142-156). New York: Basic Books, Inc.

Johnson, B. (1993, January 18). The gay quandary: Advertising's most elusive, yet lucrative, target market proved difficult to measure. *Advertising Age, 64,* 29, 35.

Kaiser, S. (1993). The circulation of style and fashion: Center/margin relationships. *Style, Fashion and the Negotiation of Identities*, Unpublished Conference Program, U. of California, Davis, CA.

Kinsey, A., Pomeroy, W. & Martin, C. (1948). *Sexual behavior in the human male.* Philadelphia: W.B. Saunders.

Kinsey, A., Pomeroy, W., Martin, C., & Gebhard, P. (1953). *Sexual behavior in the human female.* Philadelphia: W.B. Saunders.

Kleinberg, S. (1980). *Alienated affections: Being gay in America.* New York: St. Martin's Press.

Kron, J. (1986, March 11). A few daring dressers risk sneers to push menswear into the future. *The Wall Street Journal*, p. 31.

Lakoff, R. & Scherr, R. (1984). *Face value, the politics of beauty.* Boston: Routledge & Kegan Press.

Levin, G. (1993, January 18). Mainstream's domino effect: Liquor, fragrance, clothing advertising ease into gay magazines. *Advertising Age, 64*, 30 & 32.

Marmor, J. (1980). Clinical aspects of male homosexuality. In Judd Marmor (Ed.), *Homosexual Behavior: A modern reappraisal.* (pp. 267-279). New York: Basic Books, Inc.

Martin, R. (1993, Spring). The gay factor in fashion. *Esquire Gentleman*, pp. 135-140.

McJimsey, H. (1993). *Art and fashion in clothing selection.* Ames, IA: Iowa State University Press.

Miller, C. (1990, December 24). Gays are affluent but often overlooked market. *Marketing News, 24*, 2.

Miller, C. (1992a, July 10). Two new firms market exclusively to gays. *Marketing News, 26*, 8.

Miller, C. (1992b, July 10). Mainstream marketers decide time is right to target gays. *Marketing News, 26*, 8, 15.

Mishkind, M., Rodin, J., Silberstein, L. & Striegel-Moore, R. (1986). The embodiment of masculinity. *American Behavioral Scientist, 29*, 545-562.

Moore, M. (1992, August 18). Retailer targets gay market: "Out" next to Banana Republic. *USA Today*, B2.

Roach-Higgins, M. E. & Eicher, J. B. (1992). Dress and identity. *Clothing and Textiles Research Journal, 10*, (4), 1-8.

Robertson, T. & Kennedy, J. (1968). Prediction of consumer innovators: Application of multiple discriminant analysis. *Journal of Marketing Research, 5*, 64-69.

Rodkin, D. (1990, July 9). Untapped niche offers markets brand loyalty: gay consumers favor

companies that don't exclude them. *Advertising Age, 61*, S2.

Rudd, N.A. (1992) . Clothing as signifier in the perceptions of college male homosexuals. *Semiotica, 91*(1/2), 67-78.

Schwartz, P. (1992). Gay consumers come out spending. *American Demographics, 14*, 10-11.

Sergios, P. & Cody, J. (1985/86). Importance of physical attractiveness and social assertiveness skills in male homosexual dating behavior and partner selection. *Journal of Homosexuality, 12* (2), 71-84.

Snezek, L. (1986). Clothing preferences and shopping behavior of male homosexual and heterosexual college students. Unpublished master's thesis, The Ohio State University, Columbus.

Stabiner, K. (1982, March). Tapping the homosexual market. *New York Times Magazine*, pp. 34-41.

Symons, D. (1979). *The evolution of human sexuality.* New York: Oxford Press.

The Alfred C. Kinsey Institute for Sex Research (1974). *Sex behavior.* Philadelphia: Author.

Triggs, T. (1992). Framing masculinity: Herb Ritts, Bruce Weber & the body perfect. In J. Ash & E. Wilson (Eds.), *Chic thrills: A fashion reader* (pp. 25-29). Berkley: University of California Press.

Troiden, R. (1989). The formation of homosexual identities. *Journal of Homosexuality, 17*(1/2), 43-73.

Voeller, B. (1980). Society and the gay movement. In Judd Marmor (Ed.), *Homosexual behavior: A modern reappraisal.* (pp. 232-252). New York: Basic Books, Inc.

Von Furstenburg, E. (1978). *The power look.* New York: Holt, Rinehart, and Winston.

Whisney, A., Winakor, G., & Wolins, L. (1979). Fashion drawings versus photographs. *Home Economics Research Journal, 8*, 138-150.

Wiens, P. & Johnson, K. (1993, November). *Exploring stereotypes of sexual orientation: Clothing vs. posture. Paper presented at the International Textiles and Apparel Association conference, White Sulphur Springs, WVa.*

Wilson, E. (1993). Interface: The boundary between body and dress. Style, Fashion and the Negotiation of Identities, Unpublished Conference Program, U. of California, Davis, CA.

Zuckerman, M. (1979). *Sensation seeking: Beyond the optimal level of arousal.* Hillsdale, NJ: Lawrence Erlbaum.

211

African-American Aesthetic of Dress:
Symmetry Through Diversity

Symmetry Through Diversity

Child (1968) defines aesthetics as the study of human behavior and experiences in creating, perceiving, understanding, and being influenced by art. Fiore, Moreno, and Kimle (in press) have defined aesthetics, for the purpose of this publication, as the study of human response to products, specifically internal processes, the product's multi-sensory characteristics, and the psychological and social-cultural factors of the individual that affect response to the non-instrumental quality of the product. Beardsley (1958) refers to non-instrumental quality as intrinsic value or beauty. Various scholars (Kaiser, 1990; Hume, 1965; McCracken, 1988; Sahlins, 1976; Storm, 1987) suggest that aesthetic evaluations are influenced by the collective taste of the group. Aesthetic values (such as beauty) are established within a cultural context (Hume, 1965; McCracken, 1988; Sahlins, 1972; Storm, 1987). While cultural forms are somewhat mobile, the undergirding structure and principles are relatively stable and are passed down from generation to generation (Johnson, 1986-1987; MacCannell & MacCannell, 1982; McCracken, 1988). In this paper dress is defined broadly as the composite of artifacts that modify, enclose, attach to, or are held by or for the body (Roach & Musa, 1979). Therefore, a discussion of an African-American aesthetic of dress will consider broadly notions of not only the product (i.e. clothing objects) but the composite of artifacts and the non-instrumental quality of intrinsic value (i.e. beauty) which encompass the totality or dress and appearance.

The main thesis of the paper is that there is an African-American aesthetic of dress that has its roots in African culture. This aesthetic of dress is shaped by the particularities of the unique "cultural" experiences of being of African decent and surviving as a disenfranchised people in a Eurocentric culture for centuries. Since expressive behavior and cultural modalities are determined by philosophical definition (Noble, 1980), I will seek to show that this aesthetic of dress has its foundation in several cultural and philosophical premises shared by peoples of West Africa and the Congo. This will be done by first, establishing the rationale for an Afrocentric perspective of African-American aesthetic of dress; second, discussing the common African ethos or philosophical linkage between Africans and African-Americans which has survived through slavery and into the twentieth century; third, exploring the survival of this ethos through its manifestation in African-American quilts; fourth, illustrating an African-American aesthetic of dress through correspondence between aesthetic principles used in quiltmaking and African-American dress; and finally, giving implications for the inclusion of African-American aesthetic of dress in a multi-cultural curriculum, and in the research agenda of textiles and clothing professionals.

The terms African-American and Afro-American are used synonymously to designate American descendants of Africans.

Part I: The Afrocentric Rationale

Eicher and her colleagues (Eicher, 1970; Pokornowski, Eicher, Harris, & Thieme, 1985; Thieme & Eicher, 1990) have compiled more than 2,300 annotated citations containing information pertinent to the study of African dress. Thieme and Eicher (1990) state that their study of African dress and adornment is built on a "sociocultural framework that integrates the individual as a physical being with his or her position within a specific social organization as influenced by cultural pattern"(p.5). African-Americans are mentioned in their work only in passing as having recently adopted African styles of dress in connection with the rediscovery of their heritage (Eicher, 1970; Pokornowski, Eicher, Harris, & Thieme, 1985; Thieme & Eicher, 1990). In other words, there is no connectedness of African-American dress to their study of African dress.[1] As a point of comparison, European Americans can trace their aesthetic preference in dress to its European roots.

In developing a conceptual framework for the history of dress of African-American women, Ware (1990) concluded with out giving convincing evidence, that "African women's dress behavior patterns provide insight regarding some of the extended patterns of dress worn by African-Americans during the slavery era" (p.46). The implications of her writings are that 1) African culture influenced slave dress, 2) the influence ended with slave dress (since no connection to modern dress is noted), and 3) there were similarities in dress among West African "clans." Ware (1990), by implication, considered aesthetic elements of African dress as temporal, or as having not survived at all. As such, African-Americans are, as Asante (1987) suggested, essentially left with a discontinuous history.

Aesthetic judgments and values (e.g., beauty) in America are centered in European philosophy, values, and ideals. Gayle (1971) pointed out that the European-American aesthetic "has always been with us: for long before Diotima pointed out the way to heavenly beauty to Socrates, the poets... were discussing beauty in terms of light and dark--the essential characteristics of a white and black aesthetic-- and establishing the dichotomy of superior vs. inferior which would assume body and form in the 18th century" (p. 40). In defining an aesthetic object, Beardsley (1958) stated that critics presuppose "that there is something that can be discriminated out from the process of creation and contemplation, something that can be experienced, studied, enjoyed, and judged" (p. 17). This notion of the aesthetic object allows for the composite of the individual's appearance to be viewed from an aesthetic perspective, primarily in terms of aesthetic value (i.e., beauty). From a Eurocentric perspective, white is beautiful, pure, good; black is ugly, bad, evil, and so forth. (Cone, 1990; Collins, 1991; Gayle, 1971; hooks, 1992; Sahlins, 1972). Such standards of beauty can only be attained by corresponding to European philosophy, values, and ideals. Consequently, by virtue of being of African descent, Eurocentric standards of beauty can never be attained by African-Americans.[2] The Eurocentric perspective suggest that African Americans must always be the other (Collins, 1991). Thus, African-Americans are socialized to perceive beauty in ways that may conflict with basic natural inclinations (Collins, 1991; hooks, 1992; Wallace, 1990). Therefore,

the combination of Eurocentric aesthetic values and a discontinuous history result in the lack of validation of aesthetic creations, judgements and experiences, and self-definition of beauty for African Americans.

Any analysis of aesthetics of dress that involves or reflects the basic nature of descendants of African people dispersed to the New World, must have an African-centered point of reference (Asante, 1980; Baldwin, 1986; Felder, 1993; Keto, 1991). Since aesthetic values are always bound to context, culture, and time, a discussion of an African-American aesthetic of dress must be placed within a cultural context. For our purpose, the cultural context is Africa centered or Afrocentric. Afrocentricity centers on African ideals. To discuss an African-American aesthetic from an Afrocentric perspective applies the African cultural history in the American context (Gayles, 1971). It suggests that elements of African aesthetic of dress survived on the American continent as African and not as Negro, Colored, or Black (Nobles, 1980).

The African-centered perspective encourages human "science" practitioners to critique the way they approach the study of descendants of Africa specifying the regional "center" on the globe which provides the basis on which they anchor human meaning and interpretation (Keto, 1991). An African-centered perspective begins with Africa as the historical core for analyzing and assessing aesthetics of dress of African-Americans. It seeks to bring to the interpretation an understanding of the events of human history in which basic values can be traced in whole or in part to African roots.

Part II: The Common Ethos

African-Americans derive their most fundamental self-definition from several cultural and philosophical premises shared with "tribes" from West Africa and the Congo (Herskovits, 1970; Keto, 1991; Nobles, 1980; Semmes, 1992; Sobel, 1979). Most Africans brought to America as slaves were from a relative small part of Africa, primarily the coastal belt of West Africa and the Congo (Asante & Asante, 1990; Curtin, 1969; Herskovits, 1970; Holloway, 1990; Nobels 1980; Keto, 1991; Sobel, 1979). Historians and anthropologists of old have suggested that the West and Central African regions have numerous "tribes," each having their own language, religion, and culture, thus placing emphasis on cultural differences. Asante and Asante (1990),

Ferris (1983), Herskovits (1970), Kochman (1981), Nobles (1980), Keto (1991), Mbiti (1970), Sobel (1979), Thompson (1983a) and others contend that there are underlying similarities in the "experiential community" of African peoples. These scholars maintain that "tribal" differences in Africa were superseded by a set of guiding beliefs akin to a spiritual disposition described by some as a "collective consciousness."[3] This collective consciousness or ethos, according to Nobles, is manifested in two ways-- the notion that people were part of the natural rhythm of nature; they were one with nature, and the notion of the survival of one's people. Baldwin (1986) expressed agreement with Nobles (1980) and others (Asante & Asante, 1990; Carruthers, 1972; Mbiti, 1970; Keto, 1991; Sobel, 1979; Thompson, 1983a) when he stated:

> Essentially, African Cosmology is governed by the overriding theme or ontological principle of "Human-Nature Unity," or "Oneness with Nature," or "Harmony with Nature"....A number of supporting principles derive from the basic theme of African Cosmology. Among these supporting themes are emphases on groupness (survival of the group), sameness and commonality; corporateness, cooperation, collective responsibility, and interdependence. (pp. 243-244)

For traditional Africans, everything was connected. God was viewed as the originator and sustainer of human beings. Nobles (1980) stated that there existed a force, a power, or energy which permeated the whole universe. God was the source and ultimate controller of the energy. The social order was projected in the individual and the individual was the product of his institution. The notion of unity was so ingrained that it resulted in a sense of collective responsibility.

According to Mbiti (1970), the individual did not and could not exist alone. The Africans believed that the community made, created, or produced the individual and only in terms of other people does the individual become conscious of his own being. At the same time, according to Collins (1989), each individual was thought to be a unique expression of the common spirit, power, or energy; and this unique individual expression was the product of the community and contributed to the good of the

community. Therefore the notion of unity or oneness with nature also meant collective kinship and individual uniqueness or expressiveness. Booker T. Washington, an inventor and descendent of enslaved Africans is credited with a contemporary expression of the same notion:

> In all things that are purely social we can be as separate as the fingers, yet as one as the hand in all things essential to mutual progress.[4]

In considering an African-American aesthetic of dress, the focus must be on the philosophical linkage between Africans and African-Americans. One must assess whether and to what extent the African aesthetic orientation has persisted. In considering the philosophical-psychological linkages between African and Afro-Americans, Nobles (1980) suggested that one must ask "How could it have been maintained?" and "What mechanism or circumstances allowed it to be maintained?" These questions seem appropriate for assessing an African-American aesthetic of dress from an Afrocentric perspective. Likewise, Nobles' answers to these questions will also suffice:

> An orientation stemming from a particular indigenous African philosophy could only be maintained when its cultural carriers were isolated (and /or insulated) from alien cultural interaction and if their behavioral expression of the orientation did not openly conflict with the cultural-behavioral elements of the "host" society. If the circumstances of the transplantation of New World Blacks met one or both of these conditions, then it is highly probable that the African orientation was retained. (p. 32)

The absence of the consideration of African aesthetics in an American context implies support of a melting pot theory: The cultural heritage of a people is lost or diffused into a larger culture. However, Andrew Hacker (1992), a noted political scientist and philosopher, provided, in his New York Times best seller, *Two Nations*, statistical data to paint the picture of a divided society in which black and white relations "have never been amiable" (p. vii). He agrees with the conclusion presented by the National Advisory Commission on Civil Disorders in 1968: "Our nation is moving toward two societies, one black, one white, separate and unequal." The notion of two nations, separate and unequal, presupposes two cultures, one dominant and one subordinate. While many have recognized that America is not a melting pot, others still hold the melting pot notion, thus opposing proponents of an African-American aesthetic.

Based on the conditions for maintenance of an orientation stemming from a particular indigenous African philosophy, African customs of dress and adornment would have had difficulty surviving during the period of African enslavement. Records of slavery clearly indicate that enslaved Africans were not allowed to bring with them their clothing or other important symbols of African culture (Starke, 1990; Warner & Parker, 1990). Dress or costume, a cultural carrier of a philosophical orientation, could only be isolated from interaction with European-American culture by slaves not being allowed to wear it. To have allowed enslaved Africans to maintain their dress and other cultural symbols would have suggested that Africans were civilized human beings with a culture. Since civilized human beings, from a Eurocentric perspective, do not treat other human beings as animals, enslaved Africans had to be considered less than human beings, thus, having no culture to be preserved.[5] The maintenance of dress and other cultural artifacts would have therefore "openly conflicted with cultural-behavioral elements of the host society" (Nobles, 1980, p. 32).

Some writers (Elkins, 1963; Frazier, 1957; Glazer & Moynihan, 1963; Silberman, 1964) suggested that because of the circumstances to which enslaved Africans were subjected, there is "zero" continuity of African tradition in the United States. Others, however, can not accept the notion that the conditions of slavery in the United States destroyed the creative memories of Africans transported to the New World so that no African influences can be found today in areas such as African-American dress.

African-American historians and writers (Asante, 1987; Gayle, 1971; Holloway, 1990; Neal, 1971; Nobles, 1980; Semmes, 1992) have recognized that much of the African culture transported to the New World has survived. The enactment of laws to separate African slaves from European-Americans and to prevent the assimilation of freemen into the dominant culture served at least two purposes: to isolate African slaves and freemen, and to preserve some cultural values and ideals. African aesthetic values and ideals have been noted in music, dance, literature, sculpture, family life, and other art forms.

Whereas experiential knowledge suggests that there is an African-American aesthetic of dress and that the quest to find it is noble, one is well aware of the dual nature of the African-American heritage with its subtleties and complexities. The reality of a disconnected history of African-American aesthetic of dress has contributed to the lack of a self-definition of beauty and the lack of validation of aesthetic experiences and expressions. It is my belief that some African aesthetic orientations in dress survived and can be seen in 20th century America if viewed from an Afrocentric perspective. Africa must be the cultural starting point and serve as the reference point in gathering and interpreting knowledge about aesthetic orientations of descendants of African people. An aesthetic orientation which might have been preserved through dress is known to have been preserved in the quiltmaking of enslaved African women in America and their descendants. Therefore, in the next section, the aesthetic of quiltmaking will be discussed.

Part III: The Aesthetic of Quiltmaking

Wahlman and Scully (1983), pointed out continuities between African textiles and Afro-American quilts. Preferred combinations of design elements in African textiles were compared to aesthetic choices made by contemporary Afro-American quiltmakers. Their symbolic research included a knowledge of the meanings encoded into African textiles used for initiation, funerals, and other ritual occasions as well as fieldwork in the American South to see how many African meanings survived or are transformed by the interactions of Afro-Americans, Native, Spanish or European Americans. Using quilts made by contemporary Southern Afro-American women[6] from Alabama, Georgia, and Mississippi, Wahlman and Scully were able to point out continuities between African textiles and Afro-American quilts. As a result of correlations between techniques employed, use of design principles, and aesthetic preferences, they offered an aesthetic framework consisting of aesthetic principles used in Afro-American quilter's work. The aesthetic principles are characterized by five elements:

1) stripes to construct and to organize quilt top design space; 2) large scale designs; 3) strong, highly contrasting colors; 4) off-beat patterns; 5) multiple rhythms. (p. 86)

Stripes to construct and organize design space. Wahlman and Scully (1983) noted that the use of strips to organize the quilt top is the most basic and predominant characteristic of Afro-American quilts. Strips are used both structurally and aesthetically and are frequently referred to as a time saving device. However, the color of the strips is considered a major element in the visual experience. "When the colors of the strips are different from the colors in the rows of blocks or designs, two distinct movements can be seen: one along the strips and the other within the designs" (p.86).

Scholars (Chase, 1978; Lamb, 1975; Sieber, 1972; Thompson, 1974; Vlach, 1978) believed that the preference for strips in quilt top design reflects a textile aesthetic which has been passed down among African-American women for generations. In testing this idea, Wahlman and Scully found that the ideal width of a strip for some Afro-American women was approximately the width of ones hand, which corresponds to the width of a single strip of West African narrow loom cloth.

Large Scale Designs. The use of large scale designs may sometimes be the results of speeding up the production process. However,

In comparison with other American quilts, except for Amish examples, most Afro-American quilts tend to emphasize large designs which carry strongly from a distance...The impression of large designs is created by the use of small patches of a similar color or by the use of large scraps. (Wahlman & Scully, 1983. p. 88)

Strong, Highly Contrasting Colors. Wahlman and Scully (1983) noted the use of contrasting, bright colors which Robert Farris Thompson calls "high affect" colors. These colors are used to "organize quilt designs; 2) stress certain elements in quilt designs; 3) emphasize improvisations upon those designs; 4) highlight the unique...phenomenon of off-beat patterns; and 5) create multiple rhythms in quilt patterns" (p.8). These uses of color in African textiles have also been noted by other researchers (Sie-

ber, 1972; Thompson, 1974). They are used in African ceremonial costumes as well as every day dress to convey a sense of vitality and power. In using the analogy of African singing in which all notes are song in a steady outpouring of even tones with no noticeable physical stress on any one note, Thompson (1974) stated about the use of color in African textiles:

The same point applies to the strong use of color in African textiles. There are two ways of preserving the full seniority of colors in textiles patterning: either through contrastive colors, hot and cool, of equal strength, or by maintaining equality of dynamics in the phrasing of light and dark colors (the textiles of the Akan of Ghana are excellent examples). Either way, full sonority and attack in the handling of color means that every line is equally emphasized. For this reason, many or most of the textile traditions of Africa seem "loud" by conventional Western standards, but this is precisely the point. Equal strength to every note parallels equal strength of every color. Yet there are probably differential limits to the amount of intensity in color preferred by different African societies... In general, however, the African usage of color in cloth is splendidly vital...(pp. 8-9).

Off-Beat Patterns. The phenomenon of "off-beat phrasing" in African textiles has been documented by Sieber (1972), Thompson (1974), Vlach (1978) and Wahlman and Scully (1983), and is generally referred to as improvisations. The term "off-beat patterning" serves to describe how Afro-American quilters control their improvisations. Wahlman and Scully suggest that while some improvisations in quilt top designs may be due to a lack of cloth in one color, the general tendency is to demonstrate how to master a pattern, and then to break or bend it. Most improvisations are accomplished by a manipulation of colored pieces. Variations, however, may be created within a strip. "When the accents in one row match the accents in another row, the design is 'on the beat.' But when the accents in one row do not match up with the accents in another row, then we have what can be termed 'off-beat' designs" and the effect is a sense of movement or direction (p.90). In discussing "off-beat patterning" in African textiles Sieber (1972) stated:

The regularity of striped patterning in Upper Volta weaving is sometimes spectacularly complicated by vibrant suspensions of expected placement of the pattern... Careful matching of the ends of the cloth dispels the impression of an uncalculated overall design (p.11)... Whereas careful measurement, precise calculations, and meticulous thread counts can create a scheme of fixed or repeated patterns, less planning may result in quite dramatic, random designs. Actually, the accidental in such cloths are not unanticipated, but are allowed for if not calculated. (p.181)

The phenomenon of "off-beat patterning" has been noted by researchers (Asante, 1987; Asante & Asante, 1990; Thompson, 1974; Vlach, 1978) in music, dance, and other art form in addition to quiltmaking.

Multiple Rhythms. The use of multiple rhythms has been found in African textiles just as is seen in African-American dance and music. Through variations in strip width, color contrast, and patch shapes, the impression of several patterns moving in different directions or multiple rhythms are created by African-American quiltmakers. While the term 'off-beat patterning' serves to describe how improvisations are controlled in quilts, the term 'multiple rhythms' describes how the quilters multiply the off-beat patterns and carry them to complex aesthetic solutions, creating the impression of several patterns moving in different directions within the context of controlled design (Wahlman & Scully, 1983).

Wahlman and Scully (1983) concluded that the aesthetic principles of the use of strong color contrasts, strips, and the impression of off-beat patterns and multiple rhythms are complex but seem most basic to Afro-American quilts. These principles are consistent with certain aesthetic principles in other Afro-American arts such as music, dance, sculpture, literature, and religious drama, and are found in the African textile tradition. While most of the quilts were made from scraps of fabrics often given by friends or employer, the end result was the production of functional beauty.

In making a direct comparison of the quilting traditions of African-Americans and European-American, Vlach (1978) asserted that the quality

of random improvisation created through the manipulation of strips, colors, and patterns sets African-American quilts apart from the European genre. A visual balance is created between precision and random variation. Brown (1989) observed that "the symmetry in African-American quilts does not come from uniformity as it does in Euro-American quilts; rather, the symmetry comes through the diversity" (p.924). Vlach (1978) concluded that

> What may in the end be regarded as the most important feature of Afro-American quilting is the apparent refusal to simply surrender an alternative aesthetic sense to the confines of mainstream expectations. Euro-American forms were converted so that African ideas would not be lost. (p.75)

Part IV: The African-American Aesthetic of Dress

Works by Thompson (1974; 1983), Vlach (1978), Sieber (1972), Ferris (1983) and others have clearly shown that the suppression of the more public African influences, such as religious rituals and forms of dress "did not still the voice of more intimate expressions." African aesthetic influences are shown to be present in verbal arts such as story telling, in healing, cuisine, singing, dance and music such as jazz and blues. For an African-American aesthetic of dress, the questions to ask are: "Did African aesthetic orientations toward dress survive the forced abandonment of native dress and ritual costume?" and "How might an African-American aesthetic of dress be manifested today?"

In answer to the first question, little primary evidence could be found relative to the survival of African dress and ritual costume. Hunt (1990) studied the influence of fashion on the dress of African-American women in Georgia, 1870-1915 and noted the use of a cloth headdress that could not be classified as European-American fashion. Hunt noted that all the rural women in the photograph she reviewed for the period 1890 to 1899 were wearing kerchiefs on their heads, however, each kerchief was arranged differently. Hunt did not attempt to explain the non-European influence in headdress nor the individuality in the arrangement of the kerchiefs worn. Is it possible that these were Africanisms? In the slave narrative, *The Fugitive Blacksmith*, Pennington (1849/1968), formally a slave in the State of Maryland, discussed the provisions given enslaved Africans:

At the beginning of winter, each slave had one pair of coarse shoes and stockings, one pair of pantaloons, and a jacket. At the beginning of summer, he had two pair of coarse linen pantaloons and two shirts.... The men had no hats, waistcoats or handkerchiefs given them, or *the women any bonnets. These they had to contrive for themselves.* (p. 66) (Italics added)

If enslaved Africans had to "contrive" their own headdress, it is possible that what Hunt found had its origin in African culture.

A Eurocentric term used to describe forms of African adornment is "mutilation." Numerous books, magazines and periodical show examples of "mutilation." To replace the term "mutilation" which has negative connotations, Eicher (1970) proposed the term body modifications to describe acts of body alteration for decorative (i.e. aesthetic) or symbolic purposes. Ear and nose piercing are two forms of body modification that obviously survived slavery, though in modified form, and is not found among ancient Europeans.

With little primary evidence available, how might an African-American aesthetic of dress be manifested today? For an answer one might consider the guiding beliefs of a people which influence the values and customs that ultimately determine the social behavior expressed in common. The African-American quiltmaking model viewed in light of the philosophical premises of oneness or unity, with the notion of the individual as a unique expression of a common spirit, might serve as a guide. In the quiltmaking model visual balance created between precision and random variation (i.e. improvisations or off-beat pattern), strong intensity or "high affect" (i.e. loud) colors, and large scale designs appear to be elements adaptable to an African-American aesthetic of dress. As noted earlier, these elements have been found previously in other African-American art forms.

Improvisations or Individual Expression. In the quiltmaking model, personal expressiveness is seen in improvisations. Wahlman and Scully (1983) suggested that the designs of these quilts were usually unplanned and that each quilter had her own discernable style in spite of the pattern variations each used. Today, this individual uniqueness is seen in the

value placed on personal expressiveness in African-American communities. Semmes (1992) stated,

that this expressiveness or "style" "powerfully attracts markets and dominates the transformation of American popular culture. Style in African American culture refers to the tradition of artfully embellishing movement, speech, and appearance.... One must inject beauty, heightened emotion or feeling, and idiosyncratic expression into a product or action. (p. 131)

Thus, what one chooses to wear or use as adornment is less important than how it is worn. This can be seen in compliments such as "Girl, you are wearing that dress." The personal expressiveness of African-Americans has been noted by some European-American writers. George Frazier, a European-American, writing in the November 1967 issue of Esquire magazine, stated that "the Negro's immense style, a style so seductive that it's little wonder that black men are, as Shakespeare puts it in *The Two Gentlemen of Verona*, 'pearls in beauteous ladies' eyes.'" The following example was used:

The formal daytime attire (black sack coats and striped trousers) the Modern Jazz Quartet wore when appearing in concert; the lazy amble with which Jimmy Brown used to return to the huddle; the delight the late "Big Daddy" Lipscomb took in making sideline tackles in full view of the crowd and the way, after crushing a ball carrier to the ground, he would chivalrously assert him to his feet; the constant cool of 'Satchel' Paige; the chic of Bobby Short; the incomparable grace of John Bubbles- things like that are style and they have nothing whatsoever to do with ability...(p. 76)

High Affect Colors and Large Scale Design. The preference for "high affect" colors was found both in African textiles and African-American quilts. The preference for "loud" colors and large bold patterns is a stereotype of African-Americans. The stereotypical notion is so ingrained in African-Americans as negative, that "loud" colors and patterns are rejected first when one attempts to assimilate into the dominant culture (i.e., become accepted by Whites). Even if there is a preference for "high affect" colors, educated African-Americans who strive to escape poverty and rise up the social and economic ladder recognize the necessity of forcing those preferences to lie dormant. Consensus has not been reached relative to African-American preferences for color. Kaiser (1990) stated that African-American females do not prefer "flashier" combinations. While Williams, Arbaugh, and Rucker (1980) suggest that African-American females prefer more intense colors and truer hues. Liebman (1987) noted blue and red as preferred colors. Also, research by Reeder and Drake (1980) suggest that African-American male athletes prefer more "attention-getting" clothing than their White counterpart. However, those preferring more attention getting clothing also exhibited feelings of a higher self-concept. No research was found in which size of design was manipulated.

Recently, marketers have concluded that aesthetic preferences of African-American women differ sufficiently to target this segment in wearing apparel, accessories, and home fashions. Spiegel and Ebony magazine jointly lunched a catalog collection for African-American women. Spokeswoman Ann Morris stated that market research found that African-American women

> wanted to see a different assortment of colors to better complement their skin--yellows, oranges, gold, fuchsia and purples. They wanted bigger and bolder prints and patterns reflecting their African heritage. (Hood, 1993, p. 2)

J.C. Penney has also produced a similar catalog which reflects a similar position. Garments with colors and patterns which create multiple rhythms are also seen. Fashions for Men, women and children are found in the J.C. Penney catalog.

Unity or Oneness. From an Afrocentric perspective, women's beauty is not based solely on physical criteria because mind, spirit, and body are not conceptualized as separate, oppositional spheres (Collins, 1991). Beauty is functional in that it has no meaning independent of the group. Asante (1987) asserts that deviating from the group "norm" is not rewarded as "beauty." Instead, participating in the group and being a functioning individual who strives for harmony is key. Participation, however, is not based on conformity but instead is seen as

individual uniqueness that enhances the overall "beauty" of the group. Collins (1991) noted that in using this criteria of beauty no one is inherently beautiful because beauty is not a state of being but is always defined in a context as a state of becoming. The notion of normative beauty is seen in what Thompson (1974) calls *mid-point mimesis*. According to Thompson, through out West Africa and the Congo moderation seems important. A representational balance which is not too real and not too abstract, but somewhere in between is found in images. To Africans, beauty is a mean. "Thus, Tutuola:[7] neither too tall and not too short, not too black and not yellow" (p. 49). This "mid-point mimesis" may be implied in recent research which indicates that African-American women tend to be more satisfied with their bodies than their European-American counterparts (Brown, 1993; Gray, Ford & Kelley, 1987; Hooper & Garner, 1986; Hsu, 1987; Pumariega, Edwards, & Mitchell, 1984; Robinson & Andersen, 1985; Silber, 1986). The quiltmaking model only serves as a starting point in assessing an African-American aesthetic of dress. At most, attempts are made to find correspondence between the observed dress of African Americans and elements of the model, and certain philosophical premises. Little is known about African-American's response to various forms of dress and appearance, internal processes, and psychological and social-cultural factors that affect responses to the aesthetic qualities of the product.

Part V: Implications

Lorenzo Turner (In Nobles, 1980) suggested that African cultural elements had a better chance of surviving where "Negroes" were in the majority. Herskovits (1958), Kochman (1981) and Valentine (1968) agree that ethnic identity and subcultural distinctness of many minority groups are greatest among the poor. Kochman (1981) stated,

> just as poor first-generation Irish, Italian, Jewish, or Ukrainian groups are likely to be more "ethnic" than their third-generation middle-class counterparts, so would poor blacks be more "ethnic" than their black middle-class counterparts whose social networks, or level of education, has brought them more within the sphere of influence of dominant white cultural norms and values. That "community"

219

blacks, even after several generations, should retain their original ethnic patterns and perspectives simply speaks to the extent to which racial segregation has kept the black rural and urban community culturally insular (p.14).

If such is the case, then evidence of African aesthetic of dress is most likely to be found where predominately African-American communities have existed historically and where cultural assimilation is minimal. The "Black" belt of Alabama and inner city areas which are known to be inhabited historically by African Americans might serve as examples. Prior to the 1950s when television was not found in nearly every home, most African Americans living in such areas had few opportunities for cultural assimilation. However, with mass media being virtually universal in the United States today, it may be difficult to distinguish preferences from fashion and other influences. It does seem possible, however, that aesthetic preferences and judgements might differ between African Americans who have greater degrees of assimilation into the dominant culture and those who have been consistently isolated.[8]

Also, in-depth interviews of African-American women might be conducted to probe aesthetic preferences and judgments relative to style, fabric, patterns, and color preferences to determine if purchasing patterns and innate preferences correspond, and the extent to which there is an awareness of differences in personal preferences and Eurocentric values and ideals of "taste."

Asante (1987) and Semmes (1992) asserted that beauty in the Western world is artifactual, but from an Afrocentric sense it is dynamic. "Expression itself can be beautiful...(Asante, 1987, p. 170). Using primarily European-American subjects, Morganosky and Postlewait (1989) found form to be a more central component of aesthetic judgments of apparel than expressive qualities. If Asante's assertion is correct, then from an Afrocentric perspective one might expect to find differences in aesthetic judgments between African Americans and European Americans.

While assumptions are made and stereotypical notions are held concerning clothing, dress and appearance preferences and aesthetic creations, judgments and experiences of Afri-

can Americans, the research support is generally unavailable. Research of body cathexis and appearance management is essentially void of discussion relative to African Americans. The noted work by Kaiser (1990), *The Social Psychology of Clothing - Symbolic Appearances in Context*, devoted approximately ten pages out of several hundred to information relative to African Americans. In reality African American and White students, faculty and researchers have all been socialized to describe, analyze, and evaluate aesthetic objects from an Eurocentric perspective. Brown (1989) suggests, however, that it is possible to have a variety of experiences, a variety of ways of understanding the world, and a variety of frameworks of operation without imposing consciously or unconsciously a notion of the norm. Brown states:

> ...I believe that all people can learn to center in another experience, validate it, and judge it by its own standards without need of comparison or need to adopt that framework as their own. Thus, one has no need to "decenter"[9] anyone in order to center someone else; one has only to constantly, appropriately, "pivot the center." (p. 922)

"Pivoting the center" is where the need is in teaching and researching African-American aesthetic of dress. One might "pivot the center" by not simply discussing differences in aesthetic preferences but by presenting the philosophical premises shared by the West African "experiential community." The European-American perspective has dominated clothing and textiles research relative to aesthetic preferences and evaluations. Presenting information and interpreting differential meanings from an Afrocentric perspective will not demand "decentering" or invalidating ones own experiences. Instead, it will serve only to aid in learning to validate another experience and in judging it by its own standards. The notion of "pivoting the center is relevant when considering any ethnic, gender, or subcultural group. However, one can only "pivot the center" when one chooses to become knowledgeable of the diverse philosophies, values, and experiences of another people.

Endnotes
[1]While the African Dress bibliographies do not deny connections between Africa and African-American dress, they do not suggest a connectedness either. The stated purpose of the bibliographies relates only to African dress. It is the

220

absence of connectedness in historic and other writings which establishes the need for work in this area.

[2]While African-American females have advanced to the finals of the Miss America pageant, these females have generally been those with distinct European-American features, thus, portraying European standards of beauty and continuing to perpetuate the beauty myth. A graphic picture of the "white aesthetic" which has been handed down from Plato to America is seen in the book, *Nojoque: A Question for a Continent*, by Hinton Helper, which was published in 1867.

[3]The question is sometimes raised as to whether "tribal" differences manifest themselves in American Culture? Much research has been conducted concerning slave history and the transmission of African Peoples. Most noted among these works are Sobel (1979), Herskovits (1970), Holloway (1990), Curtin (1969), Mbiti (1970), Asante (1987), and Engerman & Genorese (1975). Sorbel (1979) capsules the essence of these scholars conclusions when he states "Blacks arriving from Africa spoke African languages and found others with whom to share discourse, either in their own tongue or in a second African tongue they had known in Africa. In the process of interrelations with different African cultures, the various African world views rapidly began to coalesce" (p.38). Herskovits (1979) states that "Instead of representing isolated cultures, their endowments, however different in detail, possessed least common denominators that permitted a consensus of experience to be drawn on in fashioning new, though still Africanlike, customs....The process of acculturation resulted in varied degrees of reinterpretation of African custom in the light of the new situation"(p.297). Nobles (1980) stateD that enslaved Africans from the same tribe were not allowed to remain together in order to break down "the collective reinforcement of a common definition. As slavery was moving closer and closer to its final definition, the slaves themselves were moving closer to African ..as the final definition of the tribe. Thus the common notion of survival of the tribe became survival of African peoples" (p.33). It is unlikely that tribal differences might be manifested in American culture.

[4]This statement is believed to have been made in a speech at the Cotton States and International Exposition, Atlanta, Georgia, September 18, 1895.

[5]In Article I, Section 2 of the Constitution of the United States of America, slaves were considered as three fifths of a person. Also see Willhelm (1983) for how the Bible was used to justify American Indians and enslaved Africans an nonhuman (especially p. 290).

[6]Wahlman and Scully (1983) noted that the survey of Literature of Afro-American quilts lack historical data from the sixteenth and seventeenth centuries. The older quilts of which they had access dated from 1886 and 1898. Nor were sufficient African textiles available from these same periods.

[7]Tutuola refers to writings by Tutuola, A. (1962). *Feather Women of the Jungle*. London: Faber and Faber.

[8]Sociologist and cultural anthropologists have described the process of "ethnic meeting" using either one or both of the terms assimilation and acculturation. Hess, Markson, and Stein (1985) use acculturation to refer to the internationalizing of values and behavioral patterns of a majority society by members of a distinct culture. Assimilation on the other hand is more encompassing and include the accepting of individuals of a subculture into major social institutions and more personal groupings. An older but most valuable and detailed explanation of assimilation is done by Gordon (1964) who makes the distinction among degrees of assimilation. His definition of acculturation (the change of cultural patterns to those of the host society) agrees with

Hess, et.al, and is seen as an aspect of assimilation. Gordon notes that acculturation might take place without structural (large scale entrance into cliques, clubs, institutions, primary groups of the host society), identificational (development of a sense of personhood), civic (absence of value and power conflict), behavioral (absence of discrimination), or attitudinal (absence of prejudice) assimilation. Other scholars (Beatty, 1985; Lott, 1992; Frazier, 1957; Lawson, 1992) agree that there are varying degrees of assimilation that might take place. Based on these ideas of degrees and types of assimilation, clearly some African Americans have become more assimilated than others. Gordon(1964) clarifies the impact of social structure of the ethnic group on assimilation and notes that despite the "Americanization" movement following WWI, "the rural Negro of the South, under both slavery and post-Reconstruction exploration and discrimination, developed a set of subcultural patterns considerably remote from those of the core society of middle-class whites... The acculturation process was retarded because of the massive size and strength of the prejudice and consequent discrimination directed toward them. (108)" While the vast majority of African Americans have assumed patterns of the dominant culture, most have not assimilated structurally or in terms of identification, attitude, and behavior. Current data to support the lack of assimilation on the part of most African Americans can be found in Hacker (1992).

[9]According to Brown (1989) to "decenter" refers to the need to invalidate the experiences of another in order to center in one's own experiences.

References

Asante, M.K. & Asante, K.W. (Eds.). (1990). *African culture: The rhythm of unity*. Trenton, New Jersey: African World Press.

Asante, M. K. (1987). *The afrocentric idea*. Philadelphia: Temple University Press.

Asante, M. K. (1980). *Afrocentricity: The theory of social change*. Buffalo: Amulefi.

Baldwin, J. A. (1986). African (Black) psychology: Issues and synthesis. *Journal of Black Studies*, 16(3), 235-249.

Beardsley, M.C. (1958). *Aesthetics*. New York: Harcourt, Brace and Company.

Beatty, J. (1985, November 17). The self-discovery of the Black middle class. *Boston Globe Magazine*, p.49.

Brown, E. B. (1989). African-American women's quilting: A framework for conceptualizing and teaching African-Americans' history. *Signs: Journal of Women in Culture and Society*, 14(4), 921-929.

Brown, M. (June 1993). "Dying to be thin." *Essence*, pp. 86-88, 125-129.

Carruthers, J. H. (1972). *Science and oppression*. Chicago: Center for Inner City Studies, Northeastern Illinois University.

Curtin, P. (1969). *The Atlantic slave trade: A census*. Madison: University of Wisconsin Press.

Chase, J. W. (1978). Afro-American heritage from ante-bellum Black craftsmen. *Southern Folklore Quarterly*, 42(2-3), 135-158.

Child, I. (1968). Aesthetics. In D. Sills (Ed.), *International Encyclopedia of the Social Sciences* (Vol. 1) (pp. 116-121). New York: MacMillan Co.

Collins, P. H. (1989). The social construction of Black feminist thought. *Signs: Journal of Women in Culture and Society, 14*(4), 745-773.

Collins, P. H. (1991). *Black feminist thought - knowledge, consciousness and the politics of empowerment.* New York: Rutledge.

Cone, J. (1990). *A Black theology of liberation.* New York: Orbis.

Elkins, S. (1963). *Slavery: A problem in American institutional and intellectual life.* New York: Universal Library Edition.

Eicher, J. B. (1970). *African dress, a selected and annotated bibliography of Subsaharan countries.* Michigan: Michigan State University Press.

Engerman, S.L. & Genorese, E. (Eds.). (1975). *Race and slavery in the western hemisphere: Quantitative studies.* Princeton, N.J.: Princeton University Press.

Ferris, W. (1983). *Afro-American folk art and craft.* Jackson, Mississippi: University Press of Mississippi.

Felder, C.H. (1993). Cultural ideology, Afrocentrism and Biblical interpretation. In J. H. Cone and G. S. Wilmore, (Eds.), *Black theology: a documentary history* (pp. 184-195). New York: Orbis Books.

Fiore, A.M., Moreno, J.M., & Kimle, P.A. (in press). Aesthetics: A comparison of the state of the art outside and inside the field of textiles and clothing. Part III: Apppreciation process, appreciator, and summary comparison. *Clothing and Textiles Research Journal.*

Frazier, E. F. (1957). *Race and culture contacts in the modern world.* Boston: Beacon Press.

Frazier, E. F. (1957). *Black bousgeoise.* New York: Free Press.

Gayle, A. (1971). *The Black aesthetic.* Garden City, NY: Doubleday.

Glazer, N. & Moynihan, D.P. (1963). *Beyond the melting pot.* Cambridge: MIT Press.

Gordon, M.M. (1964). *Assimilation in American life.* New York: Oxford University Press.

Gray, J.J., Ford, K., & Kelly, L.M. (1987). The prevalence of bulimia in a Black college population. *International Journal of Eating Disorders, 6* (6), 733-740.

Hacker, A. (1992). *Two nations: Black and White, separate, hostile, unequal.* New York: Ballantine Books.

Herskovits, M. J. (1970). *The myth of the negro past.* Gloucester, Mass.: Peter Smith.

Hess, B.B., Markson, E.W. & Stein, P.J. (1985). *Sociology.* 2nd. Ed. New York: Macmillan.

Holloway, J. E. (1990). The origin of African-American culture. In J. E. Holloway, (Ed). *Africanisms in American culture* (1-18). Bloomington: Indiana University Press.

Hood, M. (1993, September 14). Colors that complement. *The Columbus Dispatch.* pp. C 1-2.

hooks, b. (1992). *Black looks.* Boston: South End Press.

Hooper, M.S. & Garner, D. M. (1986). Application of the eating disorders inventory to a sample of black, white, and mixed race schoolgirls in Zimbabwe. *International Journal of Eating Disorders, 5* (1), 161-168.

Hume, D. (1965). Of the standards of taste. In J. Stolnitz, *Aesthetics* (pp. 86-97). New York: MacMillan Publishing Co.

Hunt, P. A. (1990). *The influence of fashion the dress of African American women in Georgia, 1870-1915.* Unpublished doctoral dissertation, The Ohio State University, Columbus.

Hsu, L.K.G. (1987). Are the eating disorders becoming more common in blacks. *International Journal of Eating Disorders, 6* (1), 113-124.

Johnson, R. (1986-1987). What is cultural studies anyway? *Social Text. 16*, 38-80.

Kaiser, S. (1990). *The social psychology of clothing.* (2nd. Ed.) New York: Macmillan Publishing Company.

Keto, C.T. (1991). *The Africa-centered perspective of history: An introduction.* Laurel Springs, New Jersey: K.A. Publishers.

Kochman, T. (1981). *Black and white styles in conflict.* Chicago: The University of Chicago Press.

Lamb, V. (1975). *West African weaving.* London: Duckworth, Gerald and Co.

Lawson, B.E. (1992). *The underclass question.* Philadelphia: Temple University Press.

Liebman, M. M. (1987). A conceptual framework for examining color preferences, importance and categorization in a multiattribute context among blacks. In R. L. King, (ed.). *Minority Marketing: Issues and Prospects, 3* 57-63. Charleston: Academy of Marketing Sciences.

Lott, T. (1992). Marooned in America: Black urban youth culture and social pathology. In B. Lawson (Ed). *The Underclass Question.* (pp. 71-89) Philadelphia: Temple University Press.

MacCannell, D., & MacCannell, J.F. (1982). *The time of the sign: A semiotic interpretation of modern culture.* Bloomington: Indiana University Press.

Mbiti, J. C. (1970). *African religions and philosophies.* Garden City, NY: Avalon Books.

McCracken, G. (1988). *Culture and consumption.* Bloomington: Indiana University Press.

Morganosky, M. A. & Postlewait, D. S. (1989). Consumers' Evaluations of apparel form, expression, and aesthetic quality. *Clothing and Textiles Research Journal, 7* (2) 11-15.

Neal, L. (1971). Some reflections on the Black aesthetic. In A. Gayle, Jr. (Ed.), *The Black Aesthetic* (pp. 13-16). New York: Doubleday & Company, Inc.

Nobles, W. (1980). African philosophy: Foundations for Black psychology. In R. L. Jones (Ed.), *Black psychology* (2nd ed.) (pp. 23-36). New York: Harper and Row Publishers.

Pennington, J.W.C. (1849/1968). The Fugitive Blacksmith; or, events in the history of James W. C. Pennington, formerly a slave in the State of Maryland, United States. In W. L. Katz, (Ed), *Five slave Narratives: A compendium*. New York: Arno Press and the New York Times.

Pokornowski, I. M., Eicher, J. B., Harris, M. F., & Thieme, O. C. (1985). *African Dress II – A Selected and Annotated Bibliography*. East Lansing, Michigan: African Studies Center.

Pumariega, A.J., Palmer, E. & Mitchell, C.B. (1984). Anorexia nervosa in black adolescents. *Journal of the American Academy of Child Psychiatry, 23* (1) 111-114.

Reeder, E. & Drake, M. F. (1980). Clothing preferences of male athletes: Actual and perceived. *Home Economics Research Journal. 8*, 339-343.

Roach, M. E. & Musa, K. (1979). *New perspectives on the history of western dress*. New York: Nutriguides.

Robinson, P. & Andersen, A. (1985). Anorexia nervosa in American blacks. *Journal of Psychiatric Research, 19* (2/3), 183-188.

Sahlins, M. (1976). *Culture and practical reason*. Chicago: University of Chicago Press.

Semmes, C.E. (1992). *Cultural hegemony and African American development*. Westport, Connecticut: Praeger.

Sieber, R. (1972). *African textiles and the decorative arts*. New York: Museum of Modern Art.

Silber, T.J. (1986). Anorexia nervosa in blacks and hispanics. *International Journal of Eating Disorders, 5* (1), 121-128.

Silberman, C. E. (1964). *Crisis in black and white*. New York: Vintage Book.

Sobel, M. (1979). *Trabelin' on*. Westport, Connecticut: Greenwood Press.

Starke, B. (1990). U. S. slave narratives: Accounts of what they wore. In B. Starke, L. Holloman, and B. Nordquist (Eds.), *African American dress and adornment: A cultural perspective* (pp.69-80). Iowa: Kendall/Hunt Publishing Co.

Storm, P. (1987). *Functions of dress*. New Jersey: Prentice-Hall, Inc.

Thieme, O. C. & Eicher, J. B. (1990). African Dress: Form, action, meaning. In B. Starke, L. Holloman, and B. Hordquist (Eds.), *African American dress and adornment: A cultural perspective*. (pp. 4-18). Iowa: Kendall/Hunt Publishing Co.

Thompson, R. F. (1974). *African art in motion*. Berkley: University of California Press.

Thompson, R. F. (1983). *Flash of the spirit: African and Afro-American art and philosophy*. New York: Ventage.

Thompson, R. F. (1983). African influence on the art of the United States. In W. Ferris (Ed.), *Afro-American folk art and craft* (pp. 27-63). Jackson, MS: University Press of Mississippi.

Valentine, C.A. (1968). *Culture and poverty*. Chicago: University of Chicago Press.

Vlach, J. M. (1978). *The Afro-American tradition in the decorative arts*.

Wahlman, M. S. and Scully, J. (1983). Aesthetic principles in Afro-American quilts. In William Ferris (Ed.), *Afro-American folk art and crafts* (pp. 79-97). Boston: G. K. Hill.

Wallace, M. (1990). *Invisibility blues*. New York: Verso.

Ware, L. (1990). African dress. In B. Starke, L. Holloman, and B. Nordquist (Eds.), *African American dress and adornment: A cultural perspective* (pp. 39-48). Iowa: Kendall/Hunt Publishing Co.

Warner, P. C. & Parker, D. (1990). Slave clothing and textiles in North Carolina 1775-1835. In B. M. Starke, L. D. Holloman, & B. K. Nordquist (Eds.), *African American dress and adornment, A cultural perspective* (pp. 82-92). Iowa: Kendall/Hunt Publishing Co.

Williams, J., Arbaugh, J., & Rucker, M. (1980). Clothing color preferences of adolescent females. *Home Economics Research Journal 9*, 57-63.

Willhelm, S. M. (1983). *Black in a White America*. Cambridge, Massachusetts: Schenkman Publishing Company, Inc.

A Systematic Analysis of the Aesthetic Experience of Korean Traditional Dress

Marilyn DeLong
University of Minnesota

Key Sook Geum
Hong-Ik University

Aesthetic experience as defined by Eaton (1988) is "experience of intrinsic features of things or events traditionally recognized as worthy of attention and reflection (p. 143)." Closely associated in definition with aesthetic experience is aesthetic value, also defined by Eaton, as the value of a thing because of its capacity to evoke pleasure arising from features traditionally considered worthy of attention and reflection. Therefore the study of the experience of visual art forms requires studying them within the cultural context because only then can we recognize what is worthy of attention and reflection. Cultural context is not only the consideration of one's own personal responses to a particular art form but also what it means to the people who use it, what its use and functions are, and by whom and where the art was made (Hatcher, 1985).

Study of objects of another culture is of value because the experience enables us to "step outside" of our native reference. Once outside certain aspects that may go unnoticed become highlighted and perceived more clearly. The broad meaning of cultural objects is not always consciously available even to its users, but when systematic comparisons are made this meaning may be better understood (Brislin, 1980; Wallendorf and Arnould, 1988). Thus by studying objects of another culture the viewer not only understands more of that culture but can better draw upon experiences within his/her own culture to interpret objects.

Authors who have examined Korean traditional dress (KTD) have concluded that its design is embedded in the Korean culture. Geum and DeLong (1992) discuss influential factors in formation of a Korean's aesthetic response to KTD: 1. tradition in connections and continuity to the past such as use of primary colors and white; 2. the close relationship with nature in frequent use of motifs such as flowers and birds, or even the curves of the silhouette resembling the curve of the hillside; 3. ties with the Korean spirits, such as the use of rainbow stripes to ward off the evil eye; and 4. the ideal Korean persona including the high value placed upon the scholar and education.

These influential factors are similar to the ones more generally associated with Korean arts as discussed by McCune (1962). Her list includes conservatism, love of nature and outdoor living, and a high respect for learning. Stylistically she maintains that Korean artists have tended to express major themes in contour or silhouette and then to reinforce the main idea by minor detail and color. Decoration appears to be subordinate to contour, and materials are strictly used according to their artistic and functional characteristics.

A characteristic of Korean art forms is the intermingling of the foreign with the familiar and the old with the new. The Japanese occupation of Korea from 1910 to 1944 followed by the Korean War created a military state and cultural deprivation. Those who lived through this experience do not take for granted the importance of tradition and continuity with the past. At the same time such a major city as Seoul has become a vibrant and modern metropolis with international visibility. Racial roots and human relationships are very important to the Korean and result in responsibilities to family as well as enduring networks of linkages with friends.

McCune (1962) discusses a pattern of silent response to foreign cultures that has allowed Koreans to tolerate foreign invasions in a nonviolent way and at the same time adopt aspects of other cultures without forfeiting their own cultural identity. This pattern of silent response has allowed Koreans to adopt several foreign religions without completely committing to any one religion. Among the religions of Korea are Buddhism, Christianity, Confusionsim, Taoism and Shamanism. Shamanism is the name given to religious practices derived from the early Koreans who began to form tribal federations in the first millennium B.C. and then kingdoms in what is now the Korean peninsula.

Koreans gain much satisfaction from their historic symbols and traditions (Park, Warner & Fitzgerald, 1993) and are often seen as unwilling to relinquish the revelations of their deepest feelings about the world they live in (McCune, 1962). This has meant that Korean art forms are imbued with more than ordinary significance. While silence is an important technique in Korean communication in art and speech, this silence may create difficulty for outsiders to learn and understand Korean arts. Therefore a study of Korean art forms requires involvement with their historical and cultural perspective to understand the aesthetic experience for the Korean people.

As with the other formative arts, Korean traditional dress reveals these deep and silent responses through its simple curvilinear silhouette, its plain surfaces, neat impression and color combinations and motifs. In Korea, women particularly wear traditional dress to show pride in their country and respect for its traditions. Korean females place importance upon their traditional dress and appearance and are proud of its symbolic nature.

In many cultures it is the female's obligation to be the conveyer of culture, the arts and traditions. Banner (1983) discusses just such a female obligation within the United States historically. Woman's position within the home was to create a pleasing environment and outside the home her special province was to pursue the arts and ideal beauty.

The objective of this research is to study female response to Korean traditional dress. This is a first step toward understanding the aesthetic experience associated with this object of tradition. By analyzing responses to photo stimuli we hope to understand something of the formal, expressive, and referential properties that are important to an aesthetic response. Ultimately we hope to understand what KTD means to Koreans.

Two distinct methodologies are utilized to examine the aesthetic response to Korean traditional dress. The first utilizes a statistical analysis of the responses of female Koreans varying in age. To measure the meaning of a concept, a series of descriptive scales defined by polar word pairs are selected to represent the major dimensions along which meaningful processes vary (Osgood 1965). Factor analysis is the logical tool for such a multidimensional exploration to provide insight of the collective response. The second methodology utilizes a more subjective means of exploring in depth one object of Korean tradition. This requires an informed viewer to follow a four step process for studying material culture.

Procedure

Six photographs of current Korean traditional dress (KTD) designed by a prominent Korean designer were selected from a group of 15 designs. The six were chosen because of their relation to the traditional, including examples that are strictly traditional, to those varying somewhat from the traditional, to those that are definitely modified from the traditional. In Figure I from top to bottom, traditional examples are TI and T2, modified traditional are MTI and MT2 and modified are MI and M2. A comparison of those within each category illustrates the degree of modification of basic contour of silhouette and detail.

Subjects were 243 females, all Korean Nationals, varying in age between 18 and 80 years located in both Korea and the United States. For the instrument, photographs of KTD, questions and word pairs were selected based upon a pilot in which word pairs used to describe traditional dress were elicited from Korean respondents. A group of American volunteers traveled to Korea and were teamed with Korean university graduate students to collect data.

The questionnaire included the six photographs and each subject responded to the 21 word pairs using each of the photographs. The questionnaire was administered to the subjects in an individual interview format. The subject physically placed each of the six photo stimuli anywhere within the 9 spaces spread out before her and according to its meaning related to each word pair. Photographs were given a random number and placed in a protective cover so that they could be handled. After the subject responded to each word pair the six stimuli were randomized. The interviews taking place in the United States and Korea were administered in the Korean language and coded by the same bilingual Korean researcher. All interviews took place within six months.

Figure 1. Stimuli from top left are T1 and top right T2, middle left MT1, MT2 and bottom left M1 and M2.

A Comparison of Stimuli Through Factor Analysis of Word Pairs

Both the six photographic stimuli in Figure I and bipolar word pairs in Table I were selected based upon a pilot. Properties of KTD crucial to an aesthetic response were derived from a factor analysis of the bipolar word pairs that were responded to by all subjects.

Table 1. Factor analysis of subject response to the bipolar word pairs

Factor Loading	Word Pairs
	Factor 1 Dignity/Evaluation
.84938	Unacceptable to me-Acceptable to me
.83032	Unattractive-Attractive
.82431	Ugly-Beautiful
.81717	Undignified-Dignified
.80454	I would not want to wear-I would want to wear
.79989	Tacky-Graceful
.77539	Offensive-Not Offensive
.77104	Impair the beauty of KTD-Enhance the beauty of KTD
.74276	Awkward-Natural
.72845	Dowdy-Polished
.72816	Uninteresting-Interesting
.69340	Easily Bored-Wearable for a long time
.68106	Unwearable for anyone-Wearable for someone
.63058	Uncolorful-colorful
9.05889	Eigen Value
43.1	Percentage of Variance
43.1	Cumulative Percentage of Variance
	Factor 2 Modernity
.69748	Modern-Traditional
.67722	Fashionable-Unfashionable
.67627	Individualized-Ordinary
.63281	Westernized-Korean like
2.57337	Eigen Value
12.3	Percentage of Variance
55.4	Cumulative Percentage of Variance
	Factor 3 Practicality
.76670	For special occasions-For every day
.60652	Uncomfortable-Comfortable
1.29097	Eigen Value
6.1	Percentage of variance
61.5	Cumulative Percentage of Variance

This procedure was similar to that of Kahng and Koh(l99l) in which responses of Koreans to their traditional dress were examined empirically. In that study female subjects were drawn from populations of students and middle aged women. Their instrument included a set of l4 bipolar word pairs and a seven point scale to measure the meaning of the stimuli. Their stimuli were line drawings of Korean traditional dress differing in silhouette and in amount, placement and type of such details as motif and color. Three factors emerged from their data: l. evaluation/prestige, 2. modernity and 3. practicality.

Though neither the KTD nor the 21 word pairs in this study were identical to those of Kahng and Koh (l99l), three similar factors important when differentiating among KTD were extracted. The word pairs associated with each factor are indicated in Table I. Factors l, 2 and 3 explained 6l.5% of the variance. Factor l la-

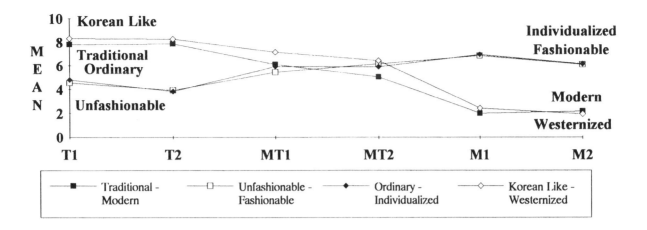

Figure 2. Display of mean response to six stimuli photographs based upon selected word pairs.

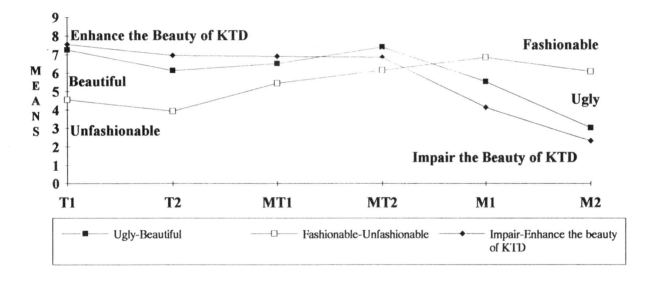

Figure 3. Display of mean response to six stimuli photographs based upon selected word pairs.

beled dignity/evaluation accounted for 43.1%, Factor 2 labeled modernity dropped to 12.3%, and Factor 3 labeled practicality, accounted for 6.1% of the response.

Responses to some of the word pairs as they relate to the six photographs are indicated in Figure 2: "Korean-like"/"westernized", "traditional"/"modern", "ordinary"/"individualized" and "unfashionable"/"fashionable". The graph is arranged according to mean responses of all subjects to "westernized"/"Korean-like", with the most "Korean-like" being Photos TI and T2 and

the most "westernized" being Photos MI and M2 (see Figure I). This graph helps to interpret traditional dress as a category. "Korean-like" and "traditional" follow similar paths in mean responses to photographs; likewise, similar paths are "ordinary" and "unfashionable". Photo stimuli considered most "Korean-like" were also considered most "traditional". When all four word pair paths are compared, subjects perceived the strictly traditional categories of stimuli as "Korean-like", "traditional", "ordinary" and "unfashionable", while the most modified are

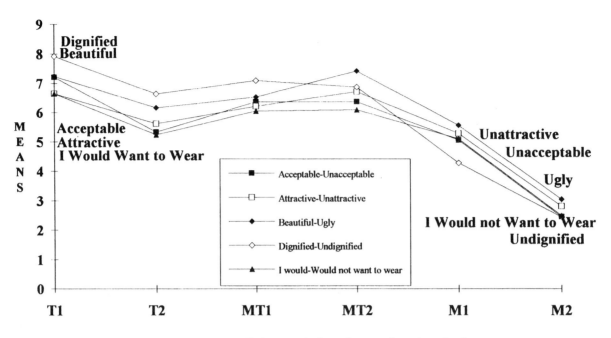

Figure 4. Display of mean response to six stimuli photographs based upon selected word pairs.

"westernized", "modern", "individualized" and "fashionable".

Figure 3 illustrates in a graph the word pairs, "enhance"/"impair the beauty of KTD", "beautiful"/"ugly" and "unfashionable"/"fashionable". When considering the evaluation of "beautiful", it does not follow the path of "fashionable". However "beautiful" and "enhance the beauty of KTD" are similar. Thus the concepts of "beautiful" and "fashionable" with regard to these six photographs are made more apparent with this display.

Figure 4 displays the similar paths of the word pairs: "dignified"/"undignified", "beautiful"/"ugly", "acceptable"/"unacceptable", "attractive"/ "unattractive" and "I would want to wear" and "I would not want to wear". This graph further illustrates the relation of these word pairs. The most traditional of the examples, Tl, is considered "dignified", "beautiful", "acceptable", "attractive" and wearable. The path is not incremental and varies with the specific stimuli. Stimulus MT2 is rated as the most "beautiful" following Tl.

This analysis of the six photographic stimuli of KTD was useful in understanding how Koreans respond to their differences. Though the

semantic procedure is meant to measure the meaning of Korean traditional dress, to attain maximum understanding of the aesthetic experience the expressive aspects require further examination utilizing another means of studying material culture.

A Method to Study Material Culture

The study of the material objects of a society is the study of material culture. When material culture is analyzed in a systematic way, reliable information about people, societies and cultures is revealed (Berger, 1992). The underlying premise is that the objects reflect the beliefs of those who made and used them. By studying such objects within a cultural context, we can gain insights about that culture and the aesthetic experience (Miller, 1987; Prown 1982).

When an individual comes into contact with an object, he/she does so in a context of cultural meanings that must be considered when interpreting the object. To use an object in a culturally appropriate way is a means of experiencing that culture directly, of understanding its signs, and becoming part of the medium of signs that makes up that culture. Cultural symbols are meaningful only when placed in the context of their contemporary culture (Csikszentimihalyi and Rochberg-Halton, 1981; Solomon, 1983).

A method of studying objects of material culture is for the viewer to take what he/she observes and knows about an object and follow a step-by-step procedure. The procedure is to first describe the physical nature of the object, and then proceed through steps of analysis, interpretation and evaluation (Prown, 1982; Fleming, 1973). In this process moving from the external manifestation to the internalization of the object, the artifact is better understood by the viewer.

The framework for visual analysis by DeLong (1987) is particularly related to dress. The framework was developed using contemporary U.S. culture because of the recognized difficulty inherent in understanding one's own perspective. However, there is no reason why the method cannot be applied to another culture since the framework involves identifying visual priorities and not cultural goals. In a cultural analysis such a procedure is more valuable when informed input from both cultures is included. The viewers in this case were the researchers, one from the Korean culture and one from the United States.

A Reference for KTD Through Analysis

One example, the most traditional KTD, will be systematically studied to determine what can be learned by beginning with the formal properties and proceeding through the analysis, interpretation and evaluation of the form. DeLong's framework (1987) was applied using the four step procedure: observation, analysis, interpretation and evaluation. This four step procedure is applied to one visual form and the unit of analysis is the Apparel-Body-Construct (ABC). Use of the term ABC is a recognition that the unit viewed by the observer involves an integral relationship of the apparel on the body. Such an analysis of one KTD will illustrate the relation of visual formal cues to cultural meaning and will provide a reference for the interpretation of the other examples. The process will include all information available to the viewer and the viewpoints of the two investigators.

Observation

In the first step of the procedure the object is described using all information at hand as well as what is directly viewed. The perspective will be that of the entire unit, the ABC and language

for the visual form (DeLong, 1987), and requires attending to and describing all aspects including the relations of the apparel to the body and the immediately surrounding space.

This selected example of KTD (Figure I, TI) was designed by Rija Lee and photographed in 1991. The ensemble is entirely of silk and the colors include the following: the top or chogore according to the Munsell System of Color Notation (1973) is 5G 9/I, the skirt or chima and cuffs are both 7.5 PB 3/12, the tie is IO RP 3/4. The circular motifs lined up on the tie, cuffs and hemline are all imprints at 2.5Y 8/8. The neckline is covered with a small band of white. The top or chogore is very defined in silhouette because of the lighter value and its contrast with the surround. The silhouette of the skirt or chima with its continuous edge is less definite because of the more closely graded values of skirt and immediately surrounding space.

The surface of the skirt has a gently rounded visual effect that appears voluminous and almost floating. Its surfaces remain somewhat determinate due to the crisp fabric. The surfaces of the chogore and chima employ the play of light and shadow in the folds of the chogore and gathers of the chima. The repetitious circular motifs also reflect the light. The tie does not reflect the light in the same way as the chogore and chima. Since it is of silk and the same texture, this may be because of the dark value, the absence of folds or gathering, or the attraction of the viewer to the motifs.

The body of the wearer is defined by her height which is not encumbered by the hair swept back and away from the face. The circular movement of the ensemble around the body invites viewing in-the-round. The body-in-the-round is emphasized by the relation of the chogore in the upper torso and the curved shape of the gathered straight-grain, three panel skirt. With its shape enclosing and covering most of the body, the clothing takes on a visual priority. The slightly curved shaping of the horizontal hemline of the chogore enhances other rounded shapes, especially that of the chima with its slightly rounding silhouette.

The ABC may be viewed as a unit from one body view. In the upper and lower torso, the chogore and chima are contrasting in value. The cuffs of the chogore contrast with the upper light value, but are the same in value as the skirt.

The border of circular floral motifs on the tie and around the cuff of the chogore and hem of the skirt provide a visual transition among the parts within the whole.

This ABC is viewed part-to-whole with a variable figure-ground relationship. For example, if the viewer concentrates on the tie, it becomes focus or figure for the rest of the ensemble as ground. If the viewer concentrates on the chogore it can also become figure while the chima becomes ground in the figure-ground relationship. Due to the similarity of value of skin surface of the head and neck and the chogore, they can be combined and viewed as a visual part with a degree of planar separation from the remainder of the ensemble. However, the tint of green of the chogore (5G 9/l) and red of the model's skin (5YR 9/2) are viewed in a complementary relationship.

Analysis

In this step of the procedure the relations among parts and the influence of one part to another are considered. The order of the parts and their position in the whole are examined. Attention is also given to how the ABC is visually organized.

To the viewers, there are five visual parts in this Apparel-Body-Construct (ABC). In order of attention they are: model's face, tie, chogore, cuffs (including hands) and chima. The tie becomes the focal point of the ensemble itself because of its reflective repetitive gold motifs and dark value. The chogore receives attention due to its light value, contrasting with the ensemble and background. The cuffs are small in size and though the cuffs are different in hue than the tie, they are visually connected by the repeat of the motif. They are noticed because of proximity to the hands, the contrast of the background of the chogore and discontinuity with the basic color and direction of the sleeve. In visual order, the chima or skirt is attended to last because of the similarity of value with the background. The repeat of the circular motifs at the hemline helps to define the extent of the ABC and a visual connection back to the motif at the chogore cuff and tie.

The organization of the parts within the whole is successive because the parts are viewed in a hierarchical relationship, especially the greater attention directed to the light-value chogore. The entirety of the visual form is at-

tended to largely because of the repetitious circular gold motifs on the tie, cuff and at the hemline.

Analysis can include what can be seen but also, if available, what can be heard and felt. Examination of the experiences of wearing KTD by both the Korean and U.S. investigator yields insight and understanding. The phenomenological experiences of wearing KTD that follow are described in first person.

The Korean researcher describes her experience wearing the traditional dress as follows:

I feel elegant and mature in KTD which I wear as formal attire a number of times a year. I am married with two teen-aged children, so am not old enough to have experienced the everyday wearing of KTD. The aged Korean over 70 may still wear traditional dress everyday. Body movements are somewhat limited while wearing because one is expected to be an elegant lady. An elegant lady takes small, slow steps and no quick movements. She carries her body in a slightly forward posture with her shoulders in a downward slope. Such a lady resembles a still and dignified image, a portrait. Activities where KTD is worn do not usually require a full range of body movement. The exception is the deep bow that is a sign of respect for the recipient and is not appropriately carried out in other forms of dress. When in motion the KTD plus its petticoat can create a pleasant rustling sound and the vertical hanging tie gently sways. For me wearing KTD can be a mood- altering experience and the result of wearing often elevates the mood of the occasion for all who participate. One must be cautious when wearing KTD because it is a symbol of our culture and the person wearing it receives added attention. As one gets older there is more responsibility and opportunity to wear KTD for many family events such as weddings and holidays, especially for hosting other family and friends.

The U.S. researcher had the opportunity to obtain her own KTD through a Korean dressmaker. The U.S. researcher described her experience in wearing KTD as follows:

Arriving at a decision from the array of colorful samples that the dressmaker displayed was difficult. First I had a conference to establish appropriate colors to age and marital status. The question of how to venerate maturity and societal status arose even for me as an outsider. Once the decision was made and the dressmaker delivered my KTD, I had the opportunity to wear KTD in public on a Korean holiday and discovered that the Korean posture must be consciously maintained: forward rounded shoulders plus short restrained steps to create the graceful floating effect of the moving woman in KTD. To my experience, the tight binding of the band of the chima slightly above full chest was unfamiliar and continual attention to the back opening of the chima was necessary. One hand remained on the wrap-around edge and the other raised the skirt to keep it from getting caught by any forward movement of the feet. Footwear consisted of padded stockings and shoes held on by the curve of the stocking toe. I felt strange in Korean society wearing my KTD, but favorable reception, even from strangers, was heartwarming. I was received with some surprise and pleasure that I believe were the result of the careful attention of the dressmaker to the nuance of message conveyed. The experience of wearing KTD was strange and did not become familiar in this wearing, but I learned the necessity of attention to detail relating to both the physical and expressive aspects. I must practice wearing my KTD to become more familiar with it.

Thus, through description of their experiences, the two researchers explained their feelings concerning the wearing of KTD. Both were caught up with the relation of the image and the prescriptions for holding and moving the body. The comfort expressed in wearing KTD was quite different for each because of the differences in cultural experiences.

Interpretation

At this step in the procedure, one looks for the associations of form and meaning that seem to summarize and explain the form. This step builds upon the previous two and continues the process.

Upon viewing this KTD we can infer certain aspects about the wearer and her culture. The priority that the clothing takes additionally gives insight as to its meaning. The natural shapes of the body are almost completely superseded by the volume of the skirt. Indeed the wearer could be pregnant or not when wearing KTD. Modesty is displayed by covering the body from head to foot with many layers of clothing including a wide underdrawer and full length underskirt. When a Korean woman is dressed, the only exposed body parts are the head and hands.

The silk used for KTD is a costly fabric and in most cultures is one of the more costly used for clothing. An ensemble made of silk, especially one requiring approximately seven yards of fabric, can represent a valuable object in monetary terms. The panels in the skirt are usually three but for very special occasions may extend to an additional fourth full length panel. This implies that the additional fabric and its effect in a fuller silhouette make the traditional dress more valued.

The rather delicate nature of this fabric indicates a restricted use. The proportions of the skirt and the contrasting close fit of the chogore would cause a decrease in some modern day physical activities when wearing this ensemble. The wearer would be somewhat inhibited when performing quick movements. Such physical limitations might indicate something of the wearer's status or the occasion of wearing.

The Korean experience of wearing traditional dress is described as disciplined, in the way of carrying oneself and displaying a neat appearance. To give a neat appearance, traditionally the hair is pulled back away from the face. The narrow white band is always worn at the neckline as a decorative aspect but also practically, as a protection of the garment from body soils. Color combinations are ordered, e.g., from a gradation of light to dark values or through complementary hues of the same intensity.

The similarity of the form of KTD may imply that the wearing of traditional dress diminishes individual personality in favor of a more uniform exterior, albeit altered by some details. Many details are used that reveal values of Koreans.

For example, motifs reveal a Korean's love of nature and often flowers, birds, clouds, and wave patterns are used. Traditional Korean motifs are intermingled with those of foreign influence. An example of such familiar motifs are Chinese characters derived from hieroglyphs indicating long life and happiness.

A Comparison Among Categories

To continue the interpretation, the traditional example T1 in Figure I can be compared to T2. Responses placed both in the same category of traditional. The greatest formal difference is the color of the skirt and the tie, while the top or chogore remains the same in hue. Upon examination, T2 is more appropriate for a younger wearer due to the bright and vibrant hue of the chima. From the position of the informed we know that T2 signifies a gown for a bride. The color combination of red and green is traditional for the bride, but the particular value and intensity of those two hues change over time. At the time of viewing, subjects responded that the wearer of this hanbok was appropriately dressed as a bride, but slightly out of fashion. The value and intensity of the red and green hues were perceived as somewhat out-of-date.

Another example, stimulus MT1 differs from T1 in formal properties. The placement and variety of surface detail and colors used are considered nontraditional. The colors are not derived from Korean history and might be most appropriate at a non-traditional event where expressing one's individuality is somewhat more important than expressing the tradition of Korea.

Variation in subject response occurred for the two examples that were considered modified traditional by the respondents. MT2 was considered the most beautiful of the two, as well as more fashionable. Photograph MT2 is traditional in silhouette and the general make-up of chogore and chima, but contains some non-traditional influence in color and motif. The fuschia color of the chima, cuffs, tie, and collar is not found in the traditional Korean color palette, but "borrowed from the West." The large scale embroidery and double layer of the chima are also non-traditional details. The fuschia color is noted as appropriate for the younger wearer and its non-traditional nature would make it appropriate for a less formal event. When consulting the Korean respondents this example is for a young woman to wear to her engagement party. This is a color and design appropriate for the younger wearer and its color is considered attractive for the physical coloring of the Korean bride-to-be and highly photogenic. The engagement party is considered a Western addition to Korean celebrations, so some non-traditional details in one's dress are viewed as more appropriate than at a more traditional Korean event, such as a Korean wedding.

The form of M1 was more familiar to the Korean viewer than M2. Many early professional women adopted a somewhat shortened and thus modified skirt to fit their lifestyle. Such a modification has been accepted widely as a sign of respect for tradition. However this example includes motifs that are not traditional such as the frog closure. The length of the jacket is another feature that is not typical of KTD. Response to M2 was mixed because many respondents could not consider it as traditional at all. Respondents acknowledged its potential comfort but also its lack of traditional beauty (Figure 4).

Evaluation

Evaluation is the final step in the systematic process of perceptual analysis. By this time the viewer can be assured that he/she is more objective after following the previous three steps. Evaluation may imply criteria derived from the cultural context. To futher understand the meaning of KTD one can assume the view of the informed.

From the view of Korean respondents, we discover that the color combination of T1 in Figure I signifies maturity and that the wearer has taken her place of responsibility within Korean society. The relationships of cuff and tie symbolize a married woman with sons. This is a highly valued position in Korea. Children are viewed as a great fortune to the family and the mother might well be proud to display this through her dress. Thus formal properties can communicate to the informed the wearer's status as a married woman who has sons.

To instill pride and continuity with the past, the traditional garment needs to be perceived as stable. The silhouette serves as the continuous and identifying property and this is in accordance with McCune's discussion of the Korean aesthetic. Tradition is maintained in silhouette and shape of the two piece chogore and chima. The design of KTD contains generations of tradition, each form evolving and expanding upon the previous one.

Formal aspects that affect the meaning of traditional dress include details of motif and color. Motifs are often related to nature such as clouds, flowers and vines intertwining on the surfaces of KTD. Certain colors are traditional, as in the colors designated for life events such as red for wedding, white for mourning. The color jade is used historically in Korea as a preferred color for objects of material culture such as pottery. Traditional colors include the colors of the rainbow and primary colors found in nature such as flowers, trees and sky. However along with recognition and use of traditional colors, a new array of colors is offered each year. Contemporary color combinations include more intense colors such as fuschia and dull colors such as olive green. Color combinations such as fuschia and grey are considered to involve a contemporary and foreign influence.

Expressive aspects include the use of KTD worn primarily for occasions of celebration and solemnity. Its use communicates the wearer's joy and respect of tradition. To the informed viewer, KTD can communicate age and status within the Korean society. For example, TI communicates maturity and pride in the status of motherhood. Finally in terms of referential aspects, that is the representation of the world in the object, KTD represents generations of tradition, each expanding upon the previous.

Thus to be valued KTD must have up-to-date colors and design motifs, yet be traditional in silhouette and layout of details. Above all, it must be grounded in the history of Korea. Beautiful KTD is dignified and Korean-like. As the photo stimuli became more traditional, generally they were considered more beautiful by the respondents. An exception, T2, perceived as somewhat out-of-date provides insights into the subject's perceptions of KTD and an understanding of the Korean aesthetic experience. Thus the example judged most traditional was not the most beautiful because of a missing fashionable component. If KTD was perceived as "dated" in some of its details, it was deemed less beautiful.

An examination of the role of KTD in Korean society can illuminate those aspects that make for traditional character. Although by definition traditional dress demands invariance, in Korea, traditional dress can change quite regularly although in subtle ways, and thus is accorded a fashionable aspect. However this change is not due to fashion as determined by New York, Paris, London or Milan, but prescribed by Korean dressmakers, designers and scholars of KTD who are continually researching Korean history.

Through interviews with Korean dressmakers and scholars of traditional dress, the researchers learned why traditional dress changes over time and yet is considered historic. They indicated that forms introduced yearly are reworked historic styles. There seems to be an unending search to find the most "historic" and therefore most "correct" or best examples. This causes the almost yearly change in the array of color combinations offered and the motifs used. Thus the concept of "fashionable" takes on a different meaning and Koreans affirm that strictly traditional KTD is relatively "unfashionable" when compared to more westernized or modified forms of dress.

Conclusions

To understand the aesthetic experience of traditional dress two methodologies were employed. Use of such diverse methodologies points out two approaches to the study of objects of material culture. The methodologies complemented each other and when applied, illustrated their utility in describing and understanding the aesthetic experience.

First we explored the use of bipolar word pairs to measure the meaning of responses of 243 Korean females to six photographs of KTD. Semantic scales and word pairs were previously tested for their appropriateness in describing KTD according to meaning. Such measurement proved to yield valuable data of the collective response that could be statistically described.

In addition a systematic method of studying material culture was used for an in-depth examination of the one example considered most traditional by the subjects. The four steps proceeded from Description to the Analysis, Interpretation and Evaluation that involved reflection about the object. Reflection required an informed viewer willing to follow the step-by-step procedure. In this way this artifact of material culture was better understood in the context of the people who use the object.

Eaton's definition of the aesthetic experience and value is enhanced through this systematic analysis of traditional dress. Both the specific examples and the category of KTD are understood within the cultural context of people who use it. Responses of individuals within the Korean culture were examined. A factor analysis helped to categorize the stimuli and confirm the responses to KTD from a previous study. Then the insights from subjective responses further placed KTD within the cultural context.

Korean traditional dress continues to be worn as formal attire. In this way its wearing is a constant reminder of Korean traditions and may even elevate the mood of the occasion. It is symbolic of the formality of the culture, yet also shows signs of the modern. This has been one of the unique characteristics of the Korean aesthetic. The design of KTD arises out of the history of the Korean culture and understanding that context is imperative to understanding aesthetic response.

McCune(1962) maintains that Korean artists have tended to express major themes in contour or silhouette and then to reinforce the main idea by minor detail and color. In this analysis the traditional aspects of KTD were its slightly curving silhouette and the two part chogore and chima that contain many curved lines and traditional shapes and proportions. This is what Korean respondents referred to when discussing the tradition in their traditional dress. The overall form of KTD remains stable along with some structural details such as the two basic pieces of chogore and chima and the neckline and tie.

Contemporary or fashionable aspects were carried out in the details of color and motif and these were often important in the message of KTD. Thus details of color and motif can signify differences in meaning. Changes that occur in the traditional dress are perhaps due to increased contact with other forms of dress. The co-existence of modified traditional dress with the strictly traditional is an indication of the flexibility of the Korean culture and their ability to adopt aspects of other cultures without forfeiting their own national identity.

References

Banner L. (1983). *American beauty.* Chicago: The University of Chicago Press.

Berger, A. A. (1992). *Reading matter: Multidisciplinary perspectives on material culture.* New Brunswick, N.J.: Transaction Publishers.

Csikszentimihalyi M. and Rochberg-Halton, E. (1981). *The meaning of things: Domestic symbols and the self.* Cambridge; Carbridge University Press.

DeLong, M.R. (1987). *The Way We Look: A framework for visual analysis of dress.* Ames, Iowa: Iowa State University Press.

Eaton, M.M. (1988). *Basic issues in aesthetics.* Belmont, CA: Wadsworth Publishing Company.

Fleming, E. M. (1973). Artifact Study: A Proposed Model. Winterthur Portfolio. 9th Ed. by Ian M.G. Quimby, Charlottesville University Press, Virginia.

Geum, K. & DeLong, M. (1992). Korean Traditional Dress as an Expression of Heritage. *Dress, 19,* 57-68.

Hatcher, E.P. (1985). *Art as culture.* New York: University Press of America.

Kahng H. & Koh, A. (1991). Effect of Design Modification and Color Scheme on Impression Formation of Traditional Korean Women's Clothing, *Journal of the Korean Society of Clothing and Textiles, 15,* 211-227.

McCune, E. (1962). *The arts of Korea: An illustrated history.* Rutland, Vermont: Charles E. Tuttle.

Miller, D. (1987). *Material culture and mass consumption.* New York: Basil Blackwell.

Munsell A.H. (1973). *Book of color,* Neighboring Hues Edition, Matte Finish Collection. Newburgh, New York: Kollmorgen.

Osgood, C.E., Suci, G.J. & Tannenbaum, P.H. (1965). *The measurement of meaning.* Urbana: University of Illinois Press.

Park S., Warner P. C. & Fitzgerald, T. K. (1993). The Process of Westernization: Adoption of Western-style Dress by Korean Woman, 1945-62. *Clothing and Textiles Research Journal, 11*(3) 39-47.

Prown, J. D. (1982). *Mind in matter: An introduction to material culture theory and method,* Winterhur Portfolio. *15* (3), 197-210.

Solomon, M.R. (1983). The Role of Products as Social Stimuli: A Symbolic Interactionism Perspective. *Journal of Consumer Research, 10,* 319-329.